Edinburgh University
Library

KV-648-901

30150 021299851

Ever Closer Partnership

Policy-Making in US-EU Relations

EDINBURGH UNIVERSITY LIBRARY
WITHDRAWN

P.I.E.-Peter Lang

Bruxelles · Bern · Berlin · Frankfurt/M · New York · Oxford · Wien

Éric PHILIPPART & Pascaline WINAND (eds.)

Ever Closer Partnership

Policy-Making in US-EU Relations

EX BIBL. UNIV. EDINBURGH

"European Policy"
No.24

Die Deutsche Bibliothek – CIP-Einheitsaufnahme

Ever closer partnership: policy-making in US-EU relations /
Éric Philippart & Pascaline Winand (ed.) –
Bruxelles ; Bern ; Berlin ; Frankfurt/M. ;
New York ; Oxford; Wien : PIE Lang, 2001
(Series European Policy ; No.24)
ISBN 90-5201-938-X

*CIP available from the British Library, GB
and the Library of Congress, USA.*

ISBN 0-8204-4666-1

© P.I.E.-Peter Lang S.A.
PRESSES INTERUNIVERSITAIRES EUROPÉENNES
Brussels, 2001
2nd printing 2002
info@peterlang.com
www.peterlang.com

No part of this book may be reproduced in any form, by print, photocopy, microfilm or any other means, without prior written permission from the publisher. All rights reserved.

ISSN 1376-0890
ISBN 90-5201-938-X
D/2001/5678/02

Table of Contents

Part II
Actors, Interests and Issues

Acknowledgements

This volume is the result of a project started in May 1996 with an international Roundtable organized in Brussels by the two co-editors in collaboration with Alberta Sbragia. We would like to thank the contributors for their commitment to a long gestation period and for having accepted several revisions of their chapters. We are also very grateful to Desmond Dinan (George Mason University), Monika Sie Dhian Ho (Scientific Council for Government Policy – The Hague) and several anonymous referees for their extensive and enlightened comments on the manuscript.

We do not forget either the valuable contribution made to our initial debates and analyses by the other speakers and paper givers of the Roundtable: Bruno Colson (Facultés Universitaires Notre Dame de la Paix à Namur), Stanley Crossick (President of the European Policy Centre – Brussels), Kusuma Cunningham (Purdue University), Georges Delcoigne (Johns Hopkins University – Bologna), Alan Donnelly (former Member of the European Parliament, Chairman of the Inter-Parliamentarian Delegation for Relations with the US Congress), Steven Ekovich (Department of Politics and International Relations, The American University of Paris), Paul Gallis (Congressional Research Service, US Congress – Washington D.C.), Marc Jorna (Policy Planning Division – DG VIII, European Commission), Bahadir Kaleagasi (Permanent Delegate of TUSIAD TISK Representation to the EU), Piers Ludlow (Balliol College, University of Oxford), Ronald W. Pruessen (Department of History, University of Toronto), Éric Remacle (Institut d'Etudes européennes, ULB), Sophie Vanhoonacker (European Institute of Public Administration EIPA – Maastricht) and Mario Zucconi (Transatlantic Studies, CeSPI – Roma).

Special thanks are due to Ove Juul Jørgensen (Director, Directorate I.B. relations with North America, Australia, New Zealand, NAFTA & APEC, European Commision), Eric Hayes (Head of Unit, European Commission), Astrid Schomaker (European Commission) and Richard Mc Polin (European Commission) for helping launch the project. The support of Geoffrey Edwards (University of Cambridge) and Alberta Sbragia (Pittsburgh University) was primordial during critical phases of the project. In addition, we would like to thank the Director, Geir Lundestad, the head of the research department, Odd Arne Westad, and the staff of the Nobel Institute in Oslo for their assistance in helping the project come to fruition at a later stage of its realization by granting Pascaline Winand a Research Fellowship. The Philippe Wiener-Maurice Anspach Foundation and its executive director, Jean-Victor Louis, were also instrumental in that respect by offering Éric Philippart a post-doctoral fellowship in 1997-8 at the Centre of International Studies, University of Cambridge.

We are indebted to the Université Libre de Bruxelles for its support, in particular André Sapir (former President of the Institut d'Études Européennes), Carine Doutreloux and Myriam Hausser for their special contribution to the practical organisation of the roundtable as well as to Michael Van Custem and Isabelle Smets for their first rate research assistance. Finally, we owe a warm thank you to Jean-Louis Migeot for helping with the mathematical aspects of this research, and to Nicola Viinikka, Catherine Closson, Kathleen Dassy, Delphine Labarde, Nicolas Leroy and Alison Whitaker for their invaluable help and patience in ushering the editors into delivering the completed manuscript.

The project could not have been completed without the generous financial support of the European Commission, the National Bank of Belgium, the Belgian National Fund for Scientific Research (Fonds National de la Recherche Scientifique) and the US Embassy to Belgium.

Preface

Alberta SBRAGIA

Pittsburgh University, West European Studies Center

The relationship between the United States and Europe has been a subject of innumerable articles and books for many decades. Repeatedly, observers and scholars have warned of a 'decoupling' within the Atlantic Alliance and multiple 'crises' within the relationship have been identified and analyzed. Whether the issue under dispute has been the construction of a pipeline from the Soviet Union, the stationing of missiles, or a trade dispute, the Euro-American relationship has often been viewed as increasingly tenuous, fraying, and vulnerable to external shocks. The institutionalization of the European Union did not significantly affect such analyses for 'Europe', in the eyes of American analysts at least, was either viewed as a collection of states or as a geopolitical construct.

In fact, an underlying theme throughout the decades has been the relative power and engagement of the United States and Europe (however defined) *vis-à-vis* each other. The United States sees 'decoupling' when the Europeans' preferences differ from those of the United States and the Europeans fear 'decoupling' when the United States seems indifferent to and aloof from European concerns. Discrete disagreements have not been treated as discrete but rather have often been viewed as indicative of the problematic health of the entire relationship.

The intensity with which the Euro-American relationship is monitored is unequalled, and that very intensity is telling. It is a platitude to say that the United States and Europe are linked in an extraordinary number of ways – but in that platitude lies a very basic truth. The United States and Europe in a sense do not have a choice of interlocutors – the relationship between the United States and Asia is fundamentally different from that with Europe. And Europe's potential relationship with Russia also differs in pivotal ways from that with the United States. The United States and Europe must engage with one other in ways which go far beyond those traditionally linked to 'international relations'. The only question, in the post-Cold War period, is how to carry out such a sophisticated engagement – rather than whether to be engaged in the first place.

Sophistication is required not only because of the substantive complexity of the Euro-American relationship but also because of the evolving nature of Europe itself. Europe is still a collection of nation-states, many of them represented in NATO, but it is also represented by the European Union. And the Union, for its part, is still in the process of formation. Thus, not only is the transatlantic relationship complex because it involves issues including military security, law enforcement, anti-trust policy, health care, environmental protection, foreign direct investment, trade in both goods and services, aviation, product and technical standards, and food safety but also because one of the interlocutors is not fully institutionalized. The legal powers of European Union are still in the process of being constructed, and the constituent units at times act collectively but outside the formal powers of the Union. Negotiations in any of the policy areas on the transatlantic agenda would be complex enough even if two traditional Westphalian states were the negotiators, but the fact that a polity in the making is one of the negotiators calls for imaginative and sophisticated policy-making on both sides.

This volume contributes to the construction of such policy-making by exploring a dimension of US-EU relations which is rarely discussed. The New Transatlantic Agenda (NTA) opened a new chapter in the relationship between the United States and the European Union but the institutional processes which were established by the NTA have been largely ignored by scholars. In a similar fashion, the NTA's actual impact on policy outcomes has also not received the kind of attention from the scholarly community which such an agreement deserves. This volume therefore illuminates several aspects of transatlantic relations which deserve far more study than they have received. First of all, the EU is treated as an interlocutor in its own right. Rather than a 'Europe' defined in various ways, the European Union as an institution with its own political and administrative capacity is central to the analysis. The New Transantlic Agenda, for its part, is set within the context of both transatlantic relations and the institutionalization of the process of European integration. Secondly, the relationship is analyzed from the perspective of very concrete actors rather than being discussed from the macro-level as is typically done. The reader comes away with a clear sense of the organizations and the interests which bear on the relationship. Thirdly, the assessment and evaluation of policy outcomes provide a grounding for those interested in further action. This volume brings together analysis and practice. The 'reflective practitioner' will find much of interest here.

As the authors make clear, the interdependence between the United States and 'Europe' is increasing dramatically. Not only is the US engaged with NATO and in bilateral relationships with European nation-states, but it is now also involved in an intensifying relationship with the European Union. The Union is not only important in trade negotiations, but its policy reach and, through the NTA, entanglement with American policies renders it a significant interlocutor for the United States. As a key institution at both the regional and global level, the European Union has organized Europe in such a way as to require American institutions, processes, and administrative procedures to adapt to a new reality. As Europe integrates, its policy-making processes change – and those of the United States must change as well. Europe and the United States are so tightly linked in so many ways that American policy-making cannot but be shaped by the kind of historic change transforming European policy-making.

INTRODUCTION

The Dynamics, Structures, Actors and Outcomes of US-EU Relations: An 'Inside-Out' Approach

Éric PHILIPPART and Pascaline WINAND

Fonds National de la Recherche Scientifique (Belgium),
Université Libre de Bruxelles,
College of Europe (Bruges)

Euro-American relations have often been described as one of the closest and most complex of all relationships in contemporary international politics. At the height of the Cold War, the Kennedy administration made a plea for a 'genuine partnership between equals'. In November 1990, in the aftermath of the Cold War, the United States, the European Community and its Member States signed a Transatlantic Declaration (TD) that sought to expand a partnership 'on an equal footing'. In December 1995, the President of the European Commission, the EU Council President and the President of the USA agreed on a 'New Transatlantic Agenda' (NTA) and a 'Joint US-EU Action Plan' (JAP) with a view primarily to widen and deepen their economic, foreign policy, defense, security, and cultural cooperation. More than 170 issues of transatlantic, international or global scope were prioritized, with an emphasis on practical approaches to these questions. The procedures were further formalized with the development and consolidation of various levels of policy-making, culminating with bi-annual summits of the Presidents of the United States, the European Council and the European Commission. The rationale behind this predefined 'serial summitry' and its cascade of preparatory levels was to increase the intensity of US-EU cooperation and to move from the 'policies of consultation' to 'the policies of joint action'.

After a long eclipse in the 1980s, the formal recognition of the EU as the third main element in the transatlantic institutional architecture, next to NATO and bilateral relationships, triggered a clear renewal of interest in the topic in the first half of the 1990s. A decade after the Transatlantic Declaration and following several years of implementation of the NTA, a number of important events, developments and adjustments affecting the US-EU relationship have taken place on both sides of the Atlantic and in the world at large. At the same time, many practitioners and observers feel that, in spite of ongoing conflicts, the relationship has reached a new plateau. All of this calls for a meaningful policy review.

Most recent books provide only a general overview of transatlantic relations, which often (over)focuses on the security dimension. Among the few who have attempted to address the US-EU relationship *stricto sensu,*[1] some, like B. Hocking and M. Smith, have approached the issue through the world politics paradigm and its new vision of global trends.[2] K. Featherstone and R. Ginsberg, using another important analytical tool in international relations – the 'complex interdependence' paradigm – have attempted to measure the intensity of interdependence between the two shores of the Atlantic and its impact on the relationship.[3] Drawing partially on 'complex interdependence' as well, J. Peterson's 'New Atlanticism' discussed the interplay between globalization and domestic political systems, the nature of US and EU respective domestic constraints, and in particular the consequences of their convergent modes of governance on the evolution of the relationship.[4] Insofar as the present book primarily explores the dynamics of policy-making, the interactions of the structures of governance, the actors and the policy outcomes, it too belongs more to the 'inside-out' than to the 'outside-in' approach in understanding foreign policy.

The ambitions of this volume are twofold. On the one hand, it seeks to study the evolution of structures and processes which characterize US-EU relations, particularly since the watershed of the TD. New US-EU institutional structures have been established to generate (greater) symmetry in the partnership. It is therefore important to examine their impact, if any, on the mode of governance of the relationship in general and, in particular, on

---

1 G. N. Yannopoulos (ed.), *Europe and America, 1992: US-EC Economic Relations and the Single European Market* (Manchester, Manchester University Press, 1991).

2 B. Hocking and M. Smith, *Beyond Foreign Economic Policy: The United States and the Single European Market in a Changing World Economy* (London, Cassell-Pinter, 1997).

3 K. Featherstone and R. Ginsberg, *The United States and the European Community – Partners in Transition* (New York, St Martin's Press, 1997, 2nd ed.).

4 J. Peterson, *Europe and America – The Prospects for Partnership* (London, Routledge, 1996, 2nd ed.).

the policy processes presiding over trade, economy, security, and development. Special attention is paid to the many institutional actors and policy-makers as they are confronted with new objectives in scope, intensity and duration, to their understanding of the issues and processes at work, and to their strategies in policy-shaping and policy-making. On the other hand, the book also aims to assess, explain and evaluate the policy outcomes of the relationship, with a focus on the post-NTA record. The emphasis is placed on methods to measure the NTA's record, as well as the relative weight and interactions of the variables affecting its results.

The book is divided into three parts. Part I, *Studying a Mature Relationship*, consists in two introductory chapters. The first one presents a review of the general historical background of transatlantic relations *lato sensu*, while identifying some of the enduring features and successive forms of the US-EU relationship, including during the run-up to the NTA. It also outlines the latter's nature and contents. The second chapter then offers a number of methodological and theoretical considerations that could contribute to explain and evaluate the policy output of the US-EU partnership. The main hypotheses of the two introductory chapters are assessed in light of the contributions of the different authors and an in-depth analysis of the NTA record in the concluding chapters of the book. Part II, *Actors, Interests, and Issues,* consists of chapters which present different levels of actorness involved in the policy-shaping of US-EU relations stricto sensu, while distinguishing between formal and informal actors. It studies the evolution of US-EC/EU relations, from the creation of the European Communities to the NTA. This is done in a comparative perspective, with a special emphasis on the genesis of the NTA on the American and on the European sides. It also undertakes a survey of sectoral studies of key policy areas and decision-making processes. Part III, *Taking Stock of US-EU Relations,* considers recent developments and challenges in EU-US economic relations and foreign policy cooperation, and their likely impact on trade and on a possible US-EU 'political partnership'. It then presents a critical evaluation of the main theses on the actual and future state of the relationship. Finally, this part summarizes the book's findings and assessments on the evolution of US-EU relations and the NTA output, and makes recommendations for improving US-EU policy processes and outputs.

Studying a Mature Relationship

In 'From "Equal Partnership" to the "New Transatlantic Agenda": The Enduring Features and Successive Forms of the US-EU Relationship', the editors open with a broad survey of US-EC/EU relations to best understand enduring features in the relationship, with a view to facilitating the analysis of the recent evolution of its structures and processes. After examining the past perceptions of the relationship's benefits, costs and dangers, the formula of cooperation that were proposed during the WWII-1990 period, as well as conflictual situations or tensions and the various strategies chosen to address them, the chapter offers a short account of the run-up to the NTA, and a general assessment of the latter's contents.

'Assessing, Evaluating and Explaining the Output of US-EU Relations' provides an analytical chart for the assessment and explanation of the US-EU policy output. It starts by defining what the essence of cooperation is and how its output could be measured and ranked. It then reviews a number of theorical approaches likely to offer some explanation for the ambitions and concrete achievements of US-EU cooperation. Four clusters of propositions are presented. The first explains how cooperation should be affected by the distribution of power, the competition for hegemony or the constellation of interests. The second revolves around the impact of the international institutional environment. The third and fourth clusters set out the inherent limitations and opportunities of the modes of governance presiding over the relationship, *i.e.* how the system of government, party systems, group politics, networks and bureaucratic politics, domestically and at the transatlantic level, could alter the course of the relationship. Finally, it considers the question of the evaluation of the decision-making performance of the system.

Actors, Interests and Issues

In his chapter, 'From the Transatlantic Declaration to the New Transatlantic Agenda: The Shaping of Institutional Mechanisms and Policy Objectives by National and Supranational Actors', Anthony Gardner gives a detailed account of the motivations and tactics of national and supranational players from the negotiations of the 1990 Transatlantic Declaration to the New Transatlantic Agenda. The author, who was directly involved in the negotiations in his capacity of Head of the European Directorate of the National Security Council from 1994-95, provides a candid analysis of the genesis of the NTA from an American perspective, which leaves few stones unturned, be it on the EU or on the US side. Shrinking foreign affairs budgets, the perception of an 'Atlantic drift', the desire to enhance the EU's foreign policy profile and its image as a global actor, Spain's domestic agenda, the threat of transatlantic trade disputes, the turn of Congress toward isolationism, are all dealt with under Anthony Gardner's incisive pen. Gardner continues with an assessment of the new policy objectives and institutional procedures for US-EU consultation and cooperation. Meetings at the level of heads of state, cabinet members, political directors and experts are examined in turn.

Pascaline Winand, in 'The US Mission to the EU in "Brussels D.C.", the European Commission Delegation in Washington D.C. and the New Transatlantic Agenda', studies the structure and activities of the US Mission to the EU (USEU) and the European Commission Delegation in Washington D.C., and their contributions to the NTA, while focusing on their organization and functions, as well as on their actions and lobbying strategies. This is done in comparative perspective with an indication of their transformation over time to keep up with evolving transatlantic relations and developments in the EU, Washington D.C., and on the world scene. The underlying assumption is that looking at these key, but little studied actors in transatlantic relations can provide challenging insights on past and current US-EC/EU relations, help identify areas where improvement might be needed in the ways these posts operate, and give some indication of how the EU and the US are developing and are being perceived by external actors. Comparing USEU with the Delegation of the European Commission in Washington can also uncover differences between the American and EU operating environments, including the nature of different actors on the lobbying scene and their interaction.

John Peterson's chapter, 'Shaping not Making: The Impact of the American Congress on US-EU Relations', assesses the impact of the US Congress on transatlantic and US-EU relations since Clinton's first term. As a consequence of the increasing 'domestication of international politics', Congress has become more active in foreign policy. The post-1994 political shift on Capitol Hill has made this evolution all the more meaningful, as the aggressive unilateralism posturing of the new Republican majority sharply contrasted with the previous long-standing internationalist consensus.

The parallel reading of the Peterson and Gardner chapters highlights an interesting discrepancy between the perceptions of the US Legislative and Executive branches: according to Peterson, NATO is central to US Congress' vision of transatlantic relations, while, according to Gardner, who represents what is probably the dominant opinion within the Clinton administration, 'trade gradually assumes a higher profile than security in transatlantic relations (and) NATO is destined to lose some of the utility it has had as the central institution for promoting and symbolizing common interests.' Peterson argues that discrepancies of views have been so far reasonably well managed and that the level of interdependence between Atlantic shores does not make room for major dramatic changes. If, as he suggests, Congress does not very often 'make' foreign policy, it nevertless often shapes it in important ways. As far as transatlantic relations are concerned, it will be a far more determinant player in the future than it has been in the past.

In 'The Role of Metropolitan Regions in Making a New Atlantic Community', Alan Henrikson builds on Jean Gottmann's concepts of 'iconography' and 'circulation'. He claims that any (social) Community needs to cohere and develop symbols which give a Community identity and meaning, and foster flows of people, trade and information which give it life. For him, subnational units in general and Metropolitan Centres in particular have a key role to play in the formation of the 'new Atlantic community': they are producers of iconography; they are hubs; and they are capable and willing to play a role internationally, having become the most significant economic concentrations in a globalized economy. Venturing on a more normative-prescriptive ground, he recommends that their involvement should be encouraged because, if left to high diplomacy, the transatlantic bond could become too formalized, structured and restrictive, limiting future growth. He therefore argues in favor of an Atlantic Community which would be characterized 'by the high degree of plurality, or multi-centredness, within it, and also by the non-hierarchical character of its structure, implying a devolution of responsibility, as well as initiative, to non-central governments (NCGs) as well as to non-governmental organizations (NGOs)'.

Maria Green Cowles examines the growing role of private actors – namely, large companies – in promoting transatlantic relations. Her chapter, 'Private Firms and US-EU Policy-Making: The Transatlantic Business Dialogue', focuses on the Transatlantic Business Dialogue (TABD) – a group of American and European companies that play a key role in shaping the transatlantic trade and investment agenda. Since their first meeting in July 1995, TABD companies have created a comprehensive set of proposals to guide government leaders in their trade negotiations. Equally important, the TABD process has emerged as a significant moderating force in transatlantic relations. Prior to its creation, the norm in US-EU trade management was often a series of global spats that soured other aspects of the transatlantic partnership. With the TABD, however, a regular forum has been established in which economic issues can be discussed on an ongoing basis. The chapter explores the development of the TABD, discusses specific TABD proposals, and highlights the significance of these private actors in furthering the transatlantic relationship.

Michael Smith, in 'The United States, the European Union and the New Transatlantic Marketplace: Public Strategy and Private Interests', evaluates the extent to which US policy towards the European Union (EU) can be given a coherent and coordinated direction. The generation of a coherent US strategy is, according to the author, confronted with multiple constraints: it requires cross-national, cross-departmental and government-business developments, not to mention various policy networks 'hardly rooted in the US at all' and that highlight the 'extra-national dimension in US policy development'. In view of this situation, the challenges for US/EU policy are as numerous as varied, including the post-Uruguay Round agenda, shaping the development of the WTO, the management of sectoral frictions as well as the implementation of the NTA and its action plan. For him, such a complex constellation of constraints and challenges creates important questions about the demand for and supply of government strategies. The 'interconnectedness, complexity and indeterminacy' of US/EU relations in general make it 'difficult to bring together an all-encompassing programme for action' and develop 'strategic behaviour, planning and interaction'. Michael Smith concludes by recommending that more attention be devoted to forms of 'learning through doing' and that a network of 'reflective practitioners' be generated both at the governmental and the private levels, as practical ways to improve transatlantic relations.

In 'European Unity in Transatlantic Commercial Diplomacy', Youri Devuyst bases his analysis on a survey of US attitudes towards the Community's commercial policy during its formative years and on several trade policy cases. He identifies three main US policy tracks in dealing with the EC as a commercial partner and rival. First, the 'pre-emptive intervention track' which aims at active involvement of the US in the EC's decision-making process, ranging from Bush's Commerce Secretary Robert Mosbacher's request for a seat at the EC bargaining table to the early warning features of the NTA. Second, the 'exploitation of European weakness track', characteristic of periods of transatlantic trade conflict, in which the United States has tended to take advantage of EC dissensions and to use unilateral sanctions to weaken the EC's common position. Finally, the 'support for unification track', in which the US supports European integration 'as a way to create a more reliable trade policy partner', notably in facilitating international trade agreements. The author argues that these various US policy tracks will succeed or fail according to the efforts of the Community and its Member States in maintaining European unity in commercial diplomacy. Thus, 'the Community largely holds the key to its own future as a player in world trade diplomacy.'

For Thomas Frellesen, in 'Processes and Procedures in EU-US Foreign Policy Cooperation: From the Transatlantic Declaration to the New Transatlantic Agenda', the NTA is remarkable for its political tone and its global approach: 'never before had the EU and the US expressed themselves so explicitly about the security aspects of their relations in a joint document'. According to the author, EU-US foreign policy cooperation has developed significantly in recent years because of the post-Cold War changes in the nature of foreign policy and security issues, on the one hand, and progress of European integration in these domains, on the other. In the process, even though disproportionate expectations should be avoided, the EU component grew in importance in the partnership. Frellesen first assesses the mechanisms of cooperation and then reviews the areas of foreign policy cooperation listed by the JAP, from Former Yugoslavia to terrorism. Besides a welcome increase in pragmatic cooperation, he sees the NTA as significant for at least four reasons: it gives focus; it gives a degree of reassurance derived from its visibility; it creates a more or less permanent EU-US dialogue; and, it allows for a better preparation of EU-US Summit meetings. Beyond that, he predicts, 'future developments will depend very much on how the EU decides to organise itself in the area of CFSP' (Common Foreign and Security Policy).

Taking Stock of US-EU Relations

In his chapter, 'EU-US Relations after Amsterdam: "Finishing Europe"', Roy Ginsberg first takes stock of the mutually beneficial and nevertheless conflictual trade and investment EU-US relationship. Although most sides have so far mostly complied with the WTO dispute settlement adjudication, he argues, 'industrial diplomacy' (notably via the Transatlantic Business Dialogue and other non-governmental dialogues) might be needed to fend off 'a new generation of trade disputes – *e.g.* electronic commerce, open skies, aircraft hush kits, and genetically-modified crops'. The author then goes on to tackle US-EU foreign policy cooperation, which he says might develop into 'a political partnership on a global scale' if the next US administration continues to support the EU as a partner in foreign policy, and, as several authors argue in this book, if the EU makes much needed decision-making and institutional reforms prior to its next wave of enlargement, and fully exploits the new CFSP instruments of the Treaty of Amsterdam. 'Finishing Europe', and especially the political union aspects of integration (CFSP and ESDI – the European Defense and Security Initiative), he claims, 'will give the EU the internal confidence required for outward confidence', thereby decreasing its overdependence on the US in times of crisis, best evidenced during the Kosovo crisis, and enhancing its role as a global partner. Yet there are limits to the EU-US political partnership: although EU leaders agreed to fold security issues into the framework of EU institutions environment in the wake of the Cologne June 1999 summit, the US, he notes, will only continue to condone the development of ESDI-CFSP as long as it is not a competitor to NATO.

René Schwok's chapter, 'Drifting apart? Dissociative and Associative Approaches', conceptualises the state of research on US-EU relations by distinguishing between two main theses or camps: the proponents of the – ineluctable – deterioration of transatlantic links (the dissociative approach) and those of a positive status quo (the associative approach). Schwok evaluates the propositions and the theoretical underpinnings of these two approaches via a number of political (the end of the Cold War; hegemonic competition) and economic (the nature of EU economic integration policy; the impact of the Economic and Monetary Union decided by the EU; the future of multilateralism and trade regimes) events and trends. He concludes that, contrary to dissociative claims and expectations, the announcement of the decline of the United States was probably premature, NATO was revitalised and the Uruguay Round successfully concluded resulting in, among other things, the creation of the World Trade Organization, while American support for the enlargement and the deepening of the European Union broadened. All these elements speak in favour of the associative thesis, *i.e.* the relative good health of transatlantic relations for now and in the future. Hence, consolidation or even upgrading are the most likely evolution for the partnership.

In the two concluding chapters of the book, the editors summarise its various findings and assessments on the evolution of the transatlantic relationship and the NTA output. The set of propositions on US-EU cooperation developed in the first two introductory chapters are confronted with these findings in order to test their validity. 'Ever Closer Partnership? Taking Stock of US-EU Relations' considers the evolution of US-EU structures and processes. Major enduring features but also discontinuities in the dynamics of US-EU policy-shaping and policy-making are identified and explained. 'Deeds not Words? Evaluating and Explaining the US-EU Policy Output' then deals with the policy outcomes of the relationship, especially in the post-NTA era. It endeavours to assess and explain what has been decided in terms of level of co-operation, while evaluating the decision-making performance of the system. The editors then venture on to examine briefly the future prospects of the US-EU partnership.

PART I

STUDYING A MATURE RELATIONSHIP

CHAPTER 1

From 'Equal Partnership' to the 'New Transatlantic Agenda': Enduring Features and Successive Forms of the US-EU Relationship[1]

Pascaline WINAND and Éric PHILIPPART

Fonds National de la Recherche Scientifique (Belgium),
Université Libre de Bruxelles,
College of Europe (Bruges)

Transatlantic relations have a long history. Looking for points of comparison in the past can but benefit the analysis of the recent evolution of structures and processes that characterise the US-EU relationship. In this instance, the points of comparison that appear the most relevant are: (1) the past perceptions of the relationship's benefits, costs and dangers; (2) the formula of cooperation (including partnership) that were proposed, accepted and rejected during the period from WWII to 1990; and (3) the tensions or conflicts during those years, as well as the ways each side managed or tried to keep the other in check. Since such an approach can only be fruitful if all terms of the comparison are properly accounted for, the concise presentation of these three points will be followed by a short account of the run-up to the NTA and a general assessment of the latter's contents.

Comparing past trends in US-EC/EU relations with the findings of the following chapters might be particularly useful when addressing one of the main questions of this book: were the highly ambitious and, at times, emphatic expressions used in the mid-1990s to describe the nature of US-EU relations merely paying lip service? If Kennedy spoke of Europe as a

---

1 The historical sections of this chapter, 'Enduring Features in US-EU Relations: "Hot" War, Cold War, Post-Cold War' and 'From New Atlanticism to the NTA', have mostly been written by Pascaline Winand. The last section, 'A First Assessment of the Contents of the NTA', was jointly written.

partner with whom one could deal 'on a basis of full equality',[2] current official speeches and documents, including the NTA, indeed speak not only of a full and equal partnership between the US and the EU, but also variably describe it as 'active', 'global', or 'vibrant'. 'Mutual generosity' or even 'joint leadership' now seem to be on the agenda. The historical comparison should enable us to assess more solidly the real motivations of both partners behind that rhetoric, the nature of transatlantic partnership(s) currently contemplated by the US and the EU (and how they tie in with leadership, 'followership'[3] or special or privileged relationships between Washington and certain national EU capitals), as well as the probability of increasing conflict and of resorting to alternative solutions (such as unilateralism or competing loci of cooperation).

Enduring Features in US-EU Relations: 'Hot' War, Cold War, Post-Cold War

Conflicting Visions of US-EC Cooperation: Fears, Challenges and Opportunities

A short examination of the not-so-distant and sometimes not-so-different past, including the World War II era, can help throw some light on the current period, while helping to identify enduring features in US-EC cooperation. Indeed, containing the Soviet Union and Communism by reinforcing the Atlantic Alliance through European prosperity and political stability was only one of the reasons for American backing of European integration. Other motivations, including the fear of political and economic isolation, existed before the Cold War, and have continued to warrant US support for European unity in the post-Cold War period. As we shall see in the concluding chapter, the Clinton administration's pronouncements about the EU now not only mimic those of Kennedy, but also hark back to expressions and motivations used in the pre-Cold War period.

During World War II, for example, US planners pondered over the pros and cons of encouraging European integration after the war. Their first query was whether this would further US interests in a liberal trading and democratic environment. On the positive side, they calculated

---

2 *Department of State Bulletin*, 23 July 1962, p.132.

3 Michael Smith and S. Woolcock, *The United States and the European Community in a Transformed World* (London, RIIA, 1993), p.10.

that the creation of a European customs union would help control protectionist forces, facilitate access of US goods to European markets and simplify commercial policy with the US, since it would possess a central authority. In addition, they were convinced that a European Union could help remove intra European trade and financial barriers. This in turn would be conducive to more European efficiency and prosperity, and more demand for imports of raw materials, food and manufactured goods of which the US would be the principal beneficiary. More economic prosperity would in turn foster political stability in Europe, thereby contributing to international and American security. In other words, markets would prime the pumps of democracy. Last but not least, during World War II as during the Cold War, the German question was central to American attitudes towards a united Europe. On the one hand, some planners anticipated that German resources were central for European recovery. On the other hand, however, Germany's independence had to be 'contained'. The preferred solution was to integrate it within an economically prosperous and politically unified Europe, which would channel German energies towards European recovery and unification, thereby contributing to political stability.

During World War II, when European integration was but a blueprint, American planners were already anticipating its Janus-like prospects. At the time, the fear was that a unified Europe might be dominated by a single power or group of powers with belligerent intentions – candidates for hegemony on the continent were either the Soviet Union or Germany, or, to a lesser extent, France. Another major concern was also that US support for European integration might upset the security preoccupations of the Soviet Union and jeopardize prospects for cooperation. Fear of a protectionist Europe, surrounded by high tariff walls – a 'Fortress Europe' as it was later called in the US in the period leading up to the Single European Act – was also predominant. A strong European regional bloc and the creation of similar entities as a reaction to it, could indeed result not so much in liberalized trade and peace as in 'the break up of the world organization in favor of a series of power blocs acting in unstable equilibrium without the ballast provided by the smaller nations'.[4] An additional concern was voiced by George Kennan

4 Subcommittee on Problems of European Organization, 'How would the Political Unification of Europe Affect the Interests of the United States' (Subcommittee on Problems of European Organization of the Advisory Committee on Post-War Foreign

in the late 1940s, notably: the preoccupation of being 'on the minority side not only in the sense of world resources but also in the sense of philosophy and outlook at the world'.[5] Decades later, in 1990, Robert Zoellick, a key adviser to US Secretary of State James Baker, and one of the masterminds behind the 1990 Declaration on US-EC relations, spoke of the necessity of an 'Alliance of values' between the EC and the US and, warned against cultural isolation.[6] What was at stake was nothing less than maintaining a congenial environment for American culture, democratic values and institutions and American capitalism.

Some of these fears have pervaded US-EC/EU relations for years: the fears of a hostile Europe, of a Fortress Europe, of an independent Europe, of Europe as a regional power. During the Cold War period, these already present fears – accompanied by some of the initial motives for US support for European integration – were being added to. Support for European integration was not a viable option as long as the US contemplated rebuilding Europe in cooperation with the Soviet Union. As the US progressively turned away from Roosevelt's globalism and his policy of conciliation with the Soviet Union, however, a united Europe came to be seen as a way of buttressing the free world against communism, of rendering American aid to Europe more efficient, of securing Franco-German reconciliation, and of keeping Western Europe, and especially West Germany and its resources, firmly anchored to the West and to the US. Yet, except for the risk of alienating the Soviet Union, the combination of fears of the earlier period persisted.

On the European side, American support for European integration, and US participation in the Atlantic Alliance and NATO, were initially mostly welcomed if not 'invited'[7] by Western Europeans. This was seen as a way of containing the Soviet Union, of bringing back economic viability and prosperity to Europe (in part by accessing American markets), and, ultimately, as a means of helping to restore the influence of the Old Continent in world councils. For some European countries, the

---

Policy, 10 December 1943, RG 59, The Records of Harley A. Notter, Box 84, R63c, National Archives).

5 Policy Planning Staff Meeting, 13 June 1949, RG 59, Box 27, PPS, National Archives.

6 Robert B. Zoellick, 'The New Europe in a New Age: Insular, Itinerant, or International? Prospects for an Alliance of Values', *US Department of State Dispatch*, 24 September 1990.

7 An expression coined by Geir Lundestad.

American military guarantee was needed to insure European recovery and unification. If those motivations very much mirrored the interests of the United States, as time went by, other European attitudes and fears joined the initial ones. In some countries, those whom we might call the 'Atlanticists', feared a European Community that would act too independently from the United States, thereby running the risk of triggering a return to US isolationism. Others were afraid that an all too exclusive concentration on the EC-US relationship, particularly in the field of trade, might not only mar the interests of other non-EC Western European countries, but also prevent optimal solutions on a world scale, thereby ultimately damaging the interests of the EC itself. Yet others feared being smothered by an overbearing American tutor, which would relegate the EC and its Member States to a second-rate status, especially in the political and defense fields, and use its military and nuclear leverage to extract economic concessions from the EC.

Moreover, if the Americans feared a 'Fortress Europe', it soon became clear that *'le défi américain'*, as Jean-Jacques Servan-Schreiber called it, could be perceived by the European side as the invasion of Europe not only by American goods but also by American industry and investments. In addition, some European leaders were apprehensive of the consequences of American spending in other parts of the world, particularly in Vietnam, which might result in either Europeans having to pay more in terms of their own defense and of aid towards developing countries, or, once again, in a return to US isolationism. Other leaders viewed things differently. For example, if Charles De Gaulle estimated that changed circumstances including *détente*, no longer warranted American hegemony in Europe via NATO, he also sought to challenge American monetary hegemony and the existence of a 'dollar area' in light of the evolution in the monetary field.

All in all changed circumstances prompted the European Communities and some of their Member States to increasingly assert their autonomy from the United States. This attitude had, to some extent, the effect of confirming and magnifying some of the aforementioned American fears.

Past Formats of the Relationship: 'Equal' Partnership, Trading Partnership, Leadership or 'Action Community'?

Different courses of action were possible in order to avert these fears. But the format of relations envisaged, proposed, accepted and rejected during the 1945-90 period often meant different things for each side of the Atlantic. These formats can broadly fall into five categories[8]: (1) no relationship, amounting for the EC to independence from the US and without influence upon it; (2) cooperation or competition, amounting to independence but with influence; (3) coalition or partnership, corresponding to a recognition by the EC and the US of their interdependence; (4) a hegemonic relationship, amounting for the EC to dependence with influence; and finally, (5) imperial relation, amounting to dependence without influence.

In general, the US attempted to 'contain' European integration with a view to making it a worthwhile enterprise to support in the best American interest. The dominant option on the European side mostly consisted of opposing American proposals susceptible to divert the development of the European Community from what was seen as in the best interests of its institutions and its Member States. Several examples will serve to illustrate this point.

Let us first consider the use of the partnership format during the Kennedy administration. In July 1962, Kennedy told one of his advisers that 'the only leverage' the US 'really [had] was nuclear knowledge and capability'. 'In the 1950s', said the President, '[the Europeans] spent their time making money: we spent our time making bombs. A partnership in the end is going to involve an exchange between their money and our bombs'.[9] That same month, Kennedy also spoke of an equal partnership. But could exchanging money for bombs possibly lead to an equal partnership?[10] And how could equal partnership possibly be compatible

8 Although several options were often simultaneously pursued throughout the period, in part because the strategies varied from one sector to another.

9 Walt Rostow, recorded interview by the John F. Kennedy Library, pp.131-132.

10 For more details, see Pascaline Winand, *Eisenhower, Kennedy and the United States of Europe* (St. Martin's Press-Macmillan, 1993 (hardback), 1997 (paperback)), pp.94-95, 129, 167. See also: Geir Lundestad, *'Empire' by Integration. The United States and European Integration, 1945-1997* (Oxford, Oxford University Press, 1998).

with American repeated claims to maintain US leadership in the Atlantic Alliance?

Of course, at the political level, a united Europe still spoke with many voices and could thus hardly claim co-leadership with the US. In the field of defense, especially nuclear defense, a better definition of the relationship from an American perspective would be integration and certainly not equal partnership. While some influential Kennedy advisers looked forward to a time when a politically united Europe could participate as a more equal partner in the nuclear field, for the time being Kennedy did not advocate the same view. For the President, greater participation did not mean giving Europeans effective control of the nuclear deterrent, despite the fact that European allies were encouraged to contribute more resources to the common defense effort. A 'trading partnership' between 'two giant markets on either side of the ocean' is all Kennedy concretely envisaged for the near future.[11]

Yet there were limits to that partnership as well. Contrary to certain quarters which urged 'joining' the Common Market or even creating strong Atlantic political institutions, Kennedy did not envisage 'joining' the Common Market. The partnership with the EC was only one of a number of the partnerships he wanted to engage in: the US was a Pacific power as well as a member of the Western Hemisphere. Establishing a 'rich man's trading community' would be detrimental to a 'new partnership between the old nations in the North and the new nations to the South'. A full-blown Atlantic Union between the EC and the US which excluded Japan or Latin America would also create economic and political problems for the US in the long run.[12] Meanwhile the EC had at heart the preservation of its privileged relationship with the Mediterranean and Africa. The evolution of the following decades made that perspective ever more problematic.

This being said, notwithstanding Kennedy's public allegations that the US did not intend to 'create an Atlantic free trade area', the dividing line between a transatlantic trading partnership and a free trade area seemed to be a tenuous one.[13] When Kennedy crusaded for the Trade Expansion Act (TEA) in the early 1960s, one of the avowed aims was to

---

11 *Department of State Bulletin*, 12 February 1962, p.233.

12 *Department of State Bulletin*, 6 March 1961, pp.330-334; Winand, *Eisenhower, Kennedy*, p.201.

13 *Ibid.*

give the US sufficient leverage to substantially lower the EEC's Common External Tariff in exchange for a comparable reduction in US tariffs. The Frenchman Jean Monnet and many of his compatriots for that matter, however, felt that some of the features of the TEA smacked of a transatlantic free trade policy which would undermine the European institutions, thereby impairing the chances of a 'real Atlantic partnership between equals'.[14] Monnet was similarly weary of the plans of some of the so-called 'Atlanticists' which contemplated pre-emptively inoculating the politically-unified Europe-to-be against bouts of neutralism by capping it with Atlantic political institutions such as an Atlantic High Council, an Atlantic Consultative Assembly and an Atlantic High Court of Justice.[15] He feared that European unity might then get lost in an Atlantic fog: 'For the present,' he insisted, 'America and Europe will come together as fast as Europe unites and no faster'. A 'more efficient Atlantic action community', be it in the economic, political or military fields, would only come about when Europe was sufficiently strong enough to be a full partner of the United States.[16]

During the Johnson administration, Charles De Gaulle seemed to agree with Monnet when he told German Chancellor Ludwig Erhard that he did not 'reject Atlantic partnership' but wanted it to be 'a partnership of equals'.[17] Yet if Monnet and De Gaulle concurred on the necessity of equality between the US and Europe, they disagreed on the degree of intimacy of the partnership with the United States. Thus, the General attempted to wean France's Western European partners from US political 'dominance', notably in NATO, which he eventually left. On the other hand, he nevertheless remained a member of the Atlantic Alliance. Meanwhile President Johnson advocated the very antithesis of De Gaulle's 'independent' Europe by sketching his own outlines of 'a new Europe': 'a stronger, increasingly united but open Europe – with Great Britain in it – and with close ties to America'.[18] This formulation encapsulated not only what the US wanted from a united Europe, but also what it did *not* want: an inward looking Europe *à la* De Gaulle,

---

14 Jean Monnet to George Ball, 18 January 1961, Max Kohnstamm's Archives (MKD).

15 Winand, *Eisenhower, Kennedy*, p.198.

16 Jean Monnet to Gene Rostow, 18 January 1961, MKD.

17 *Foreign Relations of the United States 1961-1963* (Vol.XIII, US Government Printing Office, Washington, 1994), p.237.

18 *Department of State Bulletin*, 24 October 1966, p.624.

closed to US interests, and ignoring 'the crucial collateral of Atlantic partnership'.[19]

If we now turn to the early 1970s, the international monetary confusion triggered by the US spurred on Europeans towards stepped up co-operation among themselves. When EC Member States sought to coordinate their foreign policies under the newly created EPC (European Political Cooperation), the Nixon administration launched the ill-fated 'Year of Europe' initiative, alongside a project for a new Atlantic charter, in part to counteract a possible challenge from EPC to American leadership in the Western Alliance. At the same time, Kissinger made less than subtle allusions to the 'regional interests' of its European allies as opposed to American 'global interests and responsibilities'.[20] The result was the June 1974 Gymnich formula, which allowed for some consultations between the EC presidency and the US. A statement of principles was all the answer the EC chose to give to Kissinger's Atlantic Charter.[21]

The Carter administration subsequently resurrected the commitment to a more equal partnership with the EC, but this time coupled with a trilateral relationship between the US, the EC and Japan. Signs of this were President Carter's visit to the Commission in 1976 and 1978, his approval of EPC, his acceptance of the Common Agricultural Policy as well as the greater importance he assigned to biannual EC-US consultations.

On the whole, 'leadership' and 'partnership' on both sides of the Atlantic were declined in modes particular not only to the US and to the European Communities, but also to the various EC Member States, whose recurring disagreements on the shape of European unity, and on the intimacy of the relationship with the United States, led to periodic crises within the EC and in the Atlantic framework. Some Member States, such as West Germany under Adenauer, were torn between the necessity of relying on the United States for their security, and a temp-

---

19 *Foreign Relations of the United States* 1964-1968 (Vol.XIII, Western European Region, US Government Printing Office, Washington 1995), p.185.

20 'Fourth Annual Report to the Congress on United States Foreign Policy, 3 May 1973', *Public Papers of the Presidents, Richard Nixon* (US Government Printing Office 1973 (141)), pp.402-405.

21 Kevin Featherstone and Roy Ginsberg, *The United States and the European Community in the 1990s, Partners in Transition* (New York, N.Y.), 1993, p.86.

tation to surrender to Gaullist sirens who called for more independence from the United States. In addition, changed or confrontational economic circumstances, periods of *détente*, as well as American attempts to bypass the Europeans in dealing with the Soviet Union, encouraged the EC and its Member States to periodically challenge US economic and political, and to a lesser extent, strategic hegemony. While both sides mostly paid lip service to the Atlantic partnership throughout the period under survey, the partnership also came to mean, on the American side, a 'financial partnership' with the Common market in which the European side might provide more monies for common endeavors, including in Vietnam, and which would undermine De Gaulle's or other similar attempts to build an independent Europe.

The 'Cold Relationship': Holding the Other Side in Check and Coping with Conflicts

For Eisenhower, 'weakness could not cooperate, weakness could only beg'.[22] A strong European Union seemed to be in the interest of the US. A European tendency to opt for an independent venture which might impede cooperation was however not. The US used different strategies to control European appetites for too much independence.

During World War II, American planners had hoped to avert the belligerent tendencies of a potentially hostile united Europe through the establishment of an effective security system. Subsequently, during the Cold War, Atlantic instruments such as the OECD and NATO were considered in part as instruments to safely contain the EC within an Atlantic framework. They were equally seen as burden-sharing exercises that would encourage Western Europe to coordinate its policies with the US and spend more money for common enterprises, including for defense and aid to the developing world. Thus, encouragement for a united Europe to develop a more 'global' orientation also meant that Europe must unite to share American burdens around the world. Atlantic instruments combined with multilateral instruments and special relationships to hold the Common Market in check. In the 1960s, American policy-makers anticipated that the 'NATO structure and joint US-UK influence' would 'prevent the Common Market from leading to any

---

22 President William Clinton, Remarks by the President to a multinational audience of future leaders of Europe, Hôtel de Ville, Brussels, 9 January 1994, *European Report*, No.1916, 12 January 1994; Geoffrey Warner, 'Eisenhower, Dulles and the Unity of Western Europe', *International Affairs*, 69:2 (1993): 325-26.

political or economic difficulties'. The GATT was seen as a handy instrument for reducing the common external tariff and avert the fear of a 'fortress Europe'. Correlatively, EC enlargement, especially to the UK, would open up prospects for more liberalization within the GATT 'with the Community acting as an institutional lever for opening a larger European market to US producers'.[23]

In the 1960s, 70s and 80s, US-EC relations had their ups and downs. The Kennedy administration had started to take a close look at the discriminatory aspects of the Common Market, notably during the 'chicken-war' and other trade disputes soon followed. Greater economic competition between the US and the EC, the US balance of payments and trade deficit, European criticism of American policy, not least in Vietnam, and a European tendency to act in an increasingly independent way in sensitive areas such as the Middle East, the Mediterranean, Africa, Eastern Europe or the Soviet Union, did much to usher in an eclipse in US support for the European Communities. Some American quarters questioned American support for European economic and political integration: not only did the EC rarely speak with one voice, but when it did so, notably via EPC, that voice failed to speak in unison with that of the US. American policy-makers thus alternatively resorted to other strategies to hold their partner, and rival, in check.

During the Nixon administration, in response to both a disunited, complex EC 'as mystifying as the Tibetan theocracy'[24] and an EC speaking out of line with the voice of the US, the temptation was great to divide and conquer or to ask for a seat at the table to maintain American leadership. So too was the temptation to reduce EC ambitions for global power status to those of a regional power. Thus, to obviate the tendency for the EC to present the US with political decisions as *faits accomplis* via EPC, Kissinger asked that the US be consulted before the EC even made those decisions. Clearly preferring to make US views known at several centers of decision rather than being 'forced to stake everything on affecting the views of a single, supranational body', he

---

23 John Peterson, *Europe and America. The Prospects for Partnership* (London and New York, Routledge, 1996), p.37.

24 Robert Schaetzel, *The Unhinged Alliance: America and the European Community* (New York, Harper and Row, 1975), p.95.

also on occasion did not shy from playing off one European country against the other.[25]

Controversies between the EC and the US, including over the Middle East, the Iranian hostage crisis and the Soviet invasion of Afghanistan, frequently marred the transatlantic relationship during the Carter years. Under the Reagan administration, trade wars continued to poison US-EC relations, as did disputes over foreign policy in the Middle East, Central America, Poland and Siberian natural gas. Monetary cooperation was at an all-time low, while a deep recession, EC enlargement to the Iberian peninsula and the prospects of 'Europe 1992' only served to amplify fears of trade loss and trade discrimination. Although the administration paid lip service to American support for European integration, it also took a sober look at US trade interests, strove to protect these from the EC, in a sometimes hostile fashion, and generally looked down on European policy, especially towards the Soviet Union.[26] During the Reagan years, as the EC developed policies independent from the US and as US hegemony eroded, the US alternatively used public support for European integration, neglect, denigration or even demonization of the EC. While lobbying the Community and its Member States on key issues, the US continued to resort both to Atlantic or multilateral instruments to control its European partners.

Throughout the period under survey, disagreements in the trade field frequently erupted in spite of several GATT rounds, especially in the agricultural field where American efforts to influence the Common Agricultural Policy to serve US interests mostly failed during the Kennedy Round and thereafter. The relative economic decline of the United States also made it less inclined to condone economic competition from the EC. This decline, perceived or real, further encouraged the United States to ask its European partners to work towards common tasks with the United States both in dealing with the developing world and on defense matters. At the political level, some of the worst tensions originated from European attempts to develop their own policies towards sensitive areas of the world without prior consultation with the United States. In the context of the Vietnam war, a US Ambassador

---

25 Henry A. Kissinger, 'What Kind of Atlantic Partnership?,' *The Atlantic Community Quarterly*, 7:1 (1969): 22.

26 For a brief review of US-EC relations from Nixon to Reagan, see: Roy H. Ginsberg, *Foreign Policy Actions of the European Community. The Politics of Scale* (Boulder, Lynne Rienner, 1989), pp.136-149.

lamented: 'the Europeans are causing problems for us in the United Nations. We no longer have a solid bloc of western allies behind us.'[27] If we take another example, that of the Middle East, conflicts frequently flared up between the US and the EC throughout the period, and the transatlantic partners mostly agreed to disagree and left it at that. Finally, European appetites for more control over their own defense, including in the nuclear field, led to recurrent tensions with the United States. For example, while the Americans spoke of 'integration' in the field of defense, De Gaulle, who detested the word 'integration' just as much as he did the expression 'common tasks' in an Atlantic framework, merely spoke of cooperation. For him, political European maturity and defense were indissolubly linked. The United States understood only too well that his opposition to NATO mainly stemmed from his belief that it was 'the symbol and the instrument for continued US political domination of Western Europe'.[28] In addition, while the United States was notably intent on avoiding nuclear proliferation in Europe via an integrated defense, the defense and economic dimensions were closely related. Both Kennedy and Johnson were opposed to an independent Europe without the Atlantic collateral not only for strategic reasons, but also for economic ones. Thus Kennedy was particularly wary of having to beg economic favors from a European Community *à la* De Gaulle possessing its own nuclear capability.

As we have seen, the US resorted to a wide range of instruments to hold its European partners in check and to prevent or diffuse crises. So too did the EC. If the US used Atlantic instruments such as the OECD and NATO to make sure that the EC continued to abide by the 'Atlantic collateral', its European partners similarly used such frameworks to have more of a say in influencing American policies, and to solve American problems with world wide consequences, including in the monetary field, together. Besides, while the US instrumentalized special relationships with key European countries such as West Germany or the United Kingdom, and in some cases, support of the European Commission positions, in order to put pressure on EC Member States, some of the latter in turn also used special relationships with the US to try to

[27] *Foreign Relations of the United States 1964-1968* (Vol.XIII, Western European Region, US Government Printing Office, Washington 1995), p.573.

[28] Thomas L. Hughes, 'De Gaulle and the North Atlantic Alliance', 4 May 1965, NSF C. File, Box 171, Europe and the USSR, 'France Memos, Vol.VI –2/65-6/65', Lyndon B. Johnson Library.

influence their EC partners into solving pressing European problems. Multilateral instruments such as the GATT or the UN were furthermore used by either side to prevent or diffuse conflicts in a wider framework.

Throughout the period, the United States continued to encourage European integration with close ties to the United States, for its economic and political role in stabilizing Europe, and thus in preventing conflicts in the region. Although some attempts were made to formalize the Atlantic relationship in an institutional way, these mostly failed. Even though the various partnerships advocated by several American leaders, Kissinger's 'Year of Europe', or the Transatlantic Declaration were all attempts to help diffuse tension, they did not result in the creation of new Atlantic institutions. Thus, as will be further illustrated below, we could argue that Atlantic organizations such as NATO, European organizations such as the CSCE, and organizations which subsequently had a more trilateral tinge such as the OECD, were the only frameworks where the United States could act as a 'European' power... with a seat at the table. The insistence on the US side on the 'Atlantic collateral' of the American partnership with the European Communities, never quite succeeded in guaranteeing such a seat.

From New Atlanticism to the NTA

New Atlanticism and the Transatlantic Declaration on US-EC Relations

At the end of the 1980s, sweeping changes in Eastern Europe and a highly volatile European situation prompted Washington to reassess its policy towards Europe. By mid-1989, the Bush administration, in spite of Congressional hearings to look into charges that the Europe 1992 program might lead to a 'Fortress Europe', appeared to have concluded that this danger was less real than previous assessments might have suggested. At the same time the success of the Single European Act, coupled with prospects for a European Economic and Monetary Union, and the decline of the importance of the security dimension in transatlantic relations as a result of the end of the Cold War, brought Washington to the sobering realization that US economic and political influence in Europe was unlikely to be maintained unless the US wholeheartedly backed European integration. Kennedy's fear that the US might have to beg economic favors from Europe once the security dimension took a back seat seemed to have come of age. In addition, with German reunification looming on the horizon, the Community's political significance was magnified as a way of forestalling a German Europe as opposed to a European Germany. Financial constraints on US foreign policy further made the EC an attractive candidate for burden-sharing, notably in Eastern and Central Europe. At the July 1989 G7 summit in Paris, the US gave its unqualified support to the European Commission to coordinate Western aid to Hungary and Poland. Increasingly, European integration came to be seen as an element of political stability and economic viability on the European continent. If, during the Cold War, American policy-makers had hoped that the EC would exert an irresistible pull on Russian satellites, the EC now held the prospect of expanding the community of 'market democracies' towards the East. An American commitment to a politically united Europe did, however, come with some strings attached. Attempts to renew Atlantic entanglements, as well as to find a seat at the table, were among them.

Simply put, the US was a member of NATO, of the CSCE, but not of the EC. The 'New Atlanticism' which Secretary of State Baker advocated in December 1989, made clear that, while supporting the EC, the US considered that NATO would 'remain North America's primary link with Europe'. A united Europe must remain 'free, democratic and closely linked to its North American partners'. It must stay 'open to cooperation with others' by maintaining its market access to third countries, including the US and neighbours to the East. Once again then American support for European political and economic integration was predicated upon embedding the EC within a tightly knit Atlantic community and making sure that it would meet common tasks. A revamped NATO, in which Washington could best communicate its views to its European partners, since it was a member of the organization, remained the principal means of influence of the US as a European power.

In December 1989, in order to strengthen the transatlantic relationship, Baker, building on a speech by President Bush, proposed that the EC and the US should 'work together to achieve, whether in treaty or some other form, a significantly strengthened set of institutional and consultative links'.[29] In February 1990, the Irish Prime Minister, as President of the Council of Ministers, made a proposal for a formalized EC-US relationship; Jacques Delors had made similar calls the previous

29 'A New Europe and a New Atlanticism', Berlin Press Club, 12 December 1989.

year.[30] The EC was indeed preparing to simplify and rationalise the management of its external relations in order to better cope with the multiplication of *ad hoc* bilateral contacts and increasing interdependence. The institutionalisation of key relationships was part of this scheme. Many European decision-makers were, however, torn between the desire to develop a more assertive EC (on trade, economic and monetary issues in particular) and the danger of accelerating US military withdrawal on a background of uncertainty and instability in the East.

In September 1990, Robert Zoellick, who exerted a key influence in the State Department, then echoed Baker's earlier speech. Fearing a Europe that might become either 'insular' by looking at its own problems or 'itinerant' by acting autonomously around the world now that anti-communism no longer tied the alliance structure together, he looked for renewed Atlantic commitments. He proposed to 'further institutionalize the US-EC relationship by negotiating a framework agreement', which 'might even evolve into a treaty' and would reflect the 'shared ideas and values' of what he called 'Euro-America'.[31] About two months later, in November 1990, the United States, the European Community and its Member States signed a 'Declaration on US-EC Relations' in Paris.

In February 1989, US Commerce Secretary Robert Mosbacher had openly asked for 'a seat at the table at least as an observer as a way 'to engage the EC in a broadened productive dialogue at all levels'[32] to best deal with the challenges of the EC 1992 program. This request met with expected opposition from the EC, yet the proposal for a 'dialogue at all levels' in order to strengthen the transatlantic relationship soon resurfaced in a different guise: the Bush administration's proposal for regular consultations between the US and the EC at various levels 'to enhance the practice and expectation of joint action – or at least avoid presenting either side with non-negotiable or surprise positions'.[33] Some Europeans, however, in particular the French, were not so keen on a dialogue

---

30 *The Washington Post*, February 28, 1990, p.A1.

31 Robert B. Zoellick, 'The New Europe in a New Age: Insular, Itinerant, or International? Prospects for an Alliance of Values', *US Department of State Dispatch*, 24 September 1990.

32 Robert Mosbacher, 'Address to the Columbia Institute Conference on the US Role in a United Europe', Washington D.C., 24 February 1990, p.5; See Youri Devuyst's chapter.

33 Robert Zoellick, 'The New Europe'.

at all levels which might amount to a thirteenth seat at the table via the back door. During the negotiations leading up to the Transatlantic Declaration, the French manoeuvred to squash attempts to include references to consultations below the political level in the declaration. On the American side, the Treasury Department strongly resisted an EC proposal to include a reference to the need for financial stability and monetary cooperation.

The final product was disappointing in terms of commitments. The declaration referred to 'common goals' such as supporting democracy or promoting market principles, as well as to the 'trans-national challenges'[34] of the post-Cold War world such as terrorism, drugs, pollution or missile technology. It did however contain more in terms of structure by codifying and formalizing existing mechanisms for regular consultations that had been agreed during the previous year – in particular the bi-annual summits. The European desire for independence transpired through the diplomatic language: both sides were to 'inform and consult each other on important matters of common interest, both political and economic, with a view to bringing their positions as close as possible, without prejudice to their respective independence'. This was a far cry from Zoellick's calls for enhancing 'the practice and expectation of joint action'.

Zoellick had hoped that the Declaration would 'plant the seeds of change'. Part of the logic of the declaration was educational: by engaging in a regular dialogue with EC institutions, Americans would further familiarize themselves with the EC decision-making process. A building block approach that would pick up sectors which had not been sufficiently liberalized by the Uruguay Round and include these in transatlantic discussions would create a process that could take on a life of its own. The idea of a treaty might resurface when the time was ripe, and, according to Zoellick, might even ultimately be merged with the Washington Treaty, so that the European pillar of NATO would reflect European integration on security and defense issues. NATO would then finally not only include European Member States, but representatives of EC institutions as well, and especially the Commission representative in charge of foreign policy, whoever that might be. More generally, the declaration, along with APEC (Asian-Pacific Economic Co-operation),

---

34 Declaration on US-EC Relations, 23 November 1990, *US Department of State Dispatch*, 26 November 1990.

NAFTA (North American Free Trade Association) and other such regional endeavors, was part of an American vision that tried to develop institutions both to bind partners closer to the United States now that the common external threat of communism had waned, and to press ahead for liberalization in trade and economics.[35]

The Run-up to the NTA

Similarly, instead of containing communism, the new Clinton administration sought to expand the community of 'market democracies' by binding partners around the world and building institutional links to the United States. Thus, the OECD could 'serve as a bridge between Atlantic and Pacific industrial economies' and 'inclusive post-Cold War security arrangements' such as the North Atlantic Co-operation Council and the Partnership for Peace could serve as a framework to 'help consolidate democracy and foster greater unity across the entire European continent'.[36]

On the other side of the Atlantic, the EU pursued the development of its presence on the international stage in the wake of the Maastricht Treaty on European Union and encouraged the pressing demands of a number of countries and regional groupings to establish or develop privileged relations with it. In the 1990s the transatlantic partners thus became enmeshed in a web of networks, regional agreements and partnerships, some of which were particular to each. By the beginning of the Clinton administration, links between the US and the EU seemed inadequate in light of frequent trade disputes. The existence of formalized agreements between the US and other regions of the world starkly contrasted with the lack thereof between transatlantic partners.

The December 1995 NTA and JAP partly strove to remedy this perceived gap. The agreement stemmed from joint concerns as well as from concerns specific to the EU and the US. Several chapters in this book look at the details of the run-up to the NTA. We shall only review its main stages here while briefly sketching out the stakes of the various participants.

---

35 Pascaline Winand, interview with Robert Zoellick, November 1995, Washington D.C.

36 Secretary Christopher, 'Toward a More Integrated World' (Statement at the OECD ministerial meeting, Paris, France, 8 June 1994, US Department of State, Bureau of Public Affairs, Office of Public Communication).

In European eyes, the Clinton administration initially unduly concentrated on domestic issues to the detriment of transatlantic ties. A general trend of American culture to move towards the South and the West worried European policy-makers, including Jacques Delors; NAFTA and APEC only seemed to magnify this trend. Trade disputes over bananas or the new head of the WTO, disagreements over NATO expansion, civil war in Bosnia or the resolution of the Mexican peso crisis corroborated the impression that the transatlantic partners were drifting apart. In the spring of 1993, however, both President Clinton and his Secretary of State made declarations which emphasised US support for European integration and a US-EU partnership especially geared towards the East. The focus on the EU was more than simply declaratory posturing.

By the end of the year, the conclusion of the Uruguay Round had cleared the air just in time for Clinton's first visit to Europe in January 1994. The Head of the US Mission to the EU (USEU) made sure that the EU would receive adequate attention during that visit. In Brussels, President Clinton showed his support for a EU that would 'develop stronger institutions of common purpose and common action' and act as a strong and equal partner.[37] The NATO Summit in mid-January signalled American support for the development of a European Security and Defense Identity (ESDI) and an integrated Eurocorps. While the Clinton administration reemphasized the necessity of a strong Atlantic link, its support for the WEU was a significant departure from the Bush administration.

The Transatlantic Declaration (TD) record had been a mixed one. While some regulatory convergence, information, and cooperative dialogue took place, and settlements were negotiated in response to various trade crises,[38] the TD experience also showed the necessity of improving the continuity between biannual US-EU summits, of tying the various levels of transatlantic consultations together, and possibly of supplementing these with additional lower-level meetings. The aspiration towards greater structure – especially on the US side – combined, perhaps antithetically, with a desire for more pragmatic, non-bureau-

---

37 The Head of USEU, Ambassador Eizenstat, then personally briefed the President; President Clinton's speech to the 'Future leaders of Europe', 9 January 1994.

38 Michael Calingaert, *European Integration Revisited – Progress, Prospects and US Interests* (Westview Press (CO), 1996).

cratic collaboration: both Delors and Clinton insisted that personal contact points between EU and US representatives were key to the success of future US-EU bilateral meetings.

Partly in response to these needs, the July 1994 US-EU Berlin Summit established three *ad hoc* senior level working groups[39] to better assure the *suivi* until the next US-EU Summit in Washington in 1995; one on cooperation in Central and Eastern Europe, another on CFSP, and lastly, a group concerning international crime, including nuclear smuggling.[40] In general, the three senior level working groups showed that another mechanism was needed which involved people closer to the working level and to the issues. They nevertheless fostered personal links between US and EU negotiators and served as a useful building block for the establishment of a new Senior Level Group while laying the ground for the NTA.

In January 1995, Spain's Foreign Minister, Carlos Westendorp, paid a visit to the US Mission to the EU to discuss ways of improving transatlantic relations during the Spanish presidency. Around the same time, the USEU Ambassador convinced the US Secretary of State that he should take the initiative in launching a new transatlantic agenda which focused on the relationship with the EU. The result was Secretary Christopher's speech on 2 June 1995 in Madrid which partly built on Leon Brittan's concept for transatlantic trade liberalisation[41] and proposed to jointly formulate a New Transatlantic Agenda for the 21st century. A Senior Level Group (SLG), with high-level officials from Spain, the European Commission, and the US was subsequently appointed at the 14 June 1995 US-EU Summit in Washington to prepare the agenda. It was assisted by lower working levels and involved a wide range of bureaucracies on both sides of the Atlantic. The European Commission then presented a Communication 'Europe and the US: the Way Forward' to the Council in July. At the same time, the Americans prepared their own paper so as to have an independent basis from which to negotiate, rather than solely relying on the Commission paper, and shared an outline of it with the Spanish Presidency in July 1995.

---

39 Meeting in a trilateral format – Representatives from the US Government, the European Commission and the country holding the presidency of the EU Council.

40 For more details on the working groups, see A. Gardner's chapter in this book.

41 'The EU-US Relationship. Will it last?', Speech to the American Club, Brussels, 27 April 1995.

On the whole, there were two general approaches. On the EU side, in keeping with the original Commission document, the idea was to give an extensive picture of the relationship to demonstrate its richness, while focusing on common actions with the US. The length of the Commission's note reflected not just the need to emphasise the EU's global responsibilities, but also its desire to satisfy EU institutions and national governments alike in order to quickly secure approval of the agenda. By contrast, the American side preferred to concentrate on major agenda points for the future, and to make a distinction between US-EU cooperation in Europe as separate from US-EU cooperation in the rest of the world. The Commission did not approve of this distinction which smacked of Kissinger's reference to Europe as a regional power, and preferred to arrange areas of cooperation thematically. The European and American concepts were ultimately merged into the NTA, a general statement about the relationship and the mutual commitment of the partners, and the JAP, a flexible document tailored to the problems of the moment and which would be periodically updated according to current problems and global challenges. The 'New Transatlantic Agenda' and the 'Joint Action Plan' were signed on 3 December 1995.[42]

Like the TD, the NTA/JAP belongs from a legal viewpoint to the category of non-binding instruments or gentleman's agreements. As an 'executive agreement', it does not amount to a set of binding rules like a treaty and does not require parliamentary ratification.[43] The deliberate choice, on both sides of the Atlantic, to opt for a light approach which eluded the need to win domestic support bears testimony to the diminished capacity of transatlantic partners to obtain ratification for new

---

42 'Documents Signed at the last Transatlantic Summit between the European Union and the United States', *Agence Europe*, 12 January 1996. The texts are also available on the homepages of the European Commission and the State Department.

43 In terms of EC practice, the negotiation of such arrangements by the European Commission nevertheless requires the authorization of the Council of Ministers, which then acts by common accord. See I. Macleod, I. D. Hendry and Stephen Hyett, *The External Relations of the European Communities – A Manual of Law and Practice* (Clarendon Press, Oxford, 1996), p.121. In terms of US practice, the main distinction between executive agreements and treaties is that the former do not require the approval of two-thirds of the Senate. Most, but not all executive agreements do not require any congressional approval. See James M. Lindsay, *Congress and the Politics of US Foreign Policy* (Baltimore, the Johns Hopkins University Press, 1994).

commitments.[44] On the European side, the preparation of the Intergovernmental Conference which led to the Amsterdam Treaty agreed in June 1997 also precluded that the formalisation of the relationship could seriously be considered in the short run, albeit the European Commission, for example, did not overrule a transatlantic treaty as a desirable long term option. For the time being however, both partners wanted at all costs to avoid creating false expectations in the general public. Small was beautiful: it was better to put an ambitious transatlantic treaty on the back burner and wait for the relationship to be revitalised to reactivate the treaty option at a later stage.

A First Assessment of the Contents of the NTA

The general aims of the NTA are as typical as they are ambitious: to realize opportunities and meet challenges in terms of security, (economic) prosperity and (democratic) values for the transatlantic partners and for the world. More crudely and concisely put, the NTA's main ambition is to deal better with the externalities of US policies for the EU, and vice versa, as well as to address the effects of third parties' actions on US-EU interests. To achieve these aims, the NTA innovates at four levels.

The NTA/JAP *creates a global and adjustable framework* for action that provides a better overview of the relationship and an opportunity for horizontal coordination. The framework can be adjusted regularly to the problems of the moment thanks to a built-in, pre-defined follow-up mechanism: a US-EU 'Senior Level Group' of sub-cabinet officials and a 'NTA Task Force' of working-level officials that prepare US-EU summits, evaluate progress on the various topics listed in the JAP, and propose new objectives. One limitation of this framework is the absence of a single policy paradigm linking its various parts into a coherent whole. As its name clearly indicates, the NTA is indeed an agenda, not a program.

Secondly, the NTA/JAP *significantly upgrades the level of mutual commitments* between the US and the EU, from information and consultation to coordination and joint action. The magnitude of this upgrade must however be put into perspective. A close reading of the JAP indeed reveals the high heterogeneity of the commitments made. For some cases, means and deadlines are clearly identified, while, for many oth-

44 See the chapter by John Peterson in this volume.

ers, goals and time frames remain vague. These variations reflect three main elements: (1) international priorities of the US and the EU (for instance, the risk of conflict in the Korean peninsula seemed to require a stronger commitment than the support for a 'smooth transition' of Hong Kong or Macao to Chinese sovereignty); (2) the degree of convergence of the partners' interests and analyses (preservation of *chasses gardées* – cf. Central America – and pre-existing policy disagreements – cf. Cuba – are easily traceable); and (3) the necessity to adopt or not a low profile – cf. the development of a 'New Transatlantic Marketplace' (NTM).[45] All in all, commitments are distributed as follows: thirty-two percent of these are restricted to exchange of information, dialogues and consultation; another twenty-seven percent consist of encouragement and coordination of initiatives; 'cooperation' accounts for another thirty-five percent; 'joint actions' represent no more than six percent. In that respect, the name given to the document is rather misleading; the targets set by the JAP have more to do with enhanced coordination and cooperation than with joint action.

Irrespective of its real magnitude, the upgrade was expected to improve not only the effectiveness but also the efficiency of US and EU policies. On the US domestic side, the NTA was indeed seen as a costs savings device. Hostile Republican majorities in the Congress have meant budgetary restrictions. Accordingly, collaborative efforts through the NTA looked particularly attractive as a way of maintaining American leadership by asking Europeans to contribute monies for joint ven-

45 The NTA approaches the issue of the NTM by focusing on technical aspects while remaining vague on key aspects of the action plan. Neither in the NTA nor in the JAP do we find a clear description of what the NTM is beyond a general intention of 'progressively reducing or eliminating barriers that hinder the flow of goods, services and capital'. Quite adroitly, the NTA simply states that a 'joint study' will be carried out to identify ways of eliminating various obstacles to trade. In this way, the joint study contemplated under the NTA does seem to leave the door open for a free trade area, while not mentioning it. This despite the fact that, in September 1995, a joint Spanish Presidency/European Commission draft EU-US action plan evidenced a clear intention to focus the joint EU-US feasibility study on including a free trade area component in a transatlantic economic space (Joint Presidency/Commission Working Paper. Draft EU-US Action Plan, 22 September 1995). Here vagueness was of the essence not only to avoid antagonizing the US Congress or some EU Member States but also to prevent, as Bart Kerremans has pointed out, 'a legal discussion about the compatibility of an NTM with the WTO provisions' (cf. article XXIV GATT and article V GATS). Bart Kerremans, 'The Limits of the Leap, Transatlantic Relations and the Transatlantic Economic Partnership', Paper prepared for the 1998 USA ECSA conference, p.10.

EDINBURGH UNIVERSITY LIBRARY
WITHDRAWN

tures, for example in the development field. For some US agencies threatened with closure by the US Congress, such as the Department of Commerce, the NTA became a way to save their bureaucratic skins. Seen from the European side, however, collaboration and burden sharing went hand in hand with equality and joint or shared leadership. Dealing jointly with transnational challenges meant graduating into the class of a global as opposed to a regional power.

Thirdly, the NTA/JAP *widens the scope of the relationship*. It assigns the rejuvenated US-EU Partnership to fulfil no less than 203 bilateral, regional and global objectives grouped around four main themes: 1) 'promoting peace and stability, democracy and development around the world'; 2) 'responding to global challenges'; 3) 'contributing to the expansion of world trade and closer economic cooperation'; and 4) 'building bridges across the Atlantic'. The third theme is clearly the centrepiece of the NTA/JAP. This comes as no surprise considering the stakes and the high interdependence of the US and the EU in trade and investment, not to mention the fact that it also corresponds to the EU's core competencies.

Some of the items listed, mostly those touching upon bilateral (trade and economic) issues as well as regional issues limited to the EU's near abroad, have of course been the focus of EU-US relations for years. The addition of issues like the reconstruction of the Former Yugoslavia and the stabilisation of relations with Central and Eastern European Countries, or even Russia, merely followed that pre-established logic. The real novelty lay in the decision to broaden the range of issue areas expressly earmarked for regular transatlantic cooperation to other regions, as well as to transnational and global issues. The newly listed countries were mainly from the Middle East, sub-Saharan Africa, Central America and South East Asia, some of which had been incorporated into the NTA because they had caused serious transatlantic wrangling in the past. As to the inclusion of global issues, it reflected the progress of European integration in several fields, as well as the US willingness to control such progress by gaining some kind of seat at the table. Most were indeed related to the powers acquired by the EU under the Maastricht Treaty in security, justice and home affairs – the so-called 'second' and 'third pillar' of the Union (non-proliferation, international disarmament and arms transfers; fight against organized crime, terrorism, drug trafficking and illegal immigration, in particular). The inclusion of development cooperation and humanitarian assistance had more to do with the prospect of cost savings already mentioned.

Other areas that would *a priori* benefit from more discussion or co-operation were left aside. Monetary issues, agriculture, hard security or so-called rogue States like Libya, Iran and Iraq are obvious cases of deliberate exclusion. Two reasons came into play: the risk of derailing or duplicating the work done properly in other international forums; and the risk of jeopardising the take-off of the entire NTA by including highly contentious issues.

All in all, the NTA/JAP offers a balanced blend: it includes consensual issues on which agreement should be relatively easy to secure and divisive issues for which increased capacity in terms of early warning system, conflict prevention and crisis management would be a plus, while excluding potentially explosive ones. Precautions taken in the definition of the NTA/JAP's scope and level of commitments indicate that the agreement was deliberately tailored to secure a globally positive report card.

Finally, the NTA/JAP *multiplies structured dialogues*, adding to the extensive consultations among officials established by the TD. This institutional option is part of a strategy intended to mobilise or shape public, business and political support, but without incurring the difficulties inherent to highly publicised negotiations. To answer 'the need to strengthen and broaden public support' for the partnership, parts of the NTA/JAP were indeed deliberately designed to have significant and positive public appeal. Using action-oriented and resolute vocabulary, they are focused on 'concrete and practical steps'. Furthermore, environment, organized crime, terrorism or drug trafficking, science and technology cooperation, development cooperation and humanitarian assistance, social policy, employment or health problems, and educational or cultural contacts were all included in the JAP partly to raise general public awareness of the potential of the US/EU relationship for solving pressing problems at home and for 'being altruistic' towards the rest of the world. Specific segments of the population in the US and EU, including opinion-shapers such as educators and scientists, as well as decision-makers were also targeted by the NTA/JAP. The European Commission, for example, anticipated great benefits from educating the US executive to the importance of European integration for international economic relations and security. Meanwhile part of the US executive itself considered the NTA as a convenient way of familiarizing more actors in its own bureaucracy with the arcane features of the EU decision-making process. The US government also expected that the NTA would serve as an educational tool to coach the EU to assume a greater international role which would match and even go beyond its new powers under the Maastricht Treaty, especially in foreign policy, as well as justice and home affairs issues. Finally, the NTA and its SLG reports were conceived as a way to raise the interest of the highest echelon for the process. By tying each US-EU summit more closely to the next, the impression of continuous progress and usefulness of these exercises was reinforced, thereby making the summits more gratifying for the participants.

Finding ways of maximising support while minimising risks of backlashes was particularly difficult for the third theme of the JAP, given the contentiousness of trade for US-EU relations. Together with deliberate vagueness in the wording of the objectives (see note 45), these concerns were addressed by the involvement of big business. It was no accident if it received prominent attention. The first Transatlantic Business Dialogue (TABD) was launched in Seville in mid-November 1995 at the initiative of US Secretary of Commerce Ron Brown and EU Commissioners Leon Brittan (trade) and Martin Bangemann (industry). Some hundred US and European business leaders pondered over ways of removing barriers to trade and investment. About sixty percent of their recommendations were later fed into the JAP.[46] The TABD's contribution was explicitly recognized in the fourth part of the NTA/JAP, EU and US officials were asked to 'work closely together' with business leaders in preparation for US-EU Summits.

Structured dialogues such as the TABD, and as we shall see in subsequent chapters, other such dialogues which emerged later, seem therefore to have been conceived as a way of helping the development of the US-EU relations 'on the cheap'. Against limited funding and no power sharing, they could provide extra-expertise, serve as additional early warning systems, pre-empt backlash from last minute exposure to the public and, last but not least, contribute to (re)create a 'vibrant' transatlantic community.

In conclusion, our first assessment of the contents of the NTA/JAP can be synthesised into five points: it has set a global and adjustable framework for the US-EU relationship; upgraded the level of commit-

46 See the chapter by Maria Green Cowles in this volume.

ments; widened the scope of items dealt at the US-EU level, and multiplied structured dialogues. According to some of its masterminds, the initiative mostly focused on process (meeting to create bonds): the new format of the relationship aimed at wider and deeper socialisation in order to improve mutual understanding and revitalise the 'Atlantic spirit', not to say nurture a sense of community. The exercise was however also about substance (meeting to decide on issues): the changes introduced by the NTA were expected to produce immediate results and concrete benefits. There is therefore a need to discuss further the question of the evaluation of the NTA's policy output. This is the task of the next chapter.

CHAPTER 2

Assessing, Evaluating and Explaining the Output of US-EU Relations

Éric PHILIPPART*

Fonds National de la Recherche Scientifique (Belgium),
Université Libre de Bruxelles,
College of Europe (Bruges)

One of the ambitions of this book is to learn more about the performance of the new US-EU system in terms both of its capacity to reach decisions and of the quality of the decisions reached, as well as how these results can be explained. This chapter prepares the ground for answering these questions. In the first section, cooperation is defined and operationalized. Knowing what the essence of cooperation is and how it can be measured is indeed indispensable for evaluating whether or not the US and the EU have established an effective system of cooperation. The evaluation of the quality of the US-EU cooperation requires more: a number of specific evaluative criteria that are proposed at the end of the section. The second section of this chapter reviews a selection of factors that could be used to explain the level of the ambitions assigned to US-EU cooperation and what was eventually achieved. Various theoretical approaches offer different sets of hypotheses. Even if this book is not meant to make a systematic contribution to a specific theoretical debate, even less to embark upon the elusive quest for a syncretic paradigm, this variety calls for some ordering device to put into perspective the findings of its various chapters. Defining an analytical framework is particularly important in the case of US-EU partnership because of its unorthodox nature and hyper-complexity. Unorthodox insofar as one of the partners, the EU, is often considered as a *sui generis* entity, a hybrid 'beast' borrowing features from the state and the

---

* This chapter benefited from the suggestions of Desmond Dinan and Sophie Vanhoonacker, as well as from the thorough comments of Monika Sie Dhian Ho.

international organization.[1] Hyper-complex insofar as the relationship is made up of many configurations of actors and issues that are sometimes driven by diametrically opposed dynamics.

Assessing and Evaluating the Outcomes of US-EU Relations

Cooperation as a generic term can have many meanings. In order to operationalize the concept and establish measurement standards, it has to be clearly defined. Robert Keohane has proposed a basic definition which has been largely accepted: 'cooperation requires that the actions of separate individuals or organizations – which are not in pre-existent harmony – be brought into conformity with one another through a process of negotiation'.[2] While there are many reasons why actors co-operate, the concrete objective of cooperation is mainly to deal with externalities (*i.e.* minimise disturbances caused by policies) or make policies mutually reinforcing. Forms of cooperation are numerous: they range from sharing information in order to narrow down the range of 'acceptable' options by pressure or persuasion, *ex ante* consultation and negotiation of mutual reinforcement (*i.e.* adopting identical, complementary or subsidiary policies), *ex post* adjustment through mutual concessions (*i.e.* avoiding or repelling antagonistic policies), up to joint-action.[3] Students of international relations have developed a number of typologies on the topic.[4] Decision-makers, however, too often discount them in favor of more 'immediate' classifications, easier to use but

---

1 T. Risse-Kappen, 'Exploring the Nature of the Beast: International Relations Theory and Comparative Policy Analysis Meet the European Union', *Journal of Common Market Studies*, 34:1 (1996) 53-80.

2 R. O. Keohane, *After Hegemony: Cooperation and Discord in the World Political Economy* (Princeton, Princeton University Press, 1984), pp.51-2.

3 On consultation and adjustment, see R. D. Putnam and N. Bayne, *Hanging Together: Cooperation and Conflict in the Seven Power Summits* (London, Sage, 1987), p.260.

4 Thomas Frellessen and Roy Ginsberg have, for instance, proposed four variants of foreign policy co-operation between the EU and the US ranging from 'coordinated action in pursuit of common objectives either through joint or separate means; complementary action taken separately but in pursuit of common objectives; coordinated declarations in which statements are issued in pursuit of common objectives either through joint or separate means; and complementary declarations, in which statements are issued separately in pursuit of common objectives'. T. Frellesen and R. Ginsberg, 'EU-US Foreign Policy Cooperation in the 1990s. Elements of Partnership', *CEPS,* Paper No.58, Brussels, 1994, p.6.

heuristically weaker. The US-EU case is no exception to this rule, the Senior Level Group Reports merely distinguishing between different levels of commitment (exchange of information, dialogue, etc.). The reports represent nevertheless a unique basis to measure the evolution of US-EU objectives and achievements. In terms of origin and format, they are indeed unusually constant: before each US-EU summit, a group of officials assess the past six months and draft 'new priorities' which will guide the work of the NTA for the next six months. Partially because of the stable make-up of the group, these assessments are written in a fairly standardised way. Accordingly, we have decided to use a scale which ranks cooperation by intensity and follows the diplomatic vocabulary in this matter.

If they offer undeniable advantages, the SLG reports also suffer from shortcomings that cannot be ignored in the analysis. First of all, as the authors and signatories of the reports are asked to pass a judgement on what is *lato sensu* their own work, they evidently have a direct stake in the assessment. Moreover, reasonably detailed definition of objectives, criteria for success or timeframe are often missing. The reports usually do not record either failures, non-actions or so-called missed opportunities in various areas listed for cooperation such as 'sharing responsibility' in Asia or on international disarmament and arms transfers. This is perhaps predictable insofar as the prime objective of diplomats and spin doctors is to produce 'safe' rather than precise prevision as well as 'useful' rather than accurate evaluation. Proper measurement of US-EU achievements however requires that negative results at least are put back into the equation. Finally, the reports give no indication as to the relative importance of each instance of cooperation. This would mean that, on aggregate, good performance in a trivial domain can compensate for underachievement on a crucial issue. Estimates of intensity of US-EU arrangements have therefore to be supplemented by assessments of their contents and scope.

If it is interesting to know what the new US-EU system has achieved exactly, it is just as important to examine how it compares in terms of performance. For example, it is not sufficient to know how many dispute settlements the US-EU partnership has succeeded in hammering out, one should in addition look at how much effort it took to reach these arrangements and what they are worth. Most analyses therefore evaluate policy decisions in terms of their effectiveness (capacity to produce a desired effect) and efficiency (amount of resources needed to deliver an effect). Their quality can also be evaluated in relation with the workability and sustainability of the arrangements, their clarity of purpose, their consistency between different elements of US-EU cooperation, their continuity (that is 'maintenance of a long-term or strategic perspective'), their compatibility with the environment and the resources available, as well as their adaptability.[5]

Explaining the Outcomes of US-EU Relations

Once cooperative endeavors are measured, ranked and evaluated, the US-EU record still needs to be explained. A straight and simple way to proceed is to focus on the factors affecting US-EU policy-making outputs. In their study of G7 summits, Robert Putnam and Nicholas Bayne, having observed that 'the degree of cooperation in international affairs is a variable, not a constant', have extracted a number of propositions from different theories. These propositions examine 'the correlation between the ups and downs of summit-linked cooperation, [...] and variations in [...] five proposed causal factors': national interests; national power; international regimes; ideas, learning and other cognitive factors; domestic politics.[6] We have adopted a similar analytical chart which questions whether, and how, distribution of power and constellation of interests, existing international institutions and modes of governance matter.[7] The following sub-sections put forward propositions spelling out how variations at these levels should *a priori* affect US-EU

---

5 The last five qualities are presented by Michael Smith as the components of a 'balanced foreign policy' (a standard notion used for comparative evaluation). M. Smith, 'Comparing Foreign Policy Systems: Problems, Processes and Performance', in M. Clarke and B. White (eds.), *Understanding Foreign Policy – The Foreign Policy Systems Approach* (Edward Elgar, Aldershot, 1989), p.206.

6 Putnam and Bayne, *Hanging Together*, p.269.

7 The propositions pertaining to power and interests have been regrouped since the borderline between their neo-realist and neo-liberal origins is often faint or blurred. 'Ideas, learning and other cognitive factors' have been divided up into the three last clusters. Widely shared 'ideas' that could fall into the cognitive or knowledge-based approach of regimes proposed for instance by Oran Young or Peter Haas, have been integrated into the propositions dealing with the 'international institutional environment'. 'Modes of governance' go well beyond the two-level games theory which constituted the basis for Putnam's discussion of the 'domestic politics' variable. The 'learning' factor has been relocated under that heading, together with propositions borrowed from neo-institutionalist theories, but also factors such as the general system of government, the development of policy networks, bureaucratic politics and the nature of each policy area.

cooperation. Assumptions and concepts are made explicit so that we may assess the internal consistency of the propositions and judge how well they correspond to the actual sequence of events.

Do the Distribution of Power and the Level of Interdependence Matter?

The Distribution of Power

Transatlantic relations have often been studied in terms of power structure and competition for world and regional hegemony.[8] The main contributions on hegemony come from systemic and realist schools of thought.[9] The realist school is more interesting for our study insofar as two of its main variants, the hegemonic stability theory[10] and the power transition theory,[11] not only focus on patterns of occurrence of major 'intra-core wars' but also on the probability of cooperation.

The views these variants have on cooperation partially differ. Both see 'state behavior as a rational response to variations in the international power structure, including the number of significant actors and their respective national power positions'.[12] Hence, the theory of

---

8 M. Kahler and W. Link, *Europe and America: A Return to History* (New York, Council on Foreign Relations Press, 1996).

9 For the main systemic contributions on hegemony and its cycles, see the world system theory of Wallerstein and the long cycle theory of Modelski: I. Wallerstein, *The Modern World-System* and *The Modern World-System II* (New York, Academic Press, 1974 and 1980); G. Modelski, *Exploring Long Cycles* (Boulder, Lynne Rienner, 1987); and G. Modelski and W. Thompson, *Seapower in Global Politics, 1494-1993* (Seattle, University of Washington Press, 1988). Incidentally, the understanding of hegemony does not necessarily gain much from the confrontation of these two views, each theory using its own definition criteria – superior economic efficiency, superiority in 'global reach', dominance in terms of relative power [...] – and developing 'laws of hegemony' whose claims are sometimes contradictory.

10 R. Gilpin, *War and Change in World Politics* (Cambridge, Cambridge University Press, 1981); R. Gilpin, *The Political Economy of International Relations* (Princeton, Princeton University Press, 1987).

11 A. F. K. Organski, *World Politics* (New York, Knopf, 1968); A. F. K. Organski and J. Kugler, *The War Ledger* (Chicago, University of Chicago Press, 1980).

12 Putnam and Bayne, *Hanging Together*, p.5. The ultimate expression of this conception is illustrated by the computing of 'power indexes' to deduce the ability of individual governments to influence the decisions. For a review of the methodological problems posed by power indexes and the limits of their explanatory capacity, see Geoffrey Garrett and George Tsebelis (Power indexes 'are a function of the portion of all mathematically possible winning coalitions to which each government

hegemonic stability maintains that cooperation is a direct function of (a)symmetry. Asymmetry in the distribution of power ('objective hegemony') combined with willingness of the most powerful actor to take the lead ('subjective hegemony') means indeed stability and peace, as well as the development of cooperation which is imposed by the hegemon and designed according to its interests. Conversely, symmetry means instability because of the absence of clear leadership able and willing to 'supply' international regimes combined with the reluctance of the other powers to simply be policy-takers. Generally speaking, cooperation is not only more difficult to achieve among states of equal power; it is all the more so when their number increases. As to the power transition theory, the explanatory variable for conflict or cooperation is the share of the economic and power resources each player has in the system, but also the level of satisfaction of great powers *vis-à-vis* the rules of the system and their position in the order. Conflict occurs when there is, at the same time, a relatively equal distribution of power and one or more dissatisfied great power(s). The probability of conflict increases when a challenger is rapidly catching up with the hegemon.

The problem is of course to agree on how to measure the respective power of major actors and their level of satisfaction with the system. If one considers, along with Organski,[13] that the power of the United States is still vastly superior to that of the other players, the international system is in equilibrium and cooperation arrangements should be numerous, easily agreed and far-reaching. The NTA framework could then be interpreted as a manifestation of US hegemonic supply of regime, in which a number of limited concessions can be offered to the European side to prevent defections and secure burden-sharing. Tensions could be interpreted as simple moments of wavering, where the hegemonic power must work harder to convince partners to accept its leadership.

If, on the contrary, one considers that the respective weights of the US, the EU and Japan are becoming similar through differentials in expansion or decline, that Europe is dissatisfied with its place in the system and that its demands are, in most cases, turned down, this should lead to fragmentary cooperation, greater competition, challenges and

---

is pivotal'. G. Garrett and G. Tsebelis, 'An Institutional Critique of Intergovernmentalism', *International Organization*, 50:2 (1996) 269-99.

13 A. F. K. Organski and M. Abertman, 'The Second American Century: The New International Order', in W. Zimmerman and H. Jacobson, *Behavior, Culture and Conflict in World Politics* (Ann Arbor, University of Michigan, 1993), p.99.

even conflicts. In an 'anarchic' world, the players should give more importance to relative gains and rule out deals which, while being beneficiary for all sides, could tilt the existing balance of power. Provided that Europeans and Asians are slowly catching up with the United States, the risk of a major clash should be very remote, but the record of US-EU relations should be meager, with recurring tensions, repeated unilateralism and a general failure to reach agreement on core issues touching on the leadership question. The weakening of the hegemonic leadership should result in the proliferation of small-group regimes with variable membership (the US-EU 'special relationship' being only one among many), and more 'ad hocery' in the international system.

A third hegemonic interpretation of the development of US-EU relations in the 1990s would be to see it as a manifestation of joint leadership in the making, feasible because the power transition is slow and the protagonists have a lot in common. One hegemon is replaced by a small group of large states taking collective responsibility for leadership. The post-NTA era should then be interpreted as the preamble to a hegemonic *directoire*. At times predatory for third parties, the development of US-EU cooperation should be steady and relatively smooth.

The Level of Interdependence

An early generation of theories based on liberalism and pluralism proposed quite a different explanation for the variations in cooperation, although they did not totally exclude power from their equation. According to these views, the degree of cooperation on specific issues is mainly determined by the extent of the convergence or complementarity of (national) interests, also called preferences. For liberals, preferences are determined by the demands of powerful domestic interests groups (we will return to this point in the discussion of 'domestic governance'). This interpretation was later refined by neo-liberals[14] and social constructivists[15] who strove to demonstrate that interests are, for a large part, malleable and subjective. According to this theory, interests change as a result of not only real but also perceived changes. Along a similar

[14] J. Goldstein and R. O. Keohane (eds.), *Ideas and Foreign Policy: Beliefs, Institutions, and Political Change* (Ithaca N.Y., Cornell University Press, 1993).

[15] P. M. Haas, 'Introduction: Epistemic Communities and International Policy Coordination', *International Organization*, 46:1 (1992) 1-35; J. G. Ruggie, 'What Makes the World Hang Together? Neo-utilitarianism and the Social Constructivist Challenge', *International Organization*, 52 (1998) 855-85, esp. 878.

line, the garbage can model has suggested that, in many instances, actors are confronted with major uncertainties and discover preferences through (decision-making) action.[16] Institutions can also influence these perceptions and uncertainties, hence the degree of cooperation (this is one of the main arguments of regime theories we will review in the next sub-section).

Thus, a first approximation of the insights offered by the complex interdependence approach could be that higher interdependence means more common and competing interests, as well as higher externalities; it therefore puts higher pressure in favor of more cooperation. In this respect, globalization should have increased the need for US-EU cooperation on issues vital for the maintaining of a liberal economic order. This being said, these theories acknowledge that not all cooperation should be interpreted as a direct response to economic interdependence. Political purposes can be equally important.[17] In addition, liberals warn that shared interests do not automatically result in cooperation because of various dilemmas inherent to collective action and highlighted by game theories. The question of defection, among others, is particularly damaging for cooperation perspectives. Under specific conditions, perceived bad faith, free-riding or unilateralism on a single issue could have a contagious effect and override much larger common interests. It is therefore necessary to amend the proposition on the interaction of interests and cooperation as follows: greater interdependence creates strong incentives to cooperate; these incentives can materialize if ways to overcome collective action dilemmas can be found.

---

16 Contrary to the rational actor assumptions, the garbage can approach posits that actors are, to a variable degree, uncertain about their own preferences, the decision-making processes, and the preferences of their counterparts. M. Cohen, J. March and J. Olsen, 'A Garbage Can Model of Organizational Choice', *Administrative Science Quarterly*, 17:1 1(972) 1-25; J. March and J. Olsen, *Ambiguity and Choice in Organizations* (Bergen, Universitetsforlaget, 1976); J. March, *Decisions and Organizations* (Oxford, Blackwell, 1988).

17 R. O. Keohane, 'International Institutions: Can Interdependence Work?', *Foreign Policy* (1998) 82-96.

Does the International Institutional Environment of US-EU Cooperation Matter?

The study of international regimes took off in the mid-1970s as an extension of liberal perspectives. Challenging the realist orthodoxy, it emphasized the importance of transnational actors, interdependence and 'low' politics – three key elements in US-EU relations. The most widely used definition of international regimes has been given by Stephen Krasner who described them as 'sets of implicit or explicit principles, norms, rules and decision-making procedures around which actors' expectations converge in a given area of international relations'.[18] The main (explicit) purpose of regimes is to enhance the capacity of international actors to cooperate in specific domains. Some, alleging that the concept needed to be refocused to avoid tautological reasoning, suggested to restrict the definition of international regimes to their measurable dimensions and to include only '(international) institutions with explicit rules, agreed upon by governments, that pertain to particular sets of issues in international relations'.[19] It was not sufficient to subdue all controversies on the origins of regimes and the conditions of their development and sustainability.[20]

Our central question here is to assess whether the output of US-EU relations can be explained by existing international regimes (the impact of US-EU regimes are discussed in a separate sub-section dedicated to the modes of governance of the relationship – see below). US-EU relations are indeed surrounded by, or even embedded in, many regimes that

---

[18] 'Principles are beliefs of fact, causation and rectitude. Norms are standards of behaviour defined in terms of rights and obligations. Rules are specific prescriptions or proscriptions for action. Decision-making procedures are prevailing practices for making and implementing collective choice.' S. Krasner, 'Structural Causes and Regime Consequences : Regimes as Intervening Variables', *International Organization*, 36:2 (1982) 185.

[19] V. Rittberger (ed.), *Regime Theory and International Relations* (Oxford, Clarendon Press, 1993). More recently, Hasenclever, Mayer and Rittberger also rightly underlined that international regime and international organization are neither synonymous nor co-extensional, 'even though in many cases regimes will be accompanied by organizations designed or employed to support them'. A. Hasenclever, P. Mayer and V. Rittberger, *Theories of International Regimes* (Cambridge, Cambridge University Press, 1997), p.10.

[20] On this, see the discussion on the three schools of thought on regimes (power-based, interest-based, and knowledge-based) in Hasenclever, Mayer and Rittberger, *Theories of International Regimes*.

could affect, actively or passively, transatlantic cooperation. These regimes can be facilitating elements, targets, alternatives, obstacles or sources of emulation. Propositions for each of these five variants are offered below.

The first proposition is building on the core assumption that international regimes foster cooperation. It implies that the degree of US-EU cooperation should be greater in issue areas where solid regimes pre-exist and can be exploited as building blocks for the partnership. In other words, international regimes should facilitate the development of US-EU cooperation by providing a number of multilateral principles which apply to bilateral relations. Strong regimes can also contribute to increase the level of cooperation by the lowering of transaction costs (among other things, they foster contacts and facilitate the exploration of possible package deals); by reducing uncertainty and risks (they enhance mutual understanding of the international context, increase mutual transparency and structure mutual expectations); and by lengthening 'the shadow of the future' (they create an incentive to abide by agreements, since, in a repeated game, credibility is a valuable asset which is worth more than the immediate gains from defection). Finally, regimes can foster cooperation by their action at a cognitive level. As illustrated by the previous chapter, the development of regimes has a lot to do with ideas, ideologies or intellectual fashions and representations of the past and the future. If international regimes suggest or reinforce positive images about US-EU cooperation, underline its healing potential and historical necessity, they help to lower transaction costs very substantially and therefore facilitate joint developments.

The second proposition looks at regimes as possible targets for US-EU cooperation and directly relates to the shared interest argument outlined in the previous section. Cooperation should increase when and where there is a need to join forces to defend, amend or create international regimes. The analysis should examine if cooperation in these domains was higher than in areas where there is no need for an international regime.

The third proposition posits that the degree of US-EU cooperation should be negatively affected by the existence of regimes which offer better alternatives for one of the partners. One illustration of this possible effect is the phenomenon of 'institutional shopping': when agreement seems too difficult, costly or time-consuming at US-EU level, the interested party starts looking for solution in other international fora. By moving the issue on the agenda of the OECD, WTO, IMF, NATO, WEU or OSCE, it becomes possible to circumvent recalcitrant actors or take advantage of specific cleavages in the coalition of the opponents (the particularly 'saturated' European institutional architecture and the multiplication of international organizations should increase the probability of such a scenario). The benefits of the various alternatives would logically not be judged only from a sectoral point of view. The implications of switching to alternative regime and coalition on US-EU relations as a whole should also be taken into account.

If regimes can be facilitators, targets and alternatives, the organizations which embody them may also become a direct obstacle or even a danger for US-EU relations. Our fourth proposition is that the proponents of an international regime could target the US-EU relationship if the latter undermines, among other things, their institutional *raison d'être* or short-circuits their normal procedures. For instance, parts of the bureaucratic elite of an international organization like the United Nations, NATO or the WEU could see themselves as engaged in direct rivalry with other organizations dealing with similar issues and be tempted to damage a competing bilateral relationship.

A fifth and final proposition revolves around the possible impact of the booming development of region to region relations and regional regimes. If regional organizations are conceived as competing and mutually exclusive entities, the development of other instances of regional cooperation should be a source of emulation and have a positive impact on US-EU cooperation. In a kind of arms race, such a context should indeed drive actors to deepen their regional privileged relationship defensively. If one of the transatlantic partners is however involved in the other regional regimes, the impact on US-EU cooperation should be mixed.

Do Domestic Modes of Governance Matter?

If foreign policy making was ever insulated from domestic political forces, it is certainly no longer the case. To comprehend and analyze states interactions, an understanding of domestic politics has become, for many, a precondition because of the evolution of foreign policy processes and the widening of the international agenda (both aspects being partially linked).[21] On the one hand, foreign policy processes are subjected to higher media exposure and, especially since the end of the Cold War, can much less operate on the basis of the consensus of small national *elites* than in the past.[22] Nowadays, ratification is often more demanding, for instance, in terms of consistency between what is said and done or of compensation for those penalized by the new arrangement. The negotiators have to play simultaneously at the international and domestic boards, the domestic front taking at times a huge amount of importance.[23] On the other hand, in parallel with this 'domestication' of international policies (such as security matters or human rights), a number of previously domestic policies (such as education) began their 'internationalisation', that is, appeared or featured more prominently on the international agenda. Mainly because of the nature of the political system of the EU and/or of some of its Member States, the level of complexity reached for some issues of the NTA can be staggering. For instance, German federate states (the *Länder*) have the exclusive competence on certain areas of immigration policy. It gives them the legal capacity to block the position of the German federal government, which in turn has the power to veto EU efforts to develop a transatlantic regime on the matter. In this hypothetical example, no less than four levels of government are interlocked. Such cases represent substantial challenges for the traditional analysis of 'state-centric realism' and its 'unitary-rational' account of the policy process.

According to the proponents of foreign policy analysis, the study of these new realities requires that some of the fundamental (neo)realist assumptions be abandoned. US policy towards the EU and EU policy towards the US should be considered, in essence, as 'a series of decisions made by a group of people who can be labeled decision-makers'. These decisions should be seen as 'processed through an identifiable

---

21 P. J. Katzenstein, R. O. Keohane and S. D. Krasner, '*International Organization* and the Study of World Politics', *International Organization*, 52:4 (1998) 645-85, 667-70; S. M. Walt, 'International Relations: One World, Many Theories', *Foreign Policy* (1998) 29-46.

22 O. R. Holsti, 'Public Opinion and Foreign Policy: Challenges to the Almond - Lippmann Consensus', *International Studies Quarterly*, 36 (1992) 439-66.

23 P. B. Evans, 'Building an Integrative Approach to International and Domestic Politics', in P. B. Evans, H. K. Jacobson, R. D. Putnam (eds.), *Double-Edged Diplomacy – International Bargaining and Domestic Politics* (Berkeley, University of California Press, 1993), pp.397-430.

machinery *within* the state' rather than simply emerging 'in response to external stimuli'. In other words, one should gear the analysis 'to the task of explaining the behavior of an individual or, more typically, a group of people operating within a structured environment who decide (or choose) to pursue one course of action rather than another'.[24]

Moreover the analysis should not focus solely on governments. New institutional approaches have indeed been progressively introduced which take into account the very fact of the relocation of authority, but which are equally in line with new methods of public management. The concept of governance is pointing to state-society relations and 'collective problem-solving in the public realm'.[25] It encompasses systems of rules which go beyond the classical 'forms of state' and system of government. Governance studies argue, among other things, that the state's role has shifted from 'authoritative allocation and mediation from 'above' (the Eastonian conception of 'command and control' politics) to the role of partner and mediator'.[26] These new forms of governance are henceforth among the institutional features which determine the way international and domestic forces are translated into foreign policy decisions. Starting with network politics, they therefore need to be reviewed alongside the possible impact of domestic systems of government, party systems, bureaucratic politics and the institutional dynamics specific to each type of policy area.

System of Government, Party Politics and Networks

With the development of the US 'new federalism' and the EU 'multi-level governance', it could be argued that there is an increasing parallelism between American and European modes of governance. Going one step further, John Peterson claims that a process of convergence is unfolding.[27] If one considers that the EU is a form of non-state federalism, both entities could indeed be defined as federal variants. All things being equal, convergence should *a priori* be conducive to more coop-

---

24 B. White, 'Analysing Foreign Policy: Problems and Approaches', in M. Clarke and B. White (eds.), *Understanding Foreign Policy – The Foreign Policy Systems Approach* (Edward Elgar, Aldershot, 1989), pp.11-12.

25 J. A. Caporaso, 'The European Union and Forms of State: Westphalian, Regulatory or Post-Modern?', *Journal of Common Market Studies*, 34:1 (1996) 29-52, 32.

26 B. Kohler-Koch, 'Catching up with Change: The Transformation of Governance in the European Union', *Journal of European Public Policy*, 3:3 (1996) 359-80.

27 Peterson, *Europe and America.*

eration, insofar as it should be easier for players from similar entities, who operate in similar environments and are confronted with similar constraints, to understand each other. The gain derived from greater mutual understanding could, however, be easily outweighed by the negative side-effects of federalism on the conduct of external relations. For Weaver, federalism is indeed the worst possible system for foreign policy, among other things because of coordination problems. If convergence means that both sides of the Atlantic are confronted, for instance, by the same vertical fragmentation of the decision-making procedure, then this evolution works against the development of US-EU policy output. Its expected consequences on cooperation might therefore need to be qualified, or even reversed accordingly.

If it is difficult to assess exactly the degree of transatlantic convergence, it is however obvious that the American and European systems still display significant idiosyncrasies. On the American side, most foreign policy analyses underline the central position of the US President, the importance of the relations between the legislative and the executive branches, as well as between the federal and federate levels of government. The American political system makes room for wide variations in the balance of power between the executive and the legislative branches in foreign policy matters, the imperial presidency having been replaced by a rather unstable equilibrium with a less deferential Congress, especially since the end of the Vietnam War. The powers of the President in foreign matters remain nevertheless such that his personal involvement is, most of the time, a necessary if insufficient condition for a pro-active American policy. If White House foreign policy orientations can be rather easily thwarted, little can happen if the President is either weak or disinterested in international affairs, or both. Party politics and electoral cycles in particular are most likely to have an impact on Congress and the presidential administration's commitment to the transatlantic relationship, and consequently on US-EU policy output. Another possible structural source of fluctuation lies with the many gray zones that exist between federal and federate level competencies. The federate states have been more and more assertive on the international stage with – mainly economic – external relations policies of their own.[28] The question of their influence on the US-EU partnership deserves to be ad-

---

[28] H. J. Michelmann and P. Soldatos (eds.), *Federalism and International Relations – The Role of Subnational Units* (Oxford, Clarendon Press, 1990); B. Hocking (ed.), *Foreign Relations and Federal States* (London, Leicester University Press, 1993).

dressed as well. All in all, the preceding assumptions suggest that no significant cooperative development should be expected as long as the US President remains indifferent or hostile to US-EU partnership; that limited cooperation is possible despite the opposition of Congress, if the project enjoys the backing of the President; and that strong cooperation can be helped by the pro-active approach of federal states but needs first and foremost the combination of a committed President and a supportive, or at least indifferent, Congress.

On the EU side, because of the *sui generis* nature of the European political construction, collective action has to reckon with many specific features. As to agenda-setting, European studies point at the shaping role played by the preparation of the decision through networks as well as by the six month rotating presidency of the Council. As to decision-making, the complex division of labor between major European institutions, the lack of mechanisms for meaningful interinstitutional bargaining[29] and the necessity to build large coalitions or even reach unanimous decisions are among the main institutional settings influencing policy outcomes.

Since the mid-1980s, the European Commission has embarked on a reform of EC policy paradigms which led to a new model of policy organization.[30] One of its major working principles is 'partnership' which means more 'strategic' relationships with policy end-users, that is, the 'cooption' of 'the outside clients of policy as the architects and engineers of policy'.[31] The establishment of specialized consultative committees is the most commonly used method to do so (cf. the so-called Commission's 'comitology'). Cooption is usually not neutral: 'the supranational institutions do not provide equal access for influencing the policy process', some interests being more closely associated than others.[32] In any case, it has turned the EU into a 'policy space' inhabited by a plurality of actors clustering around specific issues and concerns.

---

29 J. Peterson and E. Bomberg, *Decision-making in the European Union* (London, Macmillan, 1999), pp.58-9.

30 L. Hooghe (ed.), *Cohesion Policy and European Integration: Building Multi-Level Governance* (Oxford, Oxford University Press, 1996).

31 H. Wallace, 'The Institutions of the EU: Experience and Experiments', in H. Wallace and W. Wallace (eds.), *Policy-making in the European Union* (Oxford, Oxford University Press, 1996), p.53.

32 S. J. Bulmer, 'New Institutionalism, the Single Market and EU Governance', *Journal of European Public Policy*, 5:3 (1998) 365-86, p.374.

Interest groups, advocacy coalitions and/or epistemic communities enter into networks, hoping to enhance their influence at agenda setting and policy implementation levels. Network analysis has shown, however, that mobilization does not necessarily equate with influence. It depends very much indeed on the composition of the network, its pattern of action and recognized role, all of which are largely determined by the nature of the policy area. These interactions are reviewed below, in 'Issue Areas and Institutional Dynamics'.

The rotating system for the presidency of the Council of Ministers is another potentially important element for the fate of US-EU arrangements. The argument goes that it compels the chair to achieve something meaningful in the space of six months and creates a salutary sense of urgency, but that it also induces discontinuities which sometimes impede effective negotiation. The sheer material and human resources a country can pool vary and obviously affect the level of preparedness and the quality of the follow-up work of the presidency. Moreover EU Member States have their own policy preferences and, as shown by the previous chapter, there are definite differences of opinion as to what US-EU relations should be. These preferences influence directly the hierarchy of those priorities the presidency defines at the start of its term. The extent of this influence is nevertheless debatable. In the highly institutionalized external relations of the EU, many topics follow a pre-established timetable or cannot be ignored. Besides, it appears that most, if not all, governments tend to take their mission of presiding over the EU destiny rather literally, putting the interests of their national constituencies on hold or even making concessions they would not have conceded to otherwise: the President is, certainly to a variable extent, a role-player. If the previous assumptions are correct, the impact of the presidency can only be in the margin. This being said, the margin is not insignificant, especially when the matter is close to the 'pole of indifference' (see below). Among the various combinations of resources and preferences, a well-endowed and pro-Washington EU presidency should correspond to the most productive periods in the US-EU relationship.

The complex division of labor and the limited mechanisms for inter-institutional bargaining which characterize the EU are *a priori* counter-productive in terms of decision-making. The dilution of responsibility and the lack of transparency of the ratification process induced by such a division of labor might nevertheless prove to be a real asset for the negotiator. The possibility of putting the blame either on other actors (the negotiator alleging he or she has his or her hands tied – cf. the Schelling conjecture[33]) or on nobody (the negotiator evoking complex interaction of many forces which makes some result ineluctable) gives additional room for manœuvre to conclude specific US-EU arrangements, but this at the expense of democratic responsiveness.[34] As to the obligation to reach unanimity, it is often judged severely as a pathological decision-making mechanism leading to 'joint-decision traps'[35] which produce policies that are both rigid and inefficient. It contributes in this respect to feed the 'Capability-Expectations Gap' which means that 'the EU continues to impress more in potential than in action'.[36] On the other hand, the consensual approach offers better perspectives in terms of US-EU policy landing. Resorting (brutally) to decision rule of majority voting in a system as divided as that of the EU might indeed lead to serious problems of implementation and enforcement: for a large part, the EU relies on its Member States at these levels and those outvoted might decide to be less than cooperative.[37] So, globally, the aforementioned features make the EU a difficult partner to deal with, although they could on occasion be a mixed blessing for US-EU cooperation.

Bureaucratic Politics

The NTA represents a very substantial task expansion which results in more bureaucracies being involved in US-EU structures. On both sides, the formal monopoly of Foreign Ministries on the conduct of

---

33 R. D. Putnam, 'Diplomacy and Domestic Politics: The Logic of Two-Level Games', *International Organization*, 42:2 (1988) 427-60.

34 The intra-EU experience has indeed shown that such a shift in the locus of policy-making power is likely to emphasize 'bargaining, complex coalition building, and consensus building in policy-making arenas somewhat distant from traditional, domestic, institutional settings. S. Mazey and J. Richardson, 'Promiscuous Policy-making: The European Policy Style?', in C. Rhodes and S. Mazey (eds.), *The State of the European Union – Building a European Polity?* (Boulder, Lynne Rienner, 1995), p.338.

35 F. Scharpf, 'The Joint-Decision Trap: Lessons from German Federalism and European Integration', *Public Administration*, 66 (1988) 239-78.

36 Ch. Hill, 'Closing the Capability-Expectations Gap?', in J. Peterson and H. Sjursen (eds.) *A Common Foreign Policy for Europe? Competing Visions of the CFSP* (New York, Routledge, 1998).

37 E. Philippart and M. Sie Dhian Ho, *Pedalling against the Wind – Strategies to Strengthen the EU's Capacity to Act in the Context of Enlargement* (The Hague, Scientific Council for Government Policy, 2001).

external relations has been directly challenged. Studies of bureaucratic politics help to delineate the possible negative side effects of this evolution.

Charles Kegley and Eugene Wittkopf have identified 'interorganizational' and 'intraorganizational' attributes of bureaucratic behavior in American foreign policy, which are presumably also valid for the EU and its Member States.[38] Bureaucratic factors can be lodged and operate at the level of the principal institutions 'taken as a whole' and the level of 'the politics of functional areas'.[39] Bureaucracies are said to have a tendency to defend and extend their own jurisdictions and rationale ('parochialism' and 'imperialist task expansion'), as well as to compete as in a zero-sum game for resources and influence. These characteristics induce a number of bureaucratic behaviors which shape both policy making and policy. For instance, attachment to routines and to peculiar and often incompatible standard operating procedures leads to resistance to change and failure to cooperate. Inter-bureaucratic competition can produce the same result. There are also behaviors which do not prevent cooperation but generate suboptimal outcomes: compartmentalization of policy-making increases the risk of inconsistencies, while turf battles lead to lamed compromises – *i.e.* satisfactory for competing bureaucracies, yet globally unmanageable or irrational.[40] In the absence of a strong central authority, coordination mechanisms or effective use of weapons like the 'divide and rule' technique classically used by political leaders, bureaucratic politics are likely to blossom at US or EU levels and to affect US-EU policy output negatively: decentralization will become synonymous with 'compartmentalization' or horizontal fragmentation resulting in inefficiency and stalemate.

---

38 B. White, 'The European Challenge to Foreign Policy Analysis', *European Journal of International Relations*, 5:1 (1999): 33-36.

39 S. Mazey and J. Richardson, 'Promiscuous Policy-making: The European Policy Style?', in C. Rhodes and S. Mazey (eds.), *The State of the European Union*, p.340. For instance, in the case of the EU, the Directorate General in charge of external relations shares some bureaucratic features common to the entire European Commission but has, in addition, developed a bureaucratic style of its own on specific points.

40 Ch. W. Kegley Jr. and E. R. Wittkopf, *American Foreign Policy* (New York, St Martin Press, 1996, 5th edition), pp.485-97.

Issue Areas and Institutional Dynamics

If, firstly, the prospects for international cooperation may be fostered or blocked by (domestic and/or transnational) organized groups; if, secondly, the mobilization of these groups is determined by the distribution of costs and benefits of cooperation; and if, thirdly, this distribution is largely affected by the nature of the policy area or policy type, then the extent to which objectives set by the NTA are met should vary according to the nature of the policy area concerned.

In the early 1970s, Theodore Lowi presented a theory linking issue-areas and policy types.[41] He argued that governmental room for manœuvre varies with issue areas, but also with crisis and non-crisis situations. For each issue area, political goods are produced. Depending on the extent and manner in which these goods can be disaggregated, he divided most issue areas into distributive, regulatory and redistributive policies.[42] In distributive policies, everybody gets more or less something and the level of mobilization is usually relatively low, which, in principle, facilitates the negotiation and the conclusion of arrangements. In redistributive policies, the net costs and benefits are often clearly identifiable, which leads to high levels of mobilization. Reaching agreement on new redistribution flows should therefore be more difficult because it supposes a possibility to forge on both sides dominant coalitions in favor of the policy, for instance through new linkages or side-payments. In regulatory policies, the mobilization is likely to remain, by comparison with the two other types of policies, at an intermediary level depending on the possibility to disaggregate the goods or to foresee their precise consequences.

According to Lowi, two poles emerge – the 'pole of indifference' and the 'pole of power' – around which governments have the largest room for manœvre. The first pole corresponds to issues for which the stakes are insignificant or imprecise and the second to crisis situations. With Lowi's typology focusing on domestic politics only, William Zimmerman suggested adding foreign policy as a fourth arena of 'pro-

---

[41] Th. J. Lowi, 'Four Systems of Policy, Politics, and Choice', *Public Administration Review* (1972) 298-310.

[42] Military or R&D programmes ('pork barrel' issues) belong to distributive policies. The establishment of trade norms is an example of regulatory policy. Development funds insofar as they involve a substantial transfer of resources are a case of redistributive policy. Monetary issues could be another example, albeit with regulatory dimension.

tection and interaction' policies. Discussing how to situate foreign policy issues between the two poles, he concluded that 'the kind of "apolitical" consensual politics associated with the protection-insuring and interaction-facilitating policies occurs when the dominant perception of all involved is that the decision will be symmetrical in its impact on the values of citizens'.[43] US-EU cooperation dealing with insignificant issues, 'symmetrical' issues or critical issues should normally benefit from a low level of (adverse) mobilization, organized groups being indifferent or rallying around the flag. Cooperation could therefore develop even if the US or EU modes of governance are characterized by a weak institutional capacity to aggregate their domestic interests.

The NTA is the expression of a very substantial task expansion in US-EU cooperation. The strength of the various driving dynamics underpinning this expansion in the US and the EU should be considered as yet another possible explanatory variable of what was achieved. Mark Pollack has followed a similar approach in his study of task expansion in the EC. Revisiting Lowi's theory, he tried to identify the driving forces behind each type of policies. For him, regulatory policies were driven by functional (or economic) spillover and by political spillover (*i.e.* the political entrepreneurship of the Commission), redistributive policies were the result of tactical or bargaining linkages, while political spillover coupled with a sense of menacing crisis led to the development of distributive policies.[44] Assuming that US-EU task expansion depends on the same types of driving forces, this would suggest that strongly entrepreneurial institutions are of critical importance for the development of cooperation in those regulatory domains where functional spillover is weak and in those distributive projects not pulled by a sense of crisis.

---

43 W. Zimmerman, 'Issue Area and Foreign-Policy Process: A Research Note in Search of a General Theory', *The American Political Science Review*, 67:4 (1973) 1207. The growing importance of 'intermestic' issues on the international agenda is blurring the neatness of this categorization. Interaction-facilitating policies were mainly about security and trade matters. For new international issues which are an extension of domestic policies, it could seem more logical to classify them with other policy types, regulatory and distributive especially.

44 M. A. Pollack, 'Creeping Competence: The Expanding Agenda of the European Community', *Journal of Public Policy*, 14:2 (1994) 97.

Do US-EU Modes of Governance Matter?

The mode of governance of the transatlantic relationship is a potentially important explanatory variable of the US-EU output. As with domestic settings, US-EU institutional rules and policy tools deserve special attention because 'the configuration of the institutions and the set of policy instruments available predispose [...] to certain types of policy action but limit the scope for others'.[45] The very same assumption underpins the TD and the NTA: they deliberately (re)designed the format of the partnership in order to improve the transatlantic institutional capacity to cooperate in several fields. The serial summitry, the trilateral format, the direct contacts between US and EU (technical) administrations, as well as the participation of non-governmental actors are indeed expected to influence different aspects of policy-making processes, which in turn should affect the substance of policy (aims and tools).

Summitry, to start with, is a very specific tool in international relations and its long record demonstrates that it is rarely unconsequential. In the present case, the choice of a series of highly structured summits with open agendas is very likely to affect the outcomes of the relationship differently than, for instance, *ad hoc*, informal and specialized summits. In theory, it should indeed generate more pressure for ambitious policy decisions with comparatively high objectives and/or demanding modes of action: one does not indeed mobilize Presidents to agree, for instance, on information sharing about education methods. It should also generate more opportunity to reach agreement on ambitious projects. US-EU bi-annual summits provide a forum where the distinct political arenas meet and have an opportunity to mesh, at an advanced stage of policy-making, different processes together. The direct involvement of the top-players allows for final concessions, linkage politics and side-payments to be decided simultaneously – even if the mode of governance of the EU has its limitations in that respect. Moreover, the formal institutionalization of the summits should *a priori* bring more stability in the processes and make them more predictable. The same actors being very regularly exposed to socialization (at times close to a club atmosphere), it should furthermore mean more lubricated, if not necessarily more harmonious, processes. Finally, summitry signifies that processes are more publicized and irreversible than might otherwise have been the case. The direct participation of heads of state or govern-

45 Bulmer, 'New Institutionalism'.

ment attracts higher media coverage. Besides sustaining 'diplomatic momentum' (insofar as a failure to announce agreement at a summit usually represents an unacceptable political cost), it makes it difficult for a country to go back on a concession made by the top-players.[46] By and large, the introduction of serial summitry should clearly boost US-EU output.

A second element of potentially great importance is the preference given to a trilateral format, *i.e.* to limit US-EU interface to representatives from the US Government, the European Commission, and the country holding the presidency of the EU Council. By reducing the number of actors, this format tends not only to lighten processes, but to leave a greater role for the Commission which is *de facto* the only 'permanent' interlocutor of the US government.[47] In terms of policy-making, priority is given to continuity over legitimacy (if one considers that the Commission is actually a 'technocratic' institution which basically eludes EU democratic control). The introduction of the trilateral format should therefore also result in more effective and efficient decision-making, if the Commission succeeds in winning the trust of Member States jealous of their prerogatives and/or suspicious of possible hidden agendas.

A third feature worth mentioning is the new mode and extent of involvement of American and European bureaucratic apparatuses. Some departments and agencies have the opportunity to establish direct contacts to prepare sectoral arrangements, which makes room for a potentially large 'bottom up' input in US-EU processes. When highly centralized decision-making units disagree, this generally leads to total stalemate, as exemplified by various episodes in the US-Soviet history. By comparison, decentralized 'pre-cooking' and brokering introduced by the new format offer more possibilities to circumvent reluctant players and to progress at sector level. The larger involvement of bureaucracies may however occasionally backlash insofar as there is no reason why the counterproductive behaviors observed at national level (cf. bureaucratic politics) should not develop when US and EU administrations interact. In particular, the number of organizations involved could raise more questions of precedence as well as problems of horizontal

---

46 G. R. Berridge, *Diplomacy – Theory and Practice* (London, Prentice Hall, 1995), pp.85-6.

47 See Gardner's chapter.

and vertical coordination. The extension of direct contacts should boost US-EU output in some sectors, if bureaucratic politics can be kept in check.

A fourth and last point, the participation of non-governmental actors in a number of sectors like trade or environment, could lead to more informal, managerial or innovative policy-making processes.[48] It might as well make them more vulnerable to disruption and fragmentation, insofar as these actors are not mandated to pursue the 'general interest' and remain outside governmental hierarchies. The involvement of these actors could also be a plus, provided that the difficulties inherent to highly publicised negotiations can be minimized (cf. third section of Chapter 1).

The following chapters, through the discussion of various categories of actors or the development in several policy areas, will directly and indirectly provide partial answers to the research questions raised in this chapter. The concluding chapter, in its second section, will summarize the book's various findings and highlight the most remarkable characteristics of the US-EU record over time and over policy areas. It will then attempt to link these characteristics with the various explanatory propositions proposed *supra*. Considering the focus of the book, the propositions revolving around the modes of governance will be examined in greater detail, although those building on power, interdependence and the international institutional environment will not be ignored.

---

48 R. A. W. Rhodes, *Understanding Governance: Policy Networks, Governance, Reflexivity, and Accountability* (Philadelphia, Open University Press, 1997). R.A.W. Rhodes, 'The New Governance: Governing without Government', *Political Studies*, 44 (1996) 652-57.

Part II

Actors, Interests and Issues

CHAPTER 3

From the Transatlantic Declaration to the New Transatlantic Agenda: The Shaping of Institutional Mechanisms and Policy Objectives by National and Supranational Actors

Anthony GARDNER*

Coudert Brothers, Paris
(Director for European Affairs,
National Security Council, 1994-1995)

Introduction

Regular consultations between the United States and the European Union have been taking place for a quarter of a century. This long history is not surprising in light of Washington's enthusiasm in the 1950s and 1960s for the European Economic Community and European integration in general. But the nature and objectives of the consultations, as well as the mechanisms with which they have been carried out, have evolved considerably. It is possible to categorize US-EU relations from 1974 to the present as a progression from *ad hoc* consultations (1974-90); structured consultations (1990-95); and consultations with a view to joint action (from 1995 onwards).

Consultations have consisted of meetings at the following levels:

- US president, president of the EU Council and President of the European Commission (summits).
- US Secretary of State with Foreign Ministers of EU Member States.

* The opinions expressed herein are entirely personal. This paper draws upon the author's book, A. Gardner, *A New Era in US-EU Relations? The Clinton Administration and the New Transatlantic Agenda* (Aldershot, Avebury Press, 1996).

- US Cabinet Members with their European Commission counterparts (now replaced by semi-annual sub-cabinet meetings).
- Meetings between US Under-Secretaries or the Assistant Secretary of State for European Affairs and Political Directors of EU Member States.
- Meetings between Department Directors ('Experts') from the Department of State and Foreign Ministries of EU Member States.

Although the New Transatlantic Agenda builds on prior mechanisms of transatlantic consultation, its real significance is that it has led to a 'widening' and 'deepening' of contacts between US and EU officials and has vastly increased the range of areas for transatlantic cooperation. Before the launching of the Agenda, consultations remained focussed between a few institutional actors: Directorate-General I (DGI) and the White House, the Department of State, the Department of Commerce and the Office of the US Trade Representative. Today the consultations encompass many other actors and include bureaucrats at far lower levels who are actively engaged in carrying out policy. Whereas transatlantic consultations used to be focussed principally on contentious issues of bilateral trade, the Agenda covers a vast spectrum of issues – including security, international trade, the environment, science, health, education and humanitarian assistance and development. Many of the regions of the world toward which the US and EU have pledged to coordinate their foreign policies have never previously been the source of systematic transatlantic cooperation.

As the contents of the Agenda have been described in other chapters, this contribution provides an American perspective on the evolution of US-EU relations from the consultation process established under the 1990 Transatlantic Declaration to the launching of the Agenda in Madrid in 1995.

The Transatlantic Declaration

One month after the fall of the Berlin Wall in November 1989, Secretary of State James Baker visited Berlin and called for closer transatlantic cooperation to keep pace with European integration and institutional reform: '[w]e propose that the United States and the European Community work together to achieve, whether it is in treaty or some other form, a significantly strengthened set of institutional and consultative links'.[1]

This echoed President Bush's earlier declaration, in response to a proposal by European Commission President Jacques Delors, that the US was prepared to develop with the Community 'new mechanisms of consultation and cooperation on political and global issues'.[2] Implicit in Baker's initiative was the concern that the Community might develop policies and institutions incompatible with American interests if the process of European integration were not accompanied by improved transatlantic dialogue.

The initiative resulted nearly one year later in the Transatlantic Declaration. The document repeats a great deal of familiar poetry about the transatlantic attachment to common values, principles and traditions, especially democratic government, human rights and market economics. More important, however, it established a mechanism for regular transatlantic consultations between heads of state, foreign ministers, other cabinet members, political directors and experts, either in a trilateral format (representatives from the US Government, the European Commission and the country holding the presidency of the EU Council) or in a troika format (representatives from the US Government, the European Commission and preceding, current and subsequent EU presidency countries).[3] In addition, the Declaration also formalized exchanges between the European Parliament and the US Congress.

---

1 United States Information Agency Press Release.

2 In an interview granted to *The Wall Street Journal* in February 1989, Delors had floated the idea of new US-EU 'partnership' which would consist of dialogue on political and security issues, in addition to trade. A. Krause, *Inside the New Europe* (New York, Harper Collins, 1991), p.294.

3 The 'troika' – a Russian word for a carriage drawn by three horses – refers to the representation of the EU Council of Ministers by three countries holding the presidency thereof in six-month rotation. The troika format was developed to ensure consistency of EU policy at Council of Ministers level notwithstanding this frequent rotation; it therefore tends to strengthen the ability of the EU Council to engage in long-term planning and strategy like the European Commission. According to the trilateral format, the EU Council is represented only by the current presidency country; since presidency countries may fail to coordinate policy with, let alone brief, their successors and may even have divergent priorities from them and their predecessors, the trilateral formatweakens the ability of the EU Council to control the European Commission's initiatives.

Held between the presidents of the United States, Commission and Council, once per six-month EU presidency and alternating between Washington and Europe (normally in the capital of the current presidency country), the US-EU summits were to provide the central direction to the entire process of consultation. The summits have varied in usefulness according to the personal chemistry between the leaders. Although relations between Presidents Bush and Delors were always correct, the two leaders did not develop the same intellectual rapport as that which existed between Presidents Clinton and Delors, who enjoyed immersing themselves in the details of public policy. One of the reasons why the summits held during the presidency of Jacques Santer were of uneven usefulness is that they have provided practically the only occasions for him and President Clinton to interact.

The summits held under the 1990 Transatlantic Declaration made a limited contribution to the advancement of US-EU relations: until the creation of 'working groups' at the Berlin Summit in July 1994 to prepare for the following summit in Washington in June 1995, they took place as isolated events which failed to build on one another. As such, the summits have been criticized as being showpieces primarily intended for consumption by the media. Nevertheless, they have served an important function by reinforcing the Commission's credentials to represent Europe when speaking with the United States. Moreover, they have regularly forced the bureaucracies on both sides of the Atlantic to define positions for their political masters on key transatlantic issues. As US-EU relations are rarely characterized by crisis, except for occasional trade disputes, they require semi-annual summit meetings to ensure they receive adequate attention.

In accordance with the Transatlantic Declaration, the US Secretary of State meets with all of the foreign ministers of the EU on the margins of the UN General Assembly meeting in the fall of each year; as they are normally accompanied by several advisers each, these meetings tend to be too crowded to lend themselves to informal discussion.[4] In the spring of each year and on an *ad hoc* basis, however, the Secretary meets with the foreign minister of the EU presidency country and the EU commis-

4 These meetings began and have continued because they provide the Secretary of State with a useful opportunity to pay a courtesy to the foreign ministers and an excuse not to spend time seeing many of them again during the course of the following twelve months. For many of the ministers, these meetings may indeed provide rare occasions to participate in discussions of substantive issues with the Secretary.

sioner in charge of relations with the United States. On the European side, the trilateral format places the European Commission in the position of ensuring continuity between successive meetings of US-EU representatives; the troika format, on the other hand, entrusts the Council of Ministers with this task. From Washington's perspective, the trilateral format is preferable to the troika format because it enhances the role of the Commission, with whose policies Washington has far more in common than with many of the individual EU Member States represented in the Council of Ministers. It is also evident that Washington finds it easier, and therefore preferable, to deal with a small and familiar group of bureaucrats from the Commission rather than with a numerous and changing cast of bureaucrats from numerous Member States.

The Transatlantic Declaration took existing mechanisms for US-EU consultations a step further. Regular but informal consultations had already taken place since 1974. In 1976 it was agreed that the head of state or government of the country holding the Community's presidency would meet once during his six month term with the US president and that the Foreign Ministry of that country would keep Washington informed both before and after meetings of political directors on European Political Cooperation (EPC). Following serious transatlantic disputes regarding East-West relations in the early 1980s, annual meetings were initiated between Troika political directors and the Assistant Secretary of State for European Affairs on the margins of the UN General Assembly. In September 1986, further structure was added to transatlantic consultations: the US and the EU agreed that the foreign minister of the country holding the Community's presidency would visit Washington at the beginning of each year and that the political directors' troika should meet during each presidency with their US counterparts at the Under-Secretary level.[5]

In addition to these growing levels of transatlantic consultation, *ad hoc* consultations between members of the US cabinet and their EU counterparts took place between 1982 and the 1990 Transatlantic Declaration. These meetings were usually held following the annual December NATO summit in Brussels and involved the Secretaries of State, Commerce, Agriculture and Treasury, together with the Trade Representative, on the US side, and the President of the European Commis-

5 R. Schwok, *US-EU Relations in the Post-Cold War Era: Conflict or Partnership?* (Boulder, Westview Press, 1991), pp.32-5.

sion, together with the respective Commissioners on the European side. Discussions at these meetings were far less substantive than the ones held at the NATO summits and rarely generated concrete policy initiatives. Although the Transatlantic Declaration called for semi-annual meetings of this kind, the practice fell into disuse since December 1991, partly because their agendas focused on topics related to the Uruguay Round (and agriculture in particular) which were being discussed intensively elsewhere.

Under the Clinton Administration, cabinet-level consultations have been substituted by semi-annual sub-cabinet meetings alternating between Brussels and Washington at which the US Under-Secretary of State for Economic and Business Affairs and the US Under-Secretary for Political Affairs have met with their counterparts in Directorate-General I (external relations) of the European Commission. The meetings between the US Under-Secretary of State for Economic and Business Affairs and the Director-General for relations with the US and other advanced industrial countries have proven particularly useful because they provide advance warning of trade disputes. Such bilateral meetings between the State Department and the European Commission are particularly appropriate in the field of international trade, where the European Commission enjoys exclusive competence under the EC Treaty and therefore enjoys the clear prerogative to represent the interests of the European Union. As the Council of Ministers is duly informed by the European Commission but not represented, such meetings tend to be attended by fewer representatives, more insulated from the changing political pressures of European Member States' parochial interests, and more focussed on specific issues. In early 1995 the practice was initiated of holding meetings between European political directors and US assistant or deputy assistant secretaries of state before the sub-cabinet meetings to further improve the latter's focus and effectiveness. Within the US Government, these meetings facilitate inter-agency coordination between the Department of State, the Office of the United States Trade Representative, the National Economic Council, National Security Council, Department of Commerce and the Department of the Treasury.[6]

---

6 The US Department of State is run by the Secretary of State, the equivalent of a European Foreign Minister. The Secretary (the equivalent of the Minister) is assisted by a Deputy Secretary of State (the equivalent of Secretary of State) and several Under-Secretaries, including the Under-Secretary for Political Affairs and the Under-

The semi-annual consultations at the level of political directors / assistant or deputy assistant secretaries of state were also to serve the function of identifying areas of shared interest and recommending specific actions at the experts level, such as the formulation of joint policies and the implementation of parallel demarches. The consultations at experts level (deputy assistant secretaries or heads of bureau) have covered a vast array of topics, including UN affairs, nuclear non-proliferation, human rights, terrorism, consular affairs, and the Organization for Security and Cooperation in Europe (OSCE), as well as numerous geographical areas, including Latin America, Russia and the NIS, the former Yugoslavia, Central and Eastern Europe, the Middle East, Africa and Asia.

Only modest results have been achieved at the experts and political directors / assistant or deputy assistant secretary level during recent years, largely in forging collaborative responses to human rights abuses and humanitarian crises in the Third World. One reason may be that these consultations have occurred in the troika format and therefore are constantly disrupted by a change in the identity of the participants on the European side. A familiar complaint by US participants is that the consultations are, in reality, briefings for their counterparts for which they obtain little in return.

Lessons from the Transatlantic Declaration

Several lessons may be drawn from the first four years of consultations conducted in accordance with the Transatlantic Declaration. The clearest is that the quality of the consultations varies according to the EU presidency country's management abilities and commitment to strengthening US-EU relations. The French EU presidency in the second half of 1994 is a good case in point: the presidential elections in March and the entry into power of a new leadership team distracted the bureaucracy of the Quai d'Orsay from its EU obligations; although France had pledged at the beginning of its presidency to build on the preceding German presidency's work to improve US-EU consultations, it delayed

Secretary for Economic and Business Affairs. These Under-Secretaries are assisted by several Assistant Secretaries, including the powerful Assistant Secretary for European Affairs. These Assistant Secretaries are assisted, in turn, by several deputy Assistant Secretaries. Under them work Office Directors for specific issues and/or regions who often represent the United States at the 'experts level' meetings with the European Union.

or blocked every concrete initiative to achieve this objective because of a Gaullist hyper-sensitivity about Washington's *droit de regard* over European affairs.

During the Presidency of The Netherlands in the second half of 1991, by contrast, The Hague often provided Washington with advance copies of the agendas of EPC meetings, transmitted Washington's input (without identifying it as such) to the Member States and briefed Washington on the results of these meetings.[7] Similarly, the Luxembourg Presidency in the first half of 1991 played an important role in keeping US and European policy toward Iraq in step. The enthusiasm of the Spanish Presidency in the second half of 1995 for reinvigorating transatlantic relations and its energetic efforts, along with the Commission, to forge intra-European consensus on the New Transatlantic Agenda (occasionally achieved by presenting the Council with *faits accomplis*) enabled US and EU negotiators to elaborate a major initiative within only five months after the end of the French Presidency.

The consultations held under the Transatlantic Declaration also showed that consultations held in the trilateral format are more effective at promoting dialogue because they maintain continuity in the identity of the participants. In order to strengthen its power within the EU institutions, and increase its international profile in particular, the Commission has sought to hold as many meetings as possible with the United States in this format. Washington has been a willing partner in this objective because of the conviction that, compared to the Council, the Commission holds views, particularly on trade, which are less likely to reflect the nationalistic perspectives of influential Member States and has greater ability to strike compromises between the Member States and the EU institutions in a manner which advances US interests.

In order to be effective, US-EU consultations must feature a two-way exchange of information. Moreover, the different levels of consultation need to be tied together so that the actors at each level are aware of the others' activities; meetings at each level must also be better linked over time. Most important, the first four years of consultations conducted in accordance with the Transatlantic Declaration indicated the need for a

---

7 In practice, Washington rarely provided The Hague with any input. But the American Embassy in The Hague was regularly briefed on Presidency and Troika trips and on meetings concerning the former Yugoslavia.

single, overarching framework for US-EU relations that was later to take the form of the Transatlantic Agenda.

Concerned that the transatlantic relationship needed greater structure in order to prevent a gradual shift in Washington's attention toward Asia and domestic economic problems, Chancellor Helmut Kohl proposed in November 1992 that relations between Europe and the United States be embodied in a comprehensive treaty. Although Washington was not prepared to engage in so ambitious an exercise, it acknowledged the need for greater structure, more continuity between US-EU summits and greater emphasis on pragmatic collaboration. Eager to avoid the uncomfortable position of having to choose between Washington, its premier international ally, and Paris, its essential partner in the promotion of European integration, Bonn wished to find a flexible mechanism for US-EU policy coordination between summits as a way of defusing transatlantic policy differences before being aired publicly. The result was the launching of the three 'working groups' by President Clinton, European Commission President Delors and Chancellor Kohl, at the US-EU Summit in July 1994 in Berlin.

The Three Berlin Working Groups

The working groups were primarily the creation of Bernhard Zepter, assistant to President Delors, Joachim Bitterlich, National Security Adviser to Chancellor Kohl, and Under-Secretary for Political Affairs Peter Tarnoff. In order to avoid creating another layer of bureaucracy and to assuage French concerns about Washington's insinuation into EU policy making, the Commission, the German Presidency and the United States agreed that the working groups would have the limited mandate of preparing the agenda for the next US-EU Summit in Washington, at which time they would disband.

Some EU Member States had urged that the full troika (Germany, France and Greece) represent the EU in the working groups; the Commission had lobbied in favor of holding the meetings in a trilateral format because it would diminish the representation of the Member States and thereby enhance its ability to act as the EU's foreign policy voice. The Commission's point of view prevailed, partly because the troika mechanism had been conceived as a device to ensure continuity for permanent arrangements and was, therefore, unsuited to working groups of limited duration.

The leaders agreed that the groups would focus on three areas: international crime, including drug trafficking, nuclear smuggling and money laundering; common foreign and security policy, particularly the means of improving coordination on humanitarian assistance to the Third World; and Central and Eastern Europe, particularly the means of improving coordination in technical assistance programs for market reform.

The working group on international crime was formed at the insistence of Chancellor Kohl, who wished to forge a transatlantic response to a serious threat emerging along Germany's eastern frontier: smuggling of plutonium, drug trafficking, money laundering and illegal immigration.

Nuclear-related smuggling presented, perhaps, the most serious risk: in 1994 alone, there were three seizures in Germany of significant amounts of weapons-grade material. The disintegration of the Soviet empire had led to a sharp reduction in the Russian military budget and a decline in living standards for scientists at research facilities and employees at nuclear installations; their access to fissionable materials and sensitive nuclear technology made them prime targets for corruption by terrorists groups and the Mafia. Moreover, Moscow's weakening grip over Russian economic and political life, combined with the sudden porousness of Central and Eastern European frontiers, had allowed local Mafia, most notably in Chechnya, to forge relationships with international crime syndicates.

The European Commission supported Germany's request for a working group on international crime, primarily as a back-door way of acquiring competencies which had been granted to the Council under the Third Pillar of the Maastricht Treaty. EU Member States had considered that 'Justice and Home Affairs', consisting of police powers and law enforcement, involved sensitive issues of sovereignty and should therefore be dealt by means of inter-governmental, rather than community, decision-making. But the Commission considered that these issues also impacted upon the Single Market and had transfrontier consequences which could only be dealt with effectively at a supranational level. From Washington's perspective, conducting a dialogue with a single European interlocutor on international crime is preferable to doing so with fifteen. That view is reflected in Washington's enthusiasm for EUROPOL, the nascent European police force. By engaging the EU on third pillar issues, moreover, the United States hoped to help the EU overcome its institutional weakness and develop into an effective interlocutor.

The working group on international crime ran into trouble almost immediately because several Member States suspected it to be part of a Commission 'plot' to bring home and justice affairs within the Community's competence in contradiction to the Maastricht Treaty's clear provisions that such affairs should be handled inter-governmentally. In addition, the French Government (Interior Minister Charles Pasqua in particular) was resolutely opposed to conducting exchanges of sensitive information regarding international crime, and terrorism in particular, with the United States. France had vigorously opposed, for example, an agreement between the Commission and the Drug Enforcement Agency (DEA) on sharing information about precursor chemical diversions.

The failure of the working group also reflected the weakness of Third Pillar cooperation and, specifically, the inability of the EU Member States to agree on the nature of information to exchange among themselves. Finally, its failure was also due to a bureaucratic tug-of-war between the coordinators for Third Pillar issues in the Council and Commission secretariats and between the EU and the interior ministries of its Member States.

As a result, initiatives of the US Department of Justice, Federal Bureau of Investigation and the Drug Enforcement Agency – calling for the establishment of a joint data bank on Russian organized crime, a clearinghouse to coordinate drug and law enforcement training programs in third countries and an agreement on sharing information on chemical precursors – were met with the refrain that intra-European coordination on Third Pillar issues was still in its infancy and that the United States needed to be patient.

The senior US representative on the CFSP working group, Principal Deputy Assistant Secretary of State John Kornblum, sought to focus the group's work on developing mechanisms for real-time operational interaction between Washington and Brussels. This focus reflected the State Department's long-standing frustration of not knowing whether to work principally with the EU Presidency or Commission during a crisis – such as Iraq's invasion of Kuwait, the conflict in Bosnia or the civil war in Rwanda. The group acknowledged the need for improved consultations between US and EU diplomatic missions in the Third World in order to predict political crises and prepare a coordinated evacuation of nationals, to provide emergency food and medical aid more quickly and in a more coordinated manner to areas afflicted by natural disasters, and to respond more effectively to the outbreak of hostilities (as in Bosnia) or political crises such as coups. But the group was unable to agree on the mechanisms for such consultation.

The group discussed how to give greater structure to the irregular pattern of consultations between the heads of mission of the EU troika and US ambassadors in unstable regions of Africa, Latin America and the Middle East. The US proposed that the EU should designate a single 'lead' EU embassy in each region for the purpose of facilitating US-EU contacts and coordination on the ground. The idea was not pursued, however, partly because it would be seen as reinforcing the special role played by certain European countries in their former colonies. The group also considered the promotion of joint demarches on human rights by the missions of the US and Commission, Presidency and Member States of the EU in third countries – such as Burma and Haiti – where their approaches were complementary.

The CFSP working group failed to live up to its aspirations. This was due in part to reticence in several Member States to granting the Commission a role in the definition and implementation of CFSP when the Council was competent under the Maastricht Treaty's Second Pillar. France did not want to grant Washington any say in the development of Europe's nascent foreign policy because it feared that that would diminish its own pre-eminence as Europe's spokesman. The group also suffered from a problem similar to that afflicting the group on international crime: transatlantic cooperation could not advance as long as intra-EU cooperation remained underdeveloped. The Second Pillar of the Maastricht Treaty dealing with CFSP had provided for cumbersome decision-making procedures and a complex division of competencies among the EU institutions which prevented the EU from acting rapidly or coherently. Finally, the group suffered from the German Presidency's fixation on procedure which resulted in 'non-papers' focusing nearly exclusively on mechanisms for cooperation – the frequency and timing of meetings, the representation required at these meetings and the chain of authority between various levels of consultation – rather than on practical areas of cooperation.

One of the original objectives of the working group on Central and Eastern Europe was to coordinate US and EU foreign aid and technical assistance programs in the region. But this coordination function was already being carried out between Deputy Director General for External

Economic Relations Robert Verrue of the European Commission, on the one hand, and Coordinator for Assistance Ralph Johnson at the State Department and Senior Director for Central Europe Ambassador Richard Schifter at the National Security Council, on the other. The group considered several valuable ideas for initiatives in the fields of politics, economics and the environment. It agreed that the United States and the European Union could more effectively promote their shared objective of consolidating political and economic reform in the region by coordinating positions in international financial institutions, such as the World Bank, International Monetary Fund, European Bank for Reconstruction and Development; by supporting regional efforts at economic integration and political cooperation; and by making complementary demarches to specific countries, such as Hungary about the need for fiscal responsibility and Slovakia about the dangers of backsliding on democracy.

The group also lent support to two regional centers in Budapest for law enforcement and the environment. It highlighted the need jointly to support training programs in Western crime prevention and investigation, due process and human rights for law enforcement officers from Central and Eastern Europe. The EU agreed that the International Law Enforcement Academy, established by the FBI in Budapest would be an appropriate platform for this exercise. The group also examined how to strengthen the Regional Environmental Center established in Budapest upon the initiative of the United States and jointly funded by it along with the EU and Japan. Several transboundary air and water cleanup projects were considered.

The working group on Central and Eastern Europe identified areas of potential cooperation, but was unable to make concrete recommendations to the June 1995 summit in Washington. One reason for this may have been the Commission's latent suspicion of US proposals for common initiatives in the region as being secretly intended to give Washington a more prominent role while leaving the EU to bear the bulk of the cost. The Commission was well aware that its financial and technical assistance to Central and Eastern European Countries (CEECs) and the former USSR Republics was one of its few foreign policy successes and, therefore, was not enthusiastic about sharing the credit with the United States. Indeed, the Commission was already bitter that Washington was getting all the credit for the Middle East peace process despite the EU's sponsorship of the Madrid Conference and significant financial support for regional economic reconstruction.

The working group shied away from making proposals for significant initiatives. In February 1994 Commissioner Sir Leon Brittan had proposed that both the European Union and the United States should eliminate subsidies for the export of agricultural products to Central and Eastern Europe, Russia and the NIS. These subsidies undermined Central and Eastern European agriculture in two ways: first, by destroying the domestic market for home-grown produce (since most CEECs had sharply cut subsidies to their own farmers); and second, by pushing CEECs produce out of its traditional export markets to the east. But the proposal was considered to be too controversial and was therefore not presented to the Washington summit for further consideration. The US Mission to the European Union favored engaging the EU in a discussion of how to develop a common position on the treatment of Central Europe for rules of origin purposes because it would promote the elimination of trade barriers between the members of the Central European Free Trade Area (CEFTA). Although the European Commission was originally in favor of the proposal, the European textile industry buried it.

The three working groups were tentative steps to add greater structure and substance to the US-EU relationship. The experience of these groups reconfirmed the importance of tying the many threads of the relationship into one tapestry which designed progress from joint consultation to collaboration. The effort to weave that tapestry became known as the New Transatlantic Agenda.

The Genesis of the New Transatlantic Agenda

The New Transatlantic Agenda was born of common concerns in Europe and the United States, as well as concerns specific to each. After the fall of the Berlin Wall, a growing chorus of leaders and commentators in Europe expressed concern that the end of the Cold War would weaken the transatlantic link by diminishing the importance of Washington's security guarantee which had underpinned US-European relations since 1945. During his visit to Washington in early 1995 Belgian Prime Minister Dehaene reiterated this point of view: 'The Cold War is over now. Very fortunately so, but at the same time [...] we have been deprived of an enemy. The glue which kept us together for so long, has lost its strength'.[8]

Many other European leaders, including British Foreign Secretary Malcolm Rifkind, German Foreign Minister Hans-Dietrich Genscher, French Foreign Minister Alain Juppé and European Commission President Jacques Santer, expressed similar thoughts. In the United States, House Speaker Newt Gingrich declared that only a transatlantic free trade agreement would help keep the US and Europe together: '[w]e will drift apart unless we have projects large enough to hold us together [...] We're not going to stay together out of nostalgia [...] And my suggestion is that we want to start looking at a free trade zone that includes the US and Europe [...].'[9]

President Clinton's emphasis on domestic economic and social renewal, and US free trade initiatives with Asia (APEC) and Latin America (NAFTA and the Free Trade Agreement of the Americas), were widely misinterpreted in Europe as being further evidence of a drift of the United States from Europe. Although this perception could be partly ascribed to the recurrent bouts of angst in Europe about America's European orientation which have repeatedly characterized transatlantic relations, it also reflected the turn of the US Congress toward isolationism and unilateralism after the November 1994 elections, as well as the reality that US-EU relations could not effectively compete for the attention of top US decision-makers at a time of numerous foreign policy crises – for example in Somalia, Haiti, Iraq/ Kuwait and, above all, Bosnia.

The perception of transatlantic 'drift' was reinforced during the course of 1994 by nagging disagreements: for example, over the Bosnian conflict, the pace and mechanics of NATO expansion, the bailout package for Mexico which Washington put together (after minimal consultation with its allies) in response to the peso crisis, the precipitous decline of the dollar, the US threat to retaliate under

8 Speech to the European Institute in Washington D.C., March 1995.

9 Quoted in G. Harrison, 'A New Transatlantic Initiative? US-EU Economic Relations in the Mid-1990s', *CRS Report for Congress*, 15 September 1995. Speech by Speaker Gingrich, 'An American Vision for the 21st Century' delivered at the Mayflower Hotel, 1 March 1995.

Section 301 of its 1974 Trade Act[10] against the EU's banana regime, and the nomination of a successor to Peter Sutherland as head of the World Trade Organization.

In light of the generally perceived weakness of CFSP and the inability of the EU to respond effectively to the Bosnian crisis, moreover, the New Transatlantic Agenda had the potential to enhance the EU's weak foreign policy profile and to stress the global nature of its activities and aspirations. In particular, the Commission saw in the Agenda an opportunity to shape a broad EU relationship with the US; this was one of the reasons for France's lukewarm attitude toward the three working groups during its EU presidency in the first half of 1995. Sir Leon Brittan was particularly eager to promote the initiative – and even instructed Colin Budd, his Chef de Cabinet, to work full time on it during the fall of 1995 – because it offered him a conspicuous international stage.[11] Finally, the Agenda also advanced the objective of Spain's ruling Socialist Party to improve its image in the face of domestic political scandals and to contribute to a successful EU presidency by bringing President Clinton to Madrid for a major summit attracting international press attention.

The factors generating interest in the United States in the New Transatlantic Agenda were rather different. Europeanists within the Clinton Administration have not, by and large, believed that the United States is drifting from Europe. However, many have been preoccupied by the potential threat that transatlantic trade disputes may re-emerge as major irritants in the transatlantic relationship (as they were before the Uruguay Round) if they cease to be imbedded in a broader relationship. As trade gradually assumes a higher profile than security in transatlantic relations, according to this view, NATO is destined to lose some of the utility it has had as the central institution for promoting and symbolizing common interests. There is therefore a need to update and reinforce the

---

10 Section 301 provides, *inter alia*, that the US Trade Representative shall take action under the section if 'an act, policy or practice of a foreign country [...] is unjustifiable and burdens or restricts United States commerce'. The Trade Representative is required to 'take all appropriate and feasible action' to obtain the elimination of any act, policy or practice which is 'unreasonable or discriminatory and burdens or restricts United States commerce' provided that action by the United States is appropriate.

11 Critics claimed that Brittan's secret agenda was to reassert his influence over the EU's relations with Central and Eastern Europe which he had lost to Commissioner van den Broek during the Commission's reshuffling of portfolios in January 1995.

structures of transatlantic cooperation which were forged during the Cold War.[12] Drawing principally on these themes, the US Mission to the European Union, and Ambassador Stuart Eizenstat in particular, actively urged the Administration in the fall of 1994 to lend its weight to the elaboration of a major transatlantic initiative.

One of the main reasons why the White House was immediately receptive to the proposal and took a close interest in its evolution thereafter had to do with domestic politics: following the election of hostile Republican majorities in the House and Senate in November 1994, the White House found that its room for maneuver on its domestic agenda had become rather restricted and that foreign policy had become doubly important as an arena for the president to look 'presidential'. The proposal also appealed to those within the Administration who felt that Clinton, as the nation's first post-Cold War president and the leader of the Free World, needed to articulate a vision of US foreign policy and a New World Order in which the containment of Soviet power ceased to play a predominant role. An important part of this vision was a Europe united around the principles of democracy and free markets and of a larger transatlantic community embracing Central and Eastern Europe through its integration into Western institutions. Inspired by the history of the transatlantic partnership, which had been the strongest force in the world over the last half century for the strengthening of democracy, the liberalization of trade and the promotion of global development and prosperity, the Administration sought to identify those areas where the US and EU could supplement their consultations with joint actions to achieve common objectives.

Elaborating on proposals made by Sir Leon Brittan for a 'building block' approach to transatlantic trade liberalization in the short-to-medium term through the reduction or elimination of regulatory obstacles[13], as well as themes elaborated by the US Mission to the European Union, Secretary of State Warren Christopher delivered a significant foreign policy address in Madrid on 2 June 1995, calling for a major transatlantic effort to define a framework for broad US-EU cooperation

---

12 The European Commission also expressed this view: 'The US-EU relationship [...] cannot be relied upon to function in the future on the basis of structures and priorities relevant to the Cold War era. European Commission, 'Europe and the United States: The Way Forward', July 1995.

13 'The EU-US Relationship: Will it Last?', Speech to the American Club, Brussels, 27 April 1995.

extending beyond trade: '[b]y the end of the year, we should have developed a broad-ranging transatlantic agenda for the new century – an agenda for common economic and political action to expand democracy, prosperity and stability'.[14]

His recommendation that a 'Senior Level Group' be appointed to carry out this task was approved at the US-EU Summit in Washington on 14 June 1995. At the press conference following the summit, President Clinton echoed the Secretary's speech by stating that over the next six months the United States looked forward 'to working together with our European partners to develop a common economic and political agenda for the 21st century'.

The New Transatlantic Agenda also responded to the perception in Washington that the US-EU relationship should be adapted to reflect the EU's newly acquired powers under the Maastricht Treaty, particularly those aimed at achieving a common foreign and defense policy and an economic and monetary union. The need for a structured transatlantic relationship was becoming increasingly important as the Member States pooled ever more economic and political competencies in the EU. Although the United States has had regularly scheduled summits and consultations with many of its allies, including Canada, Mexico and Japan, relations with the European Union appeared to require greater coordination within the US Government and a specific diplomatic initiative: in addition to being the United States' largest trading partner and most important political ally, the EU poses unique challenges to US foreign policy because it is a *sui generis* entity without precedent in political history in which sovereignty has been pooled in some areas but not in others and in which the balance between intergovernmentalism, federalism and supranationalism is constantly evolving.

By defining a wide range of collaborative projects between the US and the EU in Europe and globally, the New Transatlantic Agenda also served to encourage the EU to assume greater international responsibility. The United States had already been pushing the EU in this direction for some time: for instance, the Bush Administration had urged the EU to assume primary responsibility for assistance to Central and Eastern Europe after the fall of the Berlin Wall and had supported its desire to lead international efforts at resolving the crisis in the former Yugoslavia.

---

14 US Department of State, 'Charting a Transatlantic Agenda for the 21st Century', Madrid, Spain, 2 June 1995.

The EU's 'go softly' approach to the integration of Central Europe and its inability to cope with the conflict in Bosnia underscored the need for an initiative that would encourage the EU to apply its financial and diplomatic resources internationally in partnership with the United States.

The central reason why the White House, through the National Security Council, became particularly engaged in the formulation of the New Transatlantic Agenda in the fall of 1995 was to encourage the EU to take a leading role in implementing the Dayton Peace Accords (particularly those provisions dealing with arms control, disarmament, confidence-building, the protection of human rights and the holding of free and fair elections) as well as in assisting the reconstruction of the Former Yugoslavia. From the Clinton Administration's perspective, the EU's contribution to Bosnian reconstruction had to reflect the fact that the Former Yugoslavia is on Europe's doorstep but distant from the United States and that Europe has a greater stake in the successful implementation of the peace.

In addition to satisfying the urgent need to advance the peace process with concrete actions on the ground, the focus on Bosnia in the first chapter of the Agenda on 'Promoting Peace and Stability, Democracy and Development Around the World' reassured the White House Press Office and domestic policy advisers that the President's trip to Madrid and the US-EU Summit would not be a complete media non-event: 'US-EU cooperation to bring peace to Bosnia' was a headline that the press, it was hoped, would extract from a document top-heavy with vague promises.

Other agencies of the US Government sought to achieve their own particular objectives in the first chapter of the Agenda. Faced with the prospect of declining resources for foreign aid, Director of USAID (US Agency for International Development) Brian Atwood was particularly enthusiastic about cooperating with Emma Bonino, Commissioner in charge of the EU's humanitarian aid program, on a transatlantic initiative to improve coordination of humanitarian assistance programs and preventive and crisis diplomacy. The Agenda highlights the establishment of a High-Level Consultative Group on Development Cooperation and Humanitarian Assistance to exchange information and coordinate policies from the stage of planning to that of execution. The central objective of the initiative is to avoid wasteful overlap and maximize existing resources available for foreign aid.

The Office of the Trade Representative, the Commerce Department and the National Economic Council were also driving forces behind the elaboration of the New Transatlantic Agenda. For them the document's third chapter on 'Contributing to the Expansion of World Trade and Closer Economic Relations' presented an opportunity to reduce tariff and non-tariff barriers to transatlantic trade, short of creating a free trade area, by implementing Uruguay Round commitments, accelerating tariff reductions in certain sectors, reinforcing international investment liberalization and protection, and improving regulatory cooperation. In particular, these three agencies were enthusiastic about the prospect of a US-EU Information Technology Agreement containing a commitment to eliminate all transatlantic tariffs in the information technology sector (where the United States remains highly competitive and generates high-wage jobs) by 1 January 2000. The Commerce Department, in particular, supported the Agenda, because it highlighted and supported the work of the Transatlantic Business Dialogue which Secretary of Commerce Ron Brown had called along with EU Commissioners Sir Leon Brittan and Martin Bangemann to gather leading representatives of the business world in Europe and the United States to propose priorities for future government-to-government trade negotiations.

In addition to its transatlantic dimension, the New Transatlantic Agenda presented a way for Washington to forge a partnership with the EU on international trade policy toward third countries. The need for greater collaboration on setting the terms for the entry of Russia and China into the WTO or on improving market access to the rapidly growing economies in Asia was self-evident. While both the European Union and the United States wish to redress their chronic and growing trade deficits with Asia, and even agree that hidden market barriers are the most important cause of these deficits, their tactics differ and occasionally work at cross-purposes. The EU has often been unwilling to support US trade initiatives aimed at improving access to key markets, such as Japan, China, South Korea, Taiwan and Malaysia. This unwillingness has exasperated some of the Administration's leading trade officials: 'the European Union has had a tendency to define its policy as the opposite of ours, even as it seeks virtually the same objectives'.[15]

---

15 Speech by Under-Secretary of Commerce Jeffrey Garten, the European Institute, 9 May 1995.

From Washington's perspective, the EU's strategy has been to let the United States take on the unpopular task of opening closed markets through threats of retaliation; after criticizing Washington for undermining the multilateral order and seeking to curry favor with the targets of such threats, the EU nonetheless benefits from the improved market access negotiated by Washington.[16]

Although strengthened transatlantic relations clearly responded to a need, launching a major new initiative just before the opening of the Inter-Governmental Conference was clearly a risk from Washington's perspective: the EU might become entirely self-absorbed with the task of defining the proper balance between inter-governmentalism and supranationalism within the Union; even if the EU had sufficient energy to devote to the initiative, it was uncertain whether the Member States would permit the Community, and the Commission in particular, to enhance its foreign policy profile. Indeed, the near failure of Maastricht ratification and growing opposition, including within the signatories to the Treaty of Rome, to further European economic and political integration indicated that the Conference might impose limits on the expansion of the Community's competence and maintain the dominance of Member States over foreign and security policy. This risk did in fact materialize, particularly with regard to the European Commission's ability to act as principal EU interlocutor with the United States. Partly due to the timid leadership of European Commission President Jacques Santer and the efforts of several Member States, especially France, to limit the Commission's margin of maneuver over a wide variety of issues, the New Transatlantic Agenda became more vulnerable than its American planners had feared to the parochial interests of the Member States and to the vicissitudes of the internal debate within the European Union regarding Community and Member State competencies.[17]

---

16 This is still a strongly felt view among leading US observers of the EU. At a farewell address at the American Chamber of Commerce in Brussels before leaving his post as US Ambassador to the EU, for example, Stuart Eizenstat stated: 'We find ourselves out front, alone, negotiating everything from intellectual property agreements with China to a set of sectoral agreements with Japan, extending them on a most-favored nation basis to the rest of the world, and finding European companies walking into the doors we open'. See 'Brussels Trade Pacts Corrosive', *Financial Times*, 9 February 1996.

17 An Advisory Opinion of the European Court of Justice in late 1994 also gave rise to concern in Washington that the European Commission would start losing its exclusive competence to represent the European Union in external trade matters. This

Notwithstanding this danger, Europeanists within the Clinton Administration were generally of the view that the United States should not wait until the end of the Intergovernmental Conference (IGC) in 1997 before beginning to engage the EU in a more structured partnership: key US interests, including NATO and EU enlargement, the stabilization of the new democracies and market economies of the former Soviet bloc, the opening of new export markets and the stabilization of the Third World were at stake in the short term. At the same time, however, the experience with the working groups confirmed that engaging the EU on some of the areas over which the Member States retained competence under the Maastricht Treaty would be a slow and laborious process.

Although the motivations of the US and EU to engage in the New Transatlantic Agenda were partly distinct, they were also partly identical. The critical motivation for a strengthened transatlantic partnership arose from the common conviction that the most pressing problems facing the US and the EU in an increasingly interdependent world are of a transnational character and cannot be addressed satisfactorily by either acting alone. On both sides of the Atlantic there is a growing desire to cooperate more effectively to combat international crime, terrorism, and the proliferation of weapons of mass destruction, to prevent or control environmental degradation, and to respond more effectively to humanitarian crises (such as the ethnic warfare in Rwanda or the outbreak of the Ebola virus in the former Zaire). Although the degree of transatlantic consensus is not nearly as high in the area of trade, it is important to note that the Commission, supported by most of the EU Member States,

---

competence had largely been responsible for the ability of the United States and the European Union to hammer out compromises on thorny issues related, for example, to agriculture, aerospace and public procurement in the Uruguay Round and previous GATT rounds. In its Opinion 1/94 of 15 November 1994, the Court found that, whereas the supply of services implying a movement of persons or an establishment within the EU falls within the concurrent competence of the EU and its Member States, those services which do not do so fall within the ambit of the common commercial policy and therefore within the exclusive competence of the Community. According to the Court, although the Community shares competence with the Member States with regard to the agreement on Trade-Related Aspects of Intellectual Property, the Community acquires exclusive competence if it has taken internal harmonization measures. The Opinion threatened a significant weakening of the European Commission's key external trade negotiating role because roughly thirty percent of all trade between the US and the EU was likely to be in services by the end of the century.

shares the Clinton Administration's strategy of pursuing further trade liberalization as a way of promoting growth and creating jobs.

Shrinking foreign affairs budgets on both sides of the Atlantic – resulting from efforts to reduce public debt and government deficits – have convinced many policy makers that independent action to address transnational crises is a wasteful luxury of the past. After the election in the November 1994 Congressional elections of hostile Republic majorities which endorsed isolationist or unilateralist foreign policies, the Clinton Administration came under particularly severe pressure to further reduce the budget for the State Department and USAID. The New Transatlantic Agenda offered the prospect of helping the United States to maintain its superpower status 'on the cheap' in the 1990s.

The Agenda was also perceived by the executive branches officials on both sides of the Atlantic as a useful mechanism to launch quickly a major transatlantic initiative which would not require lengthy parliamentary ratification. As two European Commission officials who were key players in the elaboration of the Agenda have accurately observed: 'In a situation where leaders on both sides of the Atlantic intended to send a political signal rapidly, an instrument which did not have to be submitted to the long and sometimes complicated approval procedures of the US Congress, the European Parliament and all the Parliaments of the Member States of the European Union was very attractive.'[18]

Had the Agenda been submitted for parliamentary ratification, it is by no means certain that it would have been approved. Unlike the French government, the French Parliament, for example, might not have been willing to compromise on its fierce opposition to the idea of further tariff reduction; similarly, those members of the US House of Representatives and Senate, elected in November 1994, who believed that the United States should retreat into isolation or only act unilaterally abroad would certainly have objected to the spirit and initiatives set forth in the Agenda.

By establishing a framework and concrete objectives for transatlantic dialogue, the New Transatlantic Agenda responded to the concerns of those on both sides of the Atlantic that the sense of common commitment and mutual attachment of Europe and the United States might fade with the rise of a new generation of leaders born after the War. As one

---

18 H. Krenzler and A. Schomaker, 'A New Transatlantic Agenda', *European Foreign Affairs Review*, 1:1 (1996) 18.

of the leading American commentators on Europe observed: 'Many of the 'old Atlanticists' are growing old, and not enough is being done to reproduce the ease of communication they gradually learned. It wasn't easy to get this far. It would be a grievous loss to let the capacity fade away. *The one permanent certainty about the future is that it will bring mutual problems to solve.*'[19] (emphasis added)

Nostalgia about the commonality of interests, values and traditions in the United States and Europe was clearly no substitute for closer collaboration. The 1990 Transatlantic Declaration and the Berlin working groups were tentative steps in this direction, but had not gone far enough. The New Transatlantic Agenda has charted the course for a partnership between the US and EU to cope more effectively with the economic and political challenges facing both sides of the Atlantic into the next century. President Clinton reminded the participants at the Madrid Summit, however, that actions speak louder than words and that the Agenda will be judged according to whether it brings concrete results. Although the Agenda has yielded significant progress on a number of trade issues, including the progressive reduction in tariff and non-tariff barriers, as well as on a number of 'soft' foreign policy issues, such as the coordination of humanitarian relief efforts and human rights initiatives, it remains largely a road-map and has yet to provide evidence that the US and the EU can forge and carry out joint actions on more controversial matters. Indeed, as the serious transatlantic frictions caused by US sanctions legislation demonstrates, there are still deep differences of opinion between the US and the EU regarding foreign policy. The New Transatlantic Agenda will not solve these differences overnight of course; but it has already helped to keep transitory disputes in the perspective of the wider, more significant and enduring interests which bind the US and EU together.

---

19 F. Lewis, 'Atlantic Connections Begin to Fray', *International Herald Tribune*, 23 June 1995.

CHAPTER 4

The US Mission to the EU in 'Brussels D.C.', the European Commission Delegation in Washington D.C. and the New Transatlantic Agenda

Pascaline WINAND

Fonds National de la Recherche Scientifique (Belgium), Université Libre de Bruxelles

The US Mission to the EU (USEU) played a decisive role in launching the NTA, while the European Commission Delegation (the Delegation) in Washington D.C. was active during the implementation phase.[1] As a first step to understanding the role of US and EU posts in European-American relations, the structure and activities of the Delegation, and especially those of the Mission – because of the key role of its Ambassador, Stuart Eizenstat[2] – will be studied here. This will be done in comparative perspective with an indication of their transformation to keep up with evolving transatlantic relations and developments in the EU, Washington D.C., and on the world scene. Looking at these key, but little studied, actors in transatlantic relations will hopefully give us fresh insights on past and current US-EC/EU relations, help us identify

---

1 This study is based in part on fourty-two interviews with officials at USEU and the Delegation of the Commission in Washington D.C., as well as with US officials in Washington, Commission officials, and centers, institutes or 'think tanks'. Most interviewees preferred not to be mentioned by name. A special thank you to Earl A. Wayne, former Deputy Chief at USEU, Astrid Schomaker, European Commission, and Nadine Bernard-Lubelski for their comments on an earlier manuscript. Thank you also to the Nobel Institute in Oslo for providing an invaluable research environment for completing this study.

2 Ambassador Eizenstat wrote: 'I was privileged to play a major role in the development of the NTA, and I consider it the most important contribution I have been able to make while serving as US Ambassador to the EU and one of the most important in all my years of public service.', A. Gardner, *A New Era in US-EU Relations? The Clinton Administration and the New Transatlantic Agenda* (Aldershot, Avebury, 1997), p.ix.

areas where improvement might be needed in the ways these posts operate, while also providing some indication of how the EU is developing and is being perceived by external actors. In addition, we may ask to what extent the Mission and the Delegation, in addition to fulfilling the functions normally expected of diplomatic posts, *i.e.* informing, reporting, doing demarches, lobbying, have also been shaping or even making policy. Last but not least, and most difficult perhaps, comparing the USEU with the European Commission Delegation in Washington could help us to uncover some differences in their respective operating environments, including the nature of different actors on the lobbying scene and their interaction.

The US Mission to the EU (USEU)

Historical Background

The US has maintained diplomatic relations with the forerunners of the EU since the time when the fledgling High Authority (HA) of the European Coal and Steel Community (ECSC) set up shop in Luxembourg under the presidency of Monnet. A close friend of US Secretary of State John Foster Dulles, Monnet recommended appointing a representative ranking above other US representatives in Europe in order to underscore the importance to the US of European integration. David Bruce, an old friend of his, was eventually designated as US Observer to the Interim Committee of the European Defence Community (EDC) and also served as US Representative to the ECSC, while observing the progress towards the creation of a European Political Community.

When the EDC met with defeat, Monnet then urged Dulles to keep the US representation to the HA separate from NATO or the OEEC as a confirmation of American commitment to supranational as opposed to intergovernmental European organisations. While Dulles hesitated, Bruce went back to the US. By then, what was popularly known as the 'Relaunching of Europe' was well on its way.

It took about ten months after Bruce's departure to offer tangible proof of US commitment to European integration: in October 1955 Eisenhower decided to establish a separate American Mission to the ECSC. The Mission opened in Luxembourg in 1956. In January 1958, the appointment of Walt Butterworth, with the special rank of Ambassador, as representative to the EEC and Euratom, in addition to the ECSC, was intended as a demonstration of American support to European supranational integration. A US Mission to the European Communities (USEC), still headed by Butterworth, was eventually established in Brussels in 1961.

Under the Kennedy administration, just as the negotiations for British entry into the EEC were marking time and the Common Agricultural Policy (CAP) was coming into effect, John W. Tuthill replaced Butterworth as US Ambassador to the European Communities in October 1962. As the 'chicken war' raged, thus epitomising mounting concern on the part of the US for the consequences of the CAP, he became one of the main architects of a compromise between the EEC and the US on the poultry issue. Tuthill's colleague Robert Schaetzel, replaced him in September 1966.

Schaetzel ran into disappointment after disappointment during his long stay at the Mission (1966-72). By the Spring of 1970, he complained of being 'almost cut off completely from Washington'. 'The highly private style of the President and the character of the State Department today', he lamented, 'produce an extraordinary chemistry which effectively blocks all communication'.[3] By the Fall of 1971, he truly despaired: 'The forces of darkness could win', he wrote, by this he meant the small groups in the Commerce, Agriculture and Treasury departments who produced 'a grab bag of maximum desires' including 'the destruction of the Common Agricultural Policy'.[4] Reflecting years later on this frustrating period, Schaetzel again displayed a talent for vivid characterisations:

> During the Rogers regime, in its isolation in Brussels the United States Mission to the European Communities might as well have been located on the upper reaches of the Orinoco. It was a world of silence. The Mission's functioning required more the anthropologist's talents than the diplomat's.[5]

So much for the chequered path of the early history of USEC. Since then ambassadors to the European Communities, have succeeded one another – Ambassador Richard L. Morningstar is the 15th US Representative to the European Communities – and the US Mission has undergone both structural and functional changes to keep in step with the evolution of European integration and to reflect US policy priorities.

---

3 Schaetzel to Acheson, 28 April 1970, Yale Library (YL).

4 Schaetzel to Acheson, 27 September, 1971, YL.

5 R. Schaetzel, *The Unhinged Alliance* (New York, Harper and Row, 1975).

One of these changes, which might appear to be cosmetic at first sight, is the new name of the Mission, which has become the US Mission to the European Union or USEU. While Monnet attempted to single out the US representation to the ECSC as showing US commitment to European integration as opposed to intergovernmental cooperation, this name symbolises the American recognition of the EU as a political force as well as an economic one.[6]

But just how well is the Mission tailored to do an effective, well-informed job? How well can it reach out to the EU and back home?

Background and Preparation

In general, most ambassadors, but not all, have been well prepared to take on their job at the Mission. Those who were possessed either an extensive background in European affairs as career officers in the State Department both in Europe and in the US or had been briefed before coming to Brussels. Ambassador Eizenstat, who avowedly did not know much about European integration before taking up his assignment, was intensely briefed in the US. Briefing books were prepared for him on major issues. He also met with those previous Ambassadors to the EC who were still alive and with senior officials from the departments[7] that had any connection with the issues he would be dealing with. This provided him with a sense of continuity. In addition, an all-day seminar on European integration issues was put together for him, with academic experts coming from all over the US, including from Brookings and the European Community Studies Association.[8] Finally, he was also briefed by the European Commission Delegation in Washington D.C.[9]

---

6 Eizenstat and some of his top advisers immediately reacted to the entry into force of the Maastricht Treaty by proposing to rename the US Mission to the European Communities the 'US Mission to the European Union', as a symbolic gesture to support European integration, including the Second and Third Pillars. This created problems with the European Commission, which pointed out that the EU had no legal personality. To this day, the Mission has a kind of split personality, where remnants of the old USEC days survive on the stationary for example.

7 Not just the State Department, but also the Departments of Commerce, Treasury and USTR.

8 Eizenstat has maintained ties with the academic world, notably by serving as Adjunct Lecturer at the JFK School of Government at Harvard University. He has also been a Guest Scholar at Brookings in Washington.

9 *I.e.* by Ambassador Van Agt, his deputy Jim Currie and Jonathan Davidson.

Backgrounds do differ, however, and are not always suited to the job or the period in hand. Although Eizenstat's predecessor James Dobbins was an eminent expert on security and foreign policy, he ended up focusing on economic and trade issues at a time when Vice-President Dan Quayle warned that the Cold War might well be followed by a trade war. Although he possessed much expertise in economics and trade, Eizenstat was principally an expert in domestic, not foreign affairs. His assignment at USEU, however, forced him to concentrate on problematic issues such as Bosnia, in addition to trade issues. Originally a political scientist and a lawyer by training, he was the chief domestic policy adviser to President Carter.[10] But he was also a top lawyer-lobbyist, representing the corporate cause, including high-tech companies. His understanding of how to 'work Washington' including Congress, and his knack for dealing with the substance of issues, was an asset to the effectiveness of the US Mission.[11]

Below the ambassadorial level, some members of Eizenstat's team were well suited for their work at the Mission, be it through previous positions in the US or in US embassies. For example, Eizenstat's Deputy Chief at USEU had been Director for Western European Security Affairs at the National Security Council where his key responsibility was to encourage a GATT agreement, and had thus spent much time dealing with EC affairs.[12]

---

10 In 1976 Eizenstat joined the Carter Presidential campaign full-time as Issues and Policy Director. In 1977, President Carter appointed him as Assistant to the President for Domestic Affairs and Policy and Executive *Director* of the Domestic Policy Staff at the White House. He continued in this capacity until 1981. At the time of his nomination (which the US Senate confirmed on 30 July 1993), he was Partner and Vice Chairman of the law firm, and Chairman of the Washington office, of Powell, Goldstein, Frazer and Murphy, where he had been since 1981.

11 If one of his former co-workers in Washington admired him for being 'one of those magical people who doesn't need to sleep', if he was described as having a 'policy gloss', in Brussels he was known by his staff for wanting to know minute details such as what hill warring factions were shooting from in Bosnia, see J. H. Birnbaum, *The Lobbyists* (New York, Random House, 1992); Eizenstat is also a pro-Israël activist.

12 Similarly, the Minister-Counselor for Economic Affairs formerly held the position of assistant to the Undersecretary of State for Economic Affairs with the Europe portfolio. On the other hand, the Minister-Counselor for Agricultural Affairs came to his new post from a previous assignment in a EU Member State, which gave him more of a Member State perspective. Those members of the Mission's staff who took on their

Most Ambassadors have been career diplomats, with some exceptions, Eizenstat being a case in point. In the early days of the Mission, the appointment of career diplomats and State Department people to key positions, translated into an atmosphere of collegiality dominated by an *esprit de corps*. This atmosphere was further intensified by the fact that the Mission was then much smaller than it is now; people were consequently physically closer to each other. For Schaetzel, the Mission had a good record within the State Department because it 'had the reputation of being manned by a small but highly competent and dedicated staff' and was an 'assignment to be sought by promising officers'.[13]

Besides backgrounds and career paths, personalities have also mattered. Under Ambassador Thomas O. Enders (1979-81), who maintained a certain distance towards his staff, the atmosphere was characterised by fear of one's superior. By contrast, George Vest (1981-85), an expert in US-European/Communities relations and a high-level State Department officer, is fondly remembered as 'the father of the Foreign Service' for his competency, his *esprit de corps*, his sense of humour, his concern for his staff and his openness. His successor, Thomas M. T. Niles (1989-91) followed in his footsteps as far as his background and *esprit de corps* were concerned. When asked what the US government should do to encourage awareness of the EC and 1992, he simply replied 'through publicity. The first thing we need to do is have more information about what is going on in Europe. We have a major outreach program that is being run by this mission'. Perhaps this would be a way of putting the idea of 'Fortress Europe' – an 'unfortunate expression' to rest?[14] Other ambassadors are remembered for peculiarities such as coming in late in the morning and working late into the night to match Washington's schedule. Finally, whereas some have shown a marked preference for working independently and establishing a divide

---

new job with little knowledge of the EU were briefed on the EU in Washington or in Brussels, or learned on the ground.

13 Schaetzel would have regretted 'seeing it enlarged very much' and did not think highly of political appointees. Hearing before the Subcommittee on Europe and the Middle East of the Committee on Foreign Affairs, House of Representatives, 99th Congress, 2nd session, 14 July 1986, pp.127, 185.

14 'View from the US Ambassador Thomas M. T. Niles, The US Mission to the EC Promotes Awareness of the 1992 Program', *Europe*, April 1990; An economic specialist, Niles used to keep 'a stock of plastic cards listing the distorting effects that the common agricultural policy had on trade. He would distribute these to visitors', 'Mr Ambassador talks tough', *The Bulletin*, 20 February 1992.

between the executive office and the staff, others have fostered a more direct relationship with their advisers, relying on their staff for ideas.

Eizenstat epitomised the interactive leader. His staff described the Mission under his guidance as a 'much more active mission' or a 'mission with a sense of mission'.[15] At the same time, he was also a work alcoholic. Work continued during working breakfasts, lunches and dinners, where guests were questioned by the Ambassador while a staff member took notes.

Organization, Functions and Actions of USEU

Adaptation and Expansion

One way of dealing with the mounting challenge of the EU has been to increase the staff. A lone exception in the constellation of US diplomatic posts abroad, many of which are being closed or experience staff cuts, USEU is expanding to reflect the new competencies of the EU. Staff numbers are growing and new agencies are being added.

Another way to measure changes at the Mission is by looking at the size of one section relative to other sections, and also at the level of representation within that section. In this respect, the political section, in line with Maastricht and the change from EPC to CFSP, has not only grown to be about equal in size with the economic section but has also upgraded the status of its political counsellor who used to be a middle-level officer and became a senior officer, thereby reflecting the fact that Pillar I[16] issues dominated the agenda less than in the past.

Although the State Department and the US Information Agency (USIA) have long been represented at the Mission, along with representatives from the Department of Agriculture – who joined the Mission in the early 1960s to meet the mounting challenge of the CAP – and USTR, representatives from the Treasury, the Department of Commerce, Customs, Justice, and USAID were all recent additions. A Third

---

[15] Contributing to the dedication of the staff were such personal attentions from the Ambassador as calling staff members to thank them, or allowing them to sign their own telegrams.

[16] Since the Maastricht Treaty, Pillar I consists of the three European Communities, the ECSC, the EC, and Euratom. The EEC dropped the word 'economic' and is now named the European Community. Pillar II deals with Common Foreign and Security Policy, while Pillar III deals with Justice and Home Affairs.

Pillar Unit, connected with the political section, was also added to the mix to deal with the Third[17] Pillar competencies of the EU.

The position of Trade Policy *Attaché* was established at the beginning of the 1980s after discussions which involved some turf rivalry between the State Department and USTR. A compromise solution was finally reached whereby the USEU Trade Policy *Attaché* came from USTR out to the Mission on a limited term of appointment (three years) but was hired into the State Department with the understanding that the person would then go back to USTR.[18]

Until recently, no Commerce Department representatives worked at the Mission, even though the Department's Foreign Commercial Service was present in twenty-two European countries, including all members of the EC, with the exception of tiny Luxembourg. Here, pressure to increase US government staff in Brussels and especially to appoint Commerce representatives to meet the mounting challenge of 'Europe 1992' by adding technical and commercial expertise to the Mission, thereby allowing small and medium-sized American companies to take advantage of a growing Single Market, came from Congress. 'When I was in Brussels', said one Senator during hearings on Europe 1992,

> It just overwhelmed me, frankly that there were 10,000, or I do not know how many thousands, of employees working for the Commission in Brussels. As you know, there is this gigantic, big black building with all these wings on it and all these people running around in Brussels. There are so many people it is like an anthill. It was my impression that our Mission over there is outgunned and frankly, did not quite know what is really going on [...]. I suspect that a lot of directives are going to come out in the end, a big flurry, and we'll say 'Oh, my gosh, where were we?'[19]

The absence of Commerce representatives at the Mission and foot-dragging on the part of the State Department, probably the result of a turf rivalry between the State and Commerce Departments, greatly dis-

---

17 See note 16. In addition, USEU added a PRM officer – a specialist on migration, asylum and related issues – to the team.

18 By contrast, for example, in Geneva at the WTO – the only other place where USTR has employees stationed overseas – employees are paid by USTR.

19 Senator Baucus in Senate Committee on Finance, 'Hearing on Europe 92 Trade Program', 101st Congress, 1st Session, 10 May 1989, quoted in Y. Devuyst, 'US Market Opening Strategies toward the European Community: The Role of GATT Customs Union Provisions and their Bilateral and Unilateral Alternatives', Doctoral Thesis, Vrije Universiteit Brussel, unpublished, 1994, p.332

turbed the members of Congress, who directed the Department of Commerce – through the State Department Authorization Bill – to assign a minimum of three Foreign Commercial Service (FCS) officers at USEC.[20] By July 1990, a commercial *attaché* was finally assigned to the Mission, which now counts several officers working under the direction of the Minister-Counselor for Commercial Affairs.[21]

The reason the US Treasury Department decided to be represented at the US Mission as of 1991, was mainly due to the progress on the Single Market: topics that were of interest to the Treasury, including financial market regulations, bank regulations etc. were now increasingly being done at the EC level. In addition, the whole EMU process meant that more and more macroeconomic issues were being discussed in Brussels. The Treasury's presence at the Mission is significant in light of the very small overseas contingent of Treasury people based overseas.

The Third Pillar Unit at the USEU is directly linked to its parent bureau in Washington D.C., the Bureau of International Narcotics and Law Enforcement at the State Department, and also has links with the Bureau of European Affairs. The position was first established in early 1991 and and was originally a narcotics affairs section and a one person position. With the collapse of the Iron Curtain, the State Department then took on the portfolio of dealing with transnational organised crime and the unit shifted its focus to deal more with Central Europe, organized crime, terrorism, and money laundering.[22]

---

20 See Youri Devuyst, 'Market Opening', pp.337-8.

21 While in Washington D.C. the dividing line between USTR and the Department of Commerce can generally be characterised as the difference between trade policy and trade promotion, the FCS staff at the Mission have tended to have more trade policy functions than is generally the case in Washington; Eizenstat had known Secretary of Commerce Ron Brown, a Democrat, for twenty years before he himself was chosen by the President to be Under Secretary of Commerce for International Trade, a position which he planned to use 'to do on a world-wide basis' what he did 'substantially in Brussels with the European Union – that is, working on a whole range of trade issues', and to open markets abroad 'as USTR has so effectively done, and as Secretary Brown has pursued' ('Eizenstat Wants More Small, Minority Firms Involved', *USIS Wireless File – European Wireless File*, No.7, p.24, 17 January 1996, NTA Transcript: 1/5 Foreign Press Center Briefing).

22 The new responsibilities of the State Department and those of Justice, which had until then been mostly responsible for transnational organised crime, created some bureaucratic problems in D.C. Not too long ago, a Justice Attorney was assigned to the Mission and worked closely with the Third Pillar Unit on law enforcement issues. In addition an officer from the State Department's Bureau of Population, Refugees

In August 1995, a representative from USAID joined the Mission to coordinate aid efforts with USAID in Washington. This assignment reflected the fact that the European Commission had long been one of the largest donors of assistance in the world. In an era of shrinking resources both in Europe and in the US, it made sense to cooperate more closely on development issues, and to avoid duplicating efforts, not only in Central Europe and the former Soviet Union, but also in Africa, for example. Thus, on the American side, adding an USAID representative to USEU was thought of not so much as an added expense but as a way of saving money by coordinating more with the EU. The USAID representative has maintained close links with USAID in Washington and played a key role in educating the USAID bureaucracy, who until recently did not know much about the EU.

As for the economic section of the Mission, which has not been much enlarged compared to the political section, it has nevertheless undergone a few organisational changes to match the structure and responsibilities of the European Commission, including in the environmental field.

Internal and External Coordination

Some Ambassadors have shown themselves to be shrewd administrators, notably by infusing the Mission and its various agencies with a cooperative spirit which is more difficult to find in Washington D.C., where turf battles and heavy bureaucratic machineries often make interagency coordination harder. During Eizenstat's ambassadorship, for example, the staff insisted that cooperation among the various US agencies represented at the Mission was better than in Washington D.C.: less jealousy here, in part because of Eizenstat's leadership but also because the Mission, despite recent additions to the staff, was still relatively small compared to other large embassies: 'we have so much to do we need each other' said one staff member. (Yet the Mission is expanding, both in terms of staff and office space.)[23] In addition, internal coordination was improved by staff meetings chaired by the Ambassador, and attended by the Minister-Counselors for economic, commercial, agri-

---

and Migration (PRM) has been added to the External Affairs Division and also cooperates closely with the Third Pillar Unit, the name of which obviously is indicative the evolution of the EU itself.

23 In March 2000, Secretary of State Madeleine Albright dedicated a new USEU Chancery at 13, rue Zinner.

cultural and political affairs, the Deputy Chief of the Mission, representatives from USTR, the US Treasury Department and other agencies, and the Ambassador's secretary.[24]

Eizenstat also put a premium on improving external coordination with US missions and embassies in Brussels and in other European capitals, especially in key countries such as Germany, France, the UK, Spain or Italy. In Brussels, he felt fortunate to have 'one of his oldest best friends' as head of the US Mission to NATO, with which USEU now shared responsibility for oversight of the Western European Union (WEU). Thus, while the NATO Mission looked at the WEU through the perspective of its link to NATO, USEU looked at it from the perspective of its relationship to the EU. During Eizenstat's ambassadorship, the two Ambassadors shared notes and entertained each other for dinner. For Eizenstat, the key problem was not between his Mission and the NATO Mission, but rather between the EU and NATO, which were 'each on parallel tracks for enlargement'.

In addition, the Mission also has links with the American Embassy to Belgium, particularly for economic and trade issues, and on Africa. Finally, it has extensive relations with the business Community, as well as with representations of US States in Brussels.

As far as communicating with Washington is concerned, while Schaetzel may have had some difficulties in making his voice heard, Eizenstat had no trouble accessing top policy-makers, some of whom were close friends. A token of its efficiency and of the political clout of its ambassador, the Mission's advice was well heeded at the State Department, still the main contact point of the Mission in the US administration, but also in other departments and agencies, and at the White House.[25] The Commerce Department, intent as it was to survive

---

24 Under Eizenstat, once a week a staff meeting enlarged to include the entire Mission. Meetings were scheduled every morning from 9:30 to about 10:15 and were part of the Ambassador's effort to talk through outstanding issues collectively, thereby allowing him and top USEU officials to have an overview of everybody's issues and contributing to the cohesion of the Mission's team. Similar co-ordination efforts took place within the various sections. For example, the Minister-Counselor for Agricultural Affairs organised short meetings with members of his staff several times a week and his section produced a weekly newsletter. The letter not only served to inform Washington and other American posts in Europe but was a good management tool to foster co-ordination within the section and keep it focused on key issues.

25 By early 1995 the White House counted two former American interns at the European Commission, one working on European trade and economic issues, the other,

Congressional moves for its suppression, was particularly receptive to helping launch a major new initiative such as the NTA. A friend of Eizenstat, the late US Commerce Secretary Ron Brown was one of the masterminds behind the Transatlantic Business Dialogue (TABD).[26]

In addition, Eizenstat's views on European affairs clearly mirrored those of the Clinton administration that, rather than seeking to contain communism, seemed committed to expand the community of 'market democracies'. This further helped oil relations between Washington and Brussels.[27]

Eizenstat used his Washington connections to make sure that the EU did receive high priority attention in US foreign policy. As Anthony Gardner has pointed out, 'working primarily with Secretary of Commerce Ron Brown, Deputy National Security Advisor Samuel Berger, Assistant Secretary of State Richard Holbrooke, the Bureau of Regional Affairs in the State Department and the Senior Directors for European Affairs in the National Security Council' he 'succeeded in crafting a strong EU element to the President's trip to Europe in January 1994'.[28] Finally, his unrelenting support for the NTA was a key factor in convincing the Clinton administration to devote 'considerable diplomatic resources' to make it happen.[29]

---

detached from the Council on Foreign Relations, holding the post of Director of European Affairs in the European Directorate of the National Security Council, with a special responsibility for relations with EU institutions and the 1996 Intergovernmental Conference.

26 According to Eizenstat, Brown 'first suggested this US-European business-government dialogue in December 1994 in Brussels and was soon joined by European Commission Vice President Brittan and Industry Commissioner Bangemann in his efforts to make the idea take shape', Gardner, *A New Era*, p.x.

27 Eizenstat's intention upon coming to Brussels was to 'infuse a sense of energy into the Mission and into the relationship'. He also felt 'very strongly that in the post-Cold War era we needed to broaden the definition of security and to develop additional non-military linkages' between the US and Europe. Finally, he was convinced of the necessity of uniting economies, and of including central European democracies 'to have a really seamless continent united around free market and democratic values'. Eizenstat, interview by Pascaline Winand, 4 May 1995; further quotes by Eizenstat in the rest of the paper refer to the same interview.

28 Gardner, *A New Era*, p.17.

29 Gardner, *A New Era*, p.vii.

Public Diplomacy: A High Public Profile and Pro-active Attitudes versus Pessimism

Convinced of the importance of the US relationship with the EU for US interests, Eizenstat saw himself both as an advocate of US policy and a 'cheerleader for the European Union'.[30] By contrast with some other ambassadors, he gave priority to public diplomacy, thereby keeping the Office of Public Affairs of the Mission exceedingly busy. The newsletter published by the Mission, the so-called 'Letter from Brussels', doubled in size. Eizenstat had numerous interviews with the press (TV, radio, journals) in Brussels, other European countries and in the US. In April 1995, he planned a tour of the US West Coast 'to bring the message to the hinterland in the States about the EU'. By that time he had already delivered about eighty speeches since he assumed office in October 1993, some of which were concentrated in the very first weeks of his new assignment, which is unusual for most ambassadors. He also contributed articles to major newspapers and periodicals such as *The International Herald Tribune*, *The Wall Street Journal*, *The Brussels Review*, *The Financial Times* and *European Voice*. In February 1996, soon to go back to Washington D.C., he insisted that a lot more must be done to educate US citizens about the EU. As part of this effort, he advocated that US publications and American television must learn to cover Europe not just from Paris, London or Frankfurt, but also from Brussels 'where the interplay of Member States occurs'.[31] In keeping with his remarks, the NTA and the Joint Action Plan, stress 'the need to strengthen and broaden public support' for the US/EU partnership.

If we now look at the vocabulary used by Ambassadors, we find that the international and domestic context of any given assignment influences an Ambassador's priorities, stamina or optimism, even though some seem to show more of a disposition for optimism or a pro-active attitude than others.

Eizenstat's speeches, for example, were riddled with action-oriented pronouncements such as 'we are optimistic about Europe, about the European Community', or 'we support unequivocally and enthusiasti-

30 Ambassador Stuart E. Eizenstat, 'Developing the Transatlantic Dialogue, Remarks to the US-EU Journalist Conference: New Dimensions in Transatlantic Relations', Dromoland Castle, Ireland, 19 November 1994.

31 Ambassador Stuart E. Eizenstat, 'Farewell Remarks to the EU Committee of the American Chamber of Commerce', Brussels, 8 February 1996, p.17.

cally the effort of European integration'.[32] His self-perceived role as cheerleader for European integration has also been characterized by frequent references to American history meant as comforting statements to soothe the growing pains of the EU. Articles entitled 'You Can Take Heart from US History',[33] 'Enlargement Has Never Been Easy'[34], or 'The Trans-Atlantic Desire for Devolution'[35] addressed issues such as the difficulty of institution building in the US and in the EU, and US and EU enlargements, and drew parallels between the recent trend towards 'subsidiarity' both in the US and in the EU.[36]

By contrast with Eizenstat's pro-active attitude, Dobbins displayed an inclination for pessimistic ruminations about the waning public support for European integration in EC countries, difficulties over the ratification of the Maastricht Treaty, and the Uruguay Round[37], although these were often tempered by statements such as 'the picture is not entirely dark'[38] or a touch of humour. For example, he told a journalist that, in the Fall of 1991, people back in Washington would cable him questions such as 'If the EC is so busy integrating, how come they always need more chairs?'[39]

---

32 In his farewell speech to the Am Cham EU Committee, he declared: 'I came to my post in 1993 as an enthusiastic supporter of the European Community and I leave an even more enthusiastic supporter of the European Union in 1996, because the EU serves the interests of the peoples of Europe, of the United States, for which the EU is an important partner, and indeed of freedom loving people throughout the world'. He further emphasised that he did not believe in 'doomsday forecasts' about the EU and '*Euro-pessimism*'. Eizenstat, 'Farewell Remarks'.

33 *International Herald Tribune*, 29 October 1993.

34 *Wall Street Journal*, 1 June 1994.

35 *The Wall Street Journal Europe*, 4 April 1995.

36 At the same time, Eizenstat carefully specified that the EU was a *sui generis* occurrence, something 'never before been accomplished in world history' and definitely '*not* a carbon copy of the United States for Europe'. Ambassador S. E. Eizenstat,' Address to the American Electronic Association Annual Conference', Brussels, 1 October 1993, p.3.

37 Asked whether he was optimistic that the GATT agreement would be concluded, he told a journalist 'he was neither optimistic nor pessimistic', *Le Soir*, 17 March 1993.

38 *Letter from Brussels*, 6 August 1993. The *Letter from Brussels* of USEU gives an overall account of major areas in which USEU has been most active during Eizenstat's ambassadorship.

39 See also: Speech by Ambassador Dobbins, CEPS Business Policy Seminar, 27 January 1992.

'Brussels D.C.' versus Washington D.C.

Upon his arrival in Brussels, Eizenstat confessed to a journalist that the US had 'a major problem in dealing with the EC. It doesn't understand quite what it is'. 'There is an information void', he complained.[40] So, is the EU an UPO (unidentified political object)? And how should the US deal with it? One staff member at USEU commented that the problem in Brussels was 'knowing the system, knowing the people to call'. Once you knew that, getting the right person to deal with was 'certainly no harder than in Washington D.C'. Another staff member, however, complained of ringing telephones, which no one answered, contrary to what happened in the US; this seemed to be a particular problem with the European Parliament (EP). When asked what differences he found in dealing with what some are now calling 'Brussels D.C.', as opposed to Washington D.C., and some other international fora, Eizenstat identified a major one: by contrast with NATO, the US is, of course, not a member of the EU. A member of his staff added that this was somewhat frustrating for the US which is used to being in the centre of things.

Another difference is the lobbying style. Admittedly lobbying has to be done with delicacy and there is always the question of 'how much, how directly' and whom one should lobby. A high-level officer at the Mission, however, noted that Brussels and Washington were actually the most similar cities in the world: power is widely disseminated – many people possess some but not much power – and information is very widely available. According to this source, the problem in both Brussels and Washington D.C. was not so much gaining access to the material, a problem you might encounter in Paris, Moscow or Beijing, but finding out who was right on an issue among countless and often dissenting information sources. In a similar vein, another staff member noted that it was somewhat difficult to find his counterparts in the different DGs at the European Commission and encountered problems in locating a good organisational chart of the EU. But then some members of USEU found it equally difficult to find their way in their own home bureaucracies. Other staff members of USEU pointed out that the EU largely differs from the US on one point: while the US system has a strong central authority, with relatively weak states, the EU has a weak central authority with strong Member States. This justifies a multi-tier lobbying

40 'US admits it still not sure how to deal with EC', *Reuter*, November 1993.

strategy, which goes much beyond simply lobbying the European Commission.

Lobbying the European Commission

The prime target of the Mission's lobbying efforts so far still seems to be the European Commission for first pillar topics. Results are generally obtained by lobbying the Commissioner in charge and sticking with him throughout the negotiations. Yet sometimes this simply is not enough, and one must go to other people on the Commission. For Eizenstat, direct lobbying of the Commission included the Directors-General, for he had 'always placed a great premium', as he did in Washington, 'on briefing staff'. 'In the end', he noted, 'politicians turn to the staff. So it's important for the staff to understand the merits of the case.' He insisted that there was 'no substitute for being knowledgeable. You can't make hysterical and emotional arguments, they have to based on facts, reason, logic.' Another top-level official at the Mission, specified that the Santer Commission, as opposed to the Delors Commission which was centralised, was more collegial, so that it did 'make sense to call a number of more places to share your point of view'. On the whole, Commission staff is rated by the Americans as being extremely professional and usually accessible, even though frequent travelling commitments make it rather difficult to contact the right person. Interestingly, in cases where information is hard to obtain on a dossier either from the Commission or the Member states' permanent representations, US officers try to piece the picture together by contacting other countries' representatives in Brussels, and this includes Canada, Australia, New Zealand, Japan, and depending on the subject, Central European, and Latin American countries.

The various sections and agencies of USEU are accustomed to dealing with Directorates General (DGs) and Cabinets at the Commission that parallel their own area of expertise. Thus, for example, the agricultural section mostly deals with Franz Fischler's Cabinet, the Agriculture DG, the External Relations DG, while the DG on Taxation and Customs Union and especially the DG on Environment also fall within its purview. The agricultural part of the Mission is also interested in food aid issues, which has generated new contacts with other parts of the EC bureaucracy.

Lobbying Member States

The Mission also lobbies the Council of Ministers through its Secretariat and through EU national embassies, while targeting foreign Ministers, even though the Mission seems to wield comparatively less influence at that level. The EU is further being lobbied through its Permanent Representations although a number of these are not really organized to deal diplomatically with other countries than the EU Member States, and are primarily focused on economic Coreper issues.[41]

Mission officials often find it hard to deal with the Permanent Representation of the presidency country because the staff is so busy. Yet lobbying efforts do intensify with that country and some presidencies have been singled out as particularly productive. In addition, larger permanent representations are usually targeted mostly because they are less thinly staffed.[42]

Lobbying the European Parliament

Since the 1970s, the Mission has devoted resources to paying one full-time officer to follow the EP, perhaps because of the implicit analogy with the US Congress.[43] During Eizenstat's stay in Brussels, USEU increasingly lobbied the EP partly as a result of the Ambassador's expertise in lobbying the US Congress. In addition to the full-time position earmarked for keeping a close watch on the EP, Eizenstat and his staff made an effort to integrate it into everybody's duties at USEU.[44]

---

41 Fortunately most countries now have a CFSP counsellor; this is especially important for the political section of the Mission, although counsellors often differ from each other in rank and influence. There is also some frustration in coping with the delicate interaction between the Coreper and the Political Committee.

42 Language also plays a role, although some officers insist that this is not always the case. English seems to be spoken at most Permanent Representations but US Mission officers speak more than one language.

43 Yet this analogy has its limits. While in Washington Congress is the prime lobbying target, by contrast, although growing in importance, notably with the co-decision procedure, 'the European Parliament is clearly not as strong an institution. It is a very difficult, very large institution, a balkanised institution and its Committee structure is not as established as in the Congress'. 'Lobbying in the European Union', *Executives*, Washington D.C., Bureau of National Affairs, 1994, and Pascaline Winand, interview with Ambassador Eizenstat.

44 Thus, while Eizenstat spoke at the EP, he also sent various officers to watch sessions according to their area of expertise. The agricultural section of USEU, for example,

According to one observer, British MEPs have tended to be more active in the EP because they represent constituencies, there are a lot of them, and they show a big interest in the US, notably by inviting the Ambassador. This has given the impression to some MEPs that the US was once again flaunting a special relationship with the UK. To this, a USEU staff member had only one answer: why don't other group members give such an invitation?[45]

A final remark about the EP: American lobbying efforts during Eizenstat's time at USEU focused mostly on the three largest political groups, mainly because, at a time of shrinking resources (the plummeting dollar and budgetary problems meant shrinking financial means at the Mission), it was possible to affect a maximum number of people that way. Some of the political groups also showed themselves to be more accessible to US queries relative to other groups.

The European Court of Justice, Europol, the European Monetary Institute and the Committee of the Regions

Eizenstat personally made an attempt to visit all of the major organs of the EU and this included the European Court of Justice, although he was originally not familiar with its crucial role for European integration. The Third Pillar unit closely followed the evolution of Europol (European Police Organisation) where the USEU Counselor for the Third Pillar Unit, was a relatively frequent visitor.[46] Under Eizenstat, USEU was also busy establishing links with the European Monetary Institute and with the Committee of the Regions.

---

had links with the EP's Committee on Agriculture, Fisheries and Rural Development and was increasingly in touch with the EP on environmental issues.

45 To tell the truth, some British MEPs have shown themselves to be extremely active and efficient in establishing relations with the US and USEU, this included James Elles (EPP-UK), the Chairman of the EU Steering Committee of the well-known Transatlantic Policy Network, who was well regarded by Eizenstat and his predecessor, who in turn participated in many of TPN's sessions. Alan Donelly, then Economic, Monetary and Industrial Affairs Coordinator for the Party of European Socialists and Chairman of the Interparliamentarian Delegation for Relations with the US Congress, was also cited as an asset in USEU relations.

46 USEU was however rather frustrated with lack of progress on that front in part because of British opposition to a role for the European Court of Justice in mediating disputes, which explained why the Third Pillar Unit was to some extent monitoring the Court of Justice's activities.

Of Think Tanks, Centers, Networks, Institutes and Euro Groups

In 1995, CEPS, the Belmont European Policy Centre (now European Policy Centre), and the Transatlantic Policy Network (TPN) were most frequently mentioned at the Mission as the organisations that were being relied upon for information. USEU did not seem to rely much on universities for advice.

A major difference between Brussels and Washington D.C. is that think tanks are not as well developed. Eizenstat called this a 'structural weakness in Brussels' since 'think tanks can contribute enormously to the policy mill'. In addition, various parts of the Mission maintain links with associations and Euro-groups. For instance, the agricultural section of USEU is in touch with the Committee of Professional Agricultural Organisations of the European Community (COPA) and other agricultural associations which have their headquarters in Brussels.

Links with the Business Community

The Mission has extensive links with the business community. When still at USEU, Eizenstat admitted that there would rarely be a day when he did not meet with some business person. He found that, contrary to what happened in Washington D.C. where lobbies attempted to put road blocks in the path of Clinton's health care plan and the NAFTA agreement, 'more often than not' the interests of US companies that came to him mostly coincided with those of the US government. The Mission generally left it up to those companies to lobby issues themselves but with USEU's coordination. USEU also relies on corporate lobbies simply for information and here again Eizenstat drew a parallel with Washington D.C.: 'We use company representatives and lobbies as we do in Washington: to alert us to issues and to provide us with information for our decision-making'.[47]

Most of USEU interaction with the private sector has been through the EU Committee of the American Chamber of Commerce (AMCHAM EU Committee), whose mission it is to represent the interests of European companies of American parentage. IBM, Exxon, Ford and other subsidiaries of US giants dominate its membership list. The EU Committee has so far been able to lobby the EC quite effectively. Not only are its members large employers in Europe, but the Committee, given

---

47 'Lobbying in the European Union' and Pascaline Winand, interview with Ambassador Eizenstat.

that it is 'totally company-driven' is able to give 'its position papers a hard edge and a tight focus'. Its organisational structure is a further asset: the Committee counts several sub-committees, task forces and working groups in a number of subject areas which produce action plans or position papers on recent developments in the EU.[48]

Almost all staff members both from higher and lower echelons of USEU are regular attendees and participants in nearly every subcommittee of the EU Committee.[49] Given the numerous and influential people involved in the Committee's structure, USEU finds it to be a good information source to follow a wide range of directives through the policy process, thereby compensating for its own comparatively small staff numbers, but then of course information goes both ways. Where else could Eizenstat have made his farewell remarks but at the Committee? Thanking key members of the Committee 'for being such faithful supporters of our Mission, of my own tenure here, and of the need to strengthen transatlantic ties', he said it had been 'a pleasure to work' with the Chamber 'to help solve the problems of US business in Europe'.[50] As a matter of course, the EU Committee, including its President, has played an influential role in the Transatlantic Business Dialogue.

Although Eizenstat wanted USEU to act as a 'cheerleader' for European integration, it also acts to protect US corporate interests, open markets abroad and of course to defend US foreign policy. In an interview he said: 'We view it as our mission to be the advocate of the American business to keep our markets open and to open the door to new markets'.[51] Shortly after his arrival in Brussels, he not only criticized the EC for allowing some of its members to reopen links with Iran,[52] but he also insisted that the US harbored fundamental objections to exempting cultural goods from GATT, and constantly pressed for

48 J. Gardner, *Effective Lobbying in the European Community* (Denver, Kluwer Law and Taxation, 1991), pp.42-3.

49 While the Deputy Chief of Mission attends the policy committee, other staff members participate in the trade subcommittee, the telecommunications committee, the environment committee and other committees according to their areas of expertise.

50 Eizenstat, 'Farewell Remarks'.

51 'Lobbying in the European Union', and Pascaline Winand, interview with Ambassador Eizenstat.

52 *International Herald Tribune*, 5 November 1993.

arriving at an agreement on the Uruguay Round before the December 15 deadline: 'We are negotiating as though we had another year', he told a journalist. 'We have (less than) ten days'.[53] The Mission was not only efficient in making recommendations to the US Trade Representative in terms of what 'would sell to the EU', it also acted as a quarterback or coordinator for US embassies in the EU states. Eizenstat confessed to having been 'constantly on the phone' with major embassies to 'keep them up to date and tell them what points we wanted to stress'. 'In that sense', he added, 'the Mission played a very vital role not only in informing Mickey Kantor, not only in helping with the negotiations directly but indirectly in setting contacts and a mood in the EU itself that was in a flexible and positive mode'. Eizenstat subsequently used the same coordination process to influence EU policy on banana imports and audio-visual policy.

The European Commission Delegation in Washington D.C. – Some Elements of Comparison with the US Mission to the EU

Prehistory: From Americanization to Europeanization

The incipient steps towards the creation of the European Commission Delegation in Washington occurred around the same period as those leading to the eventual establishment of a US Mission in Brussels: the EDC and its aftermath. Monnet and some of his American friends again played a key role in launching what was at first only a Community information office run by Americans, but financed by the High Authority (HA) of the ECSC. In mid-December 1952, the US Secretary of State had a conversation with Monnet. Concerned, as Monnet was, that debates surrounding the EDC might undermine support for Euro-

[53] S. Nisbet, 'Progress on EC Audiovisual Row', Reuter, 22 October 1993. Retrospectively, Eizenstat acknowledged that it was obvious to Mickey Kantor and himself from the start of the Clinton administration that 'at the end of the day we would have to make concessions in Blair House, but we kept a very firm line against that, holding out so we would get the maximum concessions from the EU on industrial tariff reductions and market access for agricultural products'. The strategy proved effective. Eizenstat added that although the US were at first very careful not to negotiate with the French on agricultural issues, thereby bypassing the EU, he and Kantor soon realized that the French had such a big stake in the issue that it would be best to establish a direct liaison with them; the administration acted upon their recommendation. That too proved effective.

pean integration in the US, he advised him to launch a heavy press campaign to publicize the achievements of the newly created ECSC in the US. Monnet chose a lawyer, George Ball, who had been helpful to him during the drafting phase of the Schuman Plan, to get the operation off the ground.[54] As part of this effort, he also asked him to set up a Community Information Office in Washington. Ball in turn hired Leonard Tennyson, a former Marshall Plan official and newspaperman. Thus Tennyson, an American, after having registered with the US Justice Department as foreign agent, found himself in the peculiar position of running the information office of the ECSC in the US. He established the office in 1954; Ball's office was right next door, which reflected his close links with Monnet. Ball, who later became one of Kennedy's top advisers in European affairs, remained close to Monnet during the Kennedy and Johnson years. The office then became some kind of 'adjunct to George Ball. It was George's community office'. Its staff members 'were clearly there to support what US foreign policy was. It was based on the idea that it was in the interest of the United States to have a community, especially in the Cold War era. So it was not a real conflict to have Americans explaining it to other Americans'. During the Kennedy administration, those working at the EC information office were 'treated as part of the family'.[55]

As we might expect, the Americanization of the Community Information Office gradually gave way to Europeanization. In the wake of the creation of Euratom and the EEC, Curt Heidenreich entered the Washington scene as representative of the Euratom supply agency office operational under the US-Euratom agreement. The Euratom section, which primarily was in charge of buying enriched Uranium from the US and sending it back to Europe, was next to but separate from Tennyson's office. The dual representation created some tension between Tennyson – who remained in his post for twenty years – and Heidenreich who both claimed the right to head the Washington office.

---

54 *Foreign Relations of the United States, 1952-1954*, Vol.VI, Western Europe and Canada, Part 1 (US GPO, Washington D.C., 1986). Memorandum of Conversation by the Special Assistant to the Secretary of State, Paris, 15 December 1952, pp.256-7.

55 Gordon Weil recalled that 'he had helped draft the communiqué when European Community President Walter Hallstein visited President Johnson in the Oval Office'. 'It was an odd experience as an American to write a *communiqué* on behalf of a foreigner.' See M. Mosettig, 'Building Ties in Washington – Europe's Delegation Forty Years later', *Europe*, Special Issue, 1995.

In the meantime, the office was yet to receive the status of a delegation. As early as 1955, though, Ball had been urging the HA to have diplomatic representation of the highest level in Washington. This was all the more imperative since key Europeanists who had functioned as contact points between Washington and the HA no longer held official functions, Monnet, for one, had left his post as President of the HA. But the French government, particularly under De Gaulle, was hardly enthused by the prospect of creating a Commission diplomatic post which might further enhance the Commission's visibility.

After De Gaulle left the political scene, the EC Member States first agreed to develop a joint approach to foreign policy issues at the 1969 The Hague Conference; this was the beginning of EPC or European Political Co-operation. In the following years the accession of new members to the European Communities, disagreements with the US on Vietnam, the Middle East, the dismantlement of the Bretton Woods System, and trade, as well as less than subtle allusions by Kissinger about the regional role of European allies, as opposed to the global responsibilities of the US, made it more pressing for EC Member States to assert their economic and political presence on the international scene *vis-à-vis* the USA as a 'distinct and original entity'.[56] In line with this situation, the Community Information Office, which by 1967 had become a 'liaison office', became a permanent Delegation to the US in 1971 with a staff of thirty-five persons. In December 1972 Richard Nixon then extended diplomatic privileges and immunities to the Delegation by executive order after the House and the Senate had authorized him to do so by the Act of 18 October 1972. A special act of Congress was required since 'under customary international law, diplomatic privileges and immunities are concomitant only of relations between States'. The Department of State, with strong backing from USEC, argued the case convincingly: not only was it fair to reciprocate the privileges and immunities granted to US representatives to the European Community, but the Community's central institutions and 'its authority to conduct a broad range of international relations on its own behalf' also made it 'clearly distinguishable from an international organization'. The House Committee on Foreign Affairs, deeply aware of the impact of

56 'Dokument über die europäische Identität' in Gasteyger, *Europe zwischen Spaltung und Einigung 1945-1990*, pp.302-5, as quoted in R. Schwok, *US-EC Relations in the Post-Cold War Era. Conflict or Partnership?* (Boulder, Westview Press, 1991), p.32, see also pp.28-33.

the Commission's activities on the US, hoped that such a move would further consolidate the role of USEC.[57]

At the same time, however, the marked propensity of the Nixon administration, and particularly of Kissinger, to maintain influence at many centers of power in Europe rather than having to deal with a single supranational body such as the Commission, meant that Washington preferred dealing directly with Member States and frequently bypassed the Commission. If US Ambassador to the European Communities Robert Schaetzel complained that the reports of his Mission were mostly ignored in Washington, the fledgling Delegation of the Commission in Washington also experienced difficulties in making its voice heard in Washington, which had not previously been the case when the Community Information Office had close ties with members of the Eisenhower and Kennedy administrations.

Background and Preparation

To be fair to the Nixon administration, however, when the Commission did obtain diplomatic representation in Washington, it took time for Brussels to define exactly what it should do: this was after all one of the very first delegations that the Commission established. To make sure that the first official representative would have ambassadorial rank, the Commission appointed Aldo Maria Mazio, who had previously held the title as Ambassador to Dublin, Tunis, The Hague and Brussels.[58] An old fashioned Italian diplomat, Mazio had been a research fellow at Yale University, had had previous experience in the US as a diplomat before World War II and had served as Consul General in New York from 1949 to 1952.[59] Yet by the time he took up his new assignment in Washington he had almost reached retirement age and this experience

---

[57] Executive Order 11689, 5 December 1972, Federal Register, Vol.37, No.236, 7 December 1972; Public Law 92-499, 92nd Congress, S. 2700, 18 October 1972; 'Diplomatic Privileges and Immunities to the Mission of the European Communities', 4 October 1972, 92nd Congress, House of Representatives, Report No.92-1521; 'By Mr. Fulbright, by Request', S. 2700, Senate, 15 October 1971, *Congressional Record*, S16310-16311; *European Community*, Press Release, 'Envoy arrives to head first permanent Common Market delegation to US', 15 October 1971. I would like to thank Marc Herrmann (DG1A) for the very useful information he gave me about the evolution of the status of the Delegation.

[58] Not too surprisingly, at the time of the appointment, an Italian, Franco Maria Malfatti, headed the European Commission, while Italy was the presidency country.

[59] Before that, he served at First Secretary of the Italian Embassy in Washington.

was rather outdated.[60] In addition, while his ambassadorial title did much to upgrade the status of the Delegation, his training as a diplomat did not make him an insider of the European Commission; he knew little about how it functioned.

Jens Otto Krag came next in 1974. A former Danish Prime Minister, he had been instrumental in bringing Denmark in the European Communities, and was in search of a job after losing an election.[61] Like his predecessor, Krag had had previous experience in the US as Economic Counselor of the Danish Embassy in Washington from 1950 to 1952. Yet, also like his predecessor, and notwithstanding his European credentials, Krag had not previously worked for the Commission.

The next appointment was different from the previous ones in one important respect: Fernand Paul Spaak came from inside the Commission and had close links with the founding fathers of the European Communities. The son of Paul-Henri Spaak, he had worked for Monnet during his HA presidency and continued thereafter to work for the HA, Euratom and the EEC Commission.[62] During his time in Washington, from January 1976 to May 1980, Spaak who, contrary to his predecessors, had not previously been stationed in Washington, put a premium on public diplomacy. Times soon also became more auspicious for close relations between the EC and the US. While Kissinger and Ford mostly ignored the European Commission, Carter was the first US President to pay official visits to it in Brussels in 1976 and 1978. The US President also welcomed the participation of the President of the Commission at G7 annual summits, accepted the CAP as a *fait accompli*, and indicated that Washington would give its 'unqualified support' for what the Community was trying to accomplish on EPC.[63] This more favorable attitude on the part of the Carter administration translated into a more prominent profile for the Delegation in Washington: whereas Krag was unable to hold a single meeting with USTR during the Nixon era, Spaak fre-

60 An admirer of Roosevelt, Ambassador Mazio frequently asked his assistants to do research on the Roosevelt administration and interpreted the issues of the day through pre-WWII eyes when reporting back to Brussels.

61 Having published several books mainly about Scandinavia, he then went on to lecture at the University of Aarhus.

62 As Director General for Energy.

63 R. Schwok, *US-EC Relations*, p.33.

quently met with the Special Trade Representative during the Carter administration.

By the time Roland de Kergolay, a French Commission *fonctionnaire,* replaced Spaak in 1980, relations with the US started deteriorating. The EPC often seemed to translate into positions that sharply differed from those of the US,[64] the Communities seemed to be mired in Eurosclerosis, and trade disputes were plentiful. Roy Denman, who replaced De Kergolay in 1982, was well suited to deal with such disputes. Trade had long been his speciality: after having been stationed in Geneva for several years, he had been a member of the negotiating delegation with the European Communities prior to British entry, and had occupied key positions in the UK as Deputy Secretary at the Department of Trade and Industry, then as Second Permanent Secretary at the Cabinet Office. Just before taking up his new assignment, he had held the position of Director General of External Relations at the European Commission from 1977 to 1982. As a former British civil servant and administrator, a chief British negotiator in GATT, and a Commission *fonctionnaire*, Sir Roy thus combined a national, a Commission and an international experience. In addition, he was well connected in the trade establishment in Washington, both private and public.

Towards the end of Denman's long tenure in Washington (1982-89), Americans grew increasingly worried lest the EC 'Europe 1992' internal market program turn the EC into 'Fortress Europe'. More 'wars' ensued including on the Second Banking Directive and its reciprocity provision, while Congress insisted on strengthening USEC in Brussels to meet the EC challenge. Yet when the Bush administration took over from the Reagan administration, American attitudes changed. Detailed studies had shown that EC 1992 might not have such deleterious effects on the US economy after all, while momentous transformations in Central and Eastern European countries warranted American support for the EC in light of its potential for attracting these countries within the safe fold of the community of market democracies. This new attitude was reflected both at the US Mission to the European Communities and at the Commission Delegation in Washington. President Bush appointed Thomas M. T. Niles, a high flying career foreign service officer and former Ambassador to Canada as a token of the administration's desire to

---

64 The Community's June 1980 Venice declaration on the Middle East supporting Palestinian participation in Arab-Israeli peace talks and a Palestinian homeland is a case in point.

increase the level of professional representation at the US Mission. In January 1990, Delors in turn appointed former Prime Minister of the Netherlands Andreas Van Agt to head the Commission Delegation in Washington as a way of demonstrating that the EC-US relationship now took on more of a political tinge as opposed to just a commercial one. In addition, Delors urged President Bush to upgrade the level of accreditation of Van Agt; USEC made similar supportive noises. As a result, the US administration decided to upgrade the diplomatic status of the Commission Delegation in Washington 'by accrediting its permanent representatives to the White House, rather than to the State Department like other heads of international organizations'; from 1990 onwards, the Head of the Delegation was accorded full ambassadorial status.[65]

A lawyer by training, and a former Professor at the Catholic University of Nijmegen, Van Agt had been a founder and leader of the Dutch Christian Democratic Party (CDA) and subsequently served as Deputy Prime Minister, Minister of Justice, Minister of Foreign Affairs and Prime Minister in the Netherlands. Just before taking up his new post in Washington, he had been Head of the Commission Delegation in Tokyo, which made him familiar with the Commission's machinery. Van Agt thus came to the job with both a Member State and a Commission perspective. However, unlike Denman, he was less well connected in Washington, and, according to one staff member, 'never quite worked up the same degree of enthusiasm for the US as for Japan'. While he planned to 'preach the political gospel of the political importance' of US-EU relations, for which his experience as Prime Minister prepared him well, he was not so well prepared to tackle wide ranging negotiations such as the Uruguay Round and did not have much interest in economics. By contrast with Denman, who was remembered 'for his unusually aggressive style of diplomacy', Van Agt was considered in

[65] Gardner, *A New Era*, p.6. See also R. Ginsberg, 'EC-US Political/Institutional Relations', in L. Hurwitz and C. Lequesne (eds.), *The State of the European Community* (Boulder, Lynne Rienner, 1991), pp.394-5; Schwok, *US-EC Relations*, pp.51-3; K. Featherstone and R. Ginsberg, *The United States and the European Union in the 1990s* (London, Macmillan, 1996), p.83. and I. Macleod, I. D. Hendry and S. Hyett, *The External Relations of the European Communities* (Oxford, Clarendon Press, 1996), p.217; Jean-Pierre Leng to Mr. Krenzler, Direction Générale Relations Extérieures, Commission des Communautés européennes, 27 September 1989; diplomatic privileges and immunities were extended to other offices of the European Commission in the US, including the UN office, and the San Francisco office in 1988, see executive order No.12651, signed by Ronald Reagan.

Washington as 'very smart', 'well briefed' but also 'very low key'[66] and much less visible than his predecessor. This was perhaps so because he tended to travel and give speeches in the whole of the US rather than staying in Washington.

In October 1995 Hugo Paemen was appointed as Van Agt's successor, after serving as the Commission's Deputy Director-General for External Relations. Although trained in philosophy, classics and political and social science, he was well suited to deal with trade since he had, in that post, been responsible for the Commission's negotiating team during most of the Uruguay Round.[67] Having served as chief of staff to EU Commission Vice-President Viscount Davignon, and as official spokesman of the first Delors Commission, he was a Commission insider. A career diplomat who worked in Washington from 1974 to 1978 as the Belgian Economic Minister, he also possessed prior Washington background and counted many friends in what he considered 'the most important capital in the world'.[68] A token of the significance of this post, Paemen was the only 'A1' (highest ranking) Commission *fonctionnaire* working outside of Brussels or Luxembourg.[69]

On the whole, recent Ambassadors have thus been well prepared to take up their assignments in Washington. However, there seems to be a lack of systematic briefings prior to leaving for Washington for both Ambassadors and staff at the Delegation. By contrast with Eizenstat's extensive preparation before coming to Brussels, there was little done in terms of preparation for Ambassador Paemen,[70] and just as little preparation for some of the staff, who, on the other hand, are generally highly

---

66 B. Stokes, 'Selling Europe outside the Beltway', *National Journal*, 15 December 1990.

67 Hugo Paemen wrote a book about these negotiations with his assistant Alexandra Bensch: H. Paemen and A. Bensch, *Du GATT à l'OMC. La Communauté européenne dans l'Uruguay Round* (Leuven, Leuven University Press, 1995).

68 'Hugo Paemen nominated Commission Head of Delegation in Washington', *European Union News*, Office of Press and Public Affairs, European Commission Delegation, 27 July 1995, No.56/95.

69 The Washington Commission representative traditionally is the highest ranking officer in the Commission's external representation system. Günter Burghardt has recently replaced Hugo Paemen.

70 On the other hand one might argue that Denman and Paemen were already well versed in US-EC/EU relations before taking up their new post since they had previously been responsible for this dossier at the European Commission.

educated, possess relevant expertise in the areas they are responsible for at the Delegation and are rated as extremely professional by outsiders. Ambassador Paemen recognized that preparation 'should be done in a much more systematic way [...] we are still in the stage of improvisation, to a large extent'.[71] Putting people in training for long periods of time as is the case for some State Department officials prior to their assignments to new posts, is apparently not yet in the cards, perhaps because of budgetary constraints and appointments which are being made on short notice.

Organization and Functions of the Delegation of the European Commission

Adaptation and Expansion

Originally an information office mostly reporting on developments in the European Communities to Washington and the US at large, the Delegation currently still has an important information function in the US, while its more recent reporting function on developments in the US to headquarters in Brussels is becoming increasingly significant. Another of its tasks is to represent the Commission to the US government, delivering demarches, instructions, lobbying. The Delegation further serves as a liaison with other international institutions in Washington D.C. Beyond that, it has recently adopted a more 'proactive' role by experimenting with developing more of a delegation view, as opposed to being a simple interface between the European Commission and the US reporting on developments in Europe and in the US. During the negotiations for the NTA and in other instances, it has, in fact, been suggesting policy decisions, as did USEU.

Much like USEU, as the range of competencies of the EU has widened, and as the EU has taken on more importance for the US not only in economic but also in political terms, the Delegation has evolved, adding new sections, upgrading the level of representation. The Office of Press and Public Affairs remains the largest section, which reflects the origins of the Delegation. The next one to come on board after press was the commerce and trade section. To this day it remains the second largest section, an indication not only of the importance of trade in USEU relations but also of the extensive competence of the European Commission in that field. A section for agriculture came afterwards,

[71] Ambassador Paemen, interview by Pascaline Winand, May 1996.

with an economic development section following thereafter. Over time, the economic development section was then split into two sections: one dealing with economic and financial affairs and reporting on the IMF and the US economy, the other being in charge of development. The Delegation also acquired a transport, energy and environment section. More recently, a political section was created to reflect the role of the Commission under the second and third pillars in the Maastricht Treaty and to enhance this role. The political section, which originally also counted a national expert, was later staffed with one and a half local staff and two Commission *fonctionnaires*, one of whom played a key role in launching the NTA, and then closely monitored its implementation. This second *fonctionnaire* post was created specifically for dealing with NTA affairs. This testified to the significance of NTA implementation for the European Commission, especially in light of the fact that many of its delegations were being closed or downgraded.[72] A token of its importance for Brussels, the Delegation has recently moved to a new set of offices, has added some staff, and has kept a rather large press and public affairs office, by contrast with many DG X (Information, Communication, Culture, Audiovisual) operations which were closed in the 1980s.

Internal and External Coordination

Internal coordination at the Delegation is reasonably good, with regular, although relatively short heads of sections meetings in the afternoon to match Brussels' schedule; mornings being often punctuated with phone calls to Brussels. Co-operation between DGs represented at the Delegation is better than in Brussels, as it was between US departments represented at USEU, and communication is easier between different hierarchical levels. Yet informal interaction between the various sections has been rendered more difficult by the Delegation's recent move which changed its configuration from a horizontal to a vertical one, with the result that sections located on a specific floor rarely interact with sections on other floors. Although the atmosphere is cordial,

---

72 Incidentally, appointments at the Delegation not only originate in the added competencies of the EU in specific fields, but also in the priorities of various DGs at the European Commission, who may or may not decide to send a *fonctionnaire* to Washington, according to the need of a DG for more information gathering for example. Budgetary considerations are a further constraint on adding staff at the Delegation.

there is also comparatively less socializing than in the early days, in part as a result of the increasing amount of work.

Dealing with headquarters in Brussels, other institutions, or with EU Member States is by no means always an easy task. The political clout of the Ambassador, as in the case of USEU, and former experience at the Commission, can go a long way in giving the Delegation a high profile *vis-à-vis* Brussels and the Member States. Although communicating with Brussels has considerably improved as a result of the introduction of technological novelties such as computers, e-mail, voice mail, videoconferences, and cheap airfares, these same technological improvements have made it easier for the Brussels headquarters to bypass the Delegation and to establish their own contacts directly with Washington. In addition, the Delegation is not always kept abreast of latest developments in Brussels by certain DGs who seem to be afraid of disseminating sensitive information, especially on CFSP and third pillar issues, or have not come to terms yet with defining the role of the Delegation. Although there are variations according to the home DGs, in some cases, while information coming from Brussels is plentiful, a lot of it is irrelevant, and Delegation officials have to prompt Brussels to send relevant documentation. Some officials also complain of getting the documents in their final version only and would like to be more useful at the policy formulation stage. The Commission's structure of contracting and slow procedures also seem to cause problems.

As far as relations with the EP are concerned, the Delegation sends information on request to the EP, organizes visits for MEPS and accompanies them.

Relations with Member States in Washington are mostly rated as more relaxed than in Brussels. Although the Delegation occasionally has to protect the prerogatives of the Commission *vis-à-vis* the Member States, on the whole, according to one source, 'embassies are more result-oriented and less jealous of their prerogatives than Member States in Brussels'. This is comparatively more so in areas where the European Commission's competencies are clear: trade is a case in point, where the Commission represents the EU and negotiates on its behalf, although on the basis of a negotiating directive from the Member States. Accordingly there seems to be a great deal of information sharing between the Delegation and trade sections from EU embassies, which all meet every month. The relationship is less relaxed in Second and Third Pillars issues, where some of the Member States' hidden agenda is to try not to involve the Commission too much and to establish privileged relations with the US bureaucracy. Yet the Delegation has frequent meetings with Member States,[73] and tries to be helpful notably by organizing briefings and debriefings for Member States when a Commissioner or a high-ranking civil servant comes to town to negotiate with the Americans. Personal chemistry, nationality, having studied at the same university also play a role, as do the size of the country holding the Council presidency and its capability to act in a decisive way. The Delegation is a relatively small operation as compared with the embassies of some Member States who use large embassies as a basis for maintaining privileged relations with the US.

On the other hand, the Commission itself also tries to establish privileged connections with Washington to enhance its clout with EU Member States, for example by making sure that the country holding the presidency of the EU Council includes the Commission in high level discussions with the US administration. In some cases the US is more than willing to do so, especially in trade, where, from an American perspective, the Commission's views on liberalization have generally accorded well with those of the US. In keeping with this attitude, the Delegation is a respected interlocutor at the Office of the Trade Representative, the Department of Commerce and the State Department on trade issues. It is less so in Second and Third Pillars issues, where the Delegation is mostly unable to speak on behalf of the Member States, even though it now does have a section dealing with such issues.[74] We should also note that national experts seconded to the Delegation from Member States administrations have to some extent helped to ease Commission/Delegation relations with Member States.

As far as international organizations and world economic summits are concerned, the Delegation's activities vary according to the level of representation of the EC/EU and its Member States in these frameworks. For example, since 1974 the Community has observer status at the United Nations but cannot vote, while an observer status has not been extended to the EU which has no legal personality. On the other hand the EC does have full membership in the Food and Agriculture

73 At least once a month EU ambassadors meet with Commission representatives in Washington.

74 See Gardner, *A New Era*, pp.25-6; pp.196-7 and M. Calingaert, *European Integration*.

Organization (FAO), which is a UN body.[75] The ability of the Delegation to follow developments in international bodies such as the IMF and the World Bank in which there is no collective EU membership, as well as in groups in which the Commission is represented such as the G7/8, is not only a function of the Commission's competencies in any given field but also of the funding it provides, and of EU Member States' attitudes towards the Commission. In the IMF, the World Bank, the G7/8,[76] and the G24[77] for instance, Americans will tend to adopt a pragmatic, *ad hoc* attitude taking into account both the advice of some EU Member States who insist on not giving much importance to the views of the Commission which they argue is not really competent to deal with macroeconomic issues, for example, and the fact that the Commission holds the purse strings and administers many programmes in Central/Eastern Europe, Africa and other areas. In the case of the IMF, the economic section[78] at the Delegation, which reports on macroeconomic issues,[79] frequently resorts to contacts with pro integrationist and generally pro-Commission EU Member States to obtain information

75 Since 1964, the Commission has a maintained an office in New York, which now serves as Delegation to the United Nations, and whose main function is not only to inform the US and the UN on EU developments but to co-ordinate EU positions in the UN. The Delegation to the UN has very close links with the Washington Delegation, especially with the Press and Public Affairs section. The Commission previously also had a bureau on the West Coast, which was closed to cut down expenses.

76 Since 1980, the Commission has participated in G7 meetings along with France, Germany, the United Kingdom and Italy, although the Commission does not participate in the G7 meetings of finance ministers and central bankers. The Commission represents the Council presidency when the EU presidency country is not currently represented in the G7, and the EU as a whole. Michael Calingaert notes that the Commission is generally 'treated as the junior member of the group' (Calingaert, *European Integration*, p.180).

77 The Group of 24, which coordinates aid to Central and Eastern Europe is chaired by the European Commission.

78 With the completion of EMU looming in the future, the IMF is taking the issue seriously, so is the US Treasury, which has been in touch with the Delegation to receive information on the Single Currency which can not only serve as an alternative currency to the dollar, but also lead to a single EMU bloc within the IMF which would have a veto power, as the US currently does. See Calingaert, *European Integration*.

79 While the economic section reports on IMF in financial and monetary matters, the development section reports on IMF debt concerns and also acts as a liaison with the World Bank.

on the IMF, which has been rated by some as the most secret non-military institution in the world.

Press and Public Affairs and Public Diplomacy

The importance of the Press and Public Affairs Office relative to other offices at the Delegation originated in part in its first avatar as ECSC Information Office. At that time, Tennyson produced a newsletter, *The Bulletin from the European Community for Coal and Steel*, which later changed names as new European Communities joined the first one and as the EU enlarged. Developing more into a magazine format, the Bulletin thus successively became *European Community* and, in 1979, *Europe*. The new name reflected the higher degree of autonomy of the magazine when a new, Irish director of communications replaced Tennyson. Although in the early days the information office could be characterized as 'free-wheeling [...] a group of Americans used to operating without hierarchy and an ocean removed from their ostensible supervisors, first in Luxembourg and then in Brussels', the situation subsequently changed with Brussels scrutinizing the reporting done by Americans, and then again when Europeans did the reporting.[80] The focus has also shifted towards more of a business audience, in part as a result of the interest sparked by the 1992 program and the EURO in the US. After the fall of Communism, *Europe* started reporting on the wider Europe, former Soviet Republics and Russia. With an enlarged team, the magazine now features articles by prominent journalists from well know newspapers such as the *International Herald Tribune*. By and large, its strategy of targeting a wider audience in the US has worked remarkably well. While winning many awards for its design and layout, it has increased its circulation from about 30,000 readers per month in 1990 to more than 75,000 today.[81]

Yet *Europe* is only one part of the Office of Press and Public Affairs,[82] which counts about twenty-six people. The Press Section in-

80 Kathleen Lynch, a former managing editor of *Europe*, recently noted: 'At that time we had an Irish head of information, we got a lot less fine tooth combing of the articles from abroad', see *Europe,* Special Issue 1995, pp.2-3.

81 In addition, *Europe* conducts a wide range of interviews of key US and European policy-makers and business people while it regularly hosts press breakfast and lunches series featuring European, American, and other countries luminaries from government, business, and culture.

82 The Delegation now has two press spokesmen which was not the case initially.

forms the media in the US, produces news releases in *EU News* and *Euromemo*, and organizes press conferences when European Commission representatives or other visitors come to town. The Speakers Bureau supports all requests for speaking engagements for visitors which are organized through particular sections at the Delegation according to their areas of expertise.[83]

Professors, researchers and students at universities and think tanks receive special treatment: a specific section is devoted to them. The academic program, in tune with the 'people to people links' part of the EU-US joint action plan, promotes cooperation between the US and the EU in education by organizing conferences on EU related topics and workshops on how to teach the EU, by helping create new courses on the EU in the US, sponsoring and guiding EU simulations projects in universities and high schools, and awarding fellowships to US students desirous to pursue their training in Europe in the field of European integration. The academic section has also organized videoconferences linking several universities and featuring prominent speakers such as Leon Brittan, Stuart Eizenstat and Hugo Paemen.[84] It has also made a serious attempt to carry the EU beyond the Washington beltway by organizing workshops and conferences in Western and Southern states that are usually less well informed about EU affairs. In a similar effort, Team Europe USA, a network of about seventy professionals knowledgeable about the EU, was formed in 1990 to address audiences in various regions of the US.[85] Finally, the EU has established an impressive network of EU depository libraries in universities throughout the US which spans thirty-six states.

Which brings us back to one specific problem, is the Delegation primarily a Washington Delegation or is it both a Washington Delegation and a wider US Delegation? During his time in Washington, Spaak put a premium on public diplomacy not only in Washington but also in the

---

83 In addition, the Public Inquiries Service, which also supports the Delegation's Library, answers all public requests for information coming to the Delegation; it operates as a filter between the public and the Delegation's diplomatic officers which would otherwise be drowned in countless requests for information from the business, international organizations, the US government and embassies.

84 For a transcript of one of the videoconferences, see 'Will Europe Work? Part 1, Transatlantic Relations', *USA Text*, 4 December 1996.

85 Team Europe, which covers the fifteen EU countries was created prior to Team Europe USA, there is also a Team Europe in Japan.

rest of the US. He and his wife were charismatic personalities and travelled all over the US to put the EC back on the map. Spaak had a set of systematic routine procedures, sent out an advance man and arranged for radio announcements, TV interviews as well as personal interviews. Yet for an Ambassador, reaching out beyond the beltway, can also easily translate into less prominence for the Delegation in Washington.

At the same time one could argue that there is a need for the general American public to be more informed about EU affairs. According to Soren Sondergaard who supervised the Office of Press and Public Affairs, the elite, 'the main policy movers and shakers' in the US, are highly knowledgeable about Europe, the EU, Asia, but 'if you go down into the lower echelons, it is almost a non-knowledge'. In general, the Delegation, which does not have a permanent relationship with individual US states for example, has focused relatively less on reaching the wider public and more on some target groups within the US leadership in a broad sense: the leadership press, business, government, academia. Given the limited amount of financial resources available, one might argue that since it is impossible to deal with the entire US, it does make sense to target specific groups.

Informing the US about the EU also faces particular problems because of the nature of the EU itself and of US/EU relations. The EU as such is not yet a unitary actor on the world scene and the American press and public tend to look at Europe as individual countries. In addition, the US seems to be relatively more important to the European press and public than the EU is to an American audience, in part because the US is a unified political actor on the world scene. As a result, the European press has many correspondents in the US while the American press has few if any bureaux or even full-time correspondents in Brussels. Furthermore, the EU competes not only with the rest of the world in American news, but also with US news which is the principal concern of much of the American public. A related problem is that good news is no news. The USEU relationship is mostly a peaceful one and this does not make for interesting headlines. When trade conflicts flare up, however, or when the EU agrees to disagree with the US on specific politico-economic issues such as the Libertad-Helms Burton or Iran/Libya legislation, conflicts become news, so too when the EU shows itself unable to cope with the intricacies of the Yugoslav conflict, for instance.

Washington D.C. versus 'Brussels D.C.'

In general, the atmosphere, the environment, and lobbying style in Washington D.C. would appear to differ from that of 'Brussels D.C.' in some respects, while being highly similar in others. The style is characterized as 'proactive', 'dynamic' or 'aggressive'. The Americans are rated as more 'result-oriented', and 'business-like' than Europeans, with an emphasis on speed rather than long-term strategy and a tendency to portray issues in black and white. The US bureaucracy is further described as 'very accessible, very open, and relatively easy to influence'. On the other hand, weak political parties, many criss-crossing alliances which change according to the issues of the day, and agencies which are being downsized or threatened with disappearance, do not make for stability and thus for stable patterns of influence, which seem relatively easier to sustain with some EU institutions. The US bureaucracy also seems to be less hierarchised than EU institutions, which in turn are comparatively less so than the IMF for example. To accusations that Brussels is a closed bureaucracy as opposed to Washington, some respondents have reacted by saying that although it is easier to find the right telephone number in Washington, with Americans having a marked propensity for publishing who is who and their numbers, Brussels is still a relatively new bureaucracy, comparatively small in numbers, and quite accessible and open to information and influence. As in Brussels, information is widely available in Washington (with think tanks playing a larger role) but the problem is again to find information that is relevant.

Dealing with the Executive Branch and Congress

If the EU's overlapping fields of competence have caused it to be branded by some Americans as a 'multiheaded octopus'[86], the US bureaucracy is equally complex and no individual or agency is solely responsible for coordinating US policy towards the EU. The State Department, while remaining the main actor in managing daily contacts with the EU, now increasingly has to share the lead with other departments and agencies concerned with US-EU relations, which frequently leads to turf battles. The Commission Delegation's contacts range from

---

86 M. Nelson and G. J. Ikenberry, *Atlantic Frontiers: A New Agenda for US-EC Relations* (Carnegie Endowment for International Peace 1993), pp.19-20, as quoted in M. Kahler, *Regional Futures and Transatlantic Economic Relations* (New York, Council of Relations Press, 1995), and Gardner, *A New Era*, p.25.

the White House, the State Department, USTR, the Commerce, Treasury, Agriculture Departments, USAID, ... to USEU and Congress. But, as we have seen, the Delegation is a more credible interlocutor in fields such as trade, where the Commission's competence is clear, than in those where it is less so. In the development field, budgetary cuts in the US as compared with the EU large contribution, have made the Delegation a desirable interlocutor for USAID, a fact that was also reflected at USEU. In some other fields, although Washington would like the EU to develop more coordinated policies and particularly on third pillar issues, the tendency is to listen less to the Commission Delegation and more to the Member States through their embassies, in international fora or during the bilateral meetings regularly taking place between the US and the EU in various formats, and at different levels.

This poses the question of whether the Delegation of the European Commission in Washington, should, in the long run, become the Representation of the EU. Although opinions vary on this score, there is a clear tendency on the part of Americans to call the Delegation's ambassador, 'EU ambassador', which he is not. A high level official at the Delegation has pointed out that a solution might be to organize the Delegation in such a way as to enable it to host national officials representing the presidency country for the duration of the presidency, as well as EP *fonctionnaires*. The recruiting pattern at the Delegation would then enlarge to encompass more national officials. With EP staff, the Delegation might also better be able to monitor and educate Congress. Indeed, whereas some Committees and staffers are very knowledgeable about the EU, others are ill informed or ignorant. Yet the sheer size of Congress and its importance in transatlantic relations, would justify sending more observers to watch developments on the Hill.

Since the end of the 1970s, the Delegation has had one person working on Congressional matters, specific sections being in touch with Congressional committees in their areas of expertise. Before that time, the State Department indicated to the European Commission – and most diplomatic entities – that it did not appreciate direct contact with Congress on their part. This being said, the EP has been dealing directly with Congress since 1974. Since then, whenever the EP's Delegation for Relations with the US come to Washington for their annual visit, they are received on the floor of the House and introduced by the Senate majority leader. As the EP increasingly deals in policy areas where Congress can have a say, certain Congressional committees such as the agricultural committees are now more open to establishing relations with the EP. Interestingly, Congress and the EP have always had a linkage in foreign policy, an area where the European Commission did not, until recently, have an outstanding role, while the relationship was more difficult in trade issues, where the Commission does have a prominent role. In general, the EP has had an easier access to Members of the House than to Senators.

At the Delegation, the person in charge of Congressional relations divides up his time between following legislation, meeting with people on Capitol Hill, organizing visits for MEPs – which often involves contacts with the private sector, meeting with officials and reporting back to Brussels. Most organizations in Washington, however, hire more than one person to do the job. Is the Delegation thus outgunned? Perhaps one solution would be to have one person dealing with the House and another with the Senate?

Think Tanks and Business

To compensate for relatively small staff numbers, to obtain information, or advocate certain policies in non-official frameworks, the Delegation has tended to rely on think tanks or fora such as the European Institute (EI)[87]. The idea for its creation developed from Jacques Delors' concern that the EC was being increasingly perceived in Washington as fortress Europe, and that the US was turning towards Asia. The future President of the Institute, Jacqueline Grapin, agreed with Delors that there was a need to create a private institute in Washington that would be able to convey information about the EC in an unofficial way, pushing for a more global and positive image of the EC in American eyes. This the Delegation could not do because of its diplomatic status and because it was mainly competent to represent the EU in trade matters. The Institute's action would thus complement that of the Delegation, while also coordinating with EC embassies. Setting up the Institute seemed urgent since Asian countries had about fifteen such institutes in Washington, with Japan being particularly active in lobbying Congress. At the Delegation, which largely favored its creation, the Institute is perceived as useful for conveying messages and for organizing debates between American and Europeans which do not appear to

87 While it does produce occasional reports, the Institute would not really qualify as a think tank, but rather as a well-connected forum, which brings Americans and Europeans together on specific topics.

be Commission or government driven. The Institute, which is funded by both public and private sources including the European Commission, European governments, non profit organizations and business, equally balanced between US and European sources, claims to be 'truly transatlantic'.[88]

This is also the claim of the European-American Chamber of Commerce in Washington, a relatively recent institution, which describes itself as 'the mind and voice of European-US business interests' and a 'truly transatlantic business organization, supported by both European and American companies [...] working independently of any national or government agency [...] to attract, contact and directly influence policy-makers'. As knowledge is power, the Chamber's goal is to be 'the definitive and up-to-date source of knowledge about US and European political activity affecting business'.[89] Seen from the Delegation, it is a useful conduit for helping to get Member States coordinated on key issues and for reaching the business community in an organized fashion, so too is the EI which does have member companies as well.[90] A token of its importance for the Delegation, staff from the trade section are regularly invited to take part in the Chamber's routine meetings, about once a month, while the Ambassador is asked to deliver speeches at lunch or breakfast. In some way this situation is thus similar to the interaction between USEU and the EU Committee in Brussels, where USEU staff frequently participate in the Committee's meetings to gather and convey information *vis-à-vis* the business community. As USEU, the Delegation also tries to develop contacts with individual firms. By contrast with USEU in Brussels though, it can rely on information from a wide array of think tanks – *i.e.* non-profit independent research institutes – in Washington, which, as we have noted, are still not as well developed in Brussels.[91]

---

88 Material for the above discussion includes an exchange of letters prior to its creation, various brochures and interviews with members of the Institute's staff.

89 Mission statement, European-American Chamber of Commerce, 1997.

90 Yet they fulfil different roles: while the Institute organizes debates which do to some extent influence policy-makers, its focus is relatively more academic and it does less lobbying and action *vis-à-vis* legislation than the European-American Chamber of Commerce which has more of a policy focus.

91 The Center for European Policy Studies and the European Policy Centre, could however to some extent be characterized as think tanks. On think tanks see, for example, R. Higgott and D. Stone, 'The Limits of Influence: Foreign Policy Think

Finally, foreign policy think tanks in Washington range from general policy institutes such as Brookings to more specialized institutes say in food policy, the environment or economics, to institutes that have been specifically created to reflect a particular political view. Brookings, the Center for Strategic and International Studies, the Carnegie Endowment for International Peace, the Council on Foreign Relations, the Progressive Policy Institute,[92] IFPRI, the Institute for International Economics, are among the think tanks most frequently mentioned at the Delegation, each section having their favorite ones.[93]

The New Transatlantic Agenda, the Joint Action Plan, and the Transatlantic Business Dialogue: From Conception to Implementation

Both USEU and the Delegation of the European Commission in Washington have played key roles at various stages of the NTA, yet they were not the only or even the most important players in the process that led to the NTA. Ultimately, their headquarters made the decisions. On the other hand, although they did not have the power to make decisions, they did contribute to shaping policy. In the earlier stages USEU played a more active role than the Delegation in launching and preparing the NTA. This was so not only because of Eizenstat's energetic support, and his influential network back in Washington, but also because the NTA became a part of the Department of Commerce's battle for survival. US business was also more active and better prepared than the European side earlier on in the preparation of the TABD, which later formed an important part of the NTA. The Commission did its very best to correct the imbalance, and stimulate Europeans to be as active as possible in the TABD and in the NTA. Throughout the process, the

---

Tanks in Britain and the USA', *Review of International Studies*, 20 (1994) 15-34; See also D. E. Abelson, *American Think Tanks and Their Role in US Foreign Policy* (New York, St Martin's Press, 1996).

92 The PPI is a think tank created by the Democratic Leadership Council which Bill Clinton presided from March 1991 to August 1991.

93 The trade and economic sections, for example, value the influential Institute for International Economics for the quality of its research, its concrete, policy focus and its free trade orientation. In addition, academic associations such as the European Community Studies Association or the Council for European Studies have developed close links with the Delegation, which partially funds some of their conferences and operating costs.

Delegation has adopted a slightly more proactive role than it was used to, *i.e.* it has developed more of a delegation view on some issues, and has suggested some of the language of the NTA.[94] Given Eizenstat's key role during the initial stages of the TABD and the NTA, as perceived by both the US and the European sides, we will give relatively more emphasis to USEU in analyzing the genesis of the TABD and the NTA.

USEU had played a vital role during Clinton's visit to Europe in January 1994, in part by ensuring that the EU would receive adequate attention: 'We did everything from the logistics to preparing the agenda, preparing his talking points, briefing him, sending him suggestions for his speech'.[95] The Mission again played a very similar role for the July 1994 Berlin summit, except for the logistics; Eizenstat then personally briefed the President. At the suggestion of USEU, with some input from the Delegation of the Commission in Washington,[96] and also at the insistence of Joachim Bitterlich, National Security adviser to Chancellor Kohl, Bernhard Zepter, assistant to Jacques Delors, and Under-Secretary for Political Affairs Peter Tarnoff, the US/EU Berlin Summit in July 1994 established three *ad hoc* senior-level working groups as an experiment to better assure the 'suivi' until the next EU/US Summit in Washington in 1995; one on cooperation in Central and Eastern Europe, another on CFSP and, lastly, a group concerning international crime.[97] USEU did not really expect to see these groups institutionalized, in part because of the bureaucratic paper this would have generated, but hoped for some modest successes that would lead to a broader effort to frame and render US-EU cooperation more effective. In general, the three-working groups experience showed that high-level working groups based in capitals made it difficult to work efficiently, and that another

---

94 A young *fonctionnaire* from DGI who took part in the NTA negotiating team under the authority of Ove Juul Jorgensen, then DG1's director for relations with North America, and subsequently was a member of the NTA monitoring task force along with Jorgensen, later acted as the NTA co-ordinator at the Delegation.

95 A member of the staff suggested including Paul-Henri Spaak, along with Monnet, Marshall and Schuman in the President's speech; the suggestion was followed.

96 Jim Currie and the Ambassador seem to have discussed this idea at the beginning of the year before the subcabinet meetings in February.

97 For more details, see the chapter by A. Gardner and the introduction in this book.

mechanism was needed which involved people closer to the working level and to the issues.[98]

Subsequently, USEU and its nine agencies had a major input and coordinating role in preparing the NTA and the Action Plan, so too did the Delegation, especially in arranging meetings with various Washington department and agencies.[99] In early 1995, USEU strongly encouraged the administration to launch a new transatlantic initiative. Eizenstat succeeded in convincing the US Secretary of State that he should take the initiative and focus on the relationship with the EU. The result was an address by Warren Christopher on 2 June 1995 in Madrid which partly built on Leon Brittan's concept for transatlantic trade liberalization[100] and proposed to jointly formulate a New Transatlantic Agenda for the 21st century. USEU worked closely with the Secretary's staff in preparing that speech by providing drafts and commenting on State Department's drafts. Key to the success of the whole operation were also meetings with Spain's Foreign Minister, Carlos Westendorp at USEU with Eizenstat and his staff. As early as January 1995, Westendorp paid a visit to the Mission to discuss ways of improving transatlantic relations during the Spanish presidency.

In the meantime, Eizenstat participated in the Senior Level Group (SLG) appointed at the 14 June 1995 US-EU Summit in Washington to prepare the agenda, alongside with high-level officials from Spain and the European Commission on the European side and Under Secretaries of State Peter Tarnoff and Joan Spero on the US side. In addition, a group – called by some the 'drafting group' although it never had an official name – was established to supplement the work of the SLG. It met about every three or four weeks and contacts with USEU were quite frequent. On the US side, the Deputy Chief of Mission, Tony Wayne, and the Political and Economic Minister-Counselors of the Mission, Jon Greenwald and Charlie Ries, worked closely with the Director for European Union Affairs (ERA) at the State Department, Bryan Samuel, who

98 In other words, on the US side, the groups must not only meet at the level of the Under Secretary of State but also involve people at the level of Office Directors and Missions.

99 Incidentally, Eizenstat was on friendly terms with Jonathan Davidson who had served in the British embassy while Eizenstat worked for the Carter administration, which subsequently eased contacts between USEU and the Delegation.

100 'The EU-US Relationship. Will it last?', Speech to the American Club, Brussels, 27 April 1995.

frequently went to Brussels; drafts were exchanged back and forth with USEU, while Samuel's office coordinated most of the work of various agencies in Washington. On the European side, representatives from the Spanish presidency worked along side with representatives from the European Commission such as Jorgensen and Astrid Schomaker, while the Delegation of the European Commission liaised with the State Department. The drafting group met in Madrid, Brussels and Washington D.C.; there was no regular schedule, but meetings intensified prior to the Madrid Summit, were the group met on a weekly or biweekly basis.[101]

The real process began in earnest in September 1995 and worked relatively smoothly in part because of Eizenstat's relentless efforts to convince higher echelons in Washington to support the project, which then made it easier for Bryan Samuel at a lower level down the hierarchy to work effectively with other agencies. As a member of USEU put it: people 'were getting vibrations down from the top that made them more cooperative'. The Mission's role was especially significant in light of Eizenstat's commitment to revive transatlantic relations by emphasizing the relationship with the EU, and not only with NATO, which nicely fit in with Clinton's concept of security that included not only military security but also trade, economic, and political aspects.

USEU also[102] closely cooperated with the Department of Commerce in coordinating the first Transatlantic Business Dialogue on 10-11 November 1995 which was originally proposed by the late US Commerce Secretary Brown in Brussels at the end of 1994. Commissioners Martin Bangemann (industry) and Sir Leon Brittan (trade) subsequently

---

[101] About half of the American papers for the NTA and the Action Plan were written by the economic and political sections of USEU. All drafted, with Charles Ries, the Minister-Counselor for Economic Affairs and Jon Greenwald, the Minister-Counselor for Political Affairs playing a leading role. Mission papers were then redrafted by the Deputy Chief of the Mission and Ambassador Eizenstat.

[102] There are other areas where USEU played a leading role. For example, working in part through the US Ambassador to Turkey and the US State Department, the Mission lobbied the EP to place less of an emphasis on human rights in Turkey and pressed for the ratification the EU-Turkey Customs Union on 13 December 1995 as a vital asset in helping to strengthen Turkish democracy and pro-Western forces in Turkey. Then, USEU played a central role in negotiating the new agreement on civilian nuclear co-operation with Euratom. On the US side, Ambassador Eizenstat signed the agreement in Brussels on 7 November 1995. In addition, as an answer to the problems caused by the most recent wave of new EU Member States on transatlantic trade, the US Mission, working hand in hand with the Office of the US Trade Representative, negotiated a major compensation agreement.

strongly supported the initiative. In order to organize the first meeting, a mixed EU-US government-business steering committee was created which met regularly in both Brussels and Washington. Here again USEU played a key role in co-chairing the steering committee. The operation was a success: some hundred European and American business leaders gathered in Seville and made recommendations to remove barriers to trade and investment some of which were then included in the NTA/Action Plan. Different agencies within USEU took part in these various actions according to their areas of expertise.[103]

Concluding Remarks

By and large, while there is always room for improvement, both the Delegation and USEU have made a positive contribution to the structure and substance of US/EU relations. They have shown themselves to be adaptable both structurally and functionally to new developments in the EU, the US and on the international scene. Of course, the picture is not entirely rosy and there are many constraints on the operation of US and EU diplomatic posts both in a transatlantic framework and in third countries. Some of these constraints are similar for both US and EU posts, so too are factors reinforcing the role of delegations and missions.

General political, economic and military developments in Europe, in the US and in the world at large, have had a significant impact on the evolution of US and EC diplomatic posts. The collapse of the Bretton Woods system, the fall of the Berlin Wall, a negative balance of payments in the US, conflicts in Africa, Europe, the Middle East, competition from Asian countries such as Japan, are cases in point. As the European Communities and the EU evolved, acquiring new competencies in the economic and political fields or stagnating, and as administrations in the US succeeded one other, as did different Commission and Council presidencies, the US periodically reassessed its attitude towards European integration, and the European Commission. This attitude ranged from support in the Monnet days, to indifference under Kissinger, to suspicion of Europe 1992 or circumspection *vis-à-vis* EMU in a later period. All of this influenced the evolution of USEU and

---

[103] For example, the Minister-Counselor for Commercial Affairs, Stephen Arlinghaus, and other officials from the Commerce Department's Foreign Commercial Service at USEU took the lead on the conception and preparation of the TABD with the help of USEU's economic section, and particularly Charles Ries, the Mission's Minister-Counselor for Economic Affairs. See *Letter from Brussels*, 2 January 1993.

the Delegation, including the level of representation, and the range of departments, agencies, or DGs being represented in these posts.

The adequacy of an Ambassador's prior background and preparation to take on his new assignment in Brussels or Washington, including his political clout with Washington or Brussels, his charisma and an aptitude for conducting public diplomacy, have also mattered considerably. On the European side, being well introduced in Washington, being a Commission insider, or being highly regarded by some Member States, have constituted definite assets in being able to work not only Washington but also Brussels.

The differences and similarities in the operating environments in Brussels and Washington D.C. have also had an influence on the information and lobbying strategies of USEU and the Commission Delegation towards business and US or EU institutions. The number of think tanks, the availability and dispersion of information, the influence of Congress as compared to the EP, strong or weak central authorities are among these factors.

More specifically, constraining factors on the US side have included turf battles between various departments, triggered in part by overlapping competencies in the EU, administrative complexity, budgetary constraints – which meant less travel for US Mission staff – election campaigns and results, diverging priorities and interests notably on certain trade issues, lack of knowledge about the EU in certain quarters including in the field, and last but not least, changes in the leadership of departments and missions which made it hard to achieve policy continuity.

On the EU side, budget constraints, lack of progress on CFSP and Third Pillar issues and conflicts over responsibilities among the various EU bodies, between the Commission and Member States or within the European Commission, have created problems for the Delegation. A lack of coordination on the EU side has been especially frustrating when decisions have had to be reached quickly in crisis situations, which has led the Americans to deal bilaterally with EU countries in a number of instances. Attempts by the European Commission to enhance its role *vis-à-vis* Member States both in the EU and in international fora, notably through the support of pro-Commission Member States, or with US backing, also had an impact on the operation of the Delegation of the Commission. In trade matters, the fact that the Commission has considerable power in the field and is sometimes perceived by the US as an ally in pushing for liberalization against the wishes of some EU Member States, has made its Delegation both a credible and useful interlocutor for the US, while it increased the suspicion of certain Member States.

In general, multi-tiered strategies have been the norm both for USEU and for the Delegation, with targets ranging from the US government and Congress, EU institutions, EU Member States, regions, business, and academia. The NTA and Action Plan have been instrumental in widening those contacts beyond the traditional array of main institutional actors on the US and EU side, to the Department of Education and DG XXII (education, training and youth – recently renamed education and culture DG), or the Department of Labor and DGV (employment, industrial relations and social affairs – recently renamed employment and social affairs DG)[104]. Yet differences in the nature of the EU, a *sui generis* occurrence with relatively strong Member States and a weak central authority in some fields but not all, and the US, a federal state with relatively weak states, have produced variations. Thus, the importance the US has accorded EU Member States, or even regions, has differed from the somewhat lower priority the European Commission Delegation has given to reaching American states beyond the beltway (budgetary and staff constraints should also be taken into account). As the EU widens and as new competences are being added in the economic or political fields, with institutions such as the EP playing more of a role, the Commission Delegation will have to come to grips with the consequences in terms of staffing and budgetary costs, perhaps by becoming more of a representation for the EU. Yet this development seems a long way off. In the meantime, both the Delegation of the Commission of the European Communities in Washington D.C. and USEU can pride themselves perhaps not for having made decisions, but for having played a considerable role in shaping policy both at the preparation and implementation stages of the NTA.*

---

[104] See Gardner, *A New Era*, p.97. An agreement on higher education and vocational training was signed in December 1995. In addition, Secretary of Labor Robert Reich and EU Commissioner Padraig Flynn launched a US-EU working group on Labor and Employment issues. The Delegation of the European Commission would seem to have played a key role in helping to launch this group.

* For an earlier and more detailed version of the first part of this chapter, see P. Winand, 'The US Mission to the EU in "Brussels D.C." and the New Transatlantic Agenda', in P.-H. Claeys, C. Gobin, I. Smets & P. Winand (eds.), *Lobbying, Pluralism and European Integration* (Brussels, P.I.E., 1998) 373-406.

CHAPTER 5

Shaping, not Making – The Impact of the American Congress on US-EU Relations

John PETERSON*

University of Glasgow, Department of Politics

Introduction

A flurry of proposals in 1994 for some type of new transatlantic 'contract' – such as a cooperation treaty or free trade area – reflected new anxieties after an ominous rift over Bosnia, and old anxieties about the durability of America's general political commitment to Europe. The proposals seemed to have little resonance in the United States. An initiative to reinvigorate relations with the EU simply did not appear on the political screen in Washington in spring 1995.[1]

Only a few months later, a significant fortification of US-EU relations was agreed at the Madrid transatlantic summit of December 1995. The New Transatlantic Agenda was unveiled, along with a related 'Ac-

* For their valued assistance in the preparation of this chapter, I am grateful to Elizabeth Bomberg, Ricardo Gomez, Christine Matthews, Clare McManus, Bob Whiteman and the editors.

1 In early 1995 the present author conducted a study for the European Commission on the likely impact of the new Republican Congressional majorities on US foreign policy and US-EU relations. Findings of the study may be gleaned from J. Peterson, *Europe and America: The Prospects for Partnership* (London and New York, Routledge, 1996, 2nd edition). See also Transatlantic Policy Network, *Towards Transatlantic Partnership: A European Strategy* (Brussels, 1994); G. Harrison, *A New Transatlantic Initiative? US-EU Economic Relations in the Mid-1990s* (Washington D.C., Congressional Research Service, 1995, 95-983 E, 15 September); S. Sloan, *European Proposals for a New Atlantic Community* (Washington D.C., Congressional Research Service, 1995, 95-374S, 10 March); W. Reinicke, *Deepening the Atlantic: Towards a New Transatlantic Marketplace?* (Gütersloh, Bertelsmann Foundation Publishers, 1996); E. Frost, *Transatlantic Trade: A Strategic Agenda* (Washington D.C., Institute for International Economics, 1997).

tion Plan'.[2] Long on aspirations and broad in scope, the NTA was signed at Madrid by Bill Clinton, Jacques Santer (the President of the European Commission) and Felipé Gonzales (the Prime Minister of Spain, which held the rotating Presidency of the EU's Council of Ministers).

Although endorsed at the highest political levels, the NTA was hardly soul-stirring in content. It overwhelmingly focused on non-controversial or technical areas such as testing and standards, humanitarian relief, banking reform in Ukraine, and police cooperation. Its economic component did little more than identify steps towards substantive cooperation. The NTA neither promised nor required new legislation to achieve its aims.

A central argument of this paper is that the obtuse composition of the Madrid agreement was not accidental. Rather, it reflected a conscious effort by administrations on both sides – particularly the American – to find and exploit productive areas of cooperation *without* attracting wider political attention, particularly given the backdrop of the creation of the World Trade Organization (WTO) and Congressional scepticism about whether it served US interests. The Clinton administration's embrace of the agreement was spurred by its belief that overarching political frameworks such as the NTA made the foreign policy agenda easier to control and 'keep away' from a hostile Congress.

The power of Congress in US foreign policy-making in the 1990s has been a subject of considerable academic debate.[3] There is little

---

2 According to insiders to the negotiations, the NTA and Action Plan were agreed after only three months of diplomacy. See Peterson, *Europe and America;* A. Gardner, *A New Era in US-EU Relations? The Clinton Administration and The New Transatlantic Agenda* (Aldershot, Avebury Press, 1996); R. Ginsberg, 'US-EU Relations' in P.-H. Laurent and M. Maresceau (eds.), *The State of the European Union, Volume 4: Widening and deepening* (Boulder CO and London, Lynne Rienner, 1998).

3 See P. Peterson, 'The President's Dominance in Foreign Policy Making', *Political Science Quarterly*, 109:2 (1994) 215-34; D. W. Rohde, 'Partisanship, leadership, and Congressional assertiveness in foreign and defense policy', in D. A. Deese (ed.), *The New Politics of American Foreign Policy* (New York, St Martin's, 1994); J. A. Tierney, 'Congressional Activism in Foreign Policy: Its Varied Forms and Stimuli', in Deese, *The New Politics*; M. Lind, 'The Out-of-Control Presidency', *The New Republic*, 14 August 1994, 18-23; E. Burgin, 'Congress and the Presidency in the Foreign Arena', *Congress and the Presidency*, 23:1 (1996) 57-64; W. C. Banks and J. D. Straussman, 'A New Imperial Presidency? Insights from US Involvement in Bosnia', *Political Science Quarterly*, 114:2 (1999) 195-217.

doubt, however, that Congress has become more active on matters of foreign policy as the line separating domestic from foreign policy has become blurred. Congress does not 'make' foreign policy very often. However, Congress – ill-disciplined, unloved by most Americans, and largely ignorant of Europe – *shapes* foreign policy in increasingly important ways. Students of US-EU relations could no longer afford to neglect the role of Congress.

US Foreign Policy, Europe and Congress in Context

To understand perceptions of the EU in Congress, the analyst must come to grips with four contextual features of the American political landscape. First and most generally, the prominence of ideals in American political culture remains difficult to overestimate. The upshot for transatlantic relations is that the US political class tends to read the EU's rhetoric about Europe's common achievements and aspirations quite literally. The gap between high expectations of the European Union and the EU's modest capabilities[4] dogs the EU's relationship with the US as much as with any other major international actor.

Second, most American elites continue to believe that European integration is a logical antidote to regional instability. This view is shared by most members of Congress who care about Europe. But members of America's political class frequently express impatience or disappointment at the EU's perceived lack of unity, particularly concerning the slow pace of eastern enlargement. An especial irritant is the Union's reluctance to embrace Turkey, which is widely viewed in Washington as a valued NATO ally, a bulwark against Islamic fundamentalism and (crucially) a friend of Israel – as opposed to a state with severe human rights problems, and the source of a serious immigration problem for the EU. (The decision taken by the European Council in December 1999 to recognize Turkey as a candidate State destined to join the Union was therefore welcome as the long-awaited first step in the right direction.)

Third, the current generation of Americans is less focused on Europe than the immediately previous generation, many of whom served in the

4 C. Hill, 'The Capability-Expectations Gap, or Conceptualising Europe's International Role', *Journal of Common Market Studies*, 31:3 (1993) 305-28; C. Hill, 'Closing the Capability-Expectations Gap?', in J. Peterson and H. Sjursen (eds.) *A Common Foreign Policy for Europe? Competing Visions of the CFSP* (London, Routledge, 1998).

armed forces in Europe or had relatives who did. The European 'imprint' on US society, mostly a product of emigration from the early part of the 20th century, is into its third or fourth generation and is thus weakening. The most active and powerful domestic ethnic lobbies in Washington are those of more recent (mostly non-European) immigrant groups: such as Israeli, Chinese, Arab, Korean and Hispanic. Meanwhile, the redistricting of Congress over the past twenty years has followed population flows, thus orienting Congress (especially the House of Representatives) far more to the South and West, areas which themselves are less concerned with Europe than the Northeast or Midwest.[5]

Fourth, very few members of Congress are very clear on the EU's powers, membership or ambitions. Congress is not unique in this respect: there are remarkably few officials in the American executive bureaucracy who work full-time on the EU (perhaps seventy-five, although precise totals are disputed), compared to thousands working exclusively on NATO.[6] No major opinion poll has ever indicated that a majority of Americans have even heard of the EU.[7] The launch of the Euro put the 'New Europe' in the US headlines briefly in early 1999, but the event was overshadowed by the resignation of the entire Santer Commission a few months later, amid charges of mismanagement and nepotism.[8] Generally, if the European Union is America's 'best partner' – as the EU was described repeatedly by Clinton after 1992 – and an international superpower (of sorts), one would hardly know it from spending time in Washington, or the US more generally.

---

5 Here I share insights that William Wallace was generous enough to share with me.

6 I am grateful to Anthony Gardner for this point.

7 To my knowledge, the largest percentage of respondents ever to indicate that they had heard of the EU or European Community in response to any major US poll was 47% in a 1990 Gallup poll. Subsequently declining numbers probably reflected confusion after the switch from 'European Community' to 'European Union' after 1993. Regardless of US public awareness of the EU *per se*, a plurality of Americans (42%) continue to consider Europe to be the most important region in the world to US interests, with only 28% choosing Asia instead (although the gap narrowed in the 1990s). See Chicago Council on Foreign Relations, 'American Public Opinion and US Foreign Policy 1999' (available from http://www.ccfr.org/publications/opinion/opinion.html).

8 See for example R. Cottrell, 'The New Conquest of Europe', *New York Review of Books*, 8 April 1999. The next issue of the *NYRB* featured a post-script article by the same author on the Santer Commission's resignation, an event generally incongruous with the tone of the first article.

Cracks in the foundations of transatlantic relations appeared in the early part of the Clinton era. The President himself appeared not to be very 'engaged or interested in the foreign policy shaping process'.[9] Insofar as it focused on foreign policy at all, his administration invested considerable political capital in regional free trade projects in Asia, North America, and Latin America. Together, these initiatives gave the impression that the administration saw America's economic future as lying almost everywhere *besides* Europe. Warren Christopher, Clinton's first Secretary of State, was primarily a Middle East specialist with little interest in the EU. He appeared almost to enjoy asserting that 'Europe is no longer the dominant area of the world'.[10]

Much changed after Clinton was re-elected in 1996. Christopher was replaced by Madeleine Albright, a European by birth and outlook, who twice insisted during her Congressional confirmation hearings that 'America must remain a European power'.[11] Bosnia was transformed from the source of the worst internal crisis in NATO's history to a significant (if still fragile) foreign policy success. During the Kosovo conflict, America's European allies displayed impressive solidarity, if also weak military firepower and (initially) disappointing levels of post-war reconstruction aid. The NTA produced significant 'deliverables', in the words of economic policy officials, particularly on certification and standards, in ways that were both extraordinary and mostly uncontroversial.[12]

Europe remained on the domestic American political agenda during the Clinton years for two fundamental reasons. The first was the Balkans. A rare act of Presidential leadership (and a lot of luck) pro-

---

9 L. Berman and E. O. Goldman, 'Clinton's Foreign Policy at Midterm' in C. Campbell and B. A. Rockman (eds.), *The Clinton Presidency: First Appraisals* (Chatham NJ, Chatham House Press, 1996).

10 Quoted in Peterson, *Europe and America*, p.137. See also W. Christopher, *In the Stream of History: Shaping Foreign Policy for a New Era* (Stanford, Stanford University Press, 1998).

11 M. Albright, 'Building a new world framework for democracy', *US Foreign Policy Agenda*, US Information Agency, March 1997 (http://www.usia.gov/journals/journals.htm), p.9.

12 For example, a 1998 bilateral mutual recognition agreement covering six sectors (including telecoms equipment, medical devices, and pharmaceuticals) saved private investors something like $1 billion annually. See D. Vogel, *Barriers or Benefits?* (Washington D.C., Brookings Institution, 1997).

duced the Dayton Peace Accord in late 1995, which Congress supported despite profound misgivings on the part of many of its members. The perception that Bosnia was a success for NATO led Congress to acquiesce to the stationing of US troops in Bosnia well beyond the Clinton administration's original putative deadline of December 1996. The continued presence of American troops in Bosnia (and Macedonia) was a factor in Clinton's decision to launch airstrikes against Yugoslavia in response to the repression of ethnic Albanians in Kosovo in 1999.[13]

The second major European issue in American politics was NATO enlargement. It moved to centre stage on the policy agenda after the 1994 mid-term elections returned Republican majorities to both the House of Representatives and the Senate, in a crushing defeat for Clinton and his Democratic party. In early 1995, the House and Senate each debated separate, Republican-sponsored bills mandating early and extensive NATO enlargement.[14] Although fought off by the Clinton administration, which favoured enlargement in principle but did not want its hands tied on timing, these bills illuminated the range of foreign policy views within the new Congress. Despite media characterisations of rising 'isolationism' in Congress, little in either the House or Senate NATO bills could have been termed isolationist. There were relatively few outright isolationists amongst Congressional Republicans.

Nonetheless, the impact of Congress on US foreign policy after 1994 was considerable. Clinton's doctrine of 'aggressive multilateralism'[15] and support for the United Nations were berated and ultimately discredited by Congressional Republicans. Clinton was forced to defend his

---

13 Before the 1999 NATO air campaign in Kosovo began, the House voted 219-191 in support of a resolution to deploy US peacekeepers if a political settlement was reached. The White House, together with Republican party grandees (such as Robert Dole and Jeanne Kirkpatrick), pleaded with House Republican leaders to postpone the vote while delicate negotiations were ongoing between the warring parties in Kosovo. Yet, the Speaker of the House, Dennis Hastert (Republican, Illinois), cited the case of Bosnia in insisting: 'When the president has moved troops into some place, we have acquiesced, just nodded our heads and done it [...]. I believe Congress must have a meaningful role in the decision, no matter how hard our task.' (quoted in *Congressional Quarterly Weekly,* 13 March 1999, p.622).

14 Both bills called for enlargement to be extended to states (such as Romania) beyond than the favoured three of Poland, Hungary and the Czech Republic, which were eventually admitted in 1999.

15 See R. Haass, 'Foreign Policy by Posse', *The National Interest* (1995) 58-64.

support for Boris Yeltsin and general tolerance of China's human rights record, as well as his advocacy of the Chemical Weapons Convention.[16] Congressional Republicans forced significant cuts in US foreign aid.

The Senate Republican party remained far less hawkish and brazen on foreign policy than its counterpart in the House. By the mid-1990s, around half of all members of the House had entered politics *after* the fall of the Berlin Wall. Inevitably, new and relatively young spokespeople emerged with non-traditional views on old issues (such as aid to Mexico, the International Monetary Fund (IMF), abortion in China etc.). If reports of rising isolationism were exaggerated, it was also true that very few 'new' Republicans were classic internationalists or Atlanticists. Many considered themselves 'Reagan Republicans', and seemed nostalgic 'for the apparent clarity and simplicity of the Cold War anti-Communist framework'.[17] Lacking such a framework, many seemed bewildered by the complexities of post-Cold War conflicts.

Congressional Republicans did not hesitate, however, to use key issues in transatlantic relations – the war in Kosovo, trade with Cuba, the Boeing-McDonnell Douglas merger – as fodder for the playing of 'wedge' or 'contrast politics'. Put simply, wedge politics means finding issues on which it is possible to strike a populist position that is clearly different from those of political enemies, and exploiting the contrast for partisan advantage. Kosovo illustrates clearly. The war broke out only eleven weeks after Clinton's impeachment trial ended in his acquittal. As the US launched airstrikes against Yugoslavia, Clinton's job approval ratings – which soared during the impeachment trial – appeared to be slipping. The Majority Whip (and a prime mover in the impeachment effort) Tom DeLay (Republican, Texas), furiously attacked Clinton's Kosovo policy and urged his Republican colleagues not to 'take ownership' of 'Clinton's war'. Yet, a House motion to endorse the air war lost on a tie vote (213-213), with thirty-one Republicans defying DeLay and voting with the President. Democrat House Minority Leader Richard Gephardt (Missouri) seized the opportunity to claim that 'the extreme right wing of the Republican Party remains in control of that party', and lambasted DeLay for instigating a 'low moment in American

---

16 See J. Helms, 'United Nations reform and the Chemical Weapons Convention', *US Foreign Policy Agenda*, US Information Agency, March 1997 (http://www.usia.gov/journals/journals.htm), 20-1.

17 T. Carothers, 'Democracy Promotion under Clinton', *The Washington Quarterly*, 18:4 (1995) 25.

foreign policy'. David Obey, a senior House Democrat (Wisconsin), lamented that 'If we cannot avoid playing politics on this issue, if we cannot avoid unnecessary divisions on this issue, then this Congress does not have the ability to play it straight on any issue, and God help the country if that is the case'.[18]

In the end, Congressional Republicans could take comfort from Kosovo (and Bosnia before it) because it highlighted how much NATO remained an institutional linchpin of America's international power. After 1994, most members of Congress – and nearly all Republicans – viewed NATO as the only multilateral organisation (including the UN) under which US forces should operate. NATO's success in bombing Milosevic's Yugoslavia into submission twice in the 1990s reinforced the perception – both in Congress and the US more generally – that NATO continued to 'come first' (that is, ahead of the EU) in transatlantic relations.

As such, the New Transatlantic Agenda attracted little attention, let alone opposition, from Congress. The support of most Republicans who cared about Europe was assured by the creation of the Transatlantic Business Dialogue, even though it was a brainchild of Ron Brown, Clinton's politically-loathed Commerce Secretary who died in 1996.[19] A rolling series of exchanges between businesspeople from the US and EU, the TABD was designed to identify barriers to transatlantic trade and investment, and then generate political momentum to eliminate them. The TABD helped pave the way for a series of successful bilateral deals, including an Information Technology Agreement (which significantly freed trade in high-tech products), a broader agreement on scientific and technological cooperation (signed in late 1997), and progress on standards recognition and regulatory harmonization.[20]

---

18 DeLay, Gephardt and Obey all quoted in *Congressional Quarterly Weekly*, 1 May 1999, pp.1038-9.

19 The TABD fit with the Clinton administration's more general 'high intensity advocacy' of the interests of US business in foreign markets. Republicans could attack the strategy only on the relatively narrow grounds that the administration – especially Ron Brown himself – was dispensing political favours via the Commerce Department to Democratic party supporters in the private sector. See J. Peterson and M. Green Cowles, 'Clinton, Europe and Economic Diplomacy: What Makes the EU Different?' *Governance*, 11:3 (1998) 251-71.

20 For an update on TABD activities in the NTA context, see statement for before the House International Relations Committee by J. M. Farren, the President of External

In contrast to the quiet, low-key cooperation spawned by the NTA, Congress often poured fuel on the flames of US-EU trade disputes over bananas, hormone-treated beef, and airplane 'hush kits' (see below). Congressional scepticism about whether the WTO served US interests intensified as the American trade deficit hit historic levels in the late 1990s. The US Trade Representative, Charlene Barshefsky, frequently cited Congressional hostility towards trade liberalisation in urging the EU to comply with WTO rulings in the banana and beef wars. 'From a strategic point of view', Barshefsky insisted, 'if Europe is concerned about US unilateralism, then it must comply with these rulings'.[21]

However, trade was never really a partisan issue during the Clinton era. More Republicans (especially in the Senate) than Democrats shared the administration's general proclivity towards liberalisation. For its part, the House voted overwhelmingly (by 289-141) to extend massive protectionism to the US steel industry in March 1999, but around half of all Republican members voted in opposition. The measure was then soundly defeated in the Senate, after Clinton administration worked hard to swing pivotal votes (such as Ted Kennedy's) against it. A subsequent WTO report on US trade policy noted rising pressure for protectionism (without mentioning Congress by name), while observing that 'by and large, the Administration has resisted such pressure'.[22]

It often seemed as if Congress had become more parochial and inward looking than the US public or especially business during the Clinton era. A broad coalition of American exporters, 'USA Engage', came together in 1997 with the explicit mission to 'educate the Congress' about the futility of imposing economic sanctions on 'rogue' states without strong support from other major allies. Even if public awareness of the EU was dim, one poll found that ordinary Americans overwhelmingly supported the notion that the US and EU should be 'equal partners' (80%). Most respondents also supported European unification to 'help balance American power in the world' (53%) and thought the US should 'work closely with the EU in coordinated efforts

---

Affairs for Xerox and TABD working chair (available from http://www.tabd.com/resources/content/Farrenspeech.html).

21 Quoted in *Financial Times*, 11 February 1999.

22 World Trade Organization, 'Trade Policy Review of the United States' (Geneva, WTO) TPRB 108 , 1 July 1999.

even if it sometimes means making compromises' (65%).[23] If such sentiments were broadly reflected in the NTA and US policy more generally during Clinton era, it was in spite of – not because of – Congress.

The Executive and Congress: Controlling the Foreign Policy Agenda

Even after the Cold War ended, Presidential prerogative in foreign policy remained powerful. Congress mostly reacted to foreign policy as designed and implemented by the executive. Still, the scope for Congressional kibitzing broadened, not least because no fundamental doctrine of US foreign policy emerged to replace 'containment' as a central organising principle. The result, in Schlesinger's view, was that 'foreign policy lobbies based on domestic constituencies rush[ed] in to fill the vacuum'.[24]

Congress was a key player in the rush. The end of the Cold War acted to lower the electoral costs of opposing the President on foreign policy, and Congress thus became more responsive to domestic lobbies (such as the steel lobby or African-American lobby) and willing to substitute its collective judgement for the President's.[25] The point was illustrated vividly by Congressional opposition to executive policies on Bosnia, Somalia, Haiti, the WTO and NAFTA (the North American Free Trade Association) even *before* Clinton lost his 'friendly' Democratic majority in Congress in 1994.

Presidential latitude in foreign policy became determined in large part by how much any given issue offered Congressional opponents scope for domestic political advantage. Generally, there was far more cooperation between the executive and Congress after 1996, as compared to Clinton's first term. However, (mostly non-trade) issues on which the President would have had considerable discretion before the late 1980s – Cuba, the IMF, Iran, the enlargement of NAFTA, Kosovo, the Comprehensive Test Ban Treaty – became 'wedge' issues.

---

23 PIPA (Program on International Policy Attitudes) 'Seeking a New Balance: A Study of American and European Public Attitudes on Transatlantic Issues' (College Park, University of Maryland, University of Maryland, June 1998 – available http://www.pipa.org/newbalance.html).

24 A. Schlesinger, Jr., 'Houdini in the White House', *Wall Street Journal*, 21 September 1994.

25 See Rohde, 'Partisanship, Leadership, and Congressional Assertiveness'.

When Congress played an important role in foreign policy decision-making, it was usually because an issue mobilised a coalition (frequently crossing parties) of members, which then was able to force policy shifts or executive activism on policies which already had been made. For example, after threatening intervention for months, Clinton's hand was forced on Haiti by the Congressional African-American caucus in 1994. Similarly, a bill on trade with Africa introduced by Jesse Jackson, Jr. – a House Democrat and son of the influential religious leader – encouraged the Clinton administration to lobby harder for its own African Growth and Opportunity Act in 1999 despite Republican and trade union opposition.

Congressional influence on policy towards Europe flowed primarily from three sources. First, American wheat and livestock farmers, especially in the northern plains states, were in grave crisis by the late 1990s. The 1996 US 'Freedom to Farm' bill (officially the Federal Agriculture Improvement and Reform Act), significantly reformed and liberalised US farm policy, thus making American farmers more dependent on foreign markets just prior to the collapse of many Asian markets. EU bashing became a cross-party pastime amongst farm state members of Congress, many of whom took up the battle cry: 'in Europe, farm policy always trumps foreign policy'.[26] In April 1998 the Head of the European Commission's delegation in Washington, Hugo Paemen, was subjected to the wrath of no less than fifteen Senators who turned up for a Capitol Hill meeting after a single boat-load of subsidised EU barley (feed for racehorses) arrived at a port in California. The Clinton administration was forced to talk tough: in congressional testimony, the deputy USTR, Richard Fisher, declared the EU's Common Agricultural Policy to be the 'world's single largest distortion of agricultural trade' and promised it would be America's 'bullseye' in the next round of global trade talks.[27]

---

26 This very language featured in a Senate Foreign Relations committee report on amendment 2321 to the NATO expansion act. See Senate Record Vote Analysis – Temporary, Vote No. 111, 105th Congress, 2nd Session, Page S-3844 Temp. Record 30 April (1998), (available from http://www.senate.gov). To get a flavour for Congressional EU-bashing, see the 11 September 1997 press release from Senator William V. Roth (Republican, Delaware) entitled 'Roth not chicken to peck a fight over EU's fowl restrictions' (available from http://www.senate.gov/~roth/press/1997/poultry.html).

27 Quoted in *Financial Times*, 29 July 1999.

Second, East European ethnic lobbies remained influential within Congress and pushed for early NATO (and EU) enlargement. Traditionally linked to the Democrats, East European lobbies gravitated towards the Republicans in the 1990s. Democratic members from districts populated by ethnic East Europeans were determined not to be outflanked by the Republicans on the expansion of NATO (or the EU).

Generally, however, the EU became something of a pawn in the Congressional debate about NATO enlargement. The debate was driven in fundamental ways by the perception that new east European democracies were being betrayed by an EU that was enlarging reluctantly and far too slowly. Many members of Congress agreed with Richard Holbrooke, the 'father' of the Dayton peace agreement, who asserted: 'almost a decade has gone by since the Berlin Wall fell and, instead of reaching out to Central Europe, the European Union turned toward a bizarre search for a common currency. So NATO enlargement had to fill the void'.[28] The US debate about NATO enlargement was informed by little, if any, appreciation of the dangers of creating new political divisions or exacerbating latent ethnic tensions in the region, by isolating Ukraine or offering membership to Hungary but not Romania. Put simply, it was a typically American debate about power, principles and morality.

Third, at least on the surface, the politics of US military spending changed remarkably little after 1989. Kosovo illustrated the point: most of the Republicans who voted in favour of US airstrikes served on defense committees. Even though it refused to endorse the air campaign, the House voted to more than double the amount requested by Clinton in May 1999 to pay for the war in Kosovo. One view was that the move was a bald attempt to jack up defense spending using the Balkans mission as a cover. Another – widely-held amongst Republicans – was

---

[28] This statement featured prominently in debates surrounding Senate Amendment 2321 – sponsored by Democrat (New York) Daniel Patrick Moynihan and Republican (Virginia) John Warner – of the NATO Expansion Act. See US Senate, 'Senate record vote analysis – temporary', vote No.111, 105th Congress, 2nd session, 30 April 1998, page S-3844 temp. Record (available from http://www.senate.gov). The Amendment mandated that eastern states should be admitted to NATO only *after* they had joined the EU. Eventually, it was rejected on a vote of 83-17. Prior to the vote, one opinion poll suggested that a majority of Americans (53%) agreed with the statement: 'We should not pressure the European Union to include these countries; it is their business when they [the Europeans] think it is best to do so.' (PIPA, 'Americans on NATO Enlargement').

that Clinton's numerous deployments of US forces abroad (Bosnia, Haiti, Kosovo etc.) had stretched US military resources to a breaking point. In any event, the notion that the defence of Europe was primarily an American prerogative remained pervasive in Congress, thus complicating hard choices the EU was just beginning to tackle concerning the upgrading and amalgamation of Europe's own defense capabilities.

Congressional support for early NATO enlargement was bolstered by close links to the Pentagon and lobbying by US arms manufacturers. It also was motivated by fear of the so-called 'nightmare scenario': that is, a process of EU enlargement which out-paced NATO enlargement. A source of considerable concern within the Pentagon, the scenario threatened to emerge if new states joined the EU, and thus the Western European Union (WEU, to which all EU Member States have a right to accede).[29] However, if new EU/WEU members chose not to join NATO, *de facto* US security guarantees would effectively be extended via a process over which the US had no control. For example, Germany's WEU commitment to defend Finland might pull the US into a military conflict through the back door given the American NATO commitment to defend Germany. Allowed to unfold, the 'nightmare scenario' would have handed Congressional populists an issue to exploit for domestic political gain by arguing that US foreign policy was being dictated elsewhere. The point here is that almost whatever the EU does – enlarge or not, deepen integration or not, upgrade its defense role or not – it risks provoking the ire of Congress.

The Electoral Equation

Whether or not the 1994 US mid-term election marked a realignment in American politics, it marked a sea change in the electoral mathematics of Congressional elections. Republican majorities were installed in both houses of Congress for the first time since the early 1950s. The Democrats suffered a 'melt-down' in the South, with Republicans winning about fifty-five per cent of the Southern vote and apparently destroying what remained of the Democratic lock on the region. If replicated in the future, these results will make it virtually impossible for the Democrats to regain control of Congress.

---

[29] G. W. Rees, *The Western European Union at the Crossroads* (Boulder and Oxford, Westview Press, 1998).

The 1996 election saw no change in the Republican majority in the Senate and only a very marginal loss (of three seats) for the Republican majority in the House, even though Clinton easily beat the Senate Majority Leader, Robert Dole, in the race for the White House. Foreign policy was barely discussed in the 1996 campaign after Dole made a brief (and lacklustre) attempt to make Clinton's record in international affairs a campaign issue. Dole was denied coveted opportunities to play wedge politics when the peace held in Bosnia and Boris Yeltsin was re-elected as Russia's President. In the case of Russia, Clinton's competence and 'Presidentialism' could have been seriously challenged by Republican allegations that he had allowed 'the return of Communism' to the Eurasian continent. Clinton was probably even more vulnerable on Bosnia: most polls in 1996 showed a clear plurality (some a majority) of voters opposing the presence of US troops in the Balkans. It was testament to Clinton's political skill that, by late 1997, clear majorities supported the American military presence in Bosnia.[30]

After the 1996 campaign, the Clinton administration could claim that: 'the fact that foreign policy wasn't an issue in last year's campaign didn't mean that it wasn't important. It meant that the big question – whether America should be engaged in the world or withdraw – has been largely decided by both parties in favour of engagement. Now we will be working with the Congress to figure out just how to do that'.[31]

Clinton used his 1997 State of the Union address to proclaim that America's 'first [foreign policy] task is to help build, for the first time, an undivided, democratic Europe. When Europe is stable, prosperous, and at peace, America is more secure.' At this point, NATO enlargement to take in Poland, Hungary and the Czech Republic became an essentially foregone conclusion.[32]

---

30 Although different polls inevitably pose different questions, it is nonetheless revealing to compare results from several polls in early 1996 (as reported in *Financial Times,* 4 April 1996) with those of PIPA, 'Americans on the NATO Operation in Bosnia' (College Park, University of Maryland, University of Maryland, 8 May 1998) (http://www.pipa.org/bosnia.html) and 'Seeking a New Balance' (June 1998).

31 D. Johnson, 'Shaping a Bipartisan Foreign Policy', *US Foreign Policy Agenda*, US Information Agency, March 1997 (http://www.usia.gov/journals/journals.htm), p.16.

32 W. J. Clinton, 'America's leadership role in the 21st century', *US Foreign Policy Agenda*, US Information Agency, March 1997 (http://www.usia.gov/journals/journals.htm), p.5. As a caveat, on 4 June 1997 the House vote was quite close (221-

Foreign policy was virtually invisible during the 1998 mid-term election campaign. The election featured very few competitive races, a large number of incumbents with weak or no opposition, and few urgent campaign issues.[33] As such, the results were surprising: the Republican Senate majority (55-45) remained unchanged, but the Democrats gained five seats in the House. On the largest turnout (39%) of any mid-term election since the 1970s, the Democrats made inroads everywhere, including in the South, and voters rejected most very conservative Republicans. The Democrats were rewarded for the healthy state of the economy, while the unpopularity of the Republican campaign to impeach Clinton was evident. Clinton became the only second-term President in the 20th century to see his party's position strengthened in a mid-term election. Afterwards, with the political 'centre' strengthened in Congress, the administration was able to take steps to settle American arrears with the UN, actively pursue China's admission to the WTO, and approve $18 billion in US funding for the IMF.

As for relations with the EU, as the end of the Clinton era approached the administration could plausibly claim that it had shown stronger support for the EU and European integration than any administration since Kennedy's. The point was evidenced by the unveiling of a peace deal at the May 1998 US-EU summit which exempted the EU from the effects of 'extra-territorial' US sanctions legislation against Cuba, Iran and Libya. Clinton's waiving of sanctions against EU investors defied the strong views of many Republican members of Congress. Benjamin Gilman (Republican, New York), chair of the House International Relations committee, spoke for many in complaining that 'the President secured little in the way of firm and binding commitments from the EU' and sent 'the wrong signal at the wrong time'.[34]

---

200) on a complex motion (HR 159) which declared – amongst other things – that 'the enlargement of [...] NATO [should] proceed in a manner consistent with United States interests'. Of course, only the Senate vote on NATO enlargement was binding under its Constitutional powers to approve treaties (including amended treaties) with foreign states.

33 R. E. Cohen and J. A. Barnes, 'The Parties Adrift', *National Journal*, 30:17 (1998) 916-20; C. Cook, 'Why the GOP stands to keep the House', *National Journal*, 30:24 (1998) 1384-97.

34 Quoted in *Financial Times*, 23 June 1998. See also M. Chapman, 'Clinton Sides with Europe and Castro against Congress', *Human Events*, 53:2 (1997) 4-5; UK Presidency of the European Union Council, 'Press Release: EU/US Summits, London, 18 May 1998 (available from http://presid.fco.gov.uk).

Republican views on the EU reflected the party's more general tilt in the 1990s towards 'aggressive unilateralism'. Its upholders insisted that the US should be active in global affairs, but should not compromise its own foreign policy interests or agenda for the sake of 'cooperation', with the EU or anyone else. During his 1996 Presidential campaign, Dole reaffirmed that 'preventing the domination of Europe by a single power' would remain a central principle of US foreign policy. The European Union, however, was cast by Dole less as a faithful ally than a potential rival to be balanced by American power: '[t]he United States, as the only global power, must lead. Europe – as individual states or as a collective – cannot.'[35]

Clinton's re-election thus was welcomed in most European capitals, not least Brussels. Still, there seemed little doubt that if Dole had been elected in 1996, foreign policy would again have become the domain of traditional, old hand, Republican internationalists. For example, Senator Richard Lugar (Republican, Indiana), one of the most thoughtful Congressional voices on foreign policy, ran a short (and barely visible) campaign against Dole for the Republican Presidential nomination, which was probably equally a bid to be Dole's Secretary of State. William Cohen, the former Republican Senator, would have been a viable candidate for Secretary of Defense in a Dole administration, as he became in the second Clinton administration.

After 1996, however, a combination of factors – Clinton's impeachment trial, generational change, and weak party leadership – produced a palpable shift to the right in the Congressional Republican party. When war erupted in Kosovo, Dole (now retired) stopped just short of condemning his former Republican colleagues for opposing the war effort.[36] The Senate (unlike the House) endorsed airstrikes in Kosovo, but

---

35 R. Dole, 'Shaping America's Global Future', *Foreign Policy*, 84:2 (1995) 31-4. See also B. W. Weinrod, 'The Need for Western Leadership', *The World & I*, 11:12 (1996) 36-41.

36 Commenting on Republican opposition to the war in Kosovo, Dole insisted that 'I don't think most Republicans are isolationist. There is a lot of mistrust of Clinton [...] But we're talking about the future of NATO and of Europe. We're talking about refugees and the 250,000 already dead in Bosnia'. Quoted in *Congressional Quarterly Weekly*, 10 April 1999, pp.835-6. Harrowing television pictures of ethnic Albanian refugees being forced to leave Kosovo – more than the Clinton administration's 'grip' on the war effort – had the effect of sustaining US public support for the 1999 air campaign against Yugoslavia. See poll results – showing that about two-thirds of Americans backed the airstrikes – as reported in

the vote (58-41 in favour) illustrated a clear generational shift in the Republican party. A total of thirty-eight Republicans voted against the President. Of the sixteen Republicans who supported Clinton, most (11) were 'old hands' who had been elected before 1994. Only five Republicans who voted against the airstrikes had served in Congress for more than five years. Many newer Republicans believed that Kosovo was 'Europe's war', which should be fought primarily by European military forces, as well as 'Clinton's war'. Whether Dole's mostly forgettable 1996 Presidential bid would end up being remembered as the final campaign by a Republican candidate who could be relied upon to turn foreign policy over to 'old hand' internationalists became an open question.[37]

Congress and Key Issues in US-EU Relations

Regardless of its rather dull content, agreement on the New Transatlantic Agenda in late 1995 was a considerable achievement, particularly given the distraction of the EU by its intergovernmental conference (which yielded the Amsterdam Treaty in 1997) and the looming US mid-term election of 1996. Steady, low-key cooperation on issues targeted by the NTA's Action Plan fortified transatlantic relations in important ways, particularly in the face of trade disputes fuelled by Congressional demands for tough US policies.

Congress continued to shape US policy and decision-making in a range of policy areas either implicated by the NTA or outside it but of importance to US-European relations. This section assesses the role of Congress in the main issue-areas that preoccupy US-EU relations.

M. A. Pomper, 'Clinton gains support on Hill for Kosovo campaign', *Congressional Quarterly Weekly*, 17 April 1999, p.905-6.

[37] On the one hand, all of the leading candidates for Presidential election in 2000 were centrists and free traders. On the other hand, a key foreign policy advisor to the clear favourite to become the Republican Presidential candidate, George W. Bush (the popular governor of Texas), was Richard Perle, a fiercely right-wing official in the Reagan administration. Meanwhile, Albright on several occasions declared herself 'very grateful to Senator Dole for his help' in diplomatic efforts to find a settlement in the Balkans. See for example Albright's statement on the State Department's fiscal year 2000 budget request to the House Appropriations Subcommittee on Commerce, Justice, and Judiciary (CJS), 10 March 1999 (available from http://www.secretary.state.gov/statements/19999/990310.html#leadership).

Trade and Economic Security

The domestic American political equation on questions of economic security is complicated and often contradictory. The Clinton administration invested considerable effort in regional free trade projects such as NAFTA and APEC, but *without* convincing clear majorities of Americans – or members of Congress – to stop associating free trade with economic insecurity.[38] Congressional input into trade policy debates was moulded by the first foreign policy experience of the large, almost exclusively Republican freshman class of 1994: the Mexican peso crisis, which required a massive, publicly-funded US-led bail-out. The peso crisis itself followed on the heels of the bruising political battle to ratify the NAFTA agreement.[39] Evidence that NAFTA had both failed to generate new jobs and damaged the environment, especially along the US-Mexican border, acted to taint NAFTA – and trade liberalisation more generally – while fuelling economic populism.[40]

Particularly in the House, younger and less-experienced Republicans tended to be social conservative populists, for whom votes on trade with China or IMF funding were viewed primarily as opportunities to draw attention to abortion rights. On the Democrat side, many centrist moderates were defeated in the 1994 election. One effect was to empower left wing, free trade sceptics in the party, with Richard Gephardt (Democrat, Missouri, and House minority leader) emerging as a capable political leader. The trade section of the 1995 New Transatlantic Agenda, which was decidedly modest in ambitions, was shaped by the administration's determination not to rile Congress.

---

38 Despite the longest and most sustained period of prosperity in American post-war history, by some estimates the economic situation of around three-quarters of the US population did not substantially improve in the ten years after 1989. See Economic Policy Institute, *The State of Working America 1998-9* (Ithaca, Cornell University Press, 1999). One poll in 1999 revealed that 54% of the US public (compared with eighty-seven percent of elite 'leaders') believed globalisation was 'mostly good for the United States'. Chicago Council on Foreign Relations, 'American Public Opinion' 1999.

39 A perceptive work on the peso crisis and NAFTA debate, by a scholar who worked on Capitol Hill during the period as an aide to Senator Bill Bradley (Democrat, New Jersey), is F. W. Mayer, *Interpreting NAFTA: The Science and Art of Political Analysis* (New York, Columbia University Press, 1998).

40 Institute for Policy Studies, *NAFTA's First Two Years: The Myths and the Realities* (Washington D.C., 1996).

The Clinton administration always struggled to convince Congress that it was defending US trade interests aggressively enough in the World Trade Organization. The creation of the WTO had the effect of uniting Republicans, many of whom were profoundly concerned about US sovereignty and/or its perceived decline as a trading power. Congress' tilt towards aggressive unilateralism on trade was particularly evident in the 1996 Helms-Burton Act (or 'Democracy in Cuba Act'), which threatened sanctions against European firms which invested in Cuba.[41] Despite hard lobbying by the EU, Clinton chose not to veto it. Besides a strong determination not to be outflanked by Congress, a key consideration was Clinton's need to win states with large Cuban émigré communities (especially Florida and New Jersey) to be re-elected in 1996.[42]

Generally, Clinton's own Democratic party showed less confidence in his administration's trade policy than did Republicans. Gephardt put aside party loyalties and opposed the administration in spearheading a successful 1997 campaign – bolstered by trades unions and environmental groups – to deny Clinton 'fast track' authority to negotiate an extension of NAFTA to include Chile.[43] Fewer than 45 of 206 Democrats in the House voted to extend fast track.[44] Clinton became the first President to be denied the authority since Congress first granted it in 1974.

---

[41] Helms-Burton was a direct Congressional response to the shooting down by Cuba in early 1996 of two Miami-based civil aircraft (which had deliberately transgressed Cuban airspace). See J. Peterson and E. Bomberg, *Decision-Making in the European Union* (London and New York, Macmillan and St Martin's Press, 1999), pp.102-3.

[42] In the event, Clinton won both states in 1996 and came close to splitting the Cuban-American vote – a traditionally reliable Republican constituency – with Robert Dole. See M. A. Pomper, 'Cuban-American Agenda Marked by New Diversity', *Congressional Quarterly Weekly*, 27 February 1999, pp.467-70.

[43] 'Fast track' originated in the US 1974 Trade Act. It seeks to give the executive broad discretion in trade negotiations while reserving for Congress a form of 'legislative veto'. Under fast track, Congress must be consulted as any trade agreement is negotiated, but it then votes 'up or down' on the resulting bill (without making amendments). Congressional committees to which the bill is referred are required to report on the bill in a short period of time and debates on the floors of both Houses are limited. See J. H. Jackson, *The World Trading System: Law and Policy of International Economic Relations* (Cambridge Mass. and London, the MIT Press, 1997), 2nd edition, pp.92-5.

[44] The House voted down fast-track by 243-180 on 25 September 1998. It was never put to a vote in the Senate, where it probably would have been approved.

Despite the dire political climate for new trade initiatives the EU's Commissioner for trade policy, Leon Brittan, produced an ambitious proposal in 1998 for a 'New Transatlantic Marketplace'. Brittan clearly calculated that the Asian financial crisis of 1997 had enhanced Europe's appeal as a stable market for US exports and investment, and that the time was right to flesh out the NTA's (rather sketchy) economic chapter. The proposal – whose primary goal was to free trade in services – was also designed to appeal to France, which exported nearly nine per cent of the world's commercial services, more than half the US total with only one-fifth of its population. Yet, before the initiative could get near Congress, it was buried by France. For one thing, French political leaders on both the right (President Jacques Chirac) and the left (Prime Minister Lionel Jospin) were profoundly and personally mistrustful of Brittan. For another, the French feared that once transatlantic trade liberalisation was out of its 'tube', it would encroach on the hyper-sensitive (for France) agriculture and audio-visual (AV) sectors. This assumption was a logical one, given the activism and effectiveness of both farm and AV industry lobbies in the US Congress.[45] In a backhanded illustration of Congress' ability to shape policy, Brittan's initiative was shelved in favour of the far less ambitious 'Transatlantic Economic Partnership' (TEP).[46] Even it was immediately condemned by William Roth (Republican, Delaware) the Chair of the Senate Finance Committee, for failing to address 'the difficult issues that divide us, particularly those of European agricultural tariffs and subsidies [...] while taking up an agenda shaped by European, not US interests'.[47] One editorial after the 1998 US-EU summit sealed agreement on the TEP bluntly asserted that, for transatlantic economic relations generally, '[t]he key problem is Congress'.[48] Its members remained far more responsive to US exporters

45 See the opening statement of Senator Tom Harkin (Democrat, Iowa) at the Agriculture Committee hearing of 7 May 1998, in which he explicitly urges 'the Administration to vigorously oppose any movement to exclude agriculture from consideration in the proposed New Transatlantic Marketplace negotiations with the European Union' (available from http://www.senate.gov/~agriculture/har98507.htm).

46 The full text of TEP is reproduced in Council of the European Union, '2129th Council Meeting – General Affairs', Brussels: General Secretariat, press release 12560/1998, Presse 369 (available from http://ue.eu.int/newsroom).

47 See Press Release #105-325, 18 May 1998 (available from http://www.senate.gov/~finance/105-325.htm).

48 *Financial Times*, 19 May 1998.

than EU investors, even though the latter acquired massive US assets after 1980 and employed huge numbers of Americans (6 million by one count), usually in good jobs. Given that the EU invested more in Texas than Japan did in the entire US, Congress' general disregard for transatlantic relations was mystifying.[49]

In this context, the role of Congress in the muscular American attack on the EU's discriminatory import regime for bananas was significant. The US-headquartered Chiquita, a large producer of bananas, lobbied hard in Congress while contributing huge amounts of campaign funds to both major parties, and was the main beneficiary of a WTO decision in favour of the US. The House came close to voting through its own retaliatory sanctions against the EU in 1998, and was headed off only by Clinton's setting of deadlines for EU compliance and threat of massive retaliation if they were not met.

Around the same time, a broad, cross-party Congressional coalition of members from farming regions was an important source of pressure on the Clinton administration over the EU's longstanding ban on imports of American hormone-treated beef. When the WTO again found in favour of the US in 1999, the Clinton administration found its room to manoeuvre in negotiating a settlement with the EU was severely proscribed by the breadth of Congressional support for nothing short of an explicit EU commitment to lift the ban. In contrast, the administration was able to deflect Congressional attacks on an EU scheme for assisting peach growers – despite very clear evidence that the scheme damaged exports of American peaches – because the US industry was very localised and relatively few members of Congress made an issue of EU support for European peach growers.[50]

Increasingly, of course, economic disputes turned less on matters of trade *per se* as 'behind the border' issues such as public procurement, standards-setting and mergers. The flap over an EU measure (agreed in 1999) to ban airplane 'hush kits', or engine mufflers, threatened $1 billion of economic harm to US aviation equipment makers and airlines. The EU directive was formulated as an environmental policy measure

---

49 Figures from European-American Business Council, *The United States and Europe: Jobs, Investment and Trade* (Washington D.C., 1999), 6th edition.

50 A dispute settlement case under the General Agreement on Tariffs and Trade (GATT), the WTO's precursor, found the EU's peach regime in violation of GATT rules. See statistics showing a massive fall in US peach exports after the 1970s as reproduced the *Financial Times*, 4 July 1999.

(older aircraft, which require hush kits to meet noise standards, pollute more) and was not primarily intended to create trade discrimination, although virtually all of its costs fell on non-EU operators. Both Houses of Congress debated retaliatory bills to ban Concorde (flown by British Airways and Air France) from landing at US airports until the Clinton administration defused the row by persuading the EU to delay the implementation of the ban. Another high profile, behind the border dispute surrounded the EU's challenge to the Boeing-McDonnell Douglas merger in 1997. A letter to Clinton from a bipartisan group of seven US Senators, which accused the EU of prejudging the merger, spurred the administration to promise, in the words of Vice-President Al Gore, to take 'whatever action is appropriate' to keep the Union from impeding the merger.[51]

Ultimately, the 'building blocks' approach of the TEP – taking small, low-profile steps (mostly on regulatory cooperation) and then building on them – kept Congress away from the centrepiece of US-EU trade and economic cooperation. As the Clinton era ended, Congress was not an inevitable barrier to new transatlantic deals on trade and investment, or US-EU cooperation in the 'Seattle Round' of global trade talks slated to begin in late 1999. But Congress had to be courted, and could be relied upon to raise the stakes and cast most trade disputes as tests of American virility.

Traditional Security

The security problems of the 1990s – Bosnia, Somalia, Haiti, Iran, Iraq, Kosovo – posed only indirect threats to American or West European security. However, they also offered valued chances to play wedge politics. A month after the Republicans' triumph in the 1994 mid-term election, Dole's European tour and ferocious attack on the UK and France over Bosnia were clearly designed to make the Republican leader appear 'Presidential', after Clinton's attempts to shift western policy on Bosnia had been stymied by European opposition. The ad-

---

[51] Quoted in *Financial Times,* 14 May 1997. The row over the merger was made moot when, essentially, Boeing backed down in the face of objections from the European Commission. The high drama of the Boeing case contrasts with a very considerable amount of routine, day-to-day co-operation and exchange according to the terms of the 1991 US-EU bilateral agreement on competition policy. For an overview, see K. Van Miert, 'Transatlantic Relations and Competition Policy', *Competition Policy Newsletter* (Brussels, European Commission DG IV), 3:2 (1996) 1-5.

ministration's own subsequent attacks on Republican 'new isolationists' suited the strategy of portraying Clinton as the 'safe' candidate in the 1996 election.[52]

With that election less than six months away, Clinton took a considerable political risk at the 1996 Berlin NATO summit in conceding that NATO could supply forces and equipment to WEU operations, over which European allies would exert 'political control and strategic direction'. Subsequently, the administration performed a tricky balancing act in responding to European moves to create what was known in policy circles as a European Security and Defence Identity (ESDI), or a more independent and integrated European defense capacity. While welcoming an ESDI in principle, the Clinton administration constantly warned that there were many members of Congress ready to misconstrue its construction as an excuse to wash their hands of Europe. To many Europeans, the US appeared schizophrenic about America's role in European security, particularly after the Anglo-Franco St. Malo Declaration in late 1998 accelerated steps towards the 'Europeanisation' of defense.[53] Albright insisted in late 1998 that the US 'strongly endorsed [...] any measures that enhance European capabilities'.[54] A few months later her deputy, Strobe Talbott, warned of the 'risks and costs' of a stronger European defense capability: 'If ESDI is misconceived, misunderstood or mishandled, it could create the impression – would could eventually lead to reality – that a new European-only alliance is being born out of the old, transatlantic one'.[55]

American schizophrenia about ESDI was mainly a product of administration fears that generational change – especially amongst Republicans – would gradually erode the Congressional commitment to America's status as a European power. Such fears were aroused in late 1997 as NATO enlargement became 'domesticated': the Senate Appro-

---

52 See Peterson, *Europe and America,* pp.84-5.

53 The Declaration was signed at a bilateral British-French summit on 3-4 December 1998 (available from the UK Foreign and Commonwealth official site at http://194.72.226.90/news/newstext.asp?1794).

54 Statement to the North Atlantic Council by Secretary of State Madeleine K. Albright (Brussels, US Department of State, Office of the Spokesman), 98/22, 8 December 1998, p.7.

55 Quoted in *Financial Times*, 11 March 1999. Talbott expressed much the same view in a speech on 7 October 1999 at the Royal Institute of International Affairs in London.

priations Committee held no less than three hearings exclusively devoted to the cost of NATO enlargement. In the event, wildly conflicting estimates of its actual costs – from the administration's $27 billion to the Congressional Budget Office's $125 billion – acted to blunt the debate. Ultimately, consensus emerged that NATO enlargement was really about ensuring geopolitical stability, and was not primarily a fiscal issue.[56] Nonetheless, the long-term durability of Congressional support for the US security commitment to Europe was not beyond question.

Preventive Security

Preventive security refers to foreign policy measures that aim to prevent conflict or international crises before they erupt. It implies proactive measures: the investment of resources today to avoid the need to spend more resources tomorrow. The EU has competence in several 'preventive security' areas.

US spending on *development aid* continued to fall after 1996. More became tied to broader US foreign policy goals, as opposed to assisting those countries most in need, as was illustrated by the miserly sums committed to Africa after Clinton's visit to the continent in 1998. Foreign aid was an issue on which many relatively new Republican members of Congress had very strong feelings (that is, they wanted to cut or even eliminate it). Closer transatlantic cooperation on aid and development issues was a key feature of the NTA, reflecting the powerful incentives the Clinton administration faced wherever savings could be made through a combination of efforts. In particular, after its budget request for emergency (non-military) aid for Kosovo was slashed by more than half by Congress in spring 1999, the administration signalled its strong desire to pool US Balkans aid efforts with those of the EU. There seemed little choice, particularly in view of comments by leading Senators: 'it's your continent, not ours' and 'we're contributing military

56 Large majorities of Americans told pollsters that they opposed spending US money to upgrade the militaries of new NATO members, but only about one-fifth apparently followed the debate on NATO enlargement. Only ten percent of Americans could name any country that was about to become a new member of NATO. See A. Richman, 'What the polls say: US public's attitude toward NATO enlargement', *US Foreign Policy Agenda* (USIA electronic journal) 2:4 (1997) (available from http://www.usia.gov/journals/itps/1097/ijpe/pj4polls.htm). See also PIPA, 'Americans on NATO enlargement'.

muscle [...The EU] should contribute the lion's share of the money' for post-war reconstruction.[57]

Far removed from the political limelight, a US-EU officials working group on *Central and Eastern Europe* had by this point made significant strides towards eliminating the rivalries and the duplication of aid efforts which seriously plagued the region's reform process in the early 1990s.[58] However, the US aid contribution was small and likely to decline further. 'Preventive security' for many Republican members of Congress was simply a matter of bringing the new eastern democracies into western institutions (especially NATO) quickly, before Russia had a chance to threaten them again.

The potential weight of the US in *international environmental diplomacy* is unquestioned, but the Clinton administration never seriously pursued the environmental policy agenda that it set for itself in the 1992 election campaign. After 1994, Republican majorities in Congress effectively precluded ambitious initiatives in this arena, as was illustrated by its refusal to ratify the targets agreed by the administration at the 1997 Kyoto summit on global warming. The Clinton administration generally remained hamstrung by a Republican, pro-business Congress on environmental questions.

In most areas of preventive security, senior Clinton administration officials tended to cite the EU's lack of competence as a stumbling block to bilateral initiatives. For example, there was considerable American interest in cooperation with the EU on international crime and terrorism, but much frustration with the Union's lack of progress on 'Communitarising' justice and home affairs policies. Again, however, the NTA did spawn a range of low-key but path-breaking joint initiatives to fight money laundering, trafficking in women and the drugs trade in the Caribbean.[59]

---

57 These comments came from two of the most 'Euro-aware' Senators: (respectively) Joseph Biden (Democrat, Delaware), the senior Democrat on the Senate Foreign Relations Committee; and Gordon Smith (Republican, Oregon), the chair of the Senate's Subcommittee on European Affairs. Both quoted in *Congressional Quarterly Weekly*, 8 May 1999.

58 See for example the White House statement (following the US-EU summit of 18 May 1998) listing ongoing and successful NTA projects which refers exclusively to projects in eastern Europe or the former Soviet Union (available from http://www.useu.be/smmit/agend518.html).

59 Monar, *The New Transatlantic Agenda*, part III.

From a US perspective, the essential obstacle to joint preventive security measures is that they usually cost something. Despite the abrupt shift from public budget deficits to huge surpluses in the late 1990s, the new American model for foreign policy during the Clinton era seemed to be 'talk about leadership, but get someone else to pay the bill'.[60] The overriding emphasis of Congress was budget-cutting, reducing the size of government and lowering taxes. The federal budget commitment to 'international affairs' (that is, non-military resources) was about half its 1984 level. The State Department 'downsized' during the Clinton era by cutting its personnel by eleven per cent. The senior Democrat on the Senate Foreign Relations Committee, Paul Sarbanes (Maryland) spoke for many when he complained that 'you can't exercise world leadership on the cheap'. For his part, a senior Republican on the House International Relations committee, Jim Leach (Iowa), retorted '[t]his administration has fairly decent instincts, but to date has shown very little willingness to risk its political capital on these matters'.[61] In her confirmation hearings before Congress in 1997, Albright acknowledged:

> One of my most important tasks will be to work with Congress to ensure that we have the superb diplomatic representation that our people deserve and our interests demand. We cannot have that on the cheap. We must invest the resources needed to maintain American leadership. Consider the stakes. We are talking here about one percent of our federal budget, but that one percent may well determine fifty percent of the history that is written about our era.[62]

In short, preventive security tended to be where European unity was most desired and least controversial in US eyes. Yet, in this area of policy, the post-1994 Republican majorities on Capitol Hill made a clear difference and generally dimmed the prospects for enhanced transatlantic cooperation.

---

60 S. Erlanger, 'Foreign Aid, Fifty Years Later, Never Looked so Good', *The New York Times*, 1 July 1997, p.3.

61 'Seizing the opportunity to foster peace and security: an interview with Senator Paul Sarbanes' and '"Standing up for what's right" in international relations': an interview with Senator James Leach', *US Foreign Policy Agenda*, US Information Agency, March 1997, pp.22-30 (available from http://www.usinfo.state.gov/journals/journals.htm).

62 M. Albright, 'Building a New World Framework for Democracy', *US Foreign Policy Agenda*, March 1997, pp.8-11.

Political Cooperation

Because of the generally low level of awareness of the EU or what it does in the US Congress, Republicans usually show less patience than Democrats when the Union's Member States either cannot agree amongst themselves or do not support the US foreign policy 'line'. Particularly amongst Republicans, Greece's flaunting of EU policy on Macedonia, French unilateralism on Algeria and Rwanda, and the refusal of all EU Member States besides the UK to support the American show of strength in the Gulf in 1997 made a mockery of the Common Foreign and Security Policy (CFSP). Increasingly during the 1990s, American analysts belittled the CFSP as a device for legitimating EU inaction.[63]

The EU's complex, often unpredictable and mercurial decision-making structures remained a source of tension in transatlantic relations.[64] Yet, the American foreign policy decision-making during the Clinton era was often chaotic, as illustrated not least during the Kosovo crisis. In spring 1999, a bipartisan group of eleven House members, led by the Russian-speaking Curt Weldon (a Republican from Pennsylvania), agreed the basic principles of a settlement for Kosovo with members of the Russian *Duma* in Vienna. In appearance, at least, the initiative helped pave the way for a remarkably similar agreement initialled by the Group of Eight nations a week later. Yet, the Congressional foray was condemned by Under Secretary of State Thomas Pickering: 'Our efforts are not helped – indeed they are hurt – by uncoordinated, free-lance efforts at negotiating with Milosevic.'[65]

An even more dramatic illustration of Congress' role in an often mercurial process of foreign policy-making was a 1999 bill sponsored by Senators Mitch McConnell (Republican, Kentucky) and Joseph Lieberman (Democrat, Connecticut) to arm the Kosovo Liberation Army

63 W. Pfaff, 'Is Liberal Internationalism Dead?', *World Policy Journal*, 19:3 (1994) 5-15; T. Judt, *A Grand Illusion? An Essay on Europe* (London: Penguin, 1997).

64 M. Kahler, *Regional Futures and Transatlantic Economic Relations* (New York, Council on Foreign Relations Press, 1995).

65 For his part, Weldon insisted that he had closely coordinated his mission with the State Department (interview with the author, 30 September 1999). Another member of the delegation, Neil Abercrombie (Democrat, Hawaii), indicated that State had given the delegation 'conflicting signals' (quoted – along with Pickering – in *Congressional Quarterly Weekly*, 15 May 1999, p.1165).

(KLA), as an alternative to continued NATO airstrikes. McConnell reported 'stunned silence' when he first raised the idea at a White House meeting in March 1999. Cohen (the Secretary of Defense) roundly condemned the idea: 'the KLA doesn't qualify as any kind of choirboy circle. There are dangerous people in the KLA.'[66] Yet, the weekend prior to a diplomatic breakthrough to end the conflict – largely engineered by the EU's envoy (and President of Finland) Martti Ahtisaari – the Clinton administration signalled that it was seriously considering the option of arming the KLA and ending the NATO air campaign.[67] The reaction in European capitals was astonishment.

The NTA gave some cause for hope that a more intensified US-EU political dialogue could avoid such policy ruptures. Still, to many in Washington, the prospect of EU enlargement acted to reinforce the primacy of NATO: as the EU enlarged, the CFSP would become progressively more unwieldy and an ESDI more crippled by national divisions. One of the best arguments for reform of the CFSP in the 1996-97 IGC was that it was a prerequisite of reinforced transatlantic relations.

In the event, the Amsterdam Treaty contained several institutional innovations.[68] The creation of a new 'High Representative' for the CFSP (which offered the US its coveted 'one number to call in Europe') and a new Policy Planning and Early Warning Unit, had potential, at least, to boost transatlantic cooperation. The 1999 appointment of Javier de Solana, who earned considerable respect in the US for his performance as NATO Secretary-General during the Kosovo crisis, as the EU's first High Representative for the CFSP was widely welcomed in Washington. So was the appointment of Chris Patten – who was particularly well connected and respected on Capitol Hill – as the EU's Commissioner for external affairs.

---

66 Quoted in *Congressional Quarterly Weekly*, 17 April 1999, p.905.

67 Author's interviews in Washington D.C., 29-30 May 1999. An op-ed piece in the Sunday *New York Times*, a leading organ of US elite opinion, endorsed the policy shift despite the KLA's widely acknowledged links to organised crime and international terrorism. See Michael W. Doyle and Stephen Holmes, 'Two Visions for Kosovo', *The New York Times*, 30 May 1999.

68 See the chapter of Th. Frellesen in this volume, and J. Peterson and H. Sjursen (eds.), *A Common Foreign Policy for Europe? Competing Visions of the CFSP* (London and New York, Routledge, 1998).

Yet, the foreign policy role of Congress meant that new links between legislators became just as important as fortifying links between agencies or officials. The NTA's chapter on 'people-to-people' links acknowledged the need for a parliamentary dialogue that could channel the input of legislators into the NTA process, and a new Transatlantic Legislative Dialogue was launched in 1999.[69] But there remained far to go before the US and EU had an equivalent of NATO's North Atlantic Assembly, which brought together representatives of over forty political parties from sixteen NATO Member States, and a clear need to have one.

Conclusion

US-EU relations will require careful management in the early 21st century. Recent political changes in the US – rising economic populism, the downsizing of government, and the Republican seizure of Congress – make more and more serious bilateral disputes likely. Arguably, the US has become a more unreliable partner because, as a former senior Clinton administration official claims, 'there is no stable coalition in this country on foreign policy issues'.[70]

When Congress tangibly shapes foreign policy, it is often because an *ad hoc*, cross-party coalition challenges existing policy. During the Clinton era, Democrats were generally more critical of the administra-

---

[69] The Dialogue built on longstanding exchanges between the House (not the Senate) and European Parliament by establishing a beefed-up set of exchanges (biannual teleconferences, links between committees, and a dedicated web-site) and instituting regular exchanges between legislators and officials prior to US-EU summits. The European Parliament continued to be far more focused on and concerned with transatlantic relations than the US Congress. An EP declaration on transatlantic relations in early 1998 insisted that the NTA negotiating process had 'to be closely monitored by parliamentary bodies', that any decision to create a 'Common Transatlantic Area' should require EP assent, and that the Commission should report to the EP on the NTA on an annual basis. See European Parliament, 'Minutes of the sitting of Thursday, 15 January 1998: Part II – Texts Adopted by the Parliament', 1998, PE 265.060. Other illustrative examples of new 'people to people' links were the creation of a new transatlantic master's degree in public policy and a series of bilateral dialogues between small businesspeople, trades unions and representatives of 'civil society', such as consumer and environmental non-governmental organisations.

[70] Peter Tarnoff, the former Undersecretary of State for Political Affairs, quoted in *Public Affairs Report*, 40: 4 (Berkeley: Institute of Governmental Studies, University of California, July 1999).

tion's trade policy than Republicans. However, the election of a new generation of Republicans to Congress in the mid-1990s still constituted a sea change in the evolution of Congress' foreign policy role. Afterwards, far fewer of its members travelled abroad. Ten-second campaign commercials that chastised incumbents for going on foreign junkets became a familiar feature of US election campaigns. Many members of Congress, in the words of a Canadian trade minister, wore 'as a badge of honour [the fact] that they have never travelled outside the US'.[71] After his election as House Majority Leader in 1994, Dick Armey (Republican, Texas), confirmed that he had been abroad only once in thirteen years. Armey explained, 'I've been to Europe once and don't see why I need to go again',[72] adding that he would only travel abroad again to visit troops or for a good barbecue.

Such statements fuelled the impression that Congress had become isolationist and obstructionist on foreign policy. Yet, the actual record of Congressional input into policy debates reveals a different, more nuanced story. In 1999 Congress endorsed a bill to give the executive more discretion in applying economic sanctions to outlaw states, and exempting food and medicine from all sanctions.[73] One study of Congressional votes on trade bills in 1996-8 found that more than ninety per cent of Senators and Representatives tended to favour trade restrictions or trade subsidies or both. Yet, its author conceded that 'sentiment is against great initiatives to expand trade, but there is no momentum for protectionism either'.[74] In a major coup for the Clinton administration, Gephardt announced his support in 1999 for China's bid to join the WTO, arguing that 'this process should and must not be politicised', while playing wedge politics in warning that 'isolationism is on the

---

71 Sergio Marchi quoted in *Financial Times*, 9 September 1997.

72 Quoted in *Financial Times*, 28 July 1998.

73 Congressional Quarterly Weekly, 30 January 1999. Of course, pressure from agricultural lobbies eager to open overseas markets at a time of depressed crop prices was an important factor in Congress' support for excluding food embargoes on foreign countries.

74 Daniel Griswold of the Cato Institute quoted in *Financial Times*, 4 February 1999. His study, 'Free Trade, Free Markets: Rating the 105th Congress' is available from http://www.freetrade.org/pubs/articles/dg-2.9.99.html. It should be noted that the study's classification scheme reflected the strong ideological bent of the Cato Institute, with a vote for funding the IMF considered 'pro-subsidy' since 'IMF loans distort rather than enhance the global market economy'.

ascent in the Republican party'.[75] Even Dick Armey found a reason to go abroad: he toured refugee camps on the Kosovo border, as well as NATO headquarters and US air bases, as part of a nineteen member cross-party House delegation to Europe in April-May 1999.

More generally, defenders of Congress could argue that its foreign policy views, when aggregated, were broadly in accord with the American public's:

- A solid majority of Americans (sixty-one per cent) believed that the US should continue to play 'an active part in world affairs'.
- Clear majorities of Americans (about two-thirds) thought that the US should stay engaged in Europe and maintain NATO.
- Protecting the jobs of American workers' remained one the most important vital policy priorities for most Americans, although apprehension about economic competition from Europe (and Japan) generally fell during 1990s.[76]

Ultimately, the most important legacy of the 1990s was that US politics no longer 'stopped at the water's edge' as they did during the Cold War. More than ever before, Congress developed alternatives, many aggressively unilateral in thrust, to the executive's foreign policy. Yet, usually such alternatives were discarded before the US, finally, opted for cooperation over conflict. Even if Congress was, on balance, more a burden than a boon to transatlantic relations it remained true – just about – that the US continued to live up to Winston Churchill's maxim: 'America always does the right thing after exhausting all the available alternatives'.

As the 1990s ended, it was plausible to suggest that America had never been more engaged in Europe. NATO was more active in Europe and widely supported in America than had been possible to imagine in the early 1990s.[77] The US and EU were linked by a complex web of

75 Gephardt quoted in *Financial Times*, 29 April 1999. The House endorsed the extension of 'most-favoured nation' status to China in July 1999 despite Congressional concerns about abortion and human rights in China, as well as charges of espionage at US nuclear laboratories.

76 Protecting jobs ranked third as a policy priority, after preventing nuclear proliferation and stemming the flow of illegal drugs. All polling data in this section from Chicago Council on Foreign Relations, 'American Public Opinion', 1999.

77 For a flavour of earlier views, see I. Kristol, 'Who now cares about NATO?', *Wall Street Journal*, 6 February 1995.

trade and investment links, which were mostly untouched by political changes. The NTA significantly upgraded political, economic and 'people to people' links. Against the odds, and in spite of Congress, US-EU relations were in generally decent shape.

CHAPTER 6

The Role of Metropolitan Regions in Making a New Atlantic Community

Alan K. HENRIKSON

Tufts University, The Fletcher School of Law and Diplomacy

The French geographer, Jean Gottmann, long ago made an arresting conceptual distinction – 'iconography' (*iconographie*) versus 'circulation' (*circulation*) – that can be used to explain the role of metropolitan centers within larger social systems, not merely national systems, or continental systems such as Europe, but, it will be argued here, even the transoceanic system that is the Atlantic community. Although, in developing this distinction, Gottmann presumably had mainly the Paris of his youth and possibly even the new 'Megalopolis' of the United States in mind,[1] he did not himself use it to connect Europe and America in a single construct – as a theoretical bridge, as it were, for analysis of the transatlantic community relationship. The role of cities, or more exactly city-regions, as foci for Atlantic identification and for American-European exchange based in part on that identification has not yet been fully defined.[2] To begin to reconceive the Atlantic community more completely in these terms is the primary purpose of this chapter.

---

1 J. Gottmann, *La Politique des États et leur Géographie* (Paris, Armand Colin, 1952). Gottmann's 'megalopolis' concept was fully articulated by him in J. Gottman, *Megalopolis: The Urbanized Northeastern Seaboard of the United States* (Cambridge, Mass., The M.I.T. Press, 1961). His interest in the subject began during World War II when he was a member of the Institute for Advanced Studies in Princeton, New Jersey. In 1950 the director of the Institute, Robert Oppenheimer, suggested the actual term, 'megalopolis', in discussion. From R. A. Harper, 'Preface', in J. Gottmann and R. A. Harper (eds.), *Since Megalopolis: The Urban Writings of Jean Gottmann* (Baltimore, The Johns Hopkins University Press, 1990), ix.

2 Gottmann, who was very interested in what he called 'transhumance over the North Atlantic', was himself very much involved in the circulation of urban ideas therein. As he wrote, 'there exists one vast transatlantic orbit in which all the main planning policies, technological innovations, and methods of management are exchanged,

First, to explain Gottmann's terms. They are correlative and, taken together, are meant to be inclusive. 'Iconography' refers to the symbols, both concrete and abstract, that give a community its identity, that signify its history and values. The Arc de Triomphe and the Statue of Liberty would be examples, of icons of the physical type. 'Circulation' refers to the flows of people, trade, and information that give a community life. Circles of activity, on every scale, generate the material energy of a community and also its excitement. The traffic flowing to and from, and around, the Arc de Triomphe in Paris would be a physical expression of such circulation. So, too, would be the movement of ships in and out of New York harbor, and other boat traffic, under the gaze of the Statue of Liberty. Iconography is static; circulation is dynamic. Gottmann calls the one a '*principe de stabilité*' and the other a '*principe de mouvement*'.[3] Both the iconographic, or symbolic, factor and the circulatory, or energizing, factor are necessary for a community – a human community on any scale – to cohere and to grow. The centripetal and the centrifugal forces must be in balance.

Gottmann's own use of this polarity was confined, as noted, largely to the national scale. The creative interplay between iconography and circulation will here be applied on the intercontinental scale, between all of Europe and North America – especially, but not only, those parts of Europe and North America that are situated on or near, and are oriented toward, the Atlantic Ocean. A particular emphasis will be placed, from the perspective of the US side of the Atlantic, on *metropolitan regions*. 'Metropolitan regions' are amalgams of local, state, and even federal authority, and are also important economic concentrations.[4] Arguably, these concentrations – 'region states', Kenichi Ohmae calls them – are the most significant ones in the rapidly globalizing world economy of today.[5] On both sides of the Atlantic, clusters of cities and regions are coming to the fore. As the current US ambassador to France, the New York financier Felix Rohatyn, told the US Conference of Mayors, 'The most important

---

attempted, at least debated'. Gottmann, 'Transatlantic Orbits: The Interplay in the Evolution of Cities', in Gottman and Harper (eds.), *Since Megalopolis*, pp.257, 260.

3 Gottmann, *La Politique des États*, p.221.

4 On the evolution of metropolitan regions and the impact of political institutions on regional economies within the United States, see H. V. Savitch and R. K. Vogel (eds.), *Regional Politics: America in a Post-City Age* (Thousand Oaks, SAGE Publications, 1996).

5 K. Ohmae, 'The Rise of the Region State', *Foreign Affairs*, 72:2 (1993) 78-87.

thing that we can do now is to think about Europe in a new way – not just as a collection of nation-states, but as a single economic space filled with a constellation of dynamic cities and economic regions, of future customers and partners.'[6]

Termed 'global cities' by the sociologist Saskia Sassen, the major urban agglomerations in the world now are (1) 'command points' in the organization of the world economy, (2) 'key locations and marketplaces' for the leading industries (finance and specialized services for firms) of the current period, and (3) 'major sites of production' for these industries, which includes the production of innovations.[7] Other theorists, too, have noted that city-regions are 'fundamental spatial units of the global economy' and, prospectively, even 'political actors on the world stage.' Far from being 'dissolved away by processes of globalization', Allen J. Scott, John Agnew, Edward W. Soja, and Michael Storper observe, city-regions

---

6 F. Rohatyn, 'Cities, Embassies, and the New Europe', *The Ambassadors Review* [Council of American Ambassadors] (Spring 1999) 15-18. Ambassador Rohatyn noted that France had 'long recognized the importance of cities outside capitals', maintaining consulates in Los Angeles, Houston, Chicago, and seven other US cities. By contrast, there were only two American consulates in France, in Marseille and in Strasbourg – insufficient in number, Rohatyn considered, for a country of sixty million. Therefore he has developed a new approach called American Presence Posts (APPs), staffed from the US Embassy in Paris and supported by modern technology. The first APP was set up in Lyon, 'not only because it is France's second largest city, but because of its regional importance'. More than a hundred American firms are doing business in Lyon, and US trade with the region amounts to some five billion dollars a year. 'We as an Embassy are simply doing what American businesses do every day', Ambassador Rohatyn explains: 'we are following our customers – and we are restructuring ourselves to do it more efficiently.' See also C. R. Whitney, 'Anxious French Mutter as US Envoy Tries to Sell Globalism', *The New York Times*, 2 December 1999. Recognizing in France a nation that sees globalization as an American takeover threat, Rohatyn contrasted the outlook of French regions. 'In the regions, people think differently', he said. 'Toulouse is an aerospace city, a combination of Silicon Valley and Southern California, where business activity is paramount and where I think there is much more admiration for the American model and less of a distancing from it.' That week he opened an APP in Toulouse. In a parallel initiative, the US Embassy in Paris, with corporate support and with Ambassador Rohatyn's wife Elizabeth prominently involved, is linking regional museums in France with similar museums in the United States. See A Riding, 'France Joins US in a Push for Midsize Museums', *The New York Times*, 26 October 1999.

7 S. Sassen, *Cities in a World Economy* (Thousand Oaks, Pine Forge Press, 1994), p.4. See also S. Sassen, *The Global City: New York, London, Tokyo* (Princeton, Princeton University Press, 1991).

are 'becoming increasingly central to modern economic and social life'. Many global city-regions and the territories surrounding them are 'beginning to consolidate politically' in response to the search by local communities for 'region-wide coalitions' as a means of dealing with the threats and the opportunities of globalization.[8]

My hypothesis is that these vital metropolitan centers and their associated hinterlands can play a role *internationally*, well beyond the limits of state (provincial), national, or continental lines. They can engage in region-wide coalition-building that is transoceanic in scope. Moreover, they can do so *directly*, without the mediation of national governments or of international or supranational bodies. A phenomenon that Gottmann himself noted in his later writing was the '*expansion of the horizons* of urban activities'. In the first instance, this meant their 'geographical horizons'. In a novel trend, cities, even those that were not of the largest size, were increasingly able to communicate with the world beyond their hinterlands. In the past, Gottmann noted: 'The range of these relations seldom extended very far, unless the city was a political capital of substance, or a very active seaport.'[9] Today, most cities and their regions have, or can have, far-flung connections.

I shall further propose in this chapter, which will focus on the international role of US subnational units – cities, states, and, as mentioned, metropolitan regions – that these entities, and their connections with Europe, are an essential part of forming what has been called – usually from too much, on the US side, a national government perspective – a *new Atlantic community*.[10] In no sense is such a community to be thought of as separate

8 A. J. Scott, J. Agnew, E. W. Soja, and M. Storper, 'Global City-Regions' (conference theme paper), Global City-Regions Conference, hosted by the School of Public Policy and Social Research, University of California at Los Angeles, Los Angeles, California, 21-23 October 1999. The authors report: 'There are now more than three hundred city-regions around the world with populations greater than one million. At least twenty city-regions have populations in excess of ten million.' They project: 'By the year 2025, the number of city-regions in each of these sizes will probably have doubled.'

9 Gottmann and Harper, 'Introduction: The Opening of an Oyster Shell', in Gottman and Harper (eds.), *Since Megalopolis*, p.11.

10 This phrase was used, for example, by US Secretary of State Warren Christopher in an address at the State Theater in Stuttgart the 6 September 1996, 'A New Atlantic Community for the 21st Century', *US Department of State Dispatch*, 7:37 (1996) 449-52. In this speech, though focused mainly on NATO, Secretary Christopher declared: 'Closer political co-operation in the European Union, and its coming

from the existing Atlantic community, which is simply a social fact that has evolved over several centuries. It is not a 'parallel' community conceived by urbanologists. Nor is it in any way a formal body of some kind – a transatlantic Hanseatic League, perhaps, although that historic notion is suggestive of the idea here being advanced.

The 'new Atlantic community' that I envision is distinguished from older conceptualizations, such as the 'Atlantica' plan put forward in 1963 by former US Secretary of State Christian A. Herter,[11] by the high degree of plurality, or multi-centeredness, within it, and also by the non-hierarchical character of its structure, which is mostly informal. The concept implies a devolution of responsibility, as well as initiative, to non-central governments (NCGs) as well as to non-governmental organizations (NGOs) and also to business enterprises. The overarching structure of the North Atlantic Treaty Organization and the channel of regularized communication that now joins the United States government to the European Union would, of course, remain in place, for the coordination of overall defense and trade policy especially. But the locus of initiative would be more and more 'localized'.

'Communities' and 'Capitals'

A true 'community', on any level, may be distinguished, partially in opposition to the above-presented Gottmann model which does have an in-built centralist bias to it, by the norms of equality of status and opportunity for participation. Wide and general involvement is required, from the so-called peripheral areas of a society no less than from its center – its predominant metropolis or, on an international scale, its most powerful country. Any human community of whatever size, almost by definition, should have more than one 'center', lest it appear an 'imperial' structure, such as the French political system, strongly centered on Paris, has over the centuries appeared to many of its critics to be. The transatlantic relationship, too, has seemed to be an 'imperial' structure, with the United States, especially during the Cold War years, predomi-

---

enlargement, will contribute to the security and prosperity of the New Atlantic Community and strengthen the partnership between Europe and the United States' (p.451). As this indicates, most US official 'Atlantic Community' thinking has emphasized alliance or partnership formation at the federal, or highest governmental authority, level.

11 C. A. Herter, 'Atlantica', *Foreign Affairs*, 41:2 (1963), 299-309.

nating heavily as the leader of NATO.[12] Both examples of dominance, though inspiring in many ways, have been, from a community perspective, somewhat dispiriting.

The United States relationship with the European Union, by contrast, has developed much more along the lines of a 'partnership' of equals. This concept of community was most influentially articulated by President John F. Kennedy in what has been called his transatlantic 'Grand Design'.[13] In an address at Independence Hall in Philadelphia on 4 July 1962, he reflected upon the American system as one whose 'checks and balances are designed to preserve the rights of the individual and the locality against preeminent central authority'. As the effort for 'independence' in the world was approaching a successful end, a great new effort for 'interdependence', an idea embodied in the US Constitution, was beginning. This could most clearly be seen 'across the Atlantic Ocean' among the nations of Western Europe. A 'strong and united Europe', as President Kennedy foresaw it, would be 'a partner with whom we can deal on a basis of full equality in all the great and burdensome tasks of building and defending a community of free nations'. Forming 'the more perfect union which will someday make this partnership possible' would not be easy, Kennedy acknowledged.

> But I will say here and now, on this Day in Independence, that the United States will be ready for a Declaration of Interdependence, that we will be prepared to discuss with a united Europe the ways and means of forming a concrete Atlantic partnership, a mutually beneficial partnership between the new union now emerging in Europe and the old American Union founded here 175 years ago.[14]

---

12 D. P. Calleo characterized NATO as 'essentially an American protectorate for Europe' in D. P. Calleo, *Beyond American Hegemony: The Future of the Western Alliance* (New York, Basic Books, 1987), p.3. For an argument aimed at broadening the leadership function within the Atlantic Alliance, see A. K. Henrikson, 'Leadership, Cooperation, and the Contribution Principle', *NATO Review*, 42:6 (1994) and 43:1 (1995), 17-21.

13 J. Kraft, *The Grand Design: From Common Market to Atlantic Partnership* (New York, Harper & Row, 1962).

14 *Public Papers of the Presidents of the United States: John F. Kennedy, Containing the Public Messages, Speeches, and Statements of the President, January 1 to December 31, 1962* (Washington D.C., United States Government Printing Office, 1963), pp.537-39.

In this design the United States would be not only connected to but also counterbalanced by a consolidating Western Europe, thus ensuring the freedom as well as the force of Atlantic civilization.

In the development of the US-EU relationship, there has been much less integration than in the NATO context. The relationship between Washington and Brussels was not even made formal until the 1990 Transatlantic Declaration. This was not given much programmatic content until the 1995 New Transatlantic Agenda and Joint Action Plan which, however, boldly envisaged a practical, participant-oriented 'New Transatlantic Marketplace'. The main emphasis of the NTA/JAP was on trade relations rather than on governmental ties, at any level. Certainly relations between NCGs were not a leading agenda item. Nonetheless, in the last part of the JAP, 'Building Bridges Across the Atlantic', there is an explicit urban provision: 'encourage "sister cities" to promote exchanges'. Referring to the twinning *(jumelage)* of cities that had been occurring across the Atlantic, as well as within Europe, in the period since the Second World War, this reference, though brief and even seemingly perfunctory, was important. It provided a formal basis for future programmatic cooperation, as well as the prospect of funding for a more general dialogue of city authorities on both sides of the Atlantic. The NTA/JAP initiative also emphasized the role of the urban-based private business sector, which through the Transatlantic Business Dialogue had actively contributed in substance to the composition of the NTA/JAP.

Communities normally have capitals – in the case of nation-states, usually one. National capitals, which are in most cases the largest cities of countries, traditionally have governed Atlantic affairs. On the American side of the Atlantic, it has been Washington D.C., an artificial capital, and sometimes New York – taken together, the 'London' or the 'Paris' of the United States – that have separately or jointly dominated the transatlantic dialogue, especially with regard to political and financial matters.[15] It is here suggested that, in order for the Atlantic world to grow further together as a community, other important urban centers – regionally prominent seaboard cities such as Boston, Philadelphia, Atlanta, and Miami, as well as powerful cities in the interior of the country such as Pittsburgh, Cleveland, Detroit, and Chicago – should be

---

[15] On Washington and its wider relationships, including that with New York, see A. K. Henrikson, '"A Small, Cozy Town, Global in Scope": Washington D.C.', *Ekistics: The Science and Study of Human Settlements*, 50:299 (1983), 123-45, 149.

recognized for also having significant relationships with Europe. They can have leading functions too. Chicago was, for example, the location of the second conference, during 8-9 November 1996, of the Transatlantic Business Dialogue, the initial, organizing conference of this group of some three hundred American and European business leaders having taken place in Seville, during 10-11 November 1995. The 'capital', in the sense of the heading-function that is pertinent at the time, of the Atlantic community can shift, in the United States no less than in Europe, from one center to another, though the term does, of course, normally refer to political headship.

In some cases – for example, Boston, which will be discussed in more detail in a later section of this chapter – transatlantic involvement, even leadership of certain kinds, is historic, and actually the basis of the city's subsequent regional and national roles within North America. Its 'iconic' status and its 'circles' activity mutually interact in subtle and often effective ways, as will be further shown. A former Governor, William F. Weld, liked to call it the 'capital of the Atlantic Rim'.[16] Boston and Massachusetts have imagined themselves as a 'Gateway to America', not merely to New England.[17] America's East Coast urban centers, for some of which external networks have remained of even greater importance than their immediate regional connections, have performed what Gottmann has termed a 'hinge' function.[18] They have

---

16 'The Hub of the Rim', *The Boston Globe*, 3 February 1993, an editorial describing a meeting of Weld with *Globe* writers in which the then Governor speculated about, *inter alia*, the greater role that Boston ('a day's sail closer to Europe than any other American port') could again play in Atlantic transportation. See also W. F. Weld, 'Logan's Runway', *The Boston Globe*, 14 June 1999, in which he argued for expenditures to improve Boston's airport, commenting: 'And we are in a unique position – right here on the Atlantic Rim – to anticipate the needs of a united Europe and profit from them. Just look at the hay made by Los Angeles, San Francisco, and Vancouver during the Asian boom of the 1980s.'

17 *Boston and Massachusetts: Gateway to America* (Boston, Massachusetts Office of Travel and Tourism, n.d.).

18 For him, within the northeast-seaboard 'Megalopolis', New York and Boston 'with their international linkages' stand out in this way (Gottmann, 'Introduction', p. 14). See also Gottmann, *Since Megalopolis*, p.156. New England is even today more dependent on foreign trade than any other part of the United States. For careful and detailed analyses, emphasizing this geographic region's adaptation of itself to new global conditions, see J. Sneddon Little, 'New England's Links to the World Economy', *New England Economic Review*, (1990), 33-50, and J. Sneddon Little, 'Necessity and Invention:

helped to swing European and other assets – investments as well as immigrants – toward America. They also have been pivots – 'hubs' – for turning the interests of the United States abroad, connecting Americans directly with port and other gateway cities on other continents, in the first instance within transatlantic 'orbits' as Gottmann described these widening spirals of urban-centered activity.[19]

The participation of cities and their surrounding regions in transatlantic community building should be direct and strong, and largely unmediated by the hierarchies of national government or international organization. At the same time, overall structures such as that of NATO and the developing US-EU relationship, do provide some guidance and encouragement for transatlantic ties, including, as suggested in the 1995 US-EU Joint Action Plan, exchanges between 'sister cities'.

American NCGs and International Relations

The range of activities of American non-central governments – city, county, state, and also metropolitan-area authorities – is increasing, and now extends into what has traditionally been the preserve of 'international relations'. In 1956 President Dwight D. Eisenhower proposed a people-to-people program at a White House conference that would, in the words of Sister Cities International (SCI), 'involve individuals and organized groups at all levels of society in citizen diplomacy, with the hope that personal relationships, fostered through sister city, county and state affiliations, would lessen the chance of future world conflicts'. This made a 'national initiative' of a movement of American NCG overseas affiliating that had begun shortly after the Second World War.[20]

Trade in High-Tech New England', *Federal Reserve Bank of Boston Regional Review*, 3:1 (1993) 6-12.

19 Gottmann, 'Transatlantic Orbits', in Gottmann and Harper, *Since Megalopolis*, pp.257-59.

20 *Directory 1999-2000* (Washington D.C., Sister Cities International, 1999), p.2. Originally part of the National League of Cities, SCI became a separate non-profit organization in 1967. It currently represents 1,283 US cities, counties, and states and their 2,390 partners in 137 countries worldwide. 'Internationally', its statement says, 'SCI is part of a global network of organizations which utilize the concept of town twinning as a means to foster deeper cross-cultural understanding and worldwide co-operation towards sustainable economic and community development.' It is the leading US organization in the field.

Of the total of some 2,020 foreign cities that are affiliated with US cities under SCI auspices, the largest number, 723, are in Europe.[21] Initially, most of the European cities chosen by US cities as partners were in Western Europe. Today there are, for instance, 104 British cities, 105 French cities, and 157 German cities with linkages to US cities, in some cases with more than one. With the end of the Cold War, and the breakup of the Soviet bloc, there has been a remarkable enlargement of US sister-city linkage into the central, eastern, and southeastern regions of Europe, including some of the newly independent states that were part of the USSR. For example, there are 9 Czech cities, 8 Hungarian cities, 31 Polish cities, 25 Ukrainian cities, and 117 Russian cities that now have official ties with American city counterparts. The newest sister-city link between the United States and Europe is one that recently has been formed between Dayton, Ohio, and Sarajevo in Bosnia-Herzegovina, formerly part of Yugoslavia. This liaison follows, and may help to reinforce, the peace agreement for Bosnia-Herzegovina that was negotiated at Wright-Patterson Air Force Base near Dayton in November 1995. The Dayton-Sarajevo connection indicates that 'citizen diplomacy' at the city level can serve, and have, a political purpose as well as those of SCI's aims of cross-cultural understanding and sustainable economic and community development.

American states and territories, too, have engaged in politically supportive action. An example is the new involvement of US National Guard units, based in states, in advising, training, and otherwise assisting countries that once belonged to the Warsaw Pact. Called the State Partnership Program (SPP), this initiative of the National Guard Bureau, dating from 1993, consists of a series of partnerships between a host nation and an American state, approved by the US ambassador to the host nation, the Joint Staff, and the National Guard Bureau. Some twenty-one partnerships have now been formed between American states and countries in Central and Eastern Europe and the former Soviet Union. For example, Illinois is associated with Poland, Ohio is associated with Hungary, Pennsylvania is associated with Lithuania, Vermont is associated with the Former Yugoslav Republic of Macedonia, and

[21] For comparison, the other foreign-city partners of US cities are located in the following regions, with the numbers indicated: Africa, 91; the Middle East, 39; the Americas, 327; the Caribbean, 25; Asia and Oceania, 645; and the New Independent States, 170. These and the statistical data that follow were provided by Sister Cities International, 8 December 1999.

Georgia is associated with the Republic of Georgia. The stated purposes of the SPP are to demonstrate military subordination to civilian authority, to provide military support to civilian authorities, to assist in the development of democratic institutions, to foster open market economies to help bring stability, and to project and represent US humanitarian values.[22] In fact, current efforts being made in the former Warsaw Pact area by American states, not merely by their National Guard units, are contributing something to these ends.

The international presence of American NCGs abroad in the past has been limited mainly to the tasks of trade promotion, investment attraction, tourism diversion, and, to some extent, cultural and educational exchange. This representational and intermediary function is well understood and is becoming well documented.[23] Many US states, and also the Commonwealth of Puerto Rico, maintain overseas offices, though not always continuously and, increasingly, in Asia and also Canada and Mexico rather than in Europe.[24] The European market, however, is relatively stable, as well as large, and therefore likely to remain a primary American focus. In the early 1970s a Council of American States in Europe (CASE) was formed as a coordinating agency for the US states, perhaps now approximately thirty, that sponsor offices in Europe. With the help of CASE a series of 'USA Trade Days' have been held.[25]

It should be recognized that, in the field of international economic policy as distinct from business promotion, the role that subnational governments can play is distinctly subordinate. For the most part, they must be content with exercising their influence, which can sometimes be

---

22 United States European Command, State Partnership Program (SPP) [http://www.eucom.mil/programs/spp/_beta].

23 See E. H. Fry, *The Expanding Role of State and Local Governments in US Foreign Affairs* (New York: The Council on Foreign Relations, 1998), D. M. Brown and E. H. Fry (eds.), *States and Provinces in the International Economy* (Berkeley, Institute of Governmental Studies Press, University of California; Kingston, Ont.: Institute of Intergovernmental Relations, Queen's University, 1993), H. J. Michelmann and P. Soldatos (eds.), *Federalism and International Relations: The Role of Subnational Units* (Oxford, Clarendon Press, 1990), and E. H. Fry, L. H. Radebaugh, and P. Soldatos (eds.), *The New International Cities Era: The Global Activities of North American Municipal Governments* (Provo, David M. Kennedy Center for International Studies, Brigham Young University, 1989).

24 Fry, *The Expanding Role of State*, pp.68-70.

25 Fry, *The Expanding Role of State*, pp.75-6.

considerable, as 'lobbies', acting either on their own or working through such groups as the National Governors' Association (NGA), US Conference of Mayors, or National League of Cities. The NGA, for example, provided strong support for passage by Congress of the Uruguay Round multilateral trade accord, and has favored renewing the 'fast track' authority of the President to negotiate further trade agreements.[26] This effort, so far, has not succeeded, owing to protectionist sentiments in Congress and outside pressures upon it.

The US Constitution assigns power over foreign relations generally, including tariff collection and trade regulation, to the US federal government. In particular, Article I, Section 8, of the Constitution gives to Congress the 'power to lay and collect taxes, duties, imposts and excises' and 'to regulate commerce with foreign nations'. There is a prevailing constitutional doctrine regarding the conduct of foreign affairs of 'one voice' – that of the government in Washington. Though the coherence of this doctrine is being relaxed somewhat by judicial decisions and actual governmental practice today, it is still the constituted authorities of the federal government that 'speak for' the United States in international matters.[27]

Nonetheless, non-central-government public authorities – principally, governors and mayors – have distinctive and important functions that can have a bearing on the international relations, even political relations, of the United States, if not on its foreign policy proper. One of these is their role, which leaders and officials at the national level must share with them, as what I would call managers of the symbols of American community,[28] including local community. There are, historically and also in current times, important signs and values – in Gottmann's portmanteau term, 'iconography' – of Atlantic community.

Many of these, especially the more concrete ones, are very specific and local – in contrast, for example, with the American Declaration of Independence or the US Constitution, although we have seen how even

---

26 Fry, *The Expanding Role of State*, p.109.

27 See C. Tiefer, 'Free Trade Agreements and the New Federalism', *Minnesota Journal of Global Trade*, 7 (1998) 45-73. For a broader legal and historical commentary on the international role of NCGs, as well as NGOs and corporations, see P. J. Spiro, 'New Players on the International Stage', *Hofstra Law & Policy Symposium*, 2 (1998) 101-17.

28 The phrase is suggested by R. L. Merritt, *Symbols of American Community, 1735-1775* (New Haven, Yale University Press, 1966).

these are identified, as they were by President Kennedy, with a particular building in the City of Philadelphia. An 'icon of the physical type' mentioned at the outset to illustrate Gottmann's idea of the iconic stasis is the Statue of Liberty, an especially powerful Atlantic-facing symbol. Designed by a Frenchman and given by the people of France to Americans in 1884 to symbolize their common love of freedom, it also has a classical significance. The poet Emma Lazarus saw it as 'The New Colossus', an almost eternal and universal figure. Her words, 'Give me your tired, your poor,/Your huddled masses yearning to breathe free', were inscribed on a tablet at the base of the Statue in 1903, making it also a symbol of America as a refuge, a home for the oppressed, and an open society. No city in America is as self-consciously symbolic as the nation's capital, Washington, District of Columbia, which was actually designed in part as an iconographic city.[29] As Gilles Paquet has pointed out, a capital city is '*a pattern of symbolic resources*' – a 'terrain of realities' but also a 'theatre of representations'.[30] The point I wish to emphasize here is that the President himself, though constitutionally representing all of the people of the United States, acts somewhat as a local official when he refers to and interprets the symbols that are situated all around him. Iconography, it is important further to note, is not in America or elsewhere the preserve only of the government, of whatever level. It also can be wielded by others speaking from positions of public trust – a Martin Luther King speaking, as a private citizen, in front of the Lincoln Memorial, for example.

Increasingly, American subnational governments are showing an interest in building upon what I have termed their iconography and using it to expand their local communities' spheres of circulation, as well as their influence. By projecting 'identity', they hope to help find markets, draw investment, and even to exert political power. A 'law and order' leader, such as Mayor Rudolph Giuliani of New York City, emanates both values, of a kind, and sheer strength. In October 1995

---

29 M. C. Cummings, Jr., and M. C. Price, 'The Creation of Washington D.C.: Political Symbolism and Practical Problem Solving in the Establishment of a Capital City for the United States of America, 1787-1850', in J. Taylor, J. G. Lengellé and C. Andrew (eds.), *Capital Cities: International Perspectives = Les capitales: perspectives internationales* (Ottawa, Carleton University Press, 1993), pp.213-49.

30 G. Paquet, 'Commentary: Capital Cities as Symbolic Resources', in Taylor, Lengellé, and Andrew (eds.), *Capital Cities*, pp.271-85. See also, at pp.7-29 in the same volume, C. Raffestin, 'Une capitale est-elle une sémiosphère nationale ou le lieu de mise en scène du pouvoir?'.

Mayor Giuliani had his aides remove the Palestine Liberation Organization leader, Yasser Arafat, from a New York Philharmonic concert at Lincoln Center. Arafat was then in New York to attend the 50th anniversary commemoration of the United Nations, whose headquarters are located in the city by international agreement.[31]

The impact abroad of such assertion of local political values and personal sway can be powerful, comparable in effect to the symbolic actions of national leaders. The 'strong mayor' system of many US cities, including New York, has itself become a subject of debate elsewhere – notably, at present, in the United Kingdom where the current Labour government of Tony Blair is attempting to strengthen local government, in order to make it more visible and accountable as well as more effective. Powerful directly elected mayors in place of the traditional town councils, it is believed partly on the basis of American experience, would be better able to form public-private partnerships and to put together other novel coalitions, including intergovernmental and even perhaps international ones. Mayor Giuliani himself has been asked to comment on the initiative. Other American urban leaders, too, have been invited to contribute to the discussion. The Local Government Association (LGA) in the UK held a seminar in March 1999 in London, titled 'Models of Local Government: A Transatlantic Exchange', in which the mayors of Baltimore and Philadelphia and other senior US local government figures participated.

The scheme that has excited by far the greatest interest is the introduction of a 'mayor plus assembly' form of governance for the greater London region. The new mayor of London will be the first directly elected executive in the United Kingdom, and will have, by British standards, a massive constituency. The 4.9 million citizens entitled to vote will be a constituency, it has been pointed out by British urban expert Robin Hambleton, equivalent to that of the seventy-four London Members of Parliament. The London mayor 'will not surprisingly have a very high national and international profile – certainly a profile which will

31 D. Firestone, 'In Mayor's Arafat Snub, a Hint of Strategy', *The New York Times*, 26 October 1995, cited in Fry, *Expanding Role of State and Local Governments*, p.98. The PLO delegation evidently had been invited to the concert by the United Nations Protocol Office, but not by the local United Nations Host Committee. Subsequently the city informed the United Nations that the PLO and seven nations not recognized by the United States would be excluded.

make most politicians in Westminster green with envy'.[32] To some extent, this represents an Americanization of British municipal government and, as such, is seen by some as threatening. In the British context especially, such deliberate strengthening of local government, though the idea for this originates with the central government which may itself in fact be strengthened thereby, may work to upset the 'natural' order of things: local democracy and parliamentary supremacy too.

The purposeful engagement by local public authorities in international relations, in a connective and not just a comparative way, might generally be called *municipal diplomacy*.[33] This can include a wide variety of representational and other activities carried out abroad, or in dealing with foreign entities. *Municipal foreign policy* would be a suitable term for the even newer phenomenon of subnational authorities, speaking for city and state governments as well, declaring formal positions regarding controversial international issues.

To date, most of the controversial position-taking by non-central governments has concerned parts of the world or substantive issues other than those relating to Europe. This observation is illustrated by the agenda of the San Francisco-based Center for Innovative Diplomacy (CID), cofounded and directed by Michael H. Shuman, which built up a network of several thousand mayors and council members who were 'eager to influence international relations' through initiatives like anti-apartheid divestment, nuclear-free zones, sister-city relationships with war-torn villages in Nicaragua and El Salvador, and stratospheric ozone-protection ordinances.[34] Other subjects on which state and local gov-

---

32 *Directly Elected Mayors: Reinvigorating the Debate*, Discussion Paper (London, Local Government Association, 1999).

33 Ivo Duchacek, using a more complex nomenclature, chooses '*global microdiplomacy*', or '*paradiplomacy*', to refer to 'processes and networks through which subnational governments search for and establish co-operative contacts and compacts on a *global* scale, usually with foreign central governments and private enterprises'. He distinguishes this from '*transborder regionalism*', by which he denotes arrangements and networks pertinent to frontier areas, such as the US-Mexican or US-Canadian borderlands. See I. D. Duchacek, 'International Competence of Subnational Governments: Borderlands and Beyond', in O. J. Martínez (ed.), *Across Borders: Transborder Interaction in Comparative Perspective* (El Paso, Texas Western Press, 1986), pp.14, 17, and also his comprehensive *The Territorial Dimension of Politics Within, Among, and Across Nations* (Boulder, Westview Press, 1986).

34 M. H. Shuman, *Going Local: Creating Self-Reliant Communities in a Global Age* (New York, The Free Press, 1998), xi.

ernments, on the East Coast as well as the West, have taken a 'foreign policy' stands are the Vietnam War, relations with Cuba, the Arab oil embargo, the status of Taiwan, the rights of Puerto Rico, recognition of 'Macedonia', Swiss banking practices, and the Northern Ireland conflict.[35] Europe, as indicated, has generally not been the focus of subnational 'foreign policy' making. Probably it is the similarity of American and European perspectives on most world issues, owing to a common democratic ideology and human-rights orientation, that has caused the thrusts of US municipal foreign policy to be directed elsewhere – against the pre-Mandela governments of South Africa, for example.

This traditional orientation, however, could change with the controversy that has arisen, putting vast economic interests potentially at stake, over the Massachusetts 'Burma Law'. In 1996 the legislature of the Commonwealth of Massachusetts passed a measure to make its own procurement decisions dependent on a foreign-policy criterion – or, in its own view, simply a moral criterion. The Massachusetts law – not a flat prohibition and not discriminatory, as between US and non-US firms that may wish to sell to it – selectively restricts the ability of the Commonwealth and its agencies to buy from individuals or companies that trade with or invest in military junta-controlled Burma (Myanmar). Such vendors would have to offer their goods or services for ten percent less than competitors' prices in order for their offers to be considered.[36] This action of the Massachusetts Great and General Court aroused the ire not only of many American and other multinational firms, whose interests were involved, but also national governments, including that in Washington, and the European Union too. They feared mainly the possible precedent-setting effects of the law, which could prompt other subnational governments to do the same and could lead to similar selective-purchasing penalties against firms dealing with, say, Indonesia

---

35 For a concise review of many of these subnational 'foreign policies', see Fry, *Expanding Role of State and Local Governments*, pp.91-100.

36 The Act Regulating State Contracts with Companies Doing Business with or in Burma (Myanmar) of June 25, 1996, ch. 130, § 1, 1996 Mass. Acts 210, Mass. Gen. Laws Ann. ch. 7, 22G-22M (West Supp. 1997) (the 'Burma Law'). The Act was sponsored by State Representative Byron Rushing, an Afro-American legislator who had been active in the antiapartheid effort. For arguments favoring the Act's constitutionality, see J. P. Trachtman, 'Nonactor States in US Foreign Relations?: The Massachusetts Burma Law', *The Challenge of Non-State Actors: Proceedings of the 92nd Annual Meeting, The American Society of International Law*, 1-4 April 1998, Washington D.C., pp.350-58.

or even China – with market sizes much greater than that of Burma. Sir Leon Brittan, as Europe's Trade Commissioner, decided to take the matter, which raised the question of the adherence of the United States of America as a whole to its international obligations, to the World Trade Organization. Within the American governmental system, the Burma Law was brought under challenge in the US District Court for Massachusetts by a business group, the National Foreign Trade Council (NFTC). The European Communities and their Member States, as *amici curiae*, joined in this legal protest.

On 4 November 1998 the District Court judge upheld the NFTC's challenge to the Burma Law on the basic ground that 'State interests, no matter how noble, do not trump the Federal Government's exclusive foreign affairs power'.[37] The European complaint about not being able to rely on the word of the United States thus also was vindicated.[38] This was not the end of the matter, however, for the Commonwealth of Massachusetts appealed the decision. Thomas A. Barnico, the Assistant Attorney General handling the case for Massachusetts, said: 'Our law is consistent with US policy and, second, our law isn't the conduct of foreign relations, it's the conduct of our own purchasing.'[39]

Although the federal government itself has expressed similar sentiments, and against Burma has actually applied various sanctions (as it also has done against Cuba, Iran, and Libya), it had to object when sub-national governments 'meddle' in a complicated process, making it even more complicated. 'Decades of international experience have shown that sanctions are most effective when they are multilateral, precisely targeted, and applied with flexibility in terms of their scope and timing, especially in a negotiating framework,' argued Congressman Lee H. Hamilton, ranking Democrat on the International Relations Committee of the US House of Representatives. 'Sanctions applied at the local level meet none of these criteria. Instead, they typically do little harm to

---

37 C. Goldberg, 'Limiting a State's Sphere of Influence: Judge Rejects Law on Myanmar as Foreign Policy Infringement', *The New York Times*, 15 November 1998.

38 Ambassador Hugo Paemen, European Commission Delegate to the United States, had also weighed in on the matter by writing a letter to Governor William Weld stating that the Burma Law was a breach of WTO agreements and advising that it would have a 'damaging effect on bilateral EU-US relations'. Quoted in 'District Court Rules in Favor of NFTC – Finds Massachusetts Burma Law Unconstitutional', US-ENGAGE press release, 4 November 1998.

39 Goldberg, 'Limiting a State's Sphere of Influence'.

their intended targets, damage the interests of US businesses and workers, and may even diminish the leverage of our diplomatic institutions.'[40] This indeed was an essential part of the finding of the three-member US Court of Appeals for the First Circuit when on 22 June 1999 it affirmed the District Court's decision invalidating the Massachusetts Burma Law. 'Additionally', the Appeals Court judges wrote, 'Massachusetts' unilateral strategy toward Burma directly contradicts the federal law's encouragement of a multilateral strategy.'[41]

This decision, too, was unacceptable to the Massachusetts State government, which resolved to take the matter all the way to the US Supreme Court. Success in that venue, however, is unlikely. As the *Boston Globe* itself argued, quoting James Madison in *The Federalist Papers*, the Constitution vests all foreign relations powers in the federal government because 'if we are to be one nation in any respect, it clearly ought to be in respect to other nations'.[42] Nonetheless, the increase of state and local governmental foreign-policy expression, direct and unmodulated by the mechanisms of political representation at the center in Washington, is a powerful phenomenon, morally legitimate even if legally impermissible in some of its forms. More than twenty other states and local governments had passed statutes regarding Burma similar to that of Massachusetts. If reformulated as resolutions, rather than laws, they would make much the same point, even though their impact on multinational business operations might be less. Among the major American and international corporations that reportedly had cited the Massachusetts law as a reason for closing down their operations in Burma are Apple Computer, Levi Strauss, Eastman Kodak, Hewlett-Packard, and Philips Electronics. Simon Billennis, a senior analyst at a social investment firm named Trillium Assets Management in Boston, asserted that the First Circuit Court of Appeals ruling would, in essence,

---

40 Lee H. Hamilton, 'Local Interference With Foreign Policy', *The Boston Globe*, 9 November 1998.

41 National Foreign Trade Council, Plaintiff, Appellee, v. Andrew S. Natsios, in his official capacity as Secretary of Administration and Finance of the Commonwealth of Massachusetts, and Philmore Anderson, III, in his official capacity as State Purchasing Agent, for the Commonwealth of Massachusetts, Defendants, Appellents, No. 98-2304, United States Court of Appeals for the First Circuit, 22 June 1999. The Foreign Operations, Export Financing, and Related Programs Appropriations Act ('Federal Burma Law'), which was passed in 1997 after the Massachusetts Burma measure, contains the instruction to pursue a multilateral strategy with regard to Burma.

42 'No Freelance Foreign Policy', *The Boston Globe*, 1 December 1999.

'require state and local governments to do business with companies that support dictators'. Representative Byron Rushing, the main and most consistent legislative proponent of the Massachusetts Burma Law, said: 'If we had rulings like this in the 1970s and 1980s, the United States would not have been able to participate in the antiapartheid movement', and added: 'I am glad these judges weren't around then or Mandela might still be in jail.'[43] Sentiments such as these, as distinct from locally enacted and conducted foreign policy, will not be suppressed by a US Supreme Court decision.

The lessons of the Massachusetts Burma Law may not be learned without more interactions, not merely between governmental levels in the United States but also between continents. The most mutually influential of these intercontinental dialogues is surely the US-European one, in which NGOs as well as governmental organizations participate. There is a larger Atlantic social sphere. If more of the polities within the United States and European Union countries become interconnected, such 'foreign policy' debates as the one over the Burma Law are likely to be not just international, transatlantically, but interlocal as well.

Models of Integration for the Atlantic Community: From 'Federation' to 'Partnership' to 'Networking'

'Although the North Atlantic area has often been called a "community", it may not actually be one.'[44] This observation, made more than forty years ago by the political scientist Karl W. Deutsch and a group of his colleagues, emphasizes an important point, still valid: in order for an Atlantic community genuinely to exist, there needs to be a certain amount of 'integration'. By this term, Deutsch and associates comprehended the need for both common institutions and a 'sense' of community. Such transatlantic 'we-feeling' could not derive merely from verbal assent to a certain set of propositions or values – from formal declarations. It must involve as well 'partial identification in terms

---

[43] F. Phillips, 'US Court Overturns Burma Law: State Purchasing Law Ruled Unconstitutional', *The Boston Globe*, 23 June 1999.

[44] K. W. Deutsch, S. A. Burrell, R. A. Kann, M. Lee, Jr., M. Lichterman, R. E. Lindgren, F. O. Loewenheim and R. W. Van Wagenen, *Political Community and the North Atlantic Area: International Organization in the Light of Historical Experience* (Princeton, Princeton University Press, 1957), p.9.

of self-images and interests'.[45] The self-images that both reflect and shape a group's identity are closely associated with the iconography that both expresses and informs the group's unity, as Gottmann conceives of that term. A sense of community was also, as Deutsch *et al.* thought, 'a matter of a perpetual dynamic process of mutual attention, communication, perception of needs, and responsiveness in the process of decision-making'.[46] This idea of communication is closely akin to Gottmann's concept of circulation. 'Integration' is a fusion of these.

The Deutsch study, carried out in the mid-1950s, understandably was focused on the 'political community' of the North Atlantic – that is, on institution-building through NATO and the common sense that the Atlantic nations had regarding their own 'security'. Deutsch and the others drew a distinction between an 'amalgamated' security-community, in which previously independent units would merge into a single larger unit, or union, and a 'pluralistic' security-community, in which the nation-states of the Atlantic would retain nearly all of their legal independence and functional autonomy.[47] In the thinking of Americans who have favored a strengthening of the Atlantic community or, more briefly, Atlanticists, there has been a trend away from the 'amalgamated' model of transatlantic cooperation to more 'pluralistic' notions of working together.

In the period after the Second World War there was considerable intellectual interest in the idea of Atlantic *federation* – essentially, to replicate the formation of the United States of America on an international level, between the USA and the democratic countries of Western Europe.[48] American federal thought was an element in the climate of opinion within which NATO was created, although the actual North Atlantic Treaty of 1949, though more than a traditional alliance, was not

45 K. W. Deutsch, S. A. Burrell, R. A. Kann, M. Lee, Jr., M. Lichterman, R. E. Lindgren, F. O. Loewenheim and R. W. Van Wagenen, *Political Community and the North Atlantic Area*, p.36.

46 Deutsch, Burrell, Kann, Lee, Jr., Lichterman, Lindgren, Loewenheim and Van Wagenen, *Political Community*, p.36.

47 Deutsch, Burrell, Kann, Lee, Jr., Lichterman, Lindgren, Loewenheim, and Van Wagenen, *Political Community*, pp.5-7.

48 See, most notably, C. K. Streit, *Union Now, A Proposal for an Atlantic Federal Union of the Free* (New York, Harper, 1949).

a federalist text.[49] An Atlantic Convention of NATO Nations, a gathering of citizens under the chairmanship of former US Secretary of State Herter that occurred during 8-20 January 1962, produced a detailed blueprint ('Declaration of Paris') for constructing a 'true Atlantic Community'.[50] This document provided for an executive body, a permanent High Council, and a High Court of Justice. An Atlantic Economic Community was also projected. Though resulting from a connection between the United States and the European Economic Community (EEC), an Atlantic Economic Community would not be closed, but 'open to other nations of the free world'.

Such a grand Atlantic Community based on the NATO Nations, had such a plan ever been adopted, would have been highly centralized, as the very notion of a High Council makes clear. The North Atlantic Treaty Organization itself would be reinforced and developed 'as a political center', capable of acting in some areas by a weighted majority vote. In some noteworthy ways, however, the vision embodied in the Declaration of Paris was pluralistic. Its authors traced the origins of the 'magnificent civilization' that Atlantic peoples shared to its origins in the 'early achievements' of the Near East, the 'classical beauty' of Greece, the 'juridical sagacity' of Rome, the 'spiritual power' of religious tradition, the 'humanism' of the Renaissance, and also the 'discoveries' of modern science – a more universal flowering. The Declaration of Paris even included what, in the nomenclature of this chapter, could be termed an iconographic proposal: '*Reconstruction of the Acropolis*', and a decision to make it 'the symbol of our culture' and 'the shrine of our Alliance'.

From the 1960s a more realistic *partnership* model came to dominate transatlantic organizational thinking. The principal expression this idea was President John F. Kennedy's so-called Grand Design of 4 July 1962 which, as already mentioned, conditionally provided for practical discussion of 'a concrete Atlantic partnership' if and as Europe moved to perfect its union, to form an entity that could deal on an equal basis, in

---

49 A. K. Henrikson, 'The Creation of the North Atlantic Alliance', in J F. Reichart and S. R. Sturm (eds.), *American Defense Policy* (Baltimore, The Johns Hopkins University Press, 1982), pp.296-320; L. S. Kaplan, *The United States and NATO: The Formative Years* (Lexington, The University Press of Kentucky, 1984).

50 'Atlantic Convention of NATO Nations: Declaration of Paris', in C. A. Herter, *Toward an Atlantic Community* (New York, Harper & Row Publishers, 1963), pp.79-90. Subsequent quotations are also from this text.

Interdependence, with the United States, the 'old American Union'.[51] Such a transatlantic partnership of equals, for many US proponents of the idea, implicitly included Canada (accustomed to dealing with the United Kingdom, France, and the rest of Europe on its own) within the North American end of a kind of Atlantic barbell, with the major and minor powers on both sides of the ocean to be consolidated for a rough overall equivalence as 'North America' and 'Western Europe'. To multilateralist Canadians, this 'dumbbell' idea as it was sometimes called, for its intellectual content as well as it shape, was simply anathema.[52] Not only for this reason, most transatlantic 'partnership' diplomacy during the 1960s, 1970s, and most of the 1980s, was conducted between the traditional nation-states,[53] rather than novel continental blocs.

By the late 1980s, with the approaching end of the Cold War and, more particularly, the European progress toward forming a Single Market and US leadership in bringing about a North American Free Trade Agreement, the prospects of an Atlantic partnership of equals improved.[54] Both the United States and Canada concluded, almost simultaneously, parallel Transatlantic Declarations (TDs) with the European Community in 1990 which provided for regular summit and other meetings with Brussels counterparts.[55] This was followed in 1995, with the United States proceeding independently with Brussels, by the business-oriented NTA and JAP, with the thought of creating a New

---

51 *Public Papers of the Presidents John F. Kennedy, 1962*, pp.537-39. The Kennedy initiative followed, and presumably was to some degree a response to, a Joint Declaration of 26 June 1962 by Jean Monnet and other members of the Action Committee for the United States of Europe. The Declaration proposed a partnership between a united Europe and the United States that 'must not be merely economic. It is necessary that it should rapidly extend to the military and political spheres.' Quoted in G. Mally, 'Proposals for Integrating the Atlantic Community', *Orbis*, 9:2 (1965) 381.

52 J. W. Holmes, 'The Dumbbell Won't Do', *Foreign Policy*, 50 (1983) 3-22.

53 For an influential realist-political analysis, see H. A. Kissinger, *The Troubled Partnership: A Reappraisal of the Atlantic Alliance* (New York, McGraw-Hill, 1965).

54 R. Wolfe, 'Atlanticism Without the Wall: Transatlantic Co-operation and the Transformation of Europe', *International Journal*, 46:1 (1990-91) 137-63.

55 These documents – the Declaration on EC-US Relations of 23 December 1990 and the Declaration on EC-Canada Relations of 22 November 1990 – are analyzed and placed in international historical context in A. K. Henrikson, 'The New Atlanticism: Western Partnership for Global Leadership', *Revue d'intégration européenne/Journal of European Integration*, 16: 2-3 (1993) 165-91.

Transatlantic Marketplace.[56] While this keeps alive the tradition of a centrally directed partnership of equals between the old American Union and a new European Union that President Kennedy foresaw, there is reason for doubt whether, in a globalizing world and under a multilateral trading regime focused on the WTO, the American-European partnership ideal will remain viable.

The concept of integration that the Atlantic countries, including peoples as well as their governments, have today, a decade after the close of the Cold War, is very different. There is now little interest in formalistic schemes of international organization on the transatlantic level, such as proposals to constitute an Atlantic 'Federation' of some kind. Even the notion of an Atlantic 'Partnership', in any binding form, increasingly seems out of date. For various reasons, surely including the diminution of the sensed need for a security-community of any type with the end of East-West nuclear confrontation, populations of what used to be called the Free World are paying less attention today to national capitals, and their policies. Concomitantly, there is a rise of interest in the efficacy of organized regions and other non-central – or subnational – jurisdictions within countries.

The most impressive of these alternative non-central centers are the leading cities or, more precisely, metropolitan regions of the Atlantic world. These are beginning, as never before, to *network*, and to institutionalize networks. This is part of a more general, indeed global phenomenon that has been called the rise of the 'network society' characterized by the flows of information, and to some degree therefore also power, according to the logic of networking, in which there are no real centers but only nodes, or intersections of communication loops. 'Networks are appropriate instruments for a capitalist economy based on innovation, globalization, and decentralized concentration', argues Manuel Castells, a leading theorist of the subject.[57] In Europe, he writes, a 'network state' – a new interactive model of social governance – is arising. The Spanish-born, California-resident Castells sees the

---

56 The remarkable alteration in style, from declaratory to pragmatic, of US-EU cooperation during the early 1990s is discussed in A. K. Henrikson, 'Atlantic Diplomacy Transformed: From the Transatlantic Declaration (1990) to the New Transatlantic Agenda (1995)', paper presented at European Community Studies Association Fifth Biennial International Conference, Seattle, Washington, 29 May-1 June 1997.

57 M. Castells, 'The Rise of the Network Society', in *The Information Age: Economy, Society and Culture* (Oxford, Blackwell Publishers, 1996) Vol.1, pp.470-1.

'key element' that is enabling the European Union to establish its legitimacy without jeopardizing its policy-making capacity as 'the ability of its institutions to link up with subnational levels of government – regional and local – by a deliberate extension of the subsidiarity principle', according to which the Union institutions only take charge of the decisions that lower levels of government cannot assume effectively. Europe's new Committee of the Regions, an advisory body representing regional and local governments from all the countries of the Union, he regards as 'the most direct institutional expression' of this concern. 'The real process of relegitimization of Europe appears to be taking place in the burgeoning of local and regional initiatives, in economic development, as well as in cultural expressions, and social rights, which link up horizontally with each other, while also linking up with European programs directly or through their respective national governments.'[58] Does a similar network-derived social and even political morphology exist today in the United States, and the rest of North America? More particularly, with respect to the Atlantic community which is the focus of this chapter, does such a structure exist, or could it exist, in relations between America and Europe? There are signs of such a development.

One of the earliest was the privately initiated First International Congress on the Atlantic Rim, convened during 11-13 November 1994 in Boston, Massachusetts. This was a meeting of several hundred government leaders, municipal association officers, academic urbanologists, businessmen, journalists, and others mainly from the United States, Canada, and European countries who gathered to discuss, both comparatively and connectively, the urban and regional elements of Atlantic life. Washington and Brussels also sent representatives to speak, including Everett M. Ehrlich, Under Secretary for Economic Affairs in the US Commerce Department, and Alan Donnelly, chairman of the European Parliament Delegation to the United States. Coming from Norfolk, Virginia, Admiral Paul David Miller, the just-retired Supreme Allied Commander Atlantic (SACLANT) of NATO, also addressed the Congress. He had been responsible for the security of the Atlantic Rim area. 'In many ways, we face the break-down of a geographic sense of community', he reflected, attributing this in part to the effects of the information-technology superhighway. 'Without constructive intervention by responsible leadership, geographic community will be replaced by strati-

58 M. Castells, 'End of Millennium', in *The Information Age: Economy, Society and Culture* (Oxford, Blackwell Publishers, 1996) Vol.3, p.331.

fied societies, marginalized workers, and alienated citizens – if we let it happen.'[59]

During the Congress, the Declaration on the Atlantic Rim was read, and symbolically signed by Mayor of Boston Thomas M. Menino and distinguished persons from other continents all around the Atlantic basin. The document affirmed:

> We, the delegates to the First International Congress on the Atlantic Rim, meeting in Boston, Massachusetts, November 11-13, 1994, recognizing that primary building blocks of the new global economy are dynamic metropolitan regions, anchored by cities, that a strong Atlantic community requires international cooperation at all governmental levels, that networks and organizations exist on either side of the Atlantic which bring together city as well as state and provincial governments and which form the basis for transatlantic cooperation, that direct exchanges between enterprises, associations, and institutions, in addition to those between individuals and informal groups, are the most vibrant forces of the transatlantic relationship, that explicit partnerships between public authorities and private entities in selected areas can demonstrate new ways of generating economic growth and other innovative and productive activity, and that, although centered on the Atlantic maritime area, the wider regionalism of the entire Atlantic sphere, extending northward and southward as well as eastward and westward, should be open and expressly welcoming to relations with other parts of the world. Hereby declare our intention to work together through existing networks and organizations to establish an Atlantic Rim Network, a center and a program of information exchange and practical cooperation, to function within the framework of principles contained in such previous transatlantic statements as the 1949 North Atlantic Treaty, the 1990 Charter of Paris for a New Europe, and the 1990 Transatlantic Declarations between the European Community and the United States and Canada.[60]

The notion of 'dynamic metropolitan regions, anchored by cities',[61] referred to in this text is vital to forming a new Atlantic community, in the more egalitarian, encompassing, and energetic sense being discussed

---

59 Remarks by Admiral Paul David Miller, USN (Ret.), at the First International Congress on the Atlantic Rim, Boston, Mass., 12 November 1994.

60 Declaration on the Atlantic Rim, presented by Professor Alan K. Henrikson, in an introductory statement for the First International Congress on the Atlantic Rim, 'Creating an Atlantic Rim Network: A New Framework for Transatlantic Cooperation', Boston, Mass, 11-13 November 1994. Local newspaper accounts of the Congress included E. Hayward, 'Hub Mayor & Reps From 20 Nations Start Work on Atlantic Rim Network', *Boston Sunday Herald*, 13 November 1994, and J. Ellement, 'Boston Named Trade Center', *The Boston Sunday Globe*, 13 November 1994.

61 The phrase is that of James H. Barron.

in this chapter. The Atlantic Rim Network (ARN) – a small-scale effort conceived of as a 'network of networks' rather than a new and separate body – that resulted from the Boston Atlantic Rim Congress is illustrative of the 'Networking' model of Atlantic integration. At the meeting an exhibition and brochure, *The Evolving Atlantic Rim*, presented in a semi-abstract graphic way the elaborate criss-cross and circular system of lines that the 'global sub-region' of the Atlantic had become from the age of sail through the age of flight to the age of the satellite and the computer. Thus to build a conceptual framework for the Atlantic Rim would be to 'redefine and re-engineer a traditional region within the context of new global realities'.

Within such a framework, a private local effort such as the ARN is less a center in its own right than a node in an expanding communications web. However intrinsically modest they may be, spontaneous networking initiatives of this kind can bring together people, often representing organizations, who would not otherwise meet, and form links, complex ones, that may last and spread.[62] Existing ties can be strengthened. In the case of the First International Congress on the Atlantic Rim, persons were present or contributed in other ways who belonged to, on the American side, the US Conference of Mayors, the National League of Cities, and many individual municipalities and, on the Europe side, Eurocities, the Club de Eurométropoles, Telecities, the Commission Arc Atlantique, the Union of Portuguese-speaking Capital Cities, Telecities, many single cities, and the International Union of Local Authorities, with headquarters in The Hague but liaisons worldwide. At the Congress in Boston, conversations were started regarding, *inter alia*, a new computer network linking European ports, designed to help assure the fullest use of space aboard ships calling there, and the possibility of making a connection to American ports, which could be joined by a similar network.[63] The main organizer of the event and founder of the Atlantic Rim Network, James Barron, emphasized: 'These just aren't

62 This chapter itself is in part a result of 'linkage' formed by work on the Atlantic Rim Congress.

63 J. Ellement, 'Boston Named Trade Center', *The Boston Globe*, 13 November 1994. Informed of the European port computer network by Alan Donnelly, Paul Cronin of the Massachusetts Port Authority reportedly said that he told Donnelly that Massport would be willing to establish a US version of the network. Massport and other US port authorities, and a number of their counterparts in Canada and Mexico, belong to the American Association of Port Authorities.

sister cities, but strategic regions with expanded economic bases that can link together for trade and economic development.'[64]

In the rush to accept a 'networking' model for the Atlantic, a strong word for traditional symbolism – for iconography, in Gottmann's sense – is in order. A community is more than circulation, or traffic in goods and data flows or even the transit of people. It must have structure, an iconographic framework to provide a guide for cooperation, to make it meaningful. A sea-focused community particularly, because (unlike a land-based social sphere) it is basically featureless,[65] must have an ideographic design. Given that an overarching 'Federation' structure for the Atlantic world is not politically or even intellectually easy to imagine today, an Atlantic pattern must be of some kind other than the constitutional-legal. A formalized 'Partnership' as a basis for Atlantic cooperation also is unlikely to carry much conviction, particularly outside the circle of political leaders and government officials. A mere 'Network', too, is inadequate. Yet a community-pattern is needed to provide coherence. Such a guide-plan, like one for an individual city, must be relatively 'readable', so as to be recognizable by all of a community's participants.[66] A new Atlantic community needs a 'mental map' of itself.[67] Modern networks of sea and air transport and, especially, electronic telecommunication are too complicated, shifting, and, essentially, imageless to provide a stabilizing symbology for such a community.

---

[64] E. Hayward, 'Hub Mayor & Reps From 20 Nations Start Work on Atlantic Rim Network', *Boston Sunday Herald*, 13 November 1994.

[65] It can be noted, however, that the most-used shipping lanes are well defined. The maritime historian Paul Butel writes: 'The "track" – the route from New York to western Europe – is by far the most important of these axes, running from the entrance of the English Channel to the east coast of the United States, passing southern Newfoundland.' P. Butel, *The Atlantic* (London, Routledge, 1999) p.293.

[66] The classic development of this idea of the 'readability', or imageability, of a geographic community, though limited to the urban scale, is K. Lynch, *The Image of the City* (Cambridge, The M.I.T. Press, 1960).

[67] On the 'mental map' concept, derived in part from the work of Kevin Lynch but applied to international relations, see A. K. Henrikson, 'Mental Maps', in M. J. Hogan and T. G. Paterson (eds.), *Explaining the History of American Foreign Relations* (Cambridge, Cambridge University Press, 1991), pp.177-92.

The Critical Role of Metropolitan Regions in Terms of Symbols and Communication: Iconography and Circulation Brought Together

European cities – 'The Museum', as they and the whole continent of Europe are too-easily sometimes collectively called – are rich in iconography. They are, in the nomenclature of the historian Pierre Nora, '*lieux de mémoire*',[68] and are indeed relatively past-oriented. The designation by the European Union since 1985 of different cities in member countries, on a regular and rotating basis, as European 'Cultural Capitals' is testimony to the awareness among Europeans of all nationalities of the value and vivacity of their shared heritage. Much of this is located in, and identified with, cities. In the year 2000, for example, the Polish city of Krakow is a European Cultural Capital – because of its large student population, described in *Europe* magazine as 'the Boston of the country'.[69] Especially now, in the still-unsettled aftermath of the Cold War, when it is necessary to find unifying symbols that can rejoin the eastern and western wings of European civilization – to rebuild a common sense of 'Europeanness' after the political, economic, and cultural ravages of communism and the internecine violence of the former Yugoslavia – the identification of 'icons' on which all or most Europeans can 'agree', thereby orienting and also reassuring themselves as a human society, is profoundly important.[70] So too, in a wider way, is it important to reconstitute the meaning of the 'West' – or, as here preferred because of its stronger reference to a geographic sense of community, 'Atlantic' civilization.

America – the New World – itself also has numerous stabilizing as well as identifying cultural symbols. Many of those, too, are located in and associated with cities. States, though they too have images, are somewhat less salient in this respect. Contrast, for example, the sobri-

---

68 P. Nora, 'Between Memory and History, Les Lieux de Mémoire', *Representations*, 26 (1989) 7-25.

69 V. Gould Stoddart, 'Krakow: City of Jazz, Poetry, and Popes', *Europe: Magazine of the European Union*, 391 (1999) 34-5.

70 This was one of the purposes of 'On Gottmann's Footsteps: The European Iconographies – Representations, Ideologies, Territories, Geopolitics', Annual International Conference of the Commission on Political Geography and the Commission on the World Political Map, University of Paris-Sorbonne, Paris, 7-9 October 1996.

quet of Philadelphia, the 'city of brotherly love', and that of Pennsylvania, the 'keystone state'. The significance – the manifold importance – of this cultural symbolism has not been at all adequately appreciated. Cultural symbols are not simply a matter of local pride or, taken all together, of a nation's identity. It is coming better to be appreciated that they are also assets having a considerable economic value, though it is not only on economic or, more narrowly, balance-sheet grounds that their worth to society must be justified.

In Europe, especially, urban culture and city economies are almost inseparable, and together constitute much of the wealth of the continent. 'Around eighty per cent of the European Union's population lives in urban areas', pointed out Bruce Millan, an EU Commissioner for Regional Policy.[71] In America too, though people are less concentrated, urban and suburban living has become the dominant place and mode of residence.[72] The United States at the turn of the century is no longer essentially a rural society. The relative amorphousness of suburban sprawl has begun to make many suburbanites, hitherto accused of being 'isolated' and self-protective, more inclined to appreciate the figurative force as well as material power of a culturally and commercially thriving urban center, or sometimes centers, at the core of the region in which they live. Heritage, in short, counts.

Some recent studies of business enterprise and economic growth have revealed a close correlation of economic vitality and urban-cultural development, with the most relevant unit of analysis being the region. The result may be a new focus on 'interregional' world trade.[73] As already noted, Kenichi Ohmae draws attention to the 'region state' as a dynamic factor.[74] Michael Porter argues: 'Competitive advantage is

---

71 B. Millan, 'The Urban Dimension in European Union Policies', *European Urban Management*, 1 (1994) 8-11.

72 Even when residing in the city, Jean Gottmann noted, Americans have a different preference from those of urban-based Europeans. 'In the United States, the middle class has always preferred to live *uptown* while working *downtown*. Not so in Europe.' Gottmann, 'Transatlantic Orbits', in Gottman and Harper, *Since Megalopolis*, p.266.

73 On the importance of developing a new theory of 'interregional trade', see A. K. Henrikson, 'The US "North American" Trade Concept: Continentalist, Hemispherist, or Globalist?', in D. Barry, with M. O. Dickerson and J. D. Gaisford (eds.), *Toward a North American Community? Canada, the United States, and Mexico* (Boulder, Westview Press, 1995), pp.155-83, especially pp.174-9.

74 Ohmae, 'The Rise of the Region State'. See also his *The Borderless World: Power and Strategy in the Interlinked Economy* (New York, Harper Business, 1990).

created and sustained through a highly localized process.'[75] Paul Krugman suggests: 'If we want to understand differences in national growth rates, a good place to start is by examining differences in regional growth; if we want to understand international specialization, a good place to start is with local specialization.'[76] Peter Karl Kresl has stressed the critical role that urban centers can play in facilitating (or, sometimes, frustrating) the changes that are produced in the economic structures and balances of a nation, or group of nations, during international trade liberalization.[77] 'Region states' in this sense are political forces as well as economic ones. This phenomenon of metropolitan region-led (or, sometimes, metropolitan region-blocked) economic change appears to be both American and European in incidence – indeed, Atlantic in scope.[78]

Most of these studies concentrate on economic processes at work in urban centers, but they generally reflect as well an appreciation of the attractions of cities as such, of their cosmopolitan qualities. It is mostly in and around cities that knowledge-workers – the producers of the information age – are found. In order to be and to feel 'world class', as Rosabeth Moss Kanter observes, such workers, either employed by or themselves starting up businesses that can compete abroad, no longer have to live in the very largest cities, notably in New York. Although 'great companies can start anywhere', she posits, there usually is some degree of local linkage, *i.e.* a specific benefit that derives from the urban-regional setting of reasonably large size that fosters a successful company. She notes, by way of illustration: 'Boston's unique advantages are in software, health care, and telecommunications; Miami's is in international trade.' Even companies in the Boston and Miami metropolitan areas that are not in those particular sectors can benefit from their physical location and socio-cultural locale. 'World-classness' thus inheres in the place as well as in the producer. 'For a place to be world

---

75 M. E. Porter, *The Competitive Advantage of Nations* (New York, The Free Press, 1990), p.19.

76 Paul Krugman, *Geography and Trade* (Cambridge, The M.I.T. Press, 1991), p.3.

77 P. K. Kresl, *The Urban Economy and Regional Trade Liberalization* (Westport, Greenwood Press, 1992).

78 See N. R. Peirce, *Citistates: How Urban America Can Prosper in a Competitive World* (Arlington, Seven Locks Press, 1993), and, for a European perspective, L. H. Klaassen, L. van den Berg and J. van der Meer (eds.), *The City: Engine Behind Economic Recovery* (Aldershot, Avebury, 1989).

class, it must feature a concentration of skills that are hard to uncouple from local assets – for example, colleges and universities in Boston, Latin American experts in Miami.'[79]

What is not sufficiently recognized in such business studies are the non-economic, particularly the symbolic, roles of the elements that give an urban setting the value it has, for those who live there and often for others, visitors and simply admirers, as well. These – the 'icons' of community – are essential for making it more than a local marketplace or communications center – a platform for 'circulation'. Urban values are more than 'magnets', to get executives, scientists, and other needed employees to migrate, or tourists to come. Their inherent content, appreciated inwardly at a personal level, may be difficult to analyze, but it is essential. Both within and from afar, the 'image of the city', in urban planner Kevin Lynch's phrase,[80] reflects a community's spirit and helps it to form purposeful, as well as profitable, relationships with other, distant communities, including counterpart communities abroad. Here it may be noted that sister-city relationships, though they may not initially have been established for strategic-economic reasons, usually are based on a careful and genuine regard for congruent symbology, as well as size comparability. The new twinning relationship between Dayton, Ohio, and Sarajevo, Bosnia-Herzegovina, is a vivid case in point.

Transatlantic 'Sub-Area of Integration': The Case of Boston and Northern Ireland

Some US cities are more 'meaningful', as distinct from being just 'imageable', than others, in part simply because they are older and more storied. Imageability alone can be just a matter of architectural profile, which New York City has on a scale above all others, either in North America or in Europe. New York's skyline image may be, if anything, more distinct for Europeans than it is for Americans, whose mental picture of the city is mediated by the desultory images of the landward

---

79 R. M. Kanter, *World Class: Thriving Locally in the World Economy* (New York, Simon & Schuster, 1995), pp.31-2. Professor Kanter cites, as examples of relatively loosely 'linked' individual companies, two large office-supply superstore chains, Staples and Office Depot. 'It would be easier for Staples to leave Boston than for an advanced technology firm; easier for Office Depot to leave south Florida than for a Latin American exporter' (p. 32). But these, too, find their respective environments generally advantageous for doing business, or congenial, and stay.

80 Lynch, *The Image of the City*.

approaches to the city. The seascape affords a greater contrast. The purely visual image of a city is, of course, important in forming an overall concept of it. In this respect, Boston, without an elevated profile and a harborfront that is only now being consciously redone, is distinctly inferior. Gottmann's idea of 'iconography', of course, involves much more than a city's physical aspect. The term connotes its entire projection, the shape of its 'idea' in every sense – architectural, economic, social, political, and even moral.

How does one know, precisely, what an urban community *stands for*, especially to others? The City of Boston, generally regarded as 'the most historic city in America',[81] stands in its own mind for a series of serious purposes. It appears to be recognized abroad, too, for its legacy of commitments – including current involvements, such as defense of the Massachusetts Burma Law. Of course, it is regarded as having a certain fusty charm as well – 'a baby London', perhaps.[82] Europeans, more than any other foreigners, find it semi-familiar, and a natural way to become introduced to the less 'European' rest of the USA.[83] It is arguably the country's foremost Atlantic City. A capsule of its history will testify to its iconography, which sometimes interferes with the growth of its circulation but can also enhance the development of it. The new Boston connection with Northern Ireland illustrates this, as well as perhaps a more general pattern of possible transatlantic integration of 'sub-areas'.

In the 17th century, Boston was a 'City Upon a Hill', a radiant theocracy. In the eighteenth century, it became the 'Cradle of Liberty', a hotbed of revolutionary ideas and agitation. This libertarian tradition continued into the 19th century, in the abolitionist movement of the Civil War period. Boston then also became the 'Athens of America' – the seat of American learning and philosophy, notably Transcen-

---

81 R. W. Apple, Jr., 'In Boston, a Boom and New Hurrahs', *The New York Times*, 29 January 1999.

82 R. W. Apple, Jr., 'In Boston, a Boom' and J. Thomas, 'An Ode to Boston: Swiss Recognize Charms We've Always Cherished', *The Boston Globe*, 26 January 1995, reporting a Swiss study that judged Boston as the American city having the highest 'quality of life'.

83 R. Doman, 'Bay State is Hot Spot With Overseas Visitors', *The Boston Globe*, 24 June 1996, noting that approximately two-thirds of foreign visitors to Boston come from western Europe, the largest numbers coming from the United Kingdom, followed by Germany.

dentalism. This image of the city as a reflective place of enlightenment had a particular architectural focal point: the now-gilded dome of the state capitol building on Beacon Hill. 'Boston State-House is the hub of the solar system', declared Oliver Wendell Holmes, Sr.[84] 'It was a symbol of our statehood', says a present-day historian of the city, Thomas O'Connor, of the Charles Bulfinch-designed dome. 'It has always struck me as the logo of Boston.'[85]

The traditions of literary Boston continued into the 20th century, in the institutional form of the Boston area's more than sixty colleges and universities as well as its many libraries and museums. With the highest percentage of students in its population, the city became the nation's 'College Capital'.[86] Its ethnic composition has changed too. Owing to a recurrent stream of Irish immigrants in particular, Boston became a place of 'Celtic pride', initially in church matters and in politics and now also in business – and, of course, in sport (the Celtics basketball team, with occasionally a few Irish names on the roster). The city's large Irish component has powerfully shaped its history and identity and, most

84 G. A. Sala, 'Introduction' in O. Wendell Holmes, *The Autocrat of the Breakfast Table* (London, John Camden Hotten, 1871), p.98. It is not widely remembered that Holmes added: 'The satire of the remark is essentially true of Boston, and of all other considerable and inconsiderable places with which I have had the privilege of being acquainted.' He explained: 'The axis of the earth sticks out visibly through the centre of each and every town or city.'

85 D. Aucoin, 'Dome in Decline: Massachusetts Landmark is in a Shambles, and the State's in no Hurry to Fix It', *The Boston Globe*, 15 February 1997. The notion of a city or state 'logo', or 'brand' image, today is a matter of intense commercial as well as cultural interest. Governments now engage in advertising. C. Reidy, 'Ads Aim to Turn Stodgy Hub Into More of a Hubba-hubba', *The Boston Globe*, 12 November 1999. At stake for New England, particularly, are tourist expenditures by British and other European visitors, as the recent economic turmoil in Asia has curtailed Asian traveling. The competition for the large number of British tourists, particularly richer younger ones, is keen. 'They view us as safe and civilized. They see the rest of America as wild, exciting, and sexy', observed Patrick B. Moscaritolo, chief executive of the Greater Boston Convention and Visitors Bureau. As a result, the Massachusetts Port Authority had developed what it calls 'the body-parts ad', according the Massport international marketing director Charles Yelen. 'And so', writes the *Globe*'s reporter, 'the image of New England as the land of the bean and the cod and the scarlet letter is giving some leeway to Boston, land of the hot bod and the red bikini.'

86 C. Goldberg, 'Moving-Madness Holiday in Nation's College Capital', *The New York Times*, 4 September 1999; A. Noble, 'Boston Loses Reputation as Best College Town to New York City: Dean of Admissions Defends Boston as Center of Education', *The Observer* [Tufts University], 21 October 1999.

importantly for the purpose of this chapter, its outward orientation and connections with the world. These are mostly transatlantic, despite a historic involvement in the China trade and continuing strong ties with Japan (*e.g.* Boston's sister-city link with culturally rich, similarly 'iconic' Kyoto and the Museum of Fine Arts' more commercial new arrangement to share its collections with Nagoya). The proper-Boston historian, Walter Muir Whitehill, wrote admiringly of Boston's emergence as a major city in 'the Age of John Fitzgerald Kennedy'.[87]

Boston holds, in fact, the largest community of Irish-Americans in the United States – viewed in Ireland as its largest 'colony'. It remains 'the most Irish of America's cities'.[88] Psychogeographically, the distance between many of its citizens and the Emerald Isle – and vice versa – is very short. The Northern Irish political leader John Hume, who grew up in Derry, noted in an interview, 'As we say in Derry, "The next parish is Boston."'[89] These connections between America and Ireland, sentimental and symbolic as well as commercial and political, have been aided by the availability of direct air access and also the telecommunications revolution. Thus contact is easier. Visits even at the top level of government have become common. Professor Mary Robinson, when President of Ireland, during a visit to Boston, which she likened to 'a visit home', spoke of the sense of 'Irishness' among a *diaspora* of some seventy million worldwide and urged those living in Ireland to use that sense as a basis of tolerance and peace.[90]

No doubt President Robinson's lesson also was intended to dissuade those Irish-Americans, in Boston and elsewhere in the country, who might be inclined to give support to the cause of the Irish Republican Army. In truth, there has been such support for the IRA, but, mainly and more recently, the contribution of Irish-Americans has been positive. A

---

87 W. M. Whitehill, *Boston in the Age of John Fitzgerald Kennedy* (Norman, University of Oklahoma Press, 1966). Cf. Apple, 'In Boston, a Boom and New Hurrahs'. *The New York Times*' Apple observes: 'For almost half a century, from the 1920's to the 1960's, Boston was a backwater of sorts, subsisting largely, it seemed, on memories. But the Kennedy Presidency, starting in 1961, brought new attention to the city.' The John F. Kennedy Presidential Library and Museum, designed by I. M. Pei, is located on Columbia Point in Boston harbor.

88 D. Aucoin, 'This Enduring Eire Hub', *The Boston Globe*, 17 March 1996.

89 'John Hume: Northern Ireland Peacemaker', *Europe: Magazine of the European Union*, 348 (1995) 12-15.

90 K. Zernike, 'Irish President Likens Hub to Home', *The Boston Globe*, 7 October 1996.

sizeable amount of investment in the business future of both Northern Ireland and the Irish Republic coming from Boston sources has helped to affirm the Irish peace process.[91] It is further helping to consolidate the 1998 Good Friday Agreement that a former US Senator from Maine, George Mitchell, facilitated. The contributors to an organization called the International Fund for Ireland have invested in numerous Irish high-technology companies, some of which are business partners with firms in New England. In June 1999 the current Governor of Massachusetts, Paul Cellucci, led a trade mission to Belfast and Derry 'to boost the peace process', he said.[92] Boston Mayor Thomas Menino himself led a mission in November, following which two participants wrote: 'We are proud to live in a city that has played a big role in stimulating business investments and job creation in Northern Ireland.'[93]

Even the Maritime region of Canada, representatives of which participated in the 1994 Boston Atlantic Rim Congress, has entered into this non-central, subnational collaboration. In November 1997 the City of Boston, represented by Mayor Menino, concluded 'a three-way,

---

[91] The pacific purpose of this business investment in Ireland, north and south, usually is made explicit. See, *e.g.* F. Costello, 'Keeping Peace Alive in Ireland', *The Boston Globe*, 3 May 1995; Costello is chairman of Boston Ireland Ventures. American 'moral' support for Ireland has taken other forms as well, including application by local and state governments of the MacBride Principles (modeled on the Sullivan Principles concerning business relations with South Africa in the apartheid period) prescribing boycott action against firms operating in Northern Ireland that provably discriminate against Catholics in employment. 'More Cities Sign on to MacBride Principles', *Bulletin of Municipal Foreign Policy*, 3:3 (1989) 33-4. As the WTO Agreement on Government Procurement (GPA) requires countries to purchase goods and services on the basis of only price and performance criteria, the international-legality of state and local government adherence to the MacBride Principles, as well as other preferential-purchasing guidelines, will be in question. R. Stumberg, 'Local Meets Global in International Negotiations', *Globecon* [National League of Cities] (1999) 4-6. Interestingly, US Senator Edward M. Kennedy from Massachusetts, relying on advice from John Hume over many years, has opposed that application of affirmative-action principles in Northern Ireland as likely to cost jobs rather than redistribute them. K. Cullen, 'Kennedy Makes First Ulster Trip at a Crucial Time', *The Boston Globe*, 9 January 1998.

[92] J. O'Farrell, 'Cellucci, in Irish Trip Sees Trade as Peace Aid: Urges Links with Massachusetts', *The Boston Globe*, 23 June 1999. The Governor planned to open a Massachusetts trade office in Derry.

[93] H. Jones and P. Guzzi, 'Looking to Belfast in Search of a Better Boston', *The Boston Globe*, 27 November 1999. Jones is special assistant to the Chancellor of the University of Massachusetts-Boston and Guzzi is president of the Greater Boston Chamber of Commerce.

cooperation-based business alliance' with Belfast in Northern Ireland and also with the Canadian province of Nova Scotia. Its official signers – besides Mayor Menino, the Lord Mayor of Belfast, Alban Maginnes, and the Nova Scotian Director of International Development, Don Robertson – termed this 'The Atlantic Rim Agreement'. The purpose of the pact was to encourage future economic growth in and among the three Atlantic regions through the sharing information, specifically, in the fields of biotechnology, aquaculture, energy technology, environmental technology, and port and harbor development. It would be 'driven by the private sector, with the three governments offering guidance'.[94]

Not only the Boston city-region but others as well along the seacoast of North America are linking up with 'significant' partners on the other side of the Atlantic. In South Carolina, for example, both the historic port city of Charleston and the inland industrial complex of Spartanburg-Greenville have developed close European ties, particularly with Germany.[95] The Boston/Massachusetts-Belfast/Northern Ireland connection, however, is perhaps the most intimate one of all, owing not merely to the ethnic bond but also to the pronounced 'Atlantic' orientations of the geographic areas involved, at the fringes of their respective continents. It is a singular tie, and one that can pay dividends, political and social as well as economic.

Under the pressures of globalization, such 'natural' advantages as Boston may have in dealing with even the proximate Irish part of Europe will be difficult to maintain. For the city and its region both to be preserved and to prosper, 'iconography', which looks to the past, and

---

94 M. A. Brunelli, 'Boston Hooks up with Nova Scotia, Belfast', *The Boston Globe*, 13 November 1997.

95 A. Brack, 'Charleston: A Fusion of Europe's Past', *Europe: Magazine of the European Union*, 371 (1997). Charleston is host to the annual Spoleto Festival USA and has the fastest-growing container port in the United States. The upcountry cities of Spartanburg and Greenville, where Bavarian Motor Works (BMW) and other German firms have located, are a transatlantic-development phenomenon. As South Carolina Governor Carroll Campbell said, in explaining BMW's move to Spartanburg County, 'You have to understand that part of the county was settled by Germans. There is a lot of German settlement in that part of South Carolina and the western part of North Carolina. This is a great comfort to BMW.' These 'ties from early times' plus other attractions make it 'just a good bond that we have between South Carolina and Germany'. 'Interview: South Carolina Governor Carroll Campbell', *Europe: Magazine of the European Community*, 320 (1992) 32-3.

'circulation', which looks to the future, must be finely balanced. 'Having lost out in the competition for economic influence, Boston sought to reinvent itself as a cultural capital', as *Boston Globe* economics writer, David Warsh, recollects its history. 'The result was the jewel box of a city as Boston exists today, with its deliberate mix of residential neighborhoods, commercial districts, and public space; its short lines of communication; its pleasing sightlines; its nearby suburbs and outlying high-tech districts.'[96]

Some of these assets, however, may be at risk if the 'competitive advantage' of the Boston city-region does not include, in particular, better transportation links to take full advantage of global economic networking. Emphasizing both inward and outward accessibility as the key to a region's success, the M.I.T. economist Robert Solow reminds his fellow Boston area residents: 'Our region will still have to move freight in the next century'.[97] In the extensive efforts currently being undertaken to expand the carrying capacity of Boston's seaport, Logan International Airport, and the region's highway system (the 'Big Dig'), fundamental issues are having to be faced. Other US cities along the Atlantic seaboard are having to confront similar dilemmas. Nearly all have decided to deepen their shipping channels through the expensive process of dredging in order to accommodate the next generation of deep-draft cargo vessels, such as the *Regina Mærsk* of the Danish shipping line, which otherwise would have to find berths in other parts of the world.[98] Earlier versions of such container ships started plying the North Atlantic in the 1960s, and containerized shipping has been concentrated on lanes between countries with the highest standards of living.[99] Yet the port of

---

96 D. Warsh, 'Boston vs. New York', *The Boston Globe*, 19 October 1999. Warsh refers to M. Domosh, *Invented Cities: The Creation of Landscape in Nineteenth-century New York and Boston* (New Haven, Yale University Press, 1996). The contemporary Boston cityscape, together with an informative text and a double map supplement showing the Boston-to-Washington 'Megalopolis', is colorfully described in W. S. Ellis, 'Boston: Breaking New Ground', photographs by J. Sartore, *National Geographic*, 186:1 (1994) 2-33.

97 R. M. Solow, 'Competition: From Idaho to Bangalore, Other Regions Are Aggressively Vying for Industry and Jobs', in 'Turning Point: Reinventing the Boston Region for an Age of Global Challenge', special section, *The Boston Globe*, 30 October 1994.

98 'US Ports Under Pressure to Dredge Shipping Channels: Race to Attract Mega-ships that Berth in North America', *Globecon* [National League of Cities] (1999) 1-2.

99 Butel, *The Atlantic*, p.291: 'The features of this traffic have brought about a concentration of the majority of the movements of containers in the northern zone of the

Boston may have fallen so far behind the commercial ports of New York/New Jersey and Halifax, and indeed others elsewhere, that such a large investment is wasteful. Related expenses include the cost of raising bridges to accommodate the passage of double-stacked containers on rail cars from new cargo-handling facilities in the harbor all the way through to the Middle West. The apparent aspiration would be to make Boston a 'circulation' hub, capable of competing globally (or perhaps not at all).

Difficult tradeoffs here are involved, such as choosing between further expenditures for dredging and more money for cleaning the harbor waters, for fishing and recreational use. An elaborate plan for a culturally rich and architecturally distinctive Seaport District with a Harborwalk, also in progress, would emphasize, by contrast, the 'iconography' of the city.[100] Just as some European cities have looked to American cities, such as Baltimore with its Harborplace,[101] as models for waterfront development, so now Boston is contemplating European models of valuable vistas to and from the sea.[102]

Conclusion: New Transatlantic Orbits, Cosmopolitan Democracy, and Participatory Citizenship

No longer do the American regions linked to Europe need to be located on the Atlantic seaboard – that which Jean Gottmann earlier called the Megalopolitan hinge of the United States.[103] These can be situated in the interior, for the pull of the 'new Atlantic community', herein described in its inclusiveness, is less and less geographical. This is emphatically not, however, to disregard the importance of a geographic

---

Atlantic in order to bind the east coast of North America – the United States and Canada – to western Europe.'

[100] S. Diesenhouse, 'Boston is Moving to Revitalize its Port', *The New York Times*, 11 October 1998; R. L. Cravatts, 'Emphasizing Arts Can Enrich Seaport District', *The Boston Globe*, 14 February 1999; B. McGrory, 'We Deserve More Out of Seaport', *The Boston Globe*, 17 December 1999.

[101] C. Belfoure, 'Baltimore's Harborside Renewal Widens', *The New York Times*, 19 September 1999.

[102] D. Z. Jackson, 'Making the Harborwalk More than a Dream', *The Boston Globe*, 24 October 1997. L. Haar, director of planning and zoning for the Boston Redevelopment Authority, talked of some of the small ports of Europe, *e.g.* Horta in the Azores, Paros in Greece, and even Marmara in Turkey.

[103] J. Gottmann, 'The Continent's Economic Hinge', in *Since Megalopolis*, ch. 3.

sense of community. Gottmann, who himself had a strong sense of place as well as space, came to realize: 'The importance of seaside location has been decreasing gradually with the constant improvement in the means of transportation by land and by air, and the networks of telecommunications. Airplanes and telephone calls now cross maritime and continental space with equal facility, though restricted by politics and organizational skills much more than by the physical features of the planet.'[104] Thus the new Atlantic community will never develop simply as a Hanseatic League, a sea-based network on a wider maritime scale.

Since Gottmann wrote, a decade ago, there has been a continuing revolution in transport and communication. Not only Cleveland, Detroit, and Chicago but also Seattle, San Francisco, and Los Angeles could be 'on the list' of metropolitan regions which, though not located on the Atlantic Ocean, are directly linked to Europe. Virtually all of the places of origin and destination in the new Atlantic community are, as noted, cities, making the Atlantic world appear at the beginning of the twenty-first century a kind of multi-centered, or even multi-nodal, cosmopolis. Within such an unbounded sphere, national identities and loyalties may become less important, for many purposes, than 'citizenship' in city-states,[105] whose 'hinterlands' are the world.

This, of course, is an ancient idea, originating in the Greek concept of the *polis*.[106] A 'cosmopolitan democracy' would be a kind of governance in which individuals and groups in localities anywhere, without much regard to state lines or the hierarchies of national or federal systems, could manage their own lives, including their relationships with each other, largely on their own. In such a world, as Scott, Agnew, Soja, and Storper comment in their essay on global city-regions, 'the city itself potentially becomes the object of primary loyalty and membership rather than the state in which it is located. With economic life and social existence increasingly tied to the fate of the city and its region rather than the state, citizenship may begin to become associated once more, as it was classically, with city-regions and not with states.' An important

---

[104] J. Gottmann and R. A. Harper, 'Introduction', in *Since Megalopolis*, p.15.

[105] B. Crossette, 'The Return of the City-State', *The New York Times*, 2 June 1996.

[106] For a brief review of the idea, and an application of it to 'European citizenship', see U. K. Preuss, 'Citizenship in the European Union: A Paradigm for Transnational Democracy?', in D. Archibugi, D. Held and M. Köhler (eds.), *Re-Imagining Political Community: Studies in Cosmopolitan Democracy* (Stanford, Stanford University Press, 1998), pp.140-4.

implication of this point is that 'residence in the city more than official state citizenship now becomes a significant basis for political activity'.[107] In particular, immigrants who may not be enfranchised to vote nationally could be allowed fully to participate in politics locally, in the *polis* where they live and may be working and otherwise contributing.

As the world globalizes further, metropolitan regions may need to repossess their locality. A networked world could become a rootless world. In the cat's cradle of shifting connections between America and Europe – eastward and westward, northward and southward – there is a place for place – for location, for history, and for culture. Cities, as relatively fixed sites on the map of the world, are still the best reference points for the interweaving of Atlantic civilization (iconography) as well as for interchanges of trade (circulation). Structured relationships between cities – not only national capitals or the great 'money centers' but also smaller metropolitan communities of definite character – can be the primary *loci* of a system of meaningful human correlation.

Many of the Atlantic world's cities are rich in both of these respects – in terms of iconography, or symbolism and associated sentiment, and in terms of circulation, or trade, travel, and communications traffic, and the resources which these both use and generate. New forms of cooperation between US and European cities may need to be devised. Under the auspices of the European Commission, frameworks of decentralized, 'horizontal' cooperation between cities, urban agglomerations, and regions in Europe and comparable urban entities in Latin America (the URB-AL Program) and also such entities in South and Southeast Asia (the ASIA-URBS Program) have been designed. Funds are already being provided for technology and experience sharing and for joint projects.[108]

American cities, which have less central, 'vertical' support from the US government, also have more political and fiscal autonomy than do European cities. This structural difference makes enhanced programmatic collaboration across a broad front between cities and regions in Europe and their counterparts in the United States improbable, if not

---

107 Scott, Agnew, Soja, and Storper, 'Global City-Regions'.

108 The website for the URB-AL Program is http://www.urb-al.com. That for the ASIA-URBS Program is http://www.asia-urbs.com.

impossible. The genius of Atlanticism does not lie, however, in programs but, rather, in people – in their connections and in their affinities. A new Atlantic community may already exist.

CHAPTER 7

Private Firms and US-EU Policy-Making: The Transatlantic Business Dialogue[1]

Maria GREEN COWLES

American University, School of International Service

In examining the US-EU partnership, one usually focuses on the interaction of government actors – whether they are from the US State Department, the European Commission, the Office of the President, or the Member States. From the Cold War to the New Transatlantic Agenda, government officials have negotiated agreements, attended summits, and developed policy agendas.

To understand the US-EU relationship in the 1990s, however, one can no longer focus solely on government elites. The creation in 1994-95 of the Transatlantic Business Dialogue (TABD) and the mobilization of private firms as important interlocutors on transatlantic trade negotiations have altered the traditional dynamics of the US-EU partnership. As one US observer noted, the TABD 'is probably the first time in American history that the private sector is determining the substance of future executive or legislative agreements.'[2]

Official documents call the TABD 'an informal process whereby European and American companies and business associations develop joint EU-US trade policy recommendations, working together with the

1 This chapter is largely drawn from M. Green Cowles, 'The Collective Action of Transatlantic Business: The Transatlantic Business Dialogue', Paper presented at the 1996 Annual Meeting of the American Political Science Association, San Francisco, CA, 31 August 1996; and M. Green Cowles, 'The Transatlantic Business Dialogue', unpublished paper prepared while at the Center for German and European Studies (CGES), Georgetown University. I thank CGES for the postdoctoral fellowship that allowed me to pursue this research. I am also grateful to the business and government officials for granting me interviews – oftentimes on several different occasions. In particular, I thank Selina Jackson, Stephen Johnston, Ted Austell, Craig Burchell, and Marino Marcich.

2 N. Levine, 'A Trans-Atlantic Bargain', *Journal of Commerce*, 10 May 1995, p.6A.

European Commission and the US Administration.'[3] At times, the TABD becomes a 'quadrilateral negotiating forum' in which business leaders and government officials sit down together to work out regulatory problems, and negotiate strategies.[4] Indeed, while governments initially proposed the TABD, industry took over its leadership. While companies are reluctant to acknowledge it, TABD has become more than a process. It has developed into a business organization (albeit unofficial) – complete with a well-developed structure, transatlantic directors and offices, and a substantial budget.[5]

In many respects, the inclusion of business as a direct interlocutor in the US-EU trade and investment negotiations is hardly surprising. As Alberta Sbragia has pointed out, 'American firms in Europe and European firms in the United States have been in some sense 'silent' members of the transatlantic community' over the years.[6] Transatlantic relations have been composed of both a 'public sphere' of government negotiations and a 'private sphere' of market activity for a number of decades. Increasingly, as Michael Smith notes in this volume, the 'public' and 'private' have to be accommodated in the US/EU relationship. The TABD has played a critical role not merely in setting the agenda for transatlantic trade discussions, but also in participating in US-EU negotiations and in shaping domestic-level support for their agenda. With the TABD, the transatlantic business community plays a

---

3 Official TABD website at TABD.COM. Interestingly, the Commerce Department website defines the TABD as 'an innovative government-business initiative to lower trade and investment barriers across the Atlantic.'

4 M. Green Cowles, 'The Collective Action of Transatlantic Business: The Transatlantic Business Dialogue', Paper presented at the 1996 Annual Meeting of the American Political Science Association, San Francisco, CA, 31 August 1996, p.2.

5 The TABD European offices are not incorporated *per se*. Rather, they receive their funding from the sponsoring lead TABD company whose CEO chairs the TABD process. Companies are reluctant to call the TABD a transatlantic business organization because they believe that such a structure would lead to a bureaucratic mindset and detract from the TABD's dynamic nature. As the US Director of the TABD has noted, 'The TABD has no formal structure and no official secretariat, nor is it a new institution or simply another business organisation designed to influence policy-makers'. S. Jackson, 'The TABD Process – A Business Approach to US-EU Trade Policy', *The European-American Business Council Newsletter*, Spring 1998, p.22.

6 A. Sbragia, 'Transatlantic Relations: An Evolving Mosaic', prepared for presentation to the international conference on 'Policy-Making and Decision-Making in Transatlantic Relations', Université Libre de Bruxelles, 3-4 May 1996, p.7.

very *public* role in what has been called 'industrial diplomacy'. Indeed, as Stuart Eizenstat, former Undersecretary for International Trade at the Commerce Department noted, 'This [TABD] process is not a fifth wheel. It has become part and parcel of the entire transatlantic agenda.'[7]

As discussed in this chapter, the TABD has prompted government and business groups alike to define new structures, new working relationships, and new policy-making processes. The chapter begins with an overview of the TABD from its origins, the early business-government relationships, and – given that TABD is a conference-driven initiative – the 1995 Seville conference that created the initial transatlantic policy recommendations. The following section highlights the events leading to the 1996 Chicago conference where business and government leaders, including EU Member State and US regulatory agency officials, met to discuss government processes. The Chicago summit led to the historic US-EU Mutual Recognition Agreement (MRA) covering seven key sectors. The next section outlines the steps taken by the TABD business community in 1997 to widen the group's membership, increase its visibility, and identify policy priorities for government officials. This section also examines the quadrilateral negotiations leading to the MRA and the achievements reached at the 1997 Rome conference. The following section highlights developments in 1998, including the TABD scorecards, the EU proposal for a New Transatlantic Marketplace, and the Transatlantic Economic Partnership that was ultimately signed by the two governments. The conclusion reexamines the TABD's contribution to the US-EU partnership, and explores some of the challenges facing industrial diplomacy in the future.

Origins of the Transatlantic Business Dialogue

On 15 December 1994, the TABD concept was formally proposed by the late Commerce Department Secretary Ron Brown at a speech sponsored by the EU Committee of AmCham in Brussels.[8] There were

---

7 Stuart Eizenstat, remarks made at the TABD outreach meeting at the US Chamber of Commerce, Washington D.C., 20 June 1997.

8 The EU Committee of AmCham is an influential lobbying organization in Brussels made up of major American companies. See M. Green Cowles, 'The EU Committee of AmCham: The Powerful Voice of American Firms in Brussels', *Journal of European Public Policy*, 3:3 (1996) 339-58. Brown's initial proposal called for meetings of the American Chambers of Commerce in Europe. At the recommendation of USEU Mission officials in Brussels, the Commerce Secretary changed his

at least two rationales behind the Commerce Secretary's 'vision' of the TABD. First was Brown's belief that international business was at least four to five years ahead of governments in its thinking on trade liberalization. Yet Brown and other Commerce Department officials found that existing US and EU lobbying organizations did not adequately coordinate their positions on transatlantic trade issues. They also believed that European firms were not sufficiently mobilized in Brussels on external trade matters. Thus, EU negotiators often based their trade positions on Member State input, but not on input from European industry *per se*. Brown believed that US and EU Chief Executive Officers (CEOs) needed to come together and develop a unified transatlantic trade agenda that neither the US nor the EU government could ignore.[9] US government officials were convinced, moreover, that their negotiating position would coincide much more closely with the US-EU business community's stance than would that of the European Commission. Consequently, the Commission as the 'outlier' would be compelled to alter its position in the negotiations.[10]

A second rationale behind the Commerce Secretary's speech related to domestic American politics. It was no coincidence that the idea was launched shortly before Congressional representatives pushed legislation to dismantle the Commerce Department. By encouraging industry involvement in transatlantic trade negotiations, Brown hoped to secure greater business support for the department.[11]

---

speech at the last minute to call for a dialogue among American and European firms. Interview with USEU Mission official, Brussels, 24 June 1996.

9 Interview with Commerce Department official, Washington D.C., 10 June 1996.

10 Interview with USTR official, Washington D.C., 29 May 1996. Several TABD participants believe that this rationale – to use TABD as 'a means to force the Commission's hand on liberalization issues' emerged only after the fact. The reason is that there was some European support – including Commission support – for TABD from the start given the economic situation in Europe. Some members of the Commission, notably Sir Leon Brittan, believed that 'a major order of liberalization' was due and that by allowing for 'outside pressure', *i.e.* the US-EU business community, the Commission would be 'allowed' to move forward. As one US business representative noted, 'If liberalization is part of the Commission's grand scheme, the TABD makes it more palatable.' Interview with US business association official, Washington D.C., 3 June 1996. This view is echoed by a Commerce Department official in an interview, Washington D.C., 10 June 1996.

11 Interview with Commerce Department official, Washington D.C., 10 June 1996.

Following Brown's speech, officials in Washington D.C., and Brussels generated a plan to create a transatlantic coalition of US and EU Chief Executive Officers who would propose measures to improve US-EU trade and investment. Stuart Eizenstat, then-US ambassador to the EU, met with Commissioners and officials from Directorate Generals I (external relations – including trade) and III (industry) to promote the plan.[12] Sir Leon Brittan, the Commissioner responsible for US-EU relations, was very receptive to the TABD concept. He wanted to involve business in trade negotiations in a more structured manner not only to create consensus and support for the talks, but to build support for Brittan's own trade agenda.[13] However, Horst Krenzler, Director General of DG I, was less enthusiastic. As one Commission official noted, 'in the initial stages, there was a certain amount of skepticism because we thought transnational relations was best done between governments [...] but the advantages of business involvement soon became apparent'.[14] Commission officials also wanted to make sure that the US government did not have a 'hidden agenda' – such as the previously proposed TransAtlantic Free Trade Agreement (TAFTA) – behind the TABD.[15] By early spring 1995, Sir Leon Brittan and Industry Commissioner Martin Bangemann agreed to the project.

In April 1995, Brown, Brittan and Bangemann sent a letter to approximately 1,800 US and European industry officials asking for sug-

---

12 The Directorate Generals (DGs) are similar to executive branch agencies in the United States. Each DG is run by Director Generals who, in turn, reports to her/his respective EU Commissioner. The Commissioners sometimes have more than one DG in their portfolio. DG I 'external relations' was split in January 1993 in DGI external economic relations and DGIA external political relations and enlargement task force. A further split occurred in 1995, with the creation of DGI, DGIA and DGIB, in charge of different sectors (commercial policy, CFSP etc.) and geographic areas. In this chapter, DG I refers to the Directorate General in charge of the external economic relations. In 1999, the Prodi Commission decided yet another restructuring, establishing a Directorate General for Trade and a single External Relations Directorate General (the numbers of the DGs have been dropped).

13 Interview with Commission official, Brussels, 18 September 1996.

14 Interview with Commission official, Brussels, 26 June 1996.

15 Interview with Commerce Department official, Washington D.C., 10 June 1996. The idea behind TAFTA was to create a free trade area similar to the US-Canadian free trade area. Many officials in both the US and the EU were unwilling to pursue a TAFTA shortly after the drawn-out Uruguay Round negotiations. In addition, French government officials were against further liberalization efforts.

gestions regarding a transatlantic business forum.[16] The famous 'Three B' letter was designed to 'test the waters' for a new initiative that would reduce tariffs and/or address other business concerns. Over 300 European and American replies were received.[17] To the surprise of both the US and EU governments, the business groups responded that the lowering of tariffs was not a high priority.[18] Rather, they argued that duplicate standards, testing, and certification procedures were far more costly and harmful to companies than the already low tariff schedules.

By July 1995, a joint US-EU steering committee comprised of government and industry officials met for the first time in Brussels.[19] The committee decided to launch a conference in Seville, Spain, four months later to bring industry officials together to develop recommendations for removing obstacles to trade and investment. Four transatlantic working groups were created to prepare working papers: (1) standards, testing/certification and regulatory issues; (2) trade liberalization; (3) investment; and (4) third country relations.

American Business-Government Relations: The 'Muffin Club'

In preparing for the November 1995 summit, American government and business officials needed to develop a strong working relationship. To do so, the government had to counter the initial reticence of the business community.

---

16 The letter to US firms was sent out on Commerce Department stationery with the three signatures. The letter to European companies was sent out on Commission stationery. Not every European government was pleased with the arrangement. The French government, for example, questioned whether it was appropriate for a US official to place his signature on Commission letterhead.

17 In the US, 400 letters were sent out to US associations and companies, of which approximately 20% responded. US Commerce Department, 'Transatlantic Business Dialogue: Initial Tabulation of US Results', June 1995. The European Commission sent letters to the top 1000 European companies based on sales, 170 medium-sized companies, and 208 business associations at the European level. As of 30 June 1995, the Commission received 230 replies of which more than one-third came from business associations. European Commission, 'TransAtlantic business Dialogue (TABD) Analysis of the EU Business Responses', undated document.

18 Interview with Commission official, 18 September 1996.

19 While the meeting was called on short notice, European officials were not pleased when the US side arrived with a handful of government officials and only two industry representatives – recruited from the Brussels offices of American companies and lobby groups.

Interestingly, despite the Commerce Department's belief that it was attuned to the needs of US business, American firms' initial response to the 'Three B' letter was rather lukewarm. First, several firms were wary that the initiative was merely a stunt to support the Commerce Department and the Clinton Administration during the run-up to an election year. Indeed, because the Republic-dominated Congress might question the TABD initiative, the companies did not want to jeopardize key legislative issues such as corporate tax cuts. Second, other firms were reluctant to find themselves caught in-between the Commerce Department and the Office of the United States Trade Representative (USTR) which had the legal authority to negotiate US-EU trade matters. Though the TABD initiative purportedly had then USTR Mickey Kantor's approval, several USTR officials were not pleased with the Commerce Department's encroachment on their turf.[20] After all, international trade negotiations – such as the agenda suggested by the 'Three B' letter – were the responsibility of the USTR, and not the Commerce Department. Third, still other business officials expressed concern that economic issues would be linked to a larger 'Atlanticist Agenda' involving military and security issues. They did not want to be 'used' by governments in the efforts to reinforce the NATO relationship, for example. Finally, many American firms questioned whether they would be embarking on anything 'new'. Most of the agenda items proposed in the 'Three B' letter – such as standards, tariff barriers and investment – were already being considered in other international fora such as the OECD and WTO. The value-added of an additional transatlantic initiative was not clear to American business.

Despite industry's initial reticence, the TABD proceeded once Commerce officials enlisted CEOs that were 'close to Commerce, friendly to Brown and the Department'.[21] Commerce sought CEOs who would be 'responsive, who could take on Commerce's mission, who could take on Brown's mission'.[22] Dana Mead of Tenneco, John Luke of Westvaco, Bill Hudson of AMP Incorporated, and Jack Murphy of

---

20 Indeed, several USTR officials found it 'odd that Commerce was running TABD because of the USTR mandate' to oversee trade negotiations. While initially strained, the relationship between USTR and Commerce on TABD matters gradually improved, notably after the November 1995 TABD conference in Seville. Interview with USTR official, Washington D.C., 29 May 1996.

21 Interview with Commerce Department official, Washington D.C., 10 June 1996.

22 Interview with Commerce Department official.

Dresser Industries joined the initiative to form the US Steering Committee. In early fall, Alex Trotman, CEO of Ford, was recruited to co-chair the US TABD Steering Committee with Allaire. Scottish born, Trotman is a naturalized US citizen whose previous post was head of Ford Europe. Thus, Trotman viewed the transatlantic initiative as an important project from both a professional and personal perspective.

Not everyone was satisfied with the TABD arrangements. Several US trade associations were less than pleased that the TABD would be a 'CEO-to-CEO dialogue' – thus shutting out groups like the National Association of Manufacturers (NAM) and the US Chamber of Commerce.[23] NAM and the US Chamber resented the exclusion in part because they already met with their European counterpart, UNICE (the Union of Industrial and Employers' Confederations of Europe), to discuss transatlantic trade and investment issues. NAM officials were somewhat placated when Dana Mead, CEO of Tenneco and incoming NAM chairman, joined the US Steering Committee.[24] In addition to the industry associations, some members of the Industry Policy Advisory Committee (IPAC), the Industry Sector Advisory Committees (ISACs), and their umbrella group, the Advisory Committee for Trade Policy and Negotiations (ACTPN) protested that TABD would bypass the legally mandated private sector advisory committee system.[25] Commerce and industry officials assured these members that they would be fully apprised of TABD activities and pointed out that there was already membership overlap between TABD and the ISACs.

Beginning in late September, a working relationship between industry and the Commerce department was underway. The US Steering Committee began to focus intensely on the preparations for the Seville conference. Every weekday morning at 8 a.m., for the following three months, the 'Muffin Club' (named after the breakfast fare) met at the Xerox government affairs office in Washington D.C. The goal of the Muffin Club was two-fold: to recruit CEOs, and to prepare working

---

23 Interview with US business association official, Washington D.C., 3 June 1996.

24 Interestingly, when Congressional leaders first attacked the Commerce Department, NAM came out in support of the agency. The US Chamber, however, chose to remain neutral. TABD insiders suggest that the NAM's presence on the US TABD steering committee was a result of the association's support.

25 IPAC and the ISACs are jointly managed by the Departments of Commerce, Agriculture, Labor and the Environmental Protection Agency. The committees provide advice on industry matters.

papers for the Seville conference. The Muffin Group participants included officials from Xerox and Ford, the representatives of four CEOs representing the Seville working groups,[26] and a newly-hired US TABD coordinator who worked out of the Xerox office in Washington D.C. In addition, Frank Vargo, the Commerce Department's Deputy Assistant Secretary-Europe, and other Commerce officials attended every meeting as 'observers'.[27] USTR and State Department officials occasionally joined the meetings. Given that the success of the Seville conference – and TABD itself – was largely dependent on the number of US CEOs who showed up for the event, Vargo's role was to assist in recruiting business leaders. Vargo regularly informed Ron Brown when telephone calls to various individuals were needed. He also served as a 'sounding board' for working group officials who questioned whether various recommendations were viable or not.[28]

While the early Muffin Club meetings were filled with concerns about CEO recruitment and complaints regarding the exhaustive workload, the group managed to pull together a high-power list of company leaders and extensive briefing papers. Participants describe the Muffin Club meetings as a 'logistical exercise'. The meetings also represented, however, the close ties forged between business and government officials on trade matters in the United States over the past few decades.[29] As discussed below, however, this same business-government relationship on trade matters was not found on the other side of the Atlantic.

---

26 Dana Mead, CEO Tenneco and incoming Chairman of NAM chaired Working Group (WG) 1 on Standards, Testing and Certification. Both Tenneco and NAM officials participated in the Muffin Meeting. John A. Luke, Jr., CEO Westvaco chaired WG 2 on Trade Liberalization; William Hudson, CEO AMP chaired WG 3 on Investment. Jack Murphy, chairman and CEO Dresser Industries chaired WG 4 on Third Country Relations. Representatives or 'sherpas' – not the CEOs – did the TABD preparatory work on both sides of the Atlantic.

27 Interview with US business representative, Washington D.C., 31 May 1996.

28 Interview with Commerce Department official, Washington D.C., 10 June 1996.

29 For an overview of growing business-government ties, see D. Vogel, *Fluctuating Fortunes: The Political Power of Business in America* (New York, Basic Books, 1989).

European Business-Government Relations: A Complicated Alliance

Following the response to the 'Three B' letter, EU Commission officials recruited Jürgen Strube, CEO of BASF who once lived in the US where he headed the firm's North American Regional Division. Officials also tapped Peter Sutherland, chairman of Goldman Sachs International. While Sutherland worked for an American firm, his 'European credentials' were firmly ensconced as former Vice President of the European Commission and Director General of GATT.

In many respects, the recruitment of European business leaders such as Strube and Sutherland was the easy step. Developing a working relationship between Commission and industry within the TABD was more difficult. Disagreements with trade associations, questions regarding the official competence of the Commission, as well as DG I's approach to external trade negotiations proved to be important obstacles.

Trade Association Disagreements

One reason for the difficulties is that Commission officials agreed with their American colleagues that CEOs should drive the TABD process – not business associations. While American associations were none too pleased with this situation, European associations were up in arms over the TABD format.[30] The reason was quite simple: the CEO-driven format defied the traditional business-government relationship long established in Europe, notably continental Europe.[31] Historically, industry associations – not CEOs – were the primary interlocutors in business-government relations.[32]

---

30 For a more detailed account on the influence of TABD on national industry associations, see M. Green Cowles, 'The TABD and Domestic Business-Government Relations: Challenge and Opportunity', in M. Green Cowles, J. Caporaso and T. Risse (eds.), *Transforming Europe: Europeanization and Domestic Change* (Ithaca (NY) Cornell University Press, 2000).

31 The composition of industry associations reinforced this pattern. Individual European firms are not direct members of the industry federations (the primary exception being Confederation of British Industry (CBI)). Instead, companies are members of various sectoral associations, which are in turn members of the national associations. See, for example, M. Green Cowles, 'German Big Business: Learning to Play the European Game', *German Politics and Society*, 14:3 (1996) 73-107.

32 However, CEOs who are members of an association's Executive Committee might become involved in these discussions indirectly. In German trade associations, for

Believing the CEO-only format would minimize the role of sectoral, national and European associations, UNICE officials held frank conversations with Commission officials as well as with Ambassador Eizenstat. While responding favorably to the '3B letter' on behalf of its membership (national industry associations), UNICE contested the new structure.[33] UNICE officials pointed out that a transatlantic industry dialogue already existed between it and American associations. They also questioned the representativeness of the TABD process, maintaining that TABD must speak on behalf of European business as a whole, and not a handful of companies.[34] Finally, UNICE officials pointed out that the TABD required individuals with specific technical expertise on trade and investment matters – an expertise usually found in the industry associations themselves in Europe.[35]

Commission officials, however, were determined that the TABD be CEO-led. They noted that UNICE's institutional format did not provide the dynamism for TABD to be successful. While undeniably 'representative', the UNICE structure could also be very time-consuming and bureaucratic. As one Commission official explained, 'We did not want the [TABD] process to be filtered by the UNICE-style process. We don't want the very correct and proper functioning of UNICE which gives you the average view'.[36] Moreover, while UNICE's expertise on transatlantic issues centered on technical details, the purpose of the TABD was to engender broader *political* initiatives. Of course, that Commissioners were more interested in working with and developing political ties to heads of major European companies than they were with leaders of national industry associations also influenced their selection of the CEO format.

---

example, when high-level ministerial meetings occur, CEOs may be present as representatives of the Executive Committee.

33 Commission officials told UNICE officials that if the associations were invited, the Americans would refuse to come to the meeting. As one association official remarked, 'they [the Commission] were had by the Americans'. Interview with EU business association official, Brussels, 1 July 1996.

34 Interviews with EU business association officials, Brussels, 1 July 1996.

35 Indeed, few European CEOs follow international trade matters closely. As one industry association official points out, 'CEOs hardly know GATT is going on [...] they leave it to the sectoral and institutional groups'. Interview with EU business association official, Brussels, 1 July 1996.

36 Interview with Commission official, Brussels, 26 June 1996.

Commission and industry officials reached a compromise in which UNICE served as a member of the European TABD steering committee while the European companies maintained the larger TABD leadership role. Strains among UNICE, individual companies and the Commission, however, persisted throughout the TABD's first year.

The Commission's Official Competence and Business's Participation

The role of the Commission *vis-à-vis* the Member States in external policy matters provided another obstacle to developing Commission-industry ties. The power of the Commission depends greatly on the policy arena at hand.[37] For example, the Commission assumes a critical role in the development of EU regulatory policy. However, EU treaties place certain restraints on the Commission's powers in external trade policy. The Commission must be given its negotiating mandate by the 113 Committee (made up of Member States) and report to the Member States regularly on the negotiation proceedings.[38] Moreover, any Commission activities must be approved by the Member States' unanimous vote.[39] Thus, the ability of the Commission to act as a legitimate partner in international trade negotiations is sometimes questioned.[40]

---

37 As Ted Lowi pointed out in American policy-making, politics makes process. The importance of any particular actor depends on the issue at hand. See T. Lowi, 'American Business, Public Policy, Case Studies and Political Theory', *World Politics*, 16 (July 1964) 677-715.

38 The (Article) 113 Committee is now referred to as the (Article) 133 Committee, following the renumbering of the TUE and TEC Treaties that entered into force in May 1999. However, for purposes of historical discussion, this chapter refers to the original name for this committee.

39 The Commission's limited trade negotiating powers frustrate American trade negotiators. Because the Commission negotiates on behalf of the Member States – and industry *per se* – American officials maintain that the voice of European business is muted. This view was reinforced during the Uruguay Round when European farmers appeared to have a far greater say in the negotiation process than did European industry. In recent years, American ambassadors to the EU have met with European industry groups to encourage greater involvement in the Uruguay round. The American officials' promotion of TABD as a means to enhance the role of large European firms in the international trade negotiations was a logical next step. From the American perspective, once these companies developed a coordinated position at the European level, they could present a more united front to the Member States.

40 M. Smith, 'Competitive Cooperation and EU-US Relations: Can the EU be a Strategic Partner for the US in the World Political Economy?', *Journal of European Public Policy*, 5:4 (1998) 561-77.

While some firms did express their interests directly to trade officials in DG I and III, Commission officials admit that it was very difficult to get a clear cut position of business on the Uruguay Round.[41] The fact that European business has not formally organized itself in Brussels to lobby Commission officials on trade issues may be one reason for the weak industry position. Another reason may be the lack of formal channels to Commission officials. US industry, for example, has direct channels to the Commerce Department and USTR on trade issues through the ISACs. European industry does not.[42] Granted, UNICE provides 'official' industry positions on trade matters. UNICE, however, is not interested in creating more formal industry inputs based on the American ISACs model for the simple reason that European-level sectoral associations would then challenge the peak association's leading role.[43]

The Approach of DG I

DG I's overall approach to trade matters also served as an impediment to closer Commission-industry ties within TABD. There are two dimensions to the DG I approach. First, DG I tends to focus on the 'wider public interest' as opposed to industry concerns *per se* in trade negotiations.[44] Commission officials draw up a work program for the negotiations based on their perceptions of what they believe are the larger societal interests – including those of labor, consumer, and environmental groups. These latter groups focus their lobbying activities on national governments, who, in turn, express their concerns in the 113 Committee. As one Commission official explains: 'Business is a major group [in external trade matters] but it is not the be all and end all. I can well imagine hearing the business contribution – but we must also take x, y and z into account. Both sides – government and business – appreciate the context in which business conclusions will be cited'.[45]

---

41 Smith, 'Competitive Cooperation'. The exception, as stated earlier, was the European chemical industry.

42 One European association member argued that ISAC members are 'nominees' and are thus not true 'representatives' of US business. Interview with EU business association official, Brussels, 3 July 1996.

43 Interview with EU business representative, Brussels, 3 July 1996.

44 Interview with Commission official, Brussels, 18 September 1996.

45 Interview with Commission official, Brussels, 26 June 1996. Some business believe that DG III has not articulated business interests as clearly to DG I as possible. Interview with EU business representative, Brussels, 3 July 1996.

Indeed, several DG I officials opposed the initial TABD concept precisely because industry groups would invariably have a greater say in trade decisions. As another official noted, 'TABD complicates life. Joint US-EU business views will carry weight. We cannot disregard them. If an organization ignores a pressure group, you make life more difficult.'[46]

The second and related dimension of DG I's approach is that it is based on a 'package approach' or 'umbrella approach' to negotiations. Rather than negotiating on a sector-by-sector basis, DG I prefers a multi-sector package. Like the 'wider public interest' argument, DG I views the package approach as a fairer means to proceed in negotiations, and a better way to gain concessions from its negotiating partners. This approach is frustrating at times to European business that desires liberalization in individual sectors. As discussed below, the package approach also complicates mutual recognition agreements with the US government.

Given these obstacles – trade association disagreements, questions regarding the Commission' competence, and DG I's approach – the working relationship between DG I and industry began very slowly. As one EU industry representative noted, 'the original involvement [of the two sides] was very difficult. Business wanted a briefing from the Commission on what the Commission was doing in these areas [of trade and investment]. The Commission expected business to tell [the Commissioners] what it wanted to do. We hadn't developed a spirit of cooperation. It didn't work too well'.[47]

Moreover, the Commission took a 'wait and see' stance, pushing industry to 'run with the process'.[48] TABD was, after all, touted as a business-to-business dialogue. Several EU business representatives, however, believed that the 'Commission wanted to place the burden of success on industry'.[49] Consequently, European industry representatives did most of the preparatory work for the Seville conference themselves.

46 Interview with Commission official, 18 September 1996.

47 Interview with EU business representative, Brussels, 3 July 1996.

48 Interview with EU business representative, Brussels, 25 June 1996.

49 Interview with EU business representative, Brussels, 25 June 1996.

The 'Spirit of Seville'

Expectations were growing by the time the Seville meeting arrived on 10 November 1995. Business leaders on both sides of the Atlantic had worked at a frenetic pace to complete the working papers that would serve as the basis of discussion. The US paper on standards, testing/certification and regulatory issues went through thirty-four revisions alone. Pressure was added when the European media labeled the conference a test for overall US-EU relations.[50]

The Seville meeting also symbolized the different cultural approaches each side brought to the business dialogue. The Americans prepared for Seville largely as a logistical exercise. 'American efficiency' was evident when each US CEO walked into the conference area with a special briefing booklet bound in a Department of Commerce folder. Muffin Club members had prepared most of the material for the booklet, notably the briefing papers. Commerce department people, however, assembled the booklets and included maps of Seville as well as an 'official welcome' from Commerce Secretary Brown. From an American perspective, the briefing booklet was a logistical necessity for CEOs traveling overseas. Of course, it also served as a nice propaganda piece for the Commerce Department. From the European perspective, however, it appeared that the Commerce Department itself had prepared the papers for the conference, and not the American companies as promised.

The European logistical preparation – according to both American and European accounts – was less obvious. There were no general briefing books, nor did every CEO or board member have a copy of the working papers before the conference (The sole exception were the European chemical CEOs who were given a preparatory book by the German chemical association, VCI.). One reason for the weaker preparation was the fact that the Commission had devoted fewer resources to TABD. Whereas the Commerce Department sent twelve people on its advance team to Seville, the Commission sent two.[51] The relative lack of coordination between the Commission and the TABD business representatives likely contributed to the situation. Of course, unlike the Americans, neither the Commission nor the industry people had any

---

50 See G. De Jonquieres and L. Barber, 'Business Meets to Revive US-EU Ties', *Financial Times*, 10 November 1995.

51 Interview with Commission official, 18 September 1996.

strong experience with the TABD's CEO-style format. As one European official noted, the TABD was 'a whole different ballgame. It was something we had not done before'.[52] Some attendees were concerned that the Europeans would be at a disadvantage in the negotiating process *vis-à-vis* the Americans as a result.[53]

Finally, there were differences in the approach taken by the two sides to the working papers. The Americans tended to focus on specific recommendations and details regarding trade and investment policy. The Europeans, on the other hand, had called attention to broader principles. The difference in approach, however, had nothing to do with preparation for the conference. As one European industry representative – who is highly regarded by his American counterparts – explained, 'As Europeans, we're different from the Americans. [In looking at the US and EU working papers, it is] not that someone was behind, or someone was leading [...] Americans love more detail, more tangibles. Europeans look for principles and visions. That won't change – but that doesn't mean we can't work together.'[54]

In fact, the many differences in tradition and culture were soon pushed aside by the accomplishments made at Seville. According to most American and European participants, the Seville conference was a great success.[55] Despite the short time frame (less than 48 hours), business participants agreed to over seventy specific recommendations in a final document for US-EU government consideration. One key recommendation put forth by the two sides was the Information Technology Agreement (ITA) slated for discussion at the 1996 WTO Singapore Ministerial meeting. The US-EU business community was united in its support for the complete elimination of residual customs tariffs on IT products by the end of the year 2000 (the united front would make it

52 Interview with EU think tank official, Brussels, 3 July 1996.

53 The night before the Seville meeting, the US and EU issue managers decided on a compromise draft paper which was then presented to people for discussion. The procedure was expeditious in that it also precluded contentious issues from reaching the floor – a point with which not every participant agreed. Interview with EU business association official, Brussels, 3 July 1996.

54 Interview with EU business representative, Brussels, 25 June 1996.

55 Not everyone was pleased with the final product. Some industry representatives pointed out that controversial non-consensus issues were not even discussed at the conference. European industry representative, correspondence with the author, 18 September 1996.

easier for US-EU negotiators to promote a global ITA to Asian and Latin American countries at the WTO Singapore meeting).

Attendees were surprised by the amount of goodwill that existed between the two business sides given that many of the companies were market competitors. The conference was also marked by the participants' willingness to focus on areas of agreement – and to not let their discussions be sidetracked by areas of disagreement. Business representatives soon referred to the cooperative working environment as the 'spirit of Seville'.

Not knowing whether the conference would be successful, government and business leaders had not made any definite plans for 'post-Seville'. Before the conference ended, however, Trotman of Ford and Strube of BASF decided to jointly continue the TABD process to ensure that their respective governments would follow through on the Seville recommendations. Indeed, the 'spirit of Seville' prompted the US-EU business to largely take over the initiative in ensuing months.

US and EU government officials were also pleased with Seville's success. Following the conference, the Commerce Department and Commission wrote extensive comments on the 70-plus recommendations. The following month, approximately sixty percent of the TABD Seville recommendations were incorporated in the NTA at the December Madrid Summit attended by President Clinton, Commission President Jacques Santer and Spanish Prime Minister and EU Council President Felipe Gonzalez.[56] Moreover, the NTA formally noted that 'the creation of the New TransAtlantic Marketplace will [...] take into consideration the recommendations of the TransAtlantic Business Dialogue'.[57] The TABD's inclusion in the NTA was further evidence that while initially viewing TABD as a separate Commerce Department undertaking, the State Department and USTR now embraced the busi-

56 Stuart Eizenstat, Undersecretary of Commerce, 'Statement at the TABD Press Briefing', Brussels, 23 May 1996. Government officials suggest that many of the proposals were already in draft form prior to the Seville conference.

57 The TABD is one component in building the New TransAtlantic Marketplace. The USTR and the Commission agreed to undertake a joint study to identify other obstacles to trade. In certain respects, the joint study was designed to 'buy time' during the US governmental elections and the EU intergovernmental conference. Most observers view TABD as the dynamic element behind the New TransAtlantic Marketplace.

ness dialogue as a positive vehicle for transatlantic economic and political relations.

1996: From Seville to Chicago

In February 1996, the government and business members of the US-EU TABD Steering Committee met to establish a follow-up program to Seville. Business leaders decided to draw up more precise statements and action plans for the Seville recommendations to preclude government backpedaling on the issues. Based on recommendations from European industry, the business leaders opted for the replacement of the original four working groups[58] and presented the Commission and US government with a new structure of fifteen issue groups: Transatlantic Committee on Standards Certification and Regulatory Policy (TACS); WTO Implementation and Expansion Issues; Trade Liberalization; Information Technology Agreement; Government Procurement; Intellectual Property; Tax Issues; Export Controls; Customs Issues; Transportation; International Business Practices; Small and Medium Sized Enterprises; Investment and R&D; Product Liability; Competition Policy.

One of the rationales for the new organizational structure was to make the process more manageable. At the same time, however, EU business participants recognized that the new structure would place pressure on DG I to move from its 'package approach' to external trade, to a sector-by-sector, issue-by-issue approach. As one European business association official noted, 'the only progress that can be made is in the sectors. The sectoral approach is best but the Commission doesn't like it. [We decided to] go for it with our American counterparts – and then push the Member States.'[59] Indeed, in later quadrilateral meetings, EU business officials were unabashed in promoting sectoral position such as 'zero-tariff' proposals in the information technology section to sometimes reluctant DG I officials.

---

58 The Transatlantic Advisory Committee on Standards, Certification and Regulatory Policy (TACS), arguably the most politically important group, was further divided into 11 sectoral groups – each with a US and EU business working chair. Two key individuals were brought in to lead the TACS: Ricardo Perissich, former director-general DG III in the Delors Commission who works with the Italian tire company, Pirelli; and Paula Stern, a former Commissioner and Chair of the US International Trade Commission.

59 Interview with EU business association official, Brussels, 3 July 1996.

Commission officials, for their part, became more responsive to the TABD process – perhaps prodded by criticism from the 113 Committee for not having briefed industry adequately prior to the Seville conference.[60] In addition to DG I and III, other DGs began to follow TABD more closely such as DG IV (competition), DG XV (intellectual property rights, procurement), and DG XXI (customs). The Commission also devised a contact list of Commission officials within the Commission services to allow for better coordination between business and the Commission. For example, there is a Commission official designated for each TABD issue group. Slowly, a more cooperative relationship developed between European industry and the Commission, notably in DG I.

The new organizational structure also created a more positive relationship between the companies and the business associations. A number of UNICE policy committee members, for example, chaired the TABD issue groups. While the companies still led the TABD initiative, the associations were now more integrated into the overall process.[61]

With the structure in place, US and EU business representatives soon pursued their own transatlantic shuttle diplomacy on behalf of the CEOs – very similar to that of their government counterparts. Meetings were held in Europe, in the US, and via transatlantic conference calls.[62] In a process that would continue over the next few years, company representatives met in individual issue groups, as part of the US or EU steering committee, and/or as part of the Joint Steering Committee to push the TABD agenda. On 23 May 1996, the TABD issued its Progress Report – a 72-pages document with specific policy recommendations. The document included suggestions for 'language to be included' in the June 1996 transatlantic government summit. In addition, a 'mes-

60 Interview with Commission official, 18 September 1996.

61 As one European industry association official noted, 'It is important to have both CEOs and organizations. You need the CEOs for the visibility but the work is done by 'sherpas' and business organizations behind [the scenes]. The originality of the TABD process is that for the first time business and organizations are working together. All four sides speak together. That is the interest, the strength of the initiatives.' Interview with EU business association official, Brussels, 1 July 1996.

62 TABD coordination offices – set up at the Ford office in Washington D.C. and at the German Chemical Industry (of which BASF is a member) office in Brussels – disseminated information and encouraged greater business participation. A TABD newsletter was launched for Seville participants and other interested parties.

sage to government on business expectations' was highlighted in virtually every subsection of the report.

The TABD Progress Report addressed several key issues including the ITA, automotive regulatory harmonization, and MRAs. The May 1996 report also reiterated the business leaders' decision to convene another conference in November. This time, CEOs and government officials – including USTR and Commission trade negotiators as well as US regulatory agency officials – would sit down to 'assess the progress' and encourage further action on TABD recommendations.

In the words of one TABD participant, the May Progress Report contained 'strident calls for government action, perhaps anticipating [what would become] the dismal June Summit'.[63] For their part, US and EU officials publicly applauded the Progress Report and cited the TABD process as one of the most positive developments in the US-EU relationship. At a 23 May 1996 press conference in Brussels, the new Undersecretary of Commerce Stuart E. Eizenstat was effusive in his praise of TABD. Eizenstat noted that:

> [...] no one would have quite imagined the degree to which this [the TABD] has influenced government decision-making on both sides of the Atlantic. It has become deeply enmeshed and embedded into the US government decision-making process on a whole range of regulatory, trade, commercial issues. It is regularly cited, often by one agency against the other [...] and is part of the ongoing discussions between the EU and the US. [...] So the TABD has had a truly remarkable impact in our country, in the Transatlantic dialogue, and multilaterally.[64]

While accepting government praise for the May 1996 Progress Report, US-EU industry groups also expected action on the TABD recommendations. Given the frenetic work and considerable resources expended on TABD, the transatlantic business community anticipated concrete results at the June 1996 government summit between US and EU leaders. The June summit, however, disappointed the business

---

63 Correspondence with the author, 18 September 1996.

64 See Eizenstat. Frank Vargo of the Commerce Department was equally supportive in his statements to American business representatives at the Washington D.C., TABD Outreach meeting in June 1996. According to Vargo, the TABD process had been moved to the 'dead center' of US government discussions. He cited Joan Spero, Undersecretary of State as saying that TABD 'is the most positive part of the US-EU relationship. Everything that comes out of TABD must be looked at first'. Presentation by Commerce Department official at TABD Outreach meeting, Washington D.C., 6 June 1996.

leaders. While President Clinton formally recognized Jürgen Schrempp of Daimler-Benz and John Luke of Westvaco at the summit press conference for their active TABD participation, the US-EU governments' disagreement over the Helms-Burton legislation on Cuban investments dominated the summit.

The June summit prompted TABD leaders to call on the governments to achieve concrete progress by the next TABD conference to be held five months later in Chicago. Industry officials warned that they might terminate the TABD process – now an important cornerstone of the New Transatlantic Marketplace – if government action was not forthcoming. In private meetings and in public fora, US and EU officials repeatedly stated their willingness to address the TABD recommendations.

Confidence Building

Business leaders – who often measure time by quarterly profit reports – were frustrated by the governments' slow response. As one Commission official noted, 'The government side [did not sell] the real necessity of time to the business side – not that we don't share their enthusiasm. It is simply that given [the potential problems], in order for whole process [to work], we need to build little by little and to get it right this first time.'

TABD business participants increasingly recognized, however, that many of the Seville and May Progress Report recommendations would take months if not years to implement. Time was necessary for government negotiators and domestic groups to grapple with some of the political initiatives. After all, transatlantic business partners required the Seville conference and almost a year of negotiations to develop a comfortable working relationship. A large part of the relationship was centered on a unique learning process. American business leaders – who knew little of the workings of the European Union – began to understand better the complicated multi-level structure in Europe. They also learned more about the specific obstacles facing European companies in the US market. As one participant noted, 'From a European perspective, the dialogue has worked very well to educate American industry to reality.'[65] In return, the Europeans discovered some of the impediments to trade facing the American companies. Equally important, the two sides

---

65 Interview with EU business representative, Brussels, 27 June 1996.

also learned how to work together in the dialogue. Americans determined that the European representatives were equally adept at 'technical details' as they were with 'overarching principles' articulated at the Seville conference. Europeans, on the other hand, learned to recognize that the Americans' 'direct, blunt' style was not designed to 'shove their views' onto the Europeans. Rather, it was simply the 'direct, blunt' style of the Americans!

As one business representative noted, 'TABD is a psychological process as much as anything.'[66] Of course, the two governments – and notably, the US regulatory agencies – needed their own confidence-building measures. As one Commission official noted: 'We are working very hard to explain how regulations work on both sides and to find a common path for a common regulatory system or a mutual regulatory system [...]. We need confidence-building measures of tremendous proportion.'[67]

Interestingly, in Europe, the confidence-building had begun several years earlier when 'mutual recognition' was enshrined as a key principle underlying the Single Market Program.

The Chicago Breakthrough

The US-EU business community's patience and confidence-building measures paid off at the November TABD conference. Approximately 300 participants attended the Chicago conference: 27 EU and 37 US CEOs, over 130 business representatives, and some 100 government officials.[68] Whereas Seville was organized primarily as a business-to-business dialogue, the Chicago TABD meeting was designed for government and business officials – including representatives from US regulatory agencies as well as from the EU Member States – to sit down and take the Seville discussions to a higher level.[69] Government officials were aware of the business community's demand for results. In a briefing prior to the Chicago conference, Frank Vargo, Deputy Assistant Secretary of Commerce for Europe, suggested that Sir Leon Brittan

66 Interview with EU business association representative, Brussels, 3 July 1996.

67 Interview with Commission official, Brussels, 26 June 1996.

68 European Commission, 'Report on the conference of the Transatlantic Business Dialogue (TABD), Chicago, 8-9 November 1995', 10 December 1996.

69 Some business representatives complained that government officials often dominated discussions in both Seville and Chicago.

captured the sentiment well when he stated that 'Wherever US and EU business agree on something, we [the governments] must act, or we must give a good explanation why not'.[70]

The conference included three roundtables: one on the Transatlantic Advisory Committee on Standards (TACS) dealing with standards, certification, and regulatory policy (with breakout groups in four sectors); a second on global issues (WTO, intellectual property and related subjects); and a third on business facilitation (investment, export controls, international business practices, etc.). TABD representatives knew that business participants were not merely interested in issuing joint recommendations as in Seville. The organizers wanted roundtable discussions in which the governments were partners in the discussions. Organizers were keen to have not only the Commerce Department and Commission at Chicago, but also the US regulatory agencies, USTR and the EU Member States. As one participant noted, 'The purpose of Chicago was to get the governments at the table and to develop the Seville-style of business/business discussions into a four-way discussion. In this discussion, business listened to the problems governments were having with various proposals, and then worked together to develop creative solutions that could address each other's concerns.'[71] Then, it would be up to the US-EU industry to respond.

The response came during the first TACs roundtable. The US and EU had been discussing MRAs for almost five years. They had been identified as a top priority at the Seville conference where the business community called on governments to accept the principle of 'approved once, accepted everywhere in the Transatlantic Marketplace'. The US government came to Chicago promoting an MRA covering five sectors where agreement could readily be reached in each sector. However, the European Commission – relying on its package approach – had insisted on an MRA covering pharmaceuticals and medical devices – two sectors where significant US-EU differences persisted.[72] In the pharmaceuticals

---

70 Comments by Frank Vargo, Deputy Assistant Secretary of Commerce for Europe, at the US Chamber of Commerce and TABD briefing on Preparations for the WTO Singapore Ministerial and TABD Conference in Chicago, 17 October 1996.

71 Interview with TABD official, Washington, 18 December 1996.

72 L. Barber and G. De Jonquieres, 'Drive to Lessen Transatlantic Trade Divisions', *Financial Times*, 8 November 1996. It is interesting to note the success of the Commission's 'package approach' despite claims by some that TABD's sector-by-sector approach is 'a new paradigm for trade liberalization'. See P. Stern, 'The

sector, the problem centered on the two sides' certification of 'good manufacturing practices' in the pharmaceuticals sector. In an opening statement, the US Food and Drug Administration noted that it 'was inexperienced in confidence building'.[73] Yet in the discussion that followed, as one FDA official recalls, 'industry leaders asked FDA officials why they were 'quibbling' over certain matters [...]. The companies' advice to the FDA was simple: 'Get on with it'.[74] A solution was proposed in which the US regulatory agency would rely on European inspection reports and vice versa, and be allowed to reinspect European plants under 'exceptional' circumstances. [75] With the FDA on board, the US and EU governments agreed to follow-up negotiations to conclude the MRA by 31 January 1997.

In addition to the MRA breakthrough, the Chicago meeting achieved success in a number of other areas. There was significant movement, for example, toward concluding an EU/US Customs Cooperation and Mutual Assistance Agreement. Following the initial efforts at Seville, business pushed the two administrations to conclude the Information Technology Agreement in the Singapore WTO Ministerial in December. The Chicago meeting also saw the creation of the Transatlantic Small Business Initiative (TASBI) – a program first promoted by the Europeans. In addition, the business community pushed for the adoption of language in the final Chicago Declaration to address the US Helms-Burton law and to encourage the withdrawal of extraterritorial provisions of the 1996 US Sanctions laws.

The appointment of two new business leaders to head the TABD was also announced at the Chicago meeting: Dana Mead, CEO of Tenneco, and Jan Timmer, Chairman of Philips. One month later, Mead and Timmer met with top-level government officials at the WTO Ministerial in Singapore where the ITA accord was signed. That same month, the two sent a letter with a copy of the Chicago Declaration to President

Transatlantic Business Dialogue: a New Paradigm for Standards and Regulatory Reform Sector-by-Sector', www.tabd.com.

73 European Commission, 'Report on the Conference of the Transatlantic Business Dialogue (TABD)', 10 December 1996, Annex 1.

74 FDA official as cited in M. Green Cowles, 'The Limits of Liberalization: Regulatory Cooperation and the New Transatlantic Agenda: A Conference Report', *American Institute for Contemporary German Studies*, Washington D.C., 16 January 1997.

75 N. Dunne, 'US, EU closer on telecoms and IT accord', *Financial Times*, 11 November 1996.

Clinton and to Sir Leon Brittan. They later met with Presidents Clinton and Santer and Irish Prime Minister Bruton during the US-EU summit in Washington D.C., to press the TABD agenda.

1997: The Road to Rome – Visibility, Priorities, and the MRA

In taking over the leadership, Timmer and Mead brought a new impetus to TABD. Timmer in particular wanted to reinvigorate the process by making the TABD 'run more efficiently by getting more companies involved and at a higher level'.[76] If Seville had launched the TABD initiative, the Chicago conference had validated the process. The two businessmen wanted to ensure that the TABD had a viable future.

Tenneco and Philips worked to widen TABD's circle by recruiting new members to become Issue Managers. The TABD's ability to speak out on behalf of industry after all depended, in part, on whether or not the wider business community found it to be representative of industry. In Europe, efforts were made to broaden the geographical reach of TABD companies – notably to France and the southern Member States who previously were not strongly involved in the process. Some European business officials had privately complained that TABD was beginning to look 'too German' in outlook with the leadership of BASF and other German companies. EU industry and government officials were also aware that TABD's continued success would depend on French participation. Until 1997, French government and industry officials were watching the process from afar. There were concerns in some French quarters that TABD was a 'Transatlantic Free Trade Agreement in disguise'.[77] To counter these perceptions, Timmer enlisted Francis Mer, CEO of Usinor-Sacilor, to head the Business Facilitation Group. Conrad Eckenschwiller from the Mouvement des Entreprises de France (MEDEF – the French national industry association) served as the working chair of the group.[78]

---

[76] Interview with EU business representative, 10 June 1997.

[77] Interview with EU business representative, 10 June 1997.

[78] The MEDEF was formerly known as the Conseil National du Patronat Français (CNPF).

The new TABD leadership also worked to increase TABD's visibility to the business community on both sides of the Atlantic.[79] Greater efforts were made to make the TABD process open, accessible, and transparent by publicizing TABD meetings, achievements, and documents. In doing so, the TABD sought to encourage companies to become more involved in the process, and to deflect criticism suggesting it was an elitist organization.

At the same time, TABD companies were reaching out not only to the US and EU administrations – but also to the Congress and the Member States. Now that the international trade agenda was set, TABD business leaders decided to redirect some of their focus on the domestic scene. They recognized that domestic groups would also mobilize to influence the government officials' negotiating positions on transatlantic matters. On the US side, business leaders stepped up efforts with members of the US House and Senate to inform them of TABD recommendations and activities. Industry officials also continued their contacts with the House Ways and Means, House International Relations, Senate Foreign Relations and Senate Finance Committees. On the EU side, TABD officials began to develop closer ties with the European Parliament and the Member States. These efforts by Philips (a Dutch company) were facilitated by the fact that the Dutch government held the EU presidency for the first six months of 1997. A representative of the Dutch Minister of Foreign Affairs soon joined the EU Steering Committee meetings in Brussels.

Finally, Tenneco and Philips worked to strengthen the TABD structure and focus on key priorities for the year to come. Instead of fifteen issue groups, the TABD was reorganized to focus on three core areas addressed at the Chicago meeting – the Transatlantic Advisory Committee on Standards, Business Facilitation, and Global Issues. In turn, each core group was further broken down into separate sectors or issues run by a US and EU issue manager. A small- and medium-sized enterprises group was also established.

While Seville had produced a 'shopping list' of recommendations, Tenneco and Philips determined that the TABD needed to prioritize its demands to encourage more direct action by the administrations. During the first four months of 1997, the US and EU Steering Committees developed their priorities by determining 'which issues have enough meat

79 Interview with US business representative, 6 January 1997.

to go forward and what new issues to embrace'.[80] Having developed its meetings and conferences around 'the rhythm of the [US-EU] summits', the TABD could thus target key issues for government leaders' attention.[81] The new priorities agenda also allowed US-EU industry to 'take control' of a process that was dominated at times by government officials' own agendas. The time had come to ensure that TABD was 'business-driven'. At the 26 February Joint Steering Committee meeting, the companies presented their plans to the governments for the year.

The MRA and the Quadrilateral Negotiating Process

The new leadership TABD team was put to task when US and EU negotiators failed to reach agreement on the MRA negotiations by 31 January 1997, as decided at the Chicago conference. A couple weeks before the deadline, the TABD became highly involved in the process, at times at the governments' request. In the midst of the MRA talks, a special quadrilateral meeting took place between the negotiators and a handful of CEOs to discuss the governmental impasse and potential business solutions. Despite the business intervention, the negotiators were unable to wrap up the MRA by the end-of-the-month deadline. A couple weeks later in February, Timmer and Mead wrote to Presidents Clinton and Santer to express their dismay that the MRA deadline had been missed, and to emphasize the importance of its completion.

Pressure for completing the MRA mounted as the two sides met on several occasions to pound out agreements both internationally and domestically. Because the MRA included a number of sectors (*i.e.* a package approach), the negotiations included US regulatory officials from a number of disparate agencies. As Stuart Eizenstat noted: 'When we launched negotiations on the MRA, I don't think any of us appreciated the difficulties we could have in this. We found that we [the US and EU] had entirely different regulatory regimes. [... The situation was compounded in the US] by having independent regulatory regimes.'[82]

The US regulatory agencies posed particular problems in the negotiations for two reasons. First, the agencies are operating under their

---

80 Interview with TABD official, 18 December 1996.

81 Interview with EU business representative, 10 June 1997.

82 S. Eizenstat, 'Building the New Transatlantic Marketplace: How Are We Doing?', presentation at TABD Midyear Report, US Chamber of Commerce, Washington D.C., 20 June 1997.

own statutory limitations imposed by Congress. Thus, there were certain things regulatory agencies such as the FDA could not do even if it wanted to due to statutory limitations. Second, the statutory independence of the agencies meant that the regulatory officials had their own independent mindset and turf to defend as well.

A week before the May US-EU summit, Commissioner Sir Leon Brittan and USTR Charlene Barshefsky met again to discuss the MRA. The TABD chairs were kept apprised of the proceedings. On 28 May, Barshefsky and Commerce Secretary William Daley announced a 'major breakthrough' on the MRA negotiations, thus allowing for an overall agreement to be reached shortly. In the USTR press release, Secretary Daley noted that 'The Trans-Atlantic Business Dialogue, in partnership with the Administration, made it possible to reach this point.'[83]

The two sides were not able to finalize the agreement before the US-EU summit. Nonetheless, for the first time, perhaps owing to Dutch government's EU presidency, TABD was an agenda item at the May US-EU summit. As another first, Timmer and Mead met briefly with Presidents Clinton and Santer, and Prime Minister Kok of the Netherlands to present the 1997 TABD *Priorities Paper* that identified 'key priorities where action is required by governments to implement the TABD recommendations'.

Finally, on 13 June, the two sides formally announced the conclusion of the MRA. Noting that the MRA covers over $40 billion of transatlantic trade a year, the two governments trumpeted the agreement. Sir Leon Brittan noted that the MRA was 'one of the crowning achievements of the new Transatlantic relationship' and that '[t]he identification of the MRA as a top priority by the business community was crucial in persuading the EU and the US to overcome bureaucratic objections and reach this hard-won agreement'.[84]

The MRA was by far the most important TABD agenda item accomplished to date. For TABD participants, the MRA's success was found

---

83 Office of the USTR, 'US-EU Achieve Breakthrough on MRA Negotiations', press release, 28 May 1997. Several EU participants found the press release premature – and potentially embarrassing if the final MRA was not concluded. Commission officials had also warned that any text had to pass by the Member States for final approval.

84 Office of Press and Public Affairs, European Commission Delegation, 'EU Reaches MRA Agreements to cut red tape with United States and Canada', press release, 13 June 1997.

not only in the potential savings to business, but in the TABD process itself. As the *Journal of Commerce* noted:

> [The MRA] took five years to negotiate, but most of the progress was made in the last eighteen months when the chief executives of some hundred European and US companies took matters into their own hands. It is a tribute to their persistence that the deal was put on the agenda of last week's trans-Atlantic summit [...]. The mutual recognition agreement, while notable on its own merits, has its greatest significance in showing where industry-government cooperation can lead.[85]

Rome: The Renewed Agenda

The 1997 TABD *Priorities Paper* presented to Clinton, Santer, and Kok, laid the groundwork for the Rome conference. The paper was not a progress report – for many in TABD business community found progress to be minimal. Rather, it was a list of issues deemed 'critical' by TABD companies to the US-EU economies. The business community cited issues in the three core TABD groups: Standards and Regulatory Policy, Business Facilitation (taxation, export controls, customs, electronic commerce, etc.), and Global Issues (WTO, Trade Related Aspects of Intellectual Property Rights Agreement (TRIPS), patent law, etc.). The paper's top priority was the implementation of the Mutual Recognition Agreement signed in June. The document also called for the US and EU governments to not merely focus on immediate concerns, but to take a longer-term perspective on regulatory cooperation by agreeing to consult with one another before adopting new or amending existing regulations.[86] Business leaders also encouraged the governments to include more sectors and product characteristics into the MRA.

The Rome summit on 6-7 November was the largest to date with 65 European, 45 American CEOs and/or company chairmen. The conference was also the largest in terms of issues and breakout groups. New issue areas included global electronic commerce, dietary supplements, food additives and flavors, fasteners, and 'metric only' labeling.

Once again, the TABD conference was successful not only in terms of what business encouraged governments to do – but also in terms of what governments agreed not to do. In the latter case, US and EU in-

---

85 'The Strength of Dialogue', *Journal of Commerce*, 5 June 1997.

86 B. Berggren, 'A Single Transatlantic Market: A Vision of Deregulation and Integration', *The European-American Business Council Newsletter*, Spring 1998, p.20.

dustry convinced the Commission to delay legislation for ten years (if not indefinitely) that would have required after 31 December 1999, for all products sold in the EU to be labeled only in metric units. 'Dual labels' with metric and non-metric (*i.e.* American measurements) would be prohibited. Industry pointed out that just as large American companies would incur significant costs in producing two different labels, so too would small European firms selling their goods to the American market. Moreover, the costs to small companies would likely be prohibitive and lessen their competitiveness.

Another important preventative action dealt with an EU directive that if enforced on 1 January, would 'block deliveries to Europe of tallow and gelatin derived from cattle carcasses because of the presumed threat of mad cow disease'. The problem is that about 'forty percent of the tallow and gelatin used in Europe to produce filler and casings for pharmaceutical products like pills and tables comes from the United States'.[87] About eighty-five percent of all medicinal products sold in Europe would be affected by the directive. The Commission agreed not to impose any ban on tallow and gelatin for the foreseeable future.

One of the most energetic sections dealt with electronic commerce where the two business communities encouraged 'industry-led, market-driven privacy protection principles'. While business and government (notably the EU) did not see eye-to-eye on the issue, it was agreed that TABD would serve as an important forum for the two sides to discuss electronic commerce.

As they did at the Chicago summit, US and EU officials, along with business leaders, openly disagreed on the American use of sanctions against Cuba, Iran and Libya.[88] The TABD promoted the idea of businesses adhering to 'global best practices' (providing non-discriminatory employment, safe places of work and other core principles of workers' rights) in all international places. While affirming that economic sanctions are necessary at times, the business leaders argued that they should then be implemented multilaterally. The TABD called for governments to terminate their individual secondary boycotts and extraterritoriality sanctions provisions.

---

87 J. Tagliabue, 'Rome Talks Seek to Defuse Trade Disputes', *The New York Times*, 8 November 1997.

88 B. Coleman, 'Trans-Atlantic Business Dialogue Gains Momentum at Rome Talks', *The Wall Street Journal Europe*, 10 November 1997, p.1.

The TABD also applauded the US announcement made at the conference of an inter-agency group, headed by the David Aaron, Under Secretary for International Trade, to ensure the implementation of TABD recommendations. The group would include key contact people in each department and regulatory agency responsible for TABD matters (In this respect, it is similar to the European Commission contact list set up after Seville.). Business officials welcomed the group as a firm commitment by the US government to support the TABD process. Some also viewed it as a Commerce Department initiative to bolster its position in a TABD turf battle with USTR now that the trade negotiators were clearly involved in TABD matters.

In the *communiqué* following the summit, business leaders praised the governments for achievements such as the MRA negotiation and worldwide Information Technology Agreement at the WTO. However, they also criticized the US and EU for the lack of progress in a number of areas such as MRA implementation (calling on the governments to provide progress reports) and taxation policies (expressing their 'strong disappointment') while stating concern for outstanding trade conflicts (notably the US sanctions policy).

The following month, Mead and Timmer again participated in the US-EU summit, promoting the TABD recommendations with President Clinton, President Santer, and Luxembourg Prime Minister Jean-Claude Juncker.

1998-99: A Continuing Partnership

In 1998, two new TABD chairmen – Jürgen Schrempp, Chairman and Chief Executive Officer of Daimler-Benz AG, and Lodewijk de Vink, President and Chief Operating Officer of Warner-Lambert – took over the leadership of the organization. The leaders determined that having enunciated TABD priorities, the organization's focus for the new year should be implementation. While US officials like to claim that eighty percent of TABD recommendations are now official US policy', most of the recommendations are in the consultation stage (The EU Commission is guilty, of course, of making similar statements). Even where agreements have been reached – such as the MRA – they have yet to be implemented.

With the theme of implementation, the TABD decided to create a 'scorecard' giving the status of each issue, an overview of what needs to be done, and a suggested date for implementation (According to a

Commission official, business adapted the Commission's own 'scorecard approach' to TABD developments.)[89] A draft scorecard was prepared for the 23-24 April Joint Steering Group meeting comprised of all issue managers and senior US and EU officials. The 1998 Mid-Year Scorecard Report was then presented by Schrempp and de Vink to Presidents Clinton and Santer, and Prime Minister Tony Blair at the 18 May US-EU summit in London. The report noted that the US and EU administrations have taken 'significant, concrete action' on almost one-third of TABD's recommendations, while more than one-half of these recommendations are 'under active discussion between business and government communities.'

As impressive as the TABD scorecard was, the business community's work was overshadowed by the US and EU administrations' own agenda-setting efforts. On 11 March 1998, the European Commission gave its support to a new plan proposed by Sir Leon Brittan to create a New Transatlantic Marketplace (NTM) – a wide-ranging plan designed to rid trade barriers from US-EU trade. Brittan had argued that under the 1995 NTA, progress was made 'through a step-by-step approach'. However, this approach proved needlessly protracted during the 1997 Mutual Recognition Agreement negotiations.[90] One of the proposed NTM's goals was to speed up the process through an extensive MRA negotiation over a number of sectors. The NTM also proposed to eliminate all industry tariffs by 2010, create a free trade area in services, and liberalize government procurement, intellectual property and investment beyond current agreements.[91]

The TABD's response to the NTM was both supportive and cautious. On one hand, the business group was 'encouraged by efforts to improve business conditions in the transatlantic region.'[92] In examining the Brittan proposal, some business leaders argued that the proposed NTM set up a broader political framework around original TABD goals. Sir Leon's proposal was a 'political top-down exercise on TABD's

89 Interview with Commission official, Brussels, 10 June 1998.

90 Commission of the European Communities, 'The New Transatlantic Marketplace', COM(1998) 125 final, Brussels, 11 March 1998.

91 Commission of the European Communities, 'The New Transatlantic', p.5.

92 TABD, 'Transatlantic Business Dialogue Encouraged by Efforts to Improve US-EU Business Conditions', Press Release, 11 March 1988.

bottom-up approach'.[93] Given the slow pace of the MRA, such a political framework was necessary to place pressure on regulatory officials to move forward and thus speed up future MRA negotiations. On the other hand, TABD expressed concern that the proposal continues to 'safeguard and improve the pragmatic results produced by TABD'.[94] In certain respects, the Brittan initiative looked like the ill-fated Transatlantic Free Trade Agreement proposals floated before the TABD's creation. TABD business leaders were wary that the NTM might detract from what were – in their view – more important TABD issues. American business representatives were also concerned that the NTM created a huge package deal.[95] As stated before, American business preferred to work on a sector-by-sector, issue-by-issue basis.

In the end, Brittan's NTM initiative was defeated by the Member States themselves at a meeting of EU foreign ministers on 27 April 1998. Less than a month later, US-EU government leaders were able to salvage the NTM debacle by agreeing to a new trade expansion initiative, contingent on compromise actions regarding the US Helms-Burton legislation. The Transatlantic Economic Partnership (TEP) was announced at the US-EU Summit in London on 18 May 1998. Initial plans call for the TEP to focus on agriculture, services, electronic commerce, and a number of other areas of interest to TABD companies. As one Commission official described it, the TEP is a rather 'innocent document' broad enough to please everyone.[96] Recognizing that the TEP is not designed to replace TABD but to add greater political impetus to trade matters, companies have been supportive of the new initiative.

With or without the TEP, the TABD has forged ahead with its agenda. At the 1998 TABD conference in Charlotte, North Carolina, US Vice President Al Gore provided the keynote address to over 500 business and government participants at the conference. The Charlotte meeting was a watershed in terms of the TABD's 'coming of age'. The fifty-two working groups allowed for more indepth and technical discussions among business and government officials. At the same time, some participants expressed concern that the TABD had become 'such a

93 Interview with US business representative, Washington D.C., 17 April 1998.

94 TABD, 'Transatlantic Business Dialogue Encouraged by Efforts to Improve US-EU Business Conditions', Press Release, 11 March 1988.

95 Interview with US business representative, Washington D.C., 17 April 1998.

96 Interview with Commission official, Brussels, 10 June 1998.

well-oiled machine that it lacked spontaneity'.[97] While several significant steps were taken on matters such as guidelines for US-EU regulatory cooperation, the implementation of the MRAs, and e-commerce, the general sentiment emerged that the TABD conferences had become too large with each CEO bringing his or her own staffer and issue manager. The political dynamics of CEO-to-CEO meetings were beginning to be overshadowed. Thus, following the December 1998 US-EU summit in Washington D.C., the new TABD co-chairs, Richard Thomas of Xerox and Jérôme Monod of Suez Lyonnaise des Eaux, determined that the TABD conferences needed to be turned back to the level of the 'decision-makers' – *i.e.* the CEOs and high-level government officials.

The new TABD leadership brought other changes to the organization in 1999. The two men decided to promote smaller, more informal meetings with senior government officials such as US Commerce Secretary Daley to promote greater dialogue on TABD priorities. In addition, small transatlantic groups of CEOs met with independent agency heads to discuss key concerns to the companies.[98] One of the TABD's more important breakthroughs occurred in May 1999, when business and government officials announced the promotion of an 'early warning system' to identify and minimize trade disputes in order to avoid any future US-EU trade wars. At the Berlin conference in October 1999, the TABD identified for government officials more than half a dozen issues that could potentially lead to transatlantic trade disputes.[99] Also at the Berlin conference, the TABD issued its recommendations on promoting private sector investment in South Eastern Europe – a new task for which President Clinton and German Prime Minister Schroeder had invited the TABD to address at the June 1999 EU-US Summit.

The TABD's primary focus in 1999, however, was the WTO ministerial in Seattle, Washington, at the end of the year. Throughout 1999, TABD working groups sought to solidify the transatlantic position on a number of key WTO-related policy areas, including TRIPs. The TABD called for the creation of a new round of multilateral trade negotiations with a built-in agenda that would last no more than three years.

97 Interview with TABD official, 25 May 1999.

98 Interview with TABD official, 12 July 1999.

99 TABD, 'Statement of Conclusions', Berlin Conference, 29-30 October 1999.

While the TABD expected 'real and concrete results at the 1999 WTO Ministerial meeting'[100] labor and environmental NGOs, and other interested parties had other plans for the Seattle meeting. The failure of the Seattle ministerial and the outcry against large multinational firms are, of course, of concern to the TABD. The Seattle debacle was not the first – and will certainly not be the last – example of protest against business-government relations. Indeed, the US-EU business community tends to view the creation of 'other dialogues' in the US-EU relationship – the Transatlantic Labor Dialogue, the Transatlantic Consumers Dialogue, the Transatlantic Legislators' Dialogue – not merely as an attempt to introduce civil society into US-EU relations, but also to counteract the growing influence of the TABD. How the TABD engages with and responds to these dialogues and developments in the future will undoubtedly be important.[101]

Assessing the Future

Through the TABD, it is clear that US and EU businesses are no longer the 'silent partners' of the transatlantic relationship. Rather, they have emerged as important political players in shaping US-EU trade relations. In doing so, the TABD takes an important first step in transcending some of the problems inherent in the US-EU relationship.

As Smith notes in his excellent piece in this book, there are a number of policy dimensions and dilemmas facing the US in its partnership with the EU – just as there are similar difficulties facing the EU in its relationship with the US. While agreeing with Smith's overall characterization of the US-EU economic partnership, I differ in his concluding assessment of US-EU trade strategies. While the TABD does not offer a 'grand strategy', the TABD can and does offer nonetheless a strategy – a limited but important one – on which to build the transatlantic economic relationship.

Smith argues, for example, that much of the complexity facing the US-EU partnership can be attributed both to the growing economic

---

100 TABD, 'Statement of Conclusion'.

101 For a discussion of the TABD's relationship with the other dialogues, see M. Green Cowles, 'The Transatlantic Business Dialogue: Transforming the New Transatlantic Dialogue', in M. Pollack and G. Shaffer, *Transatlantic Governance in a Global Economy*, forthcoming. For an overview of the other dialogues, see F. Bignami and S. Charnovitz, 'A Transatlantic Civil Society' in the same volume.

interdependence between the two as well as to the divergent regulatory structures and industrial cultures ('system friction'). It is not surprising that internationally oriented firms are far more attuned to this dimension of transatlantic relations than are the regulatory officials or public servants who purportedly represent their interests in trade discussions. Because they rely on global sourcing and imports in the face of growing cost pressures and international competition, TABD companies recognize the need for transatlantic regulatory cooperation.[102] Because they have considerable investments in each other's markets, they have a political interest in transatlantic developments.[103] The TABD has thus played an important proactive role in promoting trade and regulatory policies that address this economic interdependence. At the same time, in the 'spirit of Seville', the TABD has worked to mitigate industrial culture differences by focusing on those issues where there is significant agreement on the two sides.

As discussed above, the TABD has created new structures and prompted new working relationships not only between US government and EU Commission, but also within the respective administrations. These structures and working relationships inform the cross-national, cross-department, intergovernmental, and, of course, government-business policy developments highlighted by Smith. As pointed out in this chapter, the TABD has created a bilateral forum for discussing multilateral (*i.e.* WTO) matters, prompted interagency regulatory coordination groups, and, quite obviously, developed novel business-government coordination on regulatory matters.

Perhaps most importantly, the TABD has engendered new policy-making processes in the transatlantic partnership. As one Commission official explained, because of the TABD, 'there is a new way of negotiating that has developed'. Prior to TABD, MRA negotiations were very combative in style. The two sides would seek concessions from each other. It was, in the words of the Commission official, very 'defensive'. However, with TABD involvement, the tone of the negotiations changed as participants recognized that 'to get the MRA working, you needed to develop very deep interrelations between two big systems. [...]

---

[102] M. Green Cowles, 'The Limits of Liberalization: Regulatory Cooperation and the New Transatlantic Agenda: A Conference Report', Washington D.C., American Institute for Contemporary German Studies, 16 January 1997, pp.3-4.

[103] J. Peterson and M. Green Cowles, 'Clinton, Europe and Economic Diplomacy: What makes the EU Different?', *Governance*, 11:3 (1998) 251-71.

The TABD was a paradigm for how this kind of exchange could take place.'[104]

In short, while the TABD process may not be a 'grand strategy' (it does not address banana regimes or worker rights etc.), the TABD is much more than an 'operational activity'. It has created a novel way of 'doing business' in transatlantic trade and regulatory negotiations. The practical, cooperative, results-oriented TABD business strategy has proven successful. In certain respects, the TABD's industrial diplomacy provides a positive 'bottom-up' approach to the traditional 'top-down' interaction of government actors in US-EU trade matters. Indeed, as evidenced by the ongoing TEP discussions, a transatlantic US-EU business-government partnership continues to be forged to focus on the complex and evolving economic ties between the United States and Europe.

Given its relative infancy, the TABD and its future cannot easily be predicted. In the short term, the TABD depends on the financial and time commitment of the companies and their CEOs as well as the political will of political leaders to follow through on TABD recommendations. One factor likely to challenge the organization will be the US and EU governments' – as well as companies' – willingness to uphold TABD recommendations in multilateral forums such as the WTO. Another factor will be the ability of the TABD organization to tackle more controversial issues which to date it has avoided. Of course, as Smith points out in his chapter, political cycles are also likely to influence the TABD's future. It is not clear that future US presidents would continue to support the TABD, nor is it a foregone conclusion that new European governments at the EU or national levels will embrace the organization's preeminence in international trade matters.

Nonetheless, the role of the TABD raises a number of implications for future research on the EU – both in terms of common commercial policy (CCP) and decision-making in general. Historically, for example, business groups have not mobilized at the EU level to influence EU common commercial policy. While groups such as UNICE have provided official comments on GATT negotiations, there were no significant consultations between large firms and the Commission during the

[104] Interview with Commission official, Brussels, 10 June 1998.

GATT rounds.[105] Now that European firms have organized themselves in the TABD and Commission contacts have been developed, the companies are poised to play a more proactive role in WTO discussions with the Commission as well as with the Article 113 Committee. The mobilization of large companies in CCP matters will likely prompt other interests – environmental, consumer, and labor – to participate more fully in European-level discussions.

The TABD also challenges the core assumption of liberal theories of European decisionmaking and international politics that domestic interests are the primary sources of government decisions.[106] As demonstrated by the TABD as well as other business groups in EU policy-making, large firms are able to organize themselves at the European (or transatlantic) level first to develop their positions, discuss strategies, and enter directly into supranational or transnational negotiations.[107] Only later do the companies focus their attention on influencing national governments and other domestic groups.

Finally, the TABD provides an interesting case study for international trade negotiations in general. Increasingly, the TABD has become a model for trade negotiations in other parts of the world.[108] Thus, how the role of business fits our models of international bargaining and cooperation remains an important research agenda to pursue.

---

105 S. Woolcock and M. Hodges, 'EU Policy in the Uruguay Round', in H. Wallace and W. Wallace (eds.), *Policy-Making in the European Union* (Oxford, Oxford University Press, 1996) pp.301-324. The exception was the chemical industry that has strong international links.

106 See A. Moravcsik, 'Preferences and Power in the European Community: A Liberal Intergovernmentalist Approach', *Journal of Common Market Studies*, 31:4 (1993) 473-524; and A. Moravcsik, 'Taking Preferences Seriously: A Liberal Theory of International Politics', *International Organization*, 51:4 (1997) 513-53.

107 See M. Green Cowles, 'Setting the Agenda for a New Europe: The ERT and EC 1992', *Journal of Common Market Studies*, 33:4 (1995) 501-26.

108 M. Green Cowles, 'The Transatlantic Business Dialogue: Business at the Negotiating Table', *The International Executive*, 38:6 (1996) 849-56.

CHAPTER 8

The United States, the European Union and the New Transatlantic Marketplace: Public Strategy and Private Interests

Michael SMITH

Loughborough University, Department of European Studies

This chapter evaluates the extent to which US policies towards the European Union can be given strategic direction. It begins by analysing a number of dimensions of the US/EU relationship; it then proceeds to assess some key dimensions of US policies towards the EU, and finally it conducts an appraisal of the current and likely future policy agenda in US/EU relations. The focus is predominantly on the United States, but many of the issues identified can equally be discerned in the making of the EU's 'US policy', which is the subject of other work by the present author.[1]

The problem addressed by the chapter is thus centred on the ways in which and the extent to which the United States can produce an 'EU policy', in the sense of a coordinated and coherent strategy, consistently pursued and implemented. Much has been written in the literature of international political economy about notions of strategic action and in particular about the idea of 'strategic trade policy'. Some of this has found its way into analysis of US/EU relations, particularly in relation to the impact of the Single Market Programme and US responses to it.[2]

---

1 M. Smith, 'The European Union, Foreign Economic Policy and the Changing World Arena', *Journal of European Public Policy*, 1:2 (1994) 283-302; M. Smith, 'Competitive Cooperation and EU-US Relations: Can the EU be a Strategic Partner for the US in the World Political Economy?', *Journal of European Public Policy*, 5:4 (1998) 561-77.

2 See for example M. Calingaert, *European Integration Revisited: Progress, Prospects and US Interests* (Boulder CO, Westview Press, 1996); B. Hocking and M. Smith, *Beyond Foreign Economic Policy: The United States and the Single European Market in a Changing World Economy* (London, Cassell/Pinter, 1997); M. Kahler, *International Institutions and the Political Economy of Integration*

During the mid-1990s there was also increasing debate in policy circles about the possibility of a new transatlantic partnership, either in the narrow sense of a 'Transatlantic Free Trade Area' (TAFTA) or in the broader sense of a transatlantic dialogue covering both economic and political concerns.[3] In December 1995, President Clinton and EU leaders signed up to a 'Joint Action Plan' covering a long list of areas of common concern. At the same time, a parallel process in the context of the Transatlantic Business Dialogue was bringing together around 100 business leaders from both the US and the EU to discuss developments in the 'transatlantic marketplace'. By early 1998, the European Commissioner responsible for external economic relations, Sir Leon Brittan, felt that the time was ripe to propose in this context the fuller development of a New Transatlantic Marketplace, in which trade and regulatory barriers would become in many areas a thing of the past. During 1998, this led to considerable debate both within the EU and across the Atlantic, and eventually the proposal transmuted into the Transatlantic Economic Partnership which was embodied in the results of the June 1998 EU-US summit meeting. This was a rather less ambitious synthesis of a number of sectoral processes, but nonetheless it represented a further significant increment in the building of a transatlantic economic and regulatory space.[4]

There is thus a strong academic and policy rationale for focusing on this area of enquiry. It is also clear that this concern with the strategy for transatlantic relations was shared by policy-makers and opinion-formers in Washington and Brussels during the mid-1990s.[5] But declarations

---

(Washington D.C., Brookings Institution, 1995); J. Peterson, *Europe and America in the 1990s: Prospects for Partnership* (London, Routledge, 1996, 2nd ed.); M. Smith and S. Woolcock, *The United States and the European Community in a Transformed World* (London, Pinter-Royal Institute of International Affairs, 1993).

3 The best short treatment of the issues raised in the 'new Transatlantic Marketplace' is M. Kahler, *Regional Futures and Transatlantic Economic Relations* (New York, European Community Studies Association-Council on Foreign Relations Press, 1995).

4 See E. Frost, *The Transatlantic Economic Partnership* (Washington D.C., Institute for International Economics, Policy Brief, 1998).

5 'We need to invest at least as much time and energy in the development of a new economic architecture as we are doing in the restructuring of NATO' [Jeffrey Garten, May 1995]. '[...] there is much which can be decided in the coming months which will enhance the relationship and prepare the ground for future decisions. Indeed it is impossible to look at the future of the [EU-US] relationship without looking at it in a comprehensive way. In this way a clear signal would be given at the highest level that

alone do not generate strategy; indeed, if they are followed by ambiguity and uncertainty, they may themselves be counter-productive. It is hoped that this brief analysis will help to identify the policy dimensions and dilemmas faced by the US in approaching its 'partnership' with the EU, and link these to the broader themes of the 'transatlantic marketplace'.

The United States and the European Union: Dimensions of a Relationship

It is clear that the relationship between the US and the EU is complex, multilayered and characterised by a number of areas of uncertainty and ambiguity. Despite frequent protestations of partnership, and despite a broad awareness of shared concerns in many areas, frictions and fluctuations continue.[6] Much of the complexity can be traced back to four elements in the changing relationship: the economics of interdependence and interpenetration; the coexistence of industrial cultures; the intersection of political cycles; and the linkage to security institutions. An appreciation of these dimensions can advance our understanding of the difficulties attending strategic thought and action.

Who Is Us? The Economics of Interdependence and Interpenetration

Many authors have pointed out the ways in which US/EU relations are characterised by growing interdependence and interpenetration.[7] As Robert Reich, the US Secretary of Labour, noted during the late 1980s, this raises the question 'who is us?' which is crucial to the generation of strategy within the world political economy; more recently, Susan Strange has reformulated Reich's question as 'Who are EU?', thereby

---

the EU and the US recognise the need to update the relationship and set in motion a credible process for achieving that goal.' [European Commission, July 1995].

6 See K. Featherstone and R. Ginsberg, *The United States and the European Union in the 1990s: Partners in Transition* (London, Macmillan, 1996), Part 1; Peterson, *Europe and America*, Part 1; M. Smith, 'The United States and Western Europe: Empire, Alliance and Interdependence' in A. McGrew (ed.), *The United States in the Twentieth Century: Empire* (London, Hodder and Stoughton, 1994), pp.97-136.

7 Featherstone and Ginsberg, *The United States and the European Union*; H. Haftendorn and C. Tuschhoff (eds.), *America and Europe in an Era of Change* (Boulder CO, Westview Press, 1993); Peterson, *Europe and America*; Smith and Woolcock, *The United States and the European Community*; M. Smith and S. Woolcock, 'Learning to Cooperate: The Clinton Administration and the EU', *International Affairs*, 70:3 (1994) 459-76.

encapsulating the parallel uncertainties about the EU's identity in the world political economy.[8] The notion of strategy includes or implies the notion of a target – a 'them' to accompany the 'us' assumed to be the US, and as Strange makes clear, this target is not always easy to locate. American administrations since the mid-1980s have thus found it very difficult to adjust to the notion that the US and the EU are so thoroughly interpenetrated that it is hard to judge the targets or the effects of any policy.

This is particularly true in areas related to market access and regulatory policy. Increasingly, the overlapping of markets and the interaction of regulatory structures makes it difficult to formulate clearcut strategies: the premium is more and more on continuous interaction through working groups and negotiating fora as a means of making progress, and the notion of strategy is replaced by one which might be described as 'learning by doing'. Effectively, in such fora, 'us is them', and this is certainly true of the methods by which the US and the EU interact in pursuit of an increasing number of technical and regulatory matters. Very often, such working arrangements also include private sector experts and interests, as for example in the development of technical standards and conformity assessment procedures.[9]

System Friction: The Coexistence of Industrial Cultures

Notions of 'system friction', and of the interaction between regulatory structures and industrial cultures, are an inseparable element of US-EU relations in the 1990s. It was argued by Michel Albert in the early 1990s that such relations can partly be understood as the interaction of different forms of capitalism: Rhineland capitalism and free-market Anglo-Saxon capitalism, to be specific. When these capitalisms collide,

---

8 R. Reich, *The Work of Nations: Preparing Ourselves for Twenty-first Century Capitalism* (New York, Knopf, 1991). For a parallel recent treatment of the EU, see S. Strange, 'Who are EU? Ambiguities in the Concept of Competitiveness', *Journal of Common Market Studies*, 36:1 (1998) 101-14.

9 The best short treatment of market access issues remains S. Woolcock, *Market Access Issues in EC-US Relations: Trading Partners or Trading Blows?* (London, Pinter-Royal Institute of International Affairs, 1991). See also D. Vogel, *Barriers or Benefits? Regulation in Transatlantic Trade* (Washington D.C., Brookings Institution Press for the European Community Studies Association, 1997); *The Limits of Liberalization: Regulatory Cooperation and the New Transatlantic Agenda* (Washington D.C., American Institute for Contemporary German Studies, Johns Hopkins University, 1997).

they produce not only specific areas of dispute but also broader frictions at the systemic level, which are to be understood in terms of relations between government and the economy, assumptions about the public and the private, and related questions.[10] If such an analysis is adopted, it has clear implications for the pursuit of national strategy within the transatlantic relationship.

In particular, the approach focuses attention upon the ways in which government itself can effectively express or represent the broader properties of a given national system and enter into the interactions between systems. In terms of US government strategies towards the EU, it has often been noted that these have to cater for a number of different levels[11] as well as many different sectors of activity. The nature of 'government' cannot be taken for granted, and the United States itself is a framework within which government can take place at several different levels. Not only this, but the links between government and business in the United States are often very different from those to be found in the EU, and the ways in which business can be recruited into any sort of national economic strategy are difficult to identify.[12]

Who's in Charge? The Intersection of Political Cycles

In attempts to manage US-EU relations, an important part is likely to be played by political cycles, both in general and in the specific form of the 'political business cycle'. Quite simply, whilst the development of strategic direction in US-EU relations is a long-term exercise to be judged over a period of years if not decades, political leaders are judged over periods of five years at most, and are often embroiled in the next election campaign very soon after the last one. In different ways, this applies both to the US presidency and to the European Commission; in the EU, however, the Commission is only part of the process by which intersecting political cycles condition policy-making. The existence of

---

10 See M. Albert, *Capitalisme contre capitalisme* (Paris, Seuil, 1992); also M. Kahler, *Regional Futures*, pp.41-58; Smith and Woolcock, 'Learning to Cooperate'.

11 See the chapter by Alan Henrikson in this volume.

12 See D. Audretsch, *The Market and the State: Government Policy Towards Business in Europe, Japan and the USA* (London, Harvester-Wheatsheaf, 1989); Hocking and Smith, *Beyond Foreign Economic Policy*; M. Smith, 'The United States and the European Single Market: Federalism and Diplomacy in a Changing Political Economy', in B. Hocking (ed.), *Foreign Relations and Federal States* (London, Leicester University Press, 1993).

fifteen national political processes alongside the process of nomination and confirmation for the Commission itself means that US-EU relations are likely to be conditioned by as many as half-a-dozen electoral campaigns at any given time. When the most important of these come together, the effects for strategic thinking at the Transatlantic level can be disabling if not devastating.[13]

Such complications interact with the differences already noted, of interdependence and interpenetration and of industrial cultures, to produce a situation in which strategic thinking and policy design can appear almost self-defeating. Yet the same political cycles which make things difficult can also be a support for strategic initiatives. Everything lies in the timing, and in the ability to focus strategically at an appropriate point in the EU and the US cycles (always assuming that events outside the transatlantic relationship are conducive to such activities). For the Clinton administration, as will be seen shortly, this has had its own complications but also its undoubted benefits.

Security Institutions and 'Security Blankets'

A final dimension of the US/EU relationship to be emphasised here concerns the ways in which they are conditioned by the security context. For many years, this could be taken as a relative constant: the Cold War system nurtured and institutionalised both US leadership and the 'civilian' role of the EC.[14] Since 1989, however, things have become much less predictable. The removal of the 'security blanket' provided not only by the Americans but also by the USSR has revealed not only the very close linkage between economic, political and security issues but also the underlying instability of many areas within the broader Europe. Not surprisingly, this has intersected with the development of the EU's 'civilian' role – and with proposals to go beyond such a role – to create new dilemmas and tensions; it has also intersected with the post-Cold War retreat of US policy to create new uncertainties in the management of post-Cold War crises, both in the 'new Europe' and in

13 See Peterson, *Europe and America*, chapter 4; Smith and Woolcock, *The United States and the European*, chapter 2.

14 See M. Smith, *Western Europe and the United States: The Uncertain Alliance* (London, George Allen and Unwin, 1984); Smith, 'The United States and Western Europe', pp.97-136; Smith and Woolcock, *The United States and the European Community*.

the wider world. The examples (former Yugoslavia, central Africa and others) are obvious, and will not be laboured here.[15]

The significance of this trend in US/EU relations is not simply to be seen in terms of the European security order, important as that is. For the purposes of this paper, it raises major questions about the ability of both the US and the EU to take institutional initiatives capable of containing or shaping the post-Cold War order and the security politics of the new millennium. Taken together with the other factors mentioned above, it adds greatly to the indeterminacy and messiness of the context for strategic developments, both by unveiling new security problems and by revealing the gaps in the existing institutional framework. Not only this, but it links economic and political stabilisation firmly to the broader security order in ways not made as explicit since the end of the Second World War.

The Dimensions of US Policy: Contributors and Constraints

From what has already been said, it should be clear that the making of the US's 'EU policy' is hedged around with a wide range of other issues. This means that the generation of a coherent national strategy is inherently complex and surrounded by the interests of a large number of domestic constituencies as well as by the several dimensions of US-EU relations already identified. For the purposes of this analysis, four such 'domestic' elements are identified: the EU as a demand for cross-national policy development; the EU as a demand for cross-departmental policy development; the EU as a demand at different levels of US government; the extra-national dimension of US strategy. As noted earlier, many of the same points could be made about the nature of policy-making and policy development in the EU, but with some crucial differences reflecting the roles of member-state authorities.[16]

---

[15] For treatments of the EC's and now the EU's role in security issues, see D. Allen and M. Smith, 'Western Europe's Presence in the Contemporary International Arena', *Review of International Studies*, 16:1 (1990) 19-37; D. Allen and M. Smith, 'The European Union's Presence in the European Security Order: Barrier, Facilitator or Manager?', in C. Rhodes (ed.), *The European Union in the World Community* (Boulder, CO, Lynne Rienner, 1998), pp. 45-64.

[16] The arguments in this section are developed at greater length and in the context of detailed empirical studies in Hocking and Smith, *Beyond Foreign Economic Policy*.

The EU as a Demand for Cross-National Policy Development

One important quality of the ways in which the EU impacts on US strategy is that it is essentially cross-national in scope. Making policy towards the EU demands an appreciation of the ways in which different national contexts are linked, and of the effects which can be transmitted between them. In many cases, it also entails the support of cross-national institutional structures, for example those involved in the operation of the multilateral trading system, and in particular the GATT/WTO 'family'. The EU and the US are locked together not only in the GATT/WTO, but also in less extensive groups such as the G8, the Quad (US, Canada, Japan, EU) and the OECD, in such a way that any notion of US national strategy has to be viewed in the light of cross-national institutional entanglements. The 'new Europe' of the 1990s has also accentuated this feature of the relationship, since it links institutions and processes in the EU with those in the broader Europe, and economic networks with those in the security sphere, in new and challenging ways.

Not only this, but the attempt to influence EU policy developments and to apply pressure on them inevitably leads to engagement by the US in a range of cross-national networks, less formal but often no less powerful than the formal institutions of the world political economy. Very often, as will shortly be seen, this can lead to policy formulation on an 'extra-national' basis. In any case, it means that the parameters of US strategy are both contributed to and constrained by the infiltration of cross-national structures; indeed, they could not be achieved without such structures.[17]

The EU as a Demand for Cross-Departmental Policy Development

The significance of cross-national policy development is enhanced in the case of the US by the ways in which the EU demands cross-departmental policy development. US foreign policy has often been analysed in terms of inter-agency relationships, or of bureaucratic politics; international economic policy is often held to be particularly subject to these kinds of processes and pressures. In important ways, the EU goes beyond this notion of international economic policy, since it encap-

---

17 Hocking and Smith, *Beyond Foreign Economic Policy*, especially chapter 8. See also Peterson, *Europe and America*, Parts 2 and 3.

sulates so many of the processes of interpenetration already noted. The US government task force set up to deal with the Single Market Programme in the late 1980s mustered well over twenty agencies, each with its own domestic constituencies and links to other bodies such as the Congress.[18] Implementation of the US-EU Action Plan agreed at Madrid in December 1995 implied much the same range of cross-departmental involvement, within the broad framework provided by the senior-level group of officials; the initiative to establish the New Transatlantic Marketplace proposed during 1998 would have had to take account of perhaps an even greater range of cross-departmental interests, as well as the layers of political interest outlined earlier. From this, it is self-evident that there are major potential problems of coordination and coherence at the level of the federal government when dealing with the EU; alongside this, the EU's move into the areas of foreign and security policy and justice/home affairs during the 1990s has only expanded the range of US government agencies with an interest in the US-EU relationship (for example, in areas such as cross-border crime and the continuing problems of economic sanctions).

From this broad context arise significant questions relating to executive leadership and inter-agency coordination, which have led to some painful learning experiences in the US case; for example, by creating tensions between the 'domestic' interests of the Department of Commerce and the 'international' interests of the Department of State and the US Trade Representative. But this is not the end of the story. Very often, the issues of cross-departmental policy development are linked strongly with the processes of cross-national policy development outlined above. For example, on the question of international standards and 'technical barriers to trade', which greatly concerns both the US and the EU, there are relevant cross-national bodies at the EU level, the global functional level and the global intergovernmental level. Not only this, but they often have powerful inputs from private-sector interests who have specific commercial aims to pursue. The net result is a myriad of contributors and constraints, with different agencies entangled in different networks and with different axes to grind.[19]

---

18 Hocking and Smith, *Beyond Foreign Economic Policy*, chapter 3. See also Calingaert, *European Integration Revisited*, chapter 10.

19 Hocking and Smith, *Beyond Foreign Economic Policy*, chapter 7. See also Woolcock, *Market Access Issues*.

The EU as a Demand at Different Levels of US Government

One of the key results of the interpenetration noted above, and of the nature of the EU as a policy challenge, is the involvement of US government at other than the Washington level in policy development. Because the impact of the EU is felt on a dispersed basis, it is inevitable that subnational government becomes involved; because of the nature of the US federal system, this involvement is particularly intense in certain areas. Recent research by Hocking and Smith indicates that the growing internationalisation of the US economy, combined with the need and desire for state governments to develop export promotion and inward investment policies, have constructed new networks of governmental involvement in a wide range of EU-related issues. Very often, the evolution of state governments' roles has brought them into close collaboration with regional and local business interests, building coalitions which depart markedly from the image of a Washington-directed trade or competitiveness strategy. Increasingly, such coalitions can operate through state government offices in the EU itself (see below).[20]

It is important to note, therefore, that the intersection of subnational government concerns with those of the US federal government and with those of key industrial or commercial players is a central feature of the context for policy development. Simply put, there are networks in which the subnational/industrial axis is much more significant on a day-to-day basis than the national/political dimension in US policy formation. What this means for strategy is a combination of diffusion, diversity and complexity which militates against the development of comprehensive programmes and prescriptive agendas.

The EU as a Demand for Government-Business Policy Development

Implicit in much of what has already been said is that the EU poses particular demands for US administrations interested in developing policy through the interaction of government and business. In part, this challenge derives from the 'competing capitalisms' argument outlined above: it may simply be that the incompatibility of notions based on Rhineland capitalism and free-market capitalism leads to significant constraints on the ability of US administrations to support or sponsor US firms in the EU context. Quite simply, they may not speak the right

20 Hocking and Smith, *Beyond Foreign Economic Policy*, chapter 5.

language. But in other respects, there are important demands for government action, particularly in the area of multilateral regime formation: the US government will be needed by US business to the extent that their interests in the EU are served by the development and maintenance of accommodating international rules and regimes, and to the extent that this demand implies action by bodies in which the US is influential. Thus, the emphasis on the GATT Uruguay Round negotiations as a vital shaping force in the Single Market Programme gave an indispensable role to Washington, and further developments in the context of the WTO have served to underline this, for example in the field of telecommunications or information technology.[21]

This government role may not be relevant or even useful when it comes to the conduct of everyday business in the EU. The diverse interests of US firms, be they exporters to the EU, investors in the EU or even long-established 'European-American' firms, mean that solutions are likely to be found on a sectoral basis and through the operation of networks in which federal government is only a background participant.[22] When it comes, for example, to the importing of automobiles into the EU, the diversity of interests between US exporters (some of whom are Japanese) and European manufacturers (some of whom are American or have US allies) provide not only a challenge to government strategy but also an argument for its irrelevance.[23] In areas such as telecommunications, the growth of cross-national alliances likewise means that the important processes of regulation and market access are taken out of the hands of 'governmental' authorities.

The Extra-National Dimension of US Strategy

Alongside the wide range of 'domestic' contributors and constraints in US policy development, it is important to note the existence of an essentially extra-national dimension to US/EU relations. US policy is made and strategy developed not only in the US but also in the EU. US firms have a long-established presence there, accompanied by a wide

21 Hocking and Smith, *Beyond Foreign Economic Policy*, chapter 3. See also Calingaert, *European Integration Revisited*; Peterson, *Europe and America*.

22 Hocking and Smith, *Beyond Foreign Economic Policy*, chapter 6. See also Calingaert, *European Integration Revisited*, Part 3.

23 A good if slightly dated treatment of the automobiles case is A. Smith and A. Venables, 'Automobiles', in G. C. Hufbauer (ed.), *Europe 1992: An American Perspective* (Washington D.C., Brookings Institution, 1990), pp.119-58.

range of trade associations and sectoral interest groups. Increasingly, the governments of the American states have both representation and promotional activities in EU capitals, and especially in Brussels. Many significant policy networks are hardly rooted in the US at all, and this has important effects in shaping US strategy. It has already been noted that there are situations in which the US federal government is not needed; now it must be noted that when it comes to representation, influence and the promotion of US interests in the EU, there are significant areas in which the government is effectively absent.[24]

This is not to say that the US government has no involvement in extra-national policy formation. The activities of the US Mission to the EU in Brussels can have an important bearing both on the level of information available to the Washington administration and on the ways in which the policy debate is conducted there. Indeed, there have been occasions on which the Mission in Brussels has acted to build coalitions in Washington against proposals which it sensed were likely to damage US interests; a reversal of the accepted notion that 'international policy begins at home', and further evidence of the extra-national dimension in US policy development.[25]

The Current Policy Agenda: Towards a Strategy, or away from One?

In the light of the discussion so far, it could fairly be concluded not only that a 'US strategy' for dealing with the EU is unlikely to emerge but also that such a strategy should not even be attempted. This is not the conclusion here: rather, it is argued that a complex constellation of needs, challenges and resources creates important questions about the demand for and supply of government strategies – questions which are highly relevant to policy judgements. In this concluding section, a brief review of the current policy agenda will highlight some of the challenges presently faced and argue that notions of strategy should be at

---

24 See for example, Cowles, 'The Collective Action'; M. Green Cowles, 'The Politics of Big Business in the Single Market Program', paper presented to the 3rd Biennial Conference of the European Community Studies Association, Washington D.C., May 1993; M. Green Cowles, 'The EU Committee of AmCham: The Powerful Voice of American Firms in Brussels', *Journal of European Public Policy*, 3:3 (1996) 339-58.

25 See the chapter by Pascaline Winand in this volume.

least modified and possibly supplanted by those of learning and 'reflective practice'.

First, the policy agenda. A summary of the major items would include:

- Following up on the Uruguay Round and launching a new round in the context of the WTO

particularly in the light of the ministerial meeting held in Seattle (December 1999) and of new sectoral policy concerns. This entangles the US and the EU at three levels: first, the level of specific disputes such as those over the EU banana regime; second, the level of sector-specific regime building, for example in telecommunications or financial services; and finally, the level of wider consideration of 'new agenda' items such as trade and the environment or worker rights. Although US and EU positions are in many ways convergent, the need to deal with them in a global context is apparent, and (most significantly) the demand for 'government services' is different in each case. The preparation for the 'Millennium Round' already indicated that EU-US approaches were significantly divergent, particularly in terms of the scope of the Round and the place of agriculture within it, and this gives further weight to the points made earlier about systemic frictions and multilayered interest representation.

- Dealing with sectoral frictions on a Transatlantic level

There are a number of these, of which the most sensitive include the negotiation of air routes and 'open skies' agreements, a range of competition and anti-trust issues, the handling of public procurement issues and the development of cultural policies in the EU. Whilst the issue of extra-territoriality in respect of US policies on Cuba and other 'pariah states' was largely defused by the end of 1990s, the underlying problems had not gone away. One of the problems is that policy within the EU develops alongside policy at the broader level, extending further the range of levels at which US policies need to be designed and implemented. The issues also often intersect with broader issues in the WTO or other fora or with the concerns of US firms operating within the EU, again creating a diverse range of demands for government.

- Absorbing the Results of Institutional Changes in the EU and Dealing with this in the Light of the 'Eastern Enlargement' of the EU

This engages the US in a wide range of monitoring and shaping activities whilst the EU is engaged in 'constitution-building'. One of the most obvious areas in which this is apparent as we approach the new millennium is that of international monetary policy. The specific financial impact of the Euro by the end of 1999 was still in many respects unclear, but its impact on political debate and planning was nonetheless significant; for example, in precipitating debate about the EU's representation in international financial institutions. In the same way, the urgent need for institutional reform as the EU contemplated both a crisis in the Commission during 1999 and the implications of an ever-more expansive enlargement was bound to have an effect on US thinking. It creates a number of issues about the extent to which the US can/should take explicit positions beyond a general support for European integration, and about the extent to which the US should anticipate problems (for example, of market access) in a Union of anything up to twenty-eight members. There are also more specific issues such as those attaching to relations between the EU and Turkey, which carry implications for US security policies as well as for the broader transatlantic political economy. As in other cases, decisions about the level and direction of government activity are not to be taken for granted and need to be carefully calibrated.

- Advancing the 'New Transatlantic Dialogue'

It was noted at the outset that this enterprise produced an elaborate plan of action, both at the governmental and at the business level, encapsulated in the Madrid agreements of December 1995 and further developed by the proposals for the New Transatlantic Marketplace and the Transatlantic Economic Partnership. Inasmuch as these documents and declarations cumulatively constitute a statement of strategy, it is clear that this is less grand strategy than operational activity and incremental institutionalisation (and many would say all the better for that). The wide range of practical collaborations involved in this growing programme have had important influences on the development of mutual understanding and learning between the US and the EU, despite the turbulence encountered in specific sectors. They also in many cases formalise the mutual entanglements of government and private interests, within a very broad framework of strategic principles. The evidence is that this mixture of the public and the private can lead to significant progress in some areas (such as mutual recognition agreements including those on standards for automobile parts), but that the irruption of 'political' issues such as those of extra-territoriality can sour progress on a broad range of less insulated agenda items.[26] These difficulties did not prevent the EU's New Transatlantic Marketplace initiative of early 1998, or the elaboration of the Transatlantic Economic Partnership. What they did mean was that responses to the larger-scale proposals were equivocal both in the US and among EU member-states.[27]

Coping with the 'Presidential Cycle'

This is clearly an issue in the US, but is nonetheless a factor in the EU context. President Clinton was unopposed for the Democratic nomination in 1996, and many might argue also for the Presidency itself; this might be thought to have given a good basis for the early generation of 'real' policy on transatlantic relations early in the second term, but it became clear that the uneasy balance of power between President and Congress could exert its influence in unpredictable ways.[28] US foreign policy initiatives between 1996 and 1999 were often aimed at holding people to their commitments in the world political economy, but these were not directed specifically at the EU. In the same way, the increasing tone of economic nationalism expressed in congressional debates on the 'Millennium Round' was targeted as much at the domestic audience as at the Union. There were other developments involving Europe more generally, such as those in former Yugoslavia and the former Soviet Union, which have had important effects for the EU, for example on security and defence policies, and also on matters of international financial regulation. In all of this, it must not be forgotten that there is a complex electoral cycle in the EU itself. This means that the IGC intersected during 1996-97 with elections in the UK and France, and the implementation of Economic and Monetary Union overlapped with 1998 elections in Germany and elsewhere. Such conjunctures underline the multilayered character of US-EU relations in a highly political way.

The overall conclusion from this discussion is that we should not look for grand and comprehensive reorientations of strategy from the US in respect of the EU. For that matter, the same applies in large measure to EU declarations about the US, despite the Commission drive

---

26 See M. Smith and M. Green Cowles, 'Public Goals and Private Strategies in the Transatlantic Economic Partnership', paper presented at the Sixth Biennial International Conference of the European Community Studies Association, Pittsburgh, PA, June 1999.

27 Smith, 'Competitive Cooperation'.

28 See the chapter of J. Peterson in this volume.

for the New Transatlantic Marketplace. We can expect a continuation of overall US support for European integration, coupled with a determination to defend and promote US interests at the sectoral level, and to hold the Europeans to their commitments. This accurately reflects the interconnectedness, the complexity and the indeterminacy of US-EU relations in general, and the difficulties of bringing together an all-encompassing programme for action. But it also reflects the increasing day-to-day and month-to-month institutionalisation (in the broadest sense) of the 'transatlantic marketplace'.

In the future as in the past, US-EU relations are less likely to reflect strategic behaviour, planning and interaction than they are to express forms of 'learning through doing', in which there is generated a network of 'reflective practitioners' both in the governmental and the private realms. This seems a more robust and practical basis on which to rely than simply on rhetoric and broad declarations of strategy which come up against the untidiness and openness of the US/EU relationship in reality.

CHAPTER 9

European Unity in Transatlantic Commercial Diplomacy

Youri DEVUYST*

Vrije Universiteit Brussel

In response to European unity in commercial diplomacy, the United States has pursued three broad policy tracks: the 'pre-emptive intervention track' (which aims at active US involvement in the European Community (EC)'s decision-making process); the 'exploitation of European weakness track' (which is characteristic for periods of transatlantic trade conflict); and the 'support for unification track' (which is intended to encourage European integration as a way of creating a more reliable trade policy partner). The success or failure of the policy tracks developed by the US largely depends on the stance taken by the Community and its Member States. The 'pre-emptive intervention track' can only work to the extent that the Community's decision-making process is open to external influence. The 'exploitation of European weakness track' will only lead to results for the US to the extent that the Member States fail to maintain a common attitude during the conflictual episodes in transatlantic relations. The 'support for integration track' makes sense only to the extent that the Community succeeds in its role as a facilitator and guarantor of trade agreements. The central theme running through these pages is that – independently of the policy tracks selected by the US – the Community largely holds the key to its own future as a player in world trade diplomacy. As the cases examined in this chapter will illustrate, maintaining European unity in commercial diplomacy requires a constant effort both by the Community's institutions and the Member States.

This chapter is sub-divided into six sections. The first section includes an introduction to the Community's common commercial policy. The second section briefly analyses the US debate regarding the consequences of European unity in commercial diplomacy during the Com-

* The views expressed in this article are purely personal.

munity's formative years. The following three sections contain a review of the three US policy tracks described above based on the analysis of several concrete trade policy cases. Finally, the last section is devoted to the impact of the new World Trade Organization (WTO) framework on transatlantic commercial diplomacy.

European Unity in Commercial Diplomacy: An Introduction to the Common Commercial Policy

By way of introduction, it is useful to recall that the European Community is based on a customs union. Customs unions have an internal and an external characteristic. Internally, as between the Member States, the EC customs union implies the elimination of customs duties and of quantitative restrictions on the import and export of goods, and of all measures having equivalent effect. Externally, in terms of relations with third countries, the customs union necessitates the establishment of a common customs tariff. The common customs tariff was integrally applied in 1968 for industrial products and in 1970 for the remaining agricultural products. The common commercial policy can be regarded as the logical corollary of the customs union's common customs tariff. By the end of the so-called transitional period, on 1 January 1970, the Community's common commercial policy was to be based on uniform principles and to be implemented by the Community's institutions in accordance with the Treaty of Rome's Article 113 (renumbered as Article 133 by the Treaty of Amsterdam). Where agreements falling under the scope of the common commercial policy need to be negotiated with third countries, the Community speaks as a single voice. The Commission conducts the negotiations within the framework of those directives issued to it by the Council. It is the Council that ultimately decides by qualified majority whether or not to conclude trade agreements. Since the Community's commercial policy powers have a so-called 'exclusive' nature, the Member States are no longer competent to act on their own in the fields covered by the common commercial policy.[1]

---

1 For an introduction to the common commercial policy see E. L. M. Völker (ed.), *Protectionism and the European Community* (Deventer, Kluwer, 1987); A. Murphy, *The European Community and the International Trading System* (Brussels, Centre for European Policy Studies, 1990), Volumes I and II; M. Maresceau (ed.), *The Community's Commercial Policy after 1992: The Legal Dimension* (Dordrecht, Martinus Nijhoff, 1993); I. Macleod, I. Hendry and S. Hyett, *The External Relations of the European Communities* (Oxford, Oxford University Press, 1996).

In view of its exclusive nature, the definition of the common commercial policy is particularly important. Unfortunately, both the Treaty of Rome's original Article 113 and the Treaty of Amsterdam's redrafted Article 133 merely include a non-exhaustive list of examples: 'changes in tariff rates, the conclusion of tariff and trade agreements, the achievement of uniformity in measures of liberalization, export policy and measures to protect trade such as those to be taken in case of dumping or subsidies'. Because of the lack of a precise definition, the scope of the common commercial policy has been the subject of persistent controversy between the Commission's broad and the Member States' restrictive point of view.[2] In its landmark Opinion 1/94 on the division of competencies between the Community and the Member States regarding the Uruguay Round's Final Act, the European Court of Justice clarified the situation.[3] According to the Court, the following subjects fall under the exclusive Community competence:

- trade in goods (the entire General Agreement on Tariffs and Trade – GATT);
- cross-frontier trade in services, but only when it does not involve any movement of persons (thereby excluding from the Community's exclusive competence the parts of the General Agreement on Trade in Services – GATS – involving consumption abroad, commercial presence through subsidiary or branch, and presence of natural persons abroad); and
- measures taken at the external frontiers of the Community regarding the prohibition of the release into free circulation of counterfeit goods (excluding practically the entire Agreement on Trade-Related Intellectual Property measures – TRIPs).

---

2 On the definition of Article 113 see C. D. Ehlermann, 'The Scope of Article 113 of the EEC Treaty', in *Études de Droit des Communautés Européennes: Mélanges offerts à Pierre-Henri Teitgen* (Paris, Pedone, 1984), p.147 and J. H. J. Bourgeois, 'The Common Commercial Policy – Scope and Nature of the Powers', in Völker (ed.), *Protectionism*, p.3.

3 European Court of Justice, Opinion 1/94 of 15 November 1994. For an interpretation of this opinion see J. H. J. Bourgeois, 'The EC in the WTO and Advisory Opinion 1/94: an Echternach Procession', *Common Market Law Review*, 32:3 (1995) 763-87; M. Hilf, 'The ECJ's Opinion 1/94 on the WTO – No Surprise, but Wise?', *European Journal of International Law*, 6 (1995) 245-59; P. Pescatore, 'Opinion 1/94 on "Conclusion" of the WTO Agreement: is there an Escape from a Programmed Disaster', *Common Market Law Review*, 36:2 (1999) 387-405.

The Court's Opinion was disappointing from the Commission's perspective because it prevented the simple extension of the traditional Community method to the 'new' trade topics. Instead, trade in services and the trade-related aspects of the protection of intellectual property had to be treated as so-called mixed competencies, involving both the Community and the individual Member States.

The issue became part of the negotiations for the Treaty of Amsterdam of 1997. During the negotiations, the Commission argued that the development of international economic relations, which increasingly involves trade in services, intellectual property protection and foreign investment, required an explicit extension of Community powers. The Commission emphasized that it was not simply trying to expand its competencies. The purpose was merely to guarantee a consistent and effective policy in the field of external economic relations. The Commission's suggestion met with resistance from such Member States as France and the United Kingdom.[4] In the end, the negotiators of the Treaty of Amsterdam simply agreed that the Council, acting unanimously on a proposal from the Commission and after consulting the European Parliament, may extend the application of the common commercial policy to international negotiations on services and intellectual property.

In addition to the explicit external Community powers mentioned in the Treaty, the European Court of Justice has developed a case-law regarding the so-called implied external Community powers.[5] These take the form of a parallelism between internal and external Community powers.[6] The two main principles governing the Court's classic case-

---

4 'IGC '96: Commission – Council Wrangle over Trade Reform', *European Report*, 7 September 1996, p.1-2; A. Dashwood, 'External Relations Provisions of the Amsterdam Treaty', *Common Market Law Review* 35:5 (1998) 1019-45.

5 For an overview of the classic case-law see P. Pescatore, 'External Relations in the Case-Law of the Court of Justice of the European Communities', *Common Market Law Review*, 16:4 (1979) 615-45. For the Court's more recent case-law, see T. Tridimas and P. Eeckhout, 'The External Competence of the Community in the Case-Law of the Court of Justice: Principle versus Pragmatism', *Yearbook of European Law*, 14 (1994) 143-77; D. O'Keeffe, 'Community and Member State Competence in External Relations Agreements of the EU', *European Foreign Affairs Review*, 4:1 (1999) 7-36.

6 On this parallelism see J. Groux, 'Le Parallélisme des Compétences Internes et Externes de la Communauté Economique Européenne', *Cahiers de Droit Européen*, 14:1 (1978) 3-33.

law on the Community's implied external powers may be summarized as follows:

- whenever Community law has conferred upon the Community institutions internal powers for the purpose of attaining a specific objective, the Community is authorized to enter into the international commitments necessary for the attainment of that objective (this is the so-called Opinion 1/76 doctrine);[7]
- where Community rules have been promulgated, the Member States cannot assume obligations which might affect those rules or alter their scope outside the framework of the Community institutions (this is the so-called AERT doctrine).[8]

Over the past decade, however, the Court has severely limited the scope of these principles by spelling out that Community power is exclusive only where the subject matter of an international agreement is already substantially covered by existing internal Community legislation. Where internal Community law determines only minimum standards, at the discretion of the Member States, the Community's external powers are not exclusive, but mixed.[9] In such areas of mixed competence, the Court has established that there is an obligation of cooperation between Member States and the Community to ensure the unity of external representation.[10] The cases reviewed in this chapter will demonstrate, however, that maintaining effective European unity in commercial diplomacy is more complicated than Court doctrine would make it appear.

---

7 European Court of Justice, 'Opinion 1/76 of 26 April 1977', *E.C.R.* (1977) 741.

8 European Court of Justice, 'Case 22/70 with judgment of 31 March 1971', *E.C.R.* (1971) 263.

9 European Court of Justice, 'Opinion 2/91 of 19 March 1993', *O.J.* 19 April 1993, C 109, p.1. On the question of mixed agreements, see D. O'Keeffe and H. G. Schermers (eds.), *Mixed Agreements* (Dordrecht, Kluwer, 1983); A. Rosas, 'Mixed Union – Mixed Agreements', in M. Koskenniemi (ed.), *International Law Aspects of the European Union* (The Hague, Kluwer, 1998), pp.125-48.

10 European Court of Justice, 'Opinion 2/91', para. 36 and 'Opinion 1/94', para. 106-109.

European Unity in Commercial Diplomacy: The Debate in the United States during the Community's Creation

When, in 1956-57, the Eisenhower Administration considered the commercial policy implications of the creation of the European Economic Community, it came to the conclusion that 'the advantages to the United States of European integration through a customs union [...] far outweigh any possible disadvantages both on economic and political grounds'.[11] It predicted 'that economic integration would lead to the development of strong, modern economies with higher productivity and consumption levels, and that this in turn would result in Europe becoming a better market for United States exports',[12] this in spite of the trade diversion risks inherent to the creation of any customs union. According to the Eisenhower Administration 'the United States would be far more likely to obtain a liberal trade policy (including a dismantling of dollar restrictions) from a strong, unified European economy than from the smaller, less efficient economies as they now exist'.[13] In this sense, economic unification was looked upon as a necessary step towards effective European participation in the multilateral trade system.[14]

That the creation of the European Economic Community in 1957 would affect the division of power and influence in transatlantic trade diplomacy was, apparently, not considered a major problem by the Eisenhower Administration. According to David P. Calleo and Benjamin M. Rowland, US policy-makers were 'so carried away by the prospects of Europe imitating [their] own continental federation that [they] overlooked the dangers of fostering so formidable a potential rival

---

11 'Report by the Chairman of the Council on Foreign Economic Policy (Randall), September 1956', Foreign Relations of the United States (*FRUS)*, 1955-57 (Vol.IX), p.24.

12 'Report by the Chairman', pp.24-5.

13 'Report by the Chairman', p.25.

14 For a more detailed treatment see P. Mélandri, *Les États-Unis et le Défi Européen, 1955-1958* (Paris, Presses Universitaires de France, 1975); P. Winand, *Eisenhower, Kennedy and the United States of Europe* (New York, St. Martin's, 1993/1997); F. Romero, 'US Attitudes towards Integration and Interdependence: the 1950s', in F. H. Heller and J. R. Gillingham (eds,), *The United States and the Integration of Europe. Legacies of the Postwar Era* (New York, St. Martin's, 1996), pp.103-21.

to [them]selves'.[15] Still, the problem had been posed in very clear terms. The writings of Harvard professor Raymond Vernon were significant in this respect. Already in 1957, Vernon had warned as follows:

> Let us suppose, for example, that a Continental European Customs Union or a proliferation of other arrangements on the lines of the European Coal and Steel Community – such as a European Atom Pool or a European Power Pool – were to come into being. Unless these developments were somehow firmly subjected to the discipline of larger global groupings, there would seem to be a substantial possibility that the resulting European economic bloc could be oriented to a policy of substantial independence from – even conceivable hostility to – the rest of the Atlantic Community. For economic fusion will bring power; and economic power will carry independence with it.[16]

Vernon's warning was in line with that of economist Jacob Viner, formulated more than a decade earlier in the framework of the Department of State's Advisory Committee on Postwar Foreign Policy.[17] Referring to the historical examples of the United States and the *Zollverein*, Viner argued that the formation of a European customs union would undoubtedly 'increase the bargaining power of the area'. Furthermore, in Viner's eyes, European unification was spurred less to achieve positive results within Europe than to 'have unity against the United States'.[18] This skeptical viewpoint, however, did not dominate the mood in Washington during the 1950s. President Eisenhower, for instance, persistently underlined 'the desirability of developing in West-

15 D. P. Calleo and B. M. Rowland, *America and the World Political Economy. Atlantic Dreams and National Realities* (Bloomington, Indiana University Press, 1973), pp.74-5.

16 R. Vernon, 'Economic Aspects of the Atlantic Community', in H. F. Haviland, Jr. (ed.), *The United States and the Western Community* (Haverford, Haverford College Press, 1957), p.61.

17 On the Advisory Committee see H. A. Notter, *Postwar Foreign Policy Preparation, 1939-1945* (Washington, D.C, Department of State Publication 3580, 1950). The minutes and reports of its Special Subcommittee on Problems of European Organization can be consulted at the National Archives in Washington D.C., General Records of the US Department of State, Records of Harley Notter, 1039-1945, Records of the Advisory Committee on Postwar Foreign Policy, Record Group Number 59, Box Number 84.

18 'Chronological Minutes of the Special Subcommittee on Problems of European Organization', *R-5*, 15 October 1943, pp.5-6.

ern Europe a third great power bloc, after which development the United States would be permitted to sit back and relax somewhat'.[19]

The 'Pre-Emptive Intervention Track'

The Difficulty of Changing Intra-European Compromises: The First Lesson

The Eisenhower Administration soon learned that dealing with the Community would not always be as simple as it had initially imagined. To protect the commercial interests of the US during the establishment of the Common Market, the Eisenhower Administration relied heavily on the GATT. In theory, customs unions and free trade areas cannot enter into force if the parties concerned are not prepared to modify their agreements in accordance with the recommendations resulting from the GATT examination.[20] In view of this GATT provision, the Eisenhower Administration assumed it held 'an indirect veto over [the creation of the EEC] because the consent of the GATT will be required'.[21]

It soon turned out, however, that once the intra-European compromises on the Rome Treaty had been hammered out, the Community's founding fathers were unwilling to accept any suggestions for change by third countries. Isaiah Frank, Chairman of the US delegation during the GATT examination of the EEC Treaty, recalls this episode as follows: '[the Rome Treaty] had been the product of difficult and delicate compromises on many vital issues on which there were sharp conflicts of interests among the Six and among various groups within individual countries – *e.g.* between the high tariff and low tariff countries, between the agricultural and industrial groups, between the colonial and non-colonial powers'. In consequence, 'the Six felt [...] they were in no position to open up such a delicately balanced document to amendments'. In view of the importance which the Community's members attached to

---

19 'Remark by President Eisenhower at the 167th meeting of the National Security Council, 21 November 1955', contained in 'Editorial Note', *FRUS*, 1955-57 (Vol.IV), pp.348-9.

20 On the theory and practice of the GATT rules on customs unions, with special reference to transatlantic trade relations, see Y. Devuyst, 'GATT Customs Union Provisions and the Uruguay Round: The European Community Experience', *Journal of World Trade*, 26:1 (1992) 15-32.

21 'Letter from the Chairman of the Council on Foreign Economic Policy (Randall) to the Secretary of State, 4 October 1956', *FRUS*, 1955-57 (Vol.IV), p.469.

their project, Frank had come to the conclusion that 'if the Six had to choose between renegotiating the Treaty and being formally declared in violation of the GATT, they would undoubtedly have let the GATT go'.[22] Isaiah Frank's experience can be interpreted as the first lesson leading towards the 'pre-emptive intervention track': once an internal agreement among the Member States had been reached, it proved extremely difficult to change the Community's position from the outside.

Kissinger's Demand for a Role within Europe's Deliberations

Washington's first public request for a formal role in the Community's decision-making process came during Henry Kissinger's term as Secretary of State. On 12 December 1973, in a famous speech to the Pilgrims of Great Britain, Kissinger explicitly argued that the US would have to be included in all major decisions which the Community was likely to take. 'To present the decisions of a unifying Europe to us as *faits accomplis* not subject to effective discussion is alien to the tradition of US-European relations', Kissinger stated while claiming that 'as an old ally, the United States should be given an opportunity to express its concerns before final decisions affecting its interests are taken'.[23] Kissinger's request was a logical consequence of his earlier observation, still as Harvard professor, that 'meaningful consultation with other nations becomes very difficult when the internal process of decision-making already has some of the characteristics of compacts between quasi-sovereign entities. [...] There is an increasing reluctance to hazard a hard-won domestic consensus in an international forum.'[24] Pre-emptive intervention seemed the only effective approach to circumvent this problem. The Community, however, showed no interest in Kissinger's arrangement. As Wilfrid L. Kohl recalls, Kissinger's proposal created the strong impression among the Europeans that it was designed as an attempt 'to reassert American influence in Europe so as to subordinate important aspects of developing intra-European coopera-

22 I. Frank, *The European Common Market. An Analysis of Commercial Policy* (New York, Praeger, 1961), pp.162 and 164.

23 H. A. Kissinger, 'US-European Relations. Address to the Pilgrims of Great Britain, London, 12 December 1973', reprinted in G. Mally (ed.), *The New Europe and the United States. Partners or Rivals* (Lexington, Lexington Books, 1974), p.42.

24 H. A. Kissinger, 'Domestic Structure and Foreign Policy', in J. N. Rosenau (ed.), *International Politics and Foreign Policy* (New York, Free Press, 1969), p.266.

tion (especially in economics and foreign policy consultations) to American and Atlantic interests'.[25]

The Bush Administration and Mosbacher's 'Seat at the Table' Request

Kissinger's theme was again adopted by the Bush Administration. Following the breakdown of the Iron Curtain and the end of the Cold War, the Bush team wanted to solidify the transatlantic relationship so as to avoid an 'insular' or 'itinerant' Europe.[26] Furthermore, the Bush Administration was most interested in being able to exert an influence on the shaping of the Community's Internal Market. It realized that this had to be done before the Community's internal compromise formula on the Internal Market directives were adopted by the Council. The Administration particularly wanted to avoid a repetition of President Reagan's bad experience regarding the agricultural consequences of the Community's enlargement with Spain and Portugal. The dispute on the occasion of the enlargement had been resolved only on the brink of a potentially damaging trade war. 'Had we been a little more alert and expressed our objections earlier, maybe we wouldn't have [had] to fight such a knock-down-drag-out fight', suggested former US Ambassador to the EC, Alfred H. Kingon.[27] The Bush Administration was determined to avoid the same problems during the creation of the Internal Market.

Bush's Commerce Secretary Robert Mosbacher was the first senior Administration spokesman to openly ask for a US seat at the EC bargaining table. In a speech on 24 February 1989, Mosbacher explained that he 'advocated a seat at the table at least as an observer' because he wanted 'to engage the EC in a broadened productive dialogue at all levels' in light of the Community's Internal Market initiative.[28] In view of Europe's negative reactions, the Bush team soon abandoned the 'seat

---

[25] W. L. Kohl, 'The Nixon-Kissinger Foreign Policy System and US-European Relations', *World Politics*, 28:1 (1975) 16.

[26] R. B. Zoellick, 'The New Europe in a New Age: Insular, Itinerant, or International? Prospects for an Alliance of Values', *Current Policy*, 1300 (1990).

[27] Cited in B. Stokes, 'Will Europe's Trading Door Slam Shut', *National Journal*, 26 March 1988, p.813.

[28] R. Mosbacher, 'Address to the Columbia Institute Conference on the US Role in a United Europe', Washington D.C., 24 February 1990, p.5.

at the table' vocabulary. Instead, President Bush stated on 21 May 1989 that the US was 'ready to develop – with the European Community and its Member States – new mechanisms of consultation and cooperation'.[29] Secretary of State James Baker clarified the President's suggestion while outlining the American blueprint for a 'New Atlanticism' on 12 December 1989. 'As Europe moves toward its goals of a common Internal Market, and as its institutions for political and security cooperation evolve, the link between the United States and the European Community will become even more important', Baker said. He therefore proposed 'that the United States and the European Community [would] work together to achieve, whether it's in treaty or some other form, a significantly strengthened set of institutional and consultative links'.[30] The Secretary suggested *inter alia* that the new transatlantic link would be used to identify potential economic conflicts before they could grow into political problems. New EC-US institutional ties would also serve as the basis for regular discussions on a number of technical issues, such as standards, before Community decisions would be made which could have far-reaching political effects.

In light of Secretary Mosbacher's earlier demands, the Community remained cautious. French Minister of Foreign Affairs Roland Dumas was convinced that the Bush Administration was trying 'to obtain an oversight over the Community's decision-taking'.[31] European Commissioner Karel Van Miert, reacting to the US suggestion that the transatlantic relationship should be institutionalized, pointed out that he did 'not believe in such formal arrangements with rigid procedures. This could imply co-decision and veto rights and risk to lead to obsessive patronizing. The seat at the table formula is not a good idea. What we need is a pragmatic partnership, open to all levels and providing for trip wires as soon as there are any signs of conflict and difficulties'.[32] Even

---

29 G. Bush, 'Boston University Commencement Address', Boston, 21 May 1989, p.2.

30 J. Baker, 'A New Europe, A New Atlanticism: Architecture for a New Europe. Address to the Berlin Press Club', *Current Policy*, 1233 (1989) 4.

31 Cited in J. Amalric, 'Les propositions de M. James Baker sur l'Europe suscitent à Paris: satisfaction et perplexité', *Le Monde,* 15 December 1989, p.3.

32 K. Van Miert, 'The Relationship between Europe and the US in the 1990s: An Economic and Political Analysis', lecture delivered at the Elsevier Seminars, Brussels, 4 April 1990, p.10. For a similar remark, see F. Andriessen, 'Address to the Columbia Institute Conference on the US Role in a United Europe', Washington D.C., 23 February 1990, p.10.

Commission President Jacques Delors stated 'there [was] something ambiguous about linking transatlantic partnership with European integration as Mr. Baker did. Some Member States might interpret it as a deliberate attempt to interfere in our affairs, something which would be unacceptable between two equal partners'.[33] The Community made clear that it was determined to remain in charge of its own internal order.

The outcome of the transatlantic discussions was a non-legally binding Declaration on EC-US Relations, released on 23 November 1990 which incorporated various aspects of the pragmatic and already existing institutional framework for EC-US consultation. It stated that '[t]o achieve their common goals, the European Community and its Member States and the United States of America w[ould] inform and consult each other on important matters of common interest, both political and economic, with a view to bringing their positions as close as possible, without prejudice to their respective independence'.[34]

The Successful Pre-Emptive Mobilization for the Internal Market

While Secretary Mosbacher's idea for a seat at the table during the creation of the Internal Market had been openly rejected by the Community, the US nevertheless succeeded in setting up an effective early warning system which enabled Washington to be a player in the decision-shaping phase of the 280 Internal Market directives. The establishment of this US 'path of influence' took place independently from the negotiations for the Declaration on EC-US Relations. Already in 1988, the Cabinet-level Economic Policy Council had established a special Interagency Task Force on EC 1992 which would become Washington's forum for strategic planning and inter-service coordination regarding the Internal Market. The Task Force played a major role

---

33 J. Delors, 'Presentation of the Annual Programme of the Commission for 1990', *Verbatim Report of Proceedings European Parliament*, 17 February 1990, p.150.

34 *Declaration on EC-US Relations* (Brussels, EPC Press Release p.83/90, 23 November 1990), p.2. On the political climate surrounding the drafting of the Declaration see H. G. Krenzler and K. Kaiser, 'The Transatlantic Declaration: A New Basis for Relations between the EC and the US', *Aussenpolitik*, 42:4 (1991) 363-72 and Y. Devuyst, 'European Community Integration and the United States: Toward a New Transatlantic Relationship?', *Journal of European Integration*, 14:1 (1990) 5-29.

in making sure that the concerns of private business associations – such as the EC Committee of the American Chamber of Commerce or the National Association of Manufacturers – were transmitted in an effective way to the Community and its Member States through US government channels. Much of the impetus for the Administration's action with regard to the Internal Market came from the US Congress which devoted numerous hearings to the defense of US interests during the establishment of the Internal Market. The strengthening of the commercial side of the US Mission to the European Communities in Brussels, for instance, was the direct result of Congressional pressure.[35]

Washington's mobilization with regard to the Internal Market proved successful. While the Commission's White Paper of 1985, which formed the basis for the Internal Market initiative, had focused largely on the internal aspects of removing the remaining barriers to trade between the Member States, the external dimension was only fully developed following US representations about the dangers of a 'Fortress Europe'.[36] These concerns were soon relieved following consultations with the US government which resulted in a number of significant changes to initial Community drafts. The original mirror-image reciprocity test in the Commission's proposal for the second banking directive, for example, was changed to accommodate US demands. In the area of product standards, the American National Standards Institute's request for observer status in the European standardization committees was rejected. Still, as a result of an EC-US agreement of June 1989 which allowed for information-sharing and indirect US input, Mosbacher admitted that the European standard-setting process 'was

---

35 On this organizational effort see *Europe 1992: Administration Views*, Hearing before the Subcommittees on Europe and the Middle East, and on International Economic Policy and Trade of the Committee on Foreign Affairs, House of Representatives, 101st Congress, 2nd session, 20 February 1990 (Washington D.C., US Government Printing Office, 1990); and *Europe 1992: A Business Guide to US Government Resources* (Washington D.C., US Department of State, 1990).

36 See Y. Devuyst, 'The United States and Europe 1992', *World Competition: Law and Economics Review*, 13:1 (1989) 29-42 for an overview of early US interventions regarding the Single Market project; P. Eeckhout, 'The External Dimension of the EC Internal Market. A Portrait', *World Competition: Law and Economics Review*, 15:2 (1991) 6, for the immediate effects of the US interventions on the Single Market project; and B. Hocking and M. Smith, *Beyond Foreign Economic Policy. The United States, the Single Market and the Changing World Economy* (London, Pinter, 1997) for a general evaluation of the US impact on the Single Market.

open and transparent' and 'at times, allowed literally a seat' for representatives of US business interests.[37]

The New Transatlantic Agenda and Early Warning

The 'pre-emptive intervention track' was further developed in the framework of the New Transatlantic Agenda as a fully reciprocal instrument to improve the capacity of each side to take the other partner's interests into account at an early stage when formulating policy.[38] Following more than two years of NTA practice, Under Secretary of Commerce for International Trade David Aaron testified that '[o]ne of the most important aspects of the NTA is the breadth of its mechanisms, providing a degree of contact among US and European government officials unparalleled in the past'.[39] Semi-annual summits at Presidential level are supplemented by meetings of the Senior Level Group (SLG), bringing together the senior trade and economic officials on both sides. The SLG in turn is supported by the NTA Task Force of working-level officials. On each occasion, time is set aside for early warning points when the two sides can raise matters of concern before they become more major grievances and a source of dispute. The principles and mechanisms for early warning and problem prevention regarding trade issues were further clarified at the EU-US Bonn Summit of 21 June 1999. The parties notably invited the Transatlantic Legislators, Business, Consumer, Environment and Labor Dialogues to contribute to the early warning effort by identifying problems and offering proposals for resolution.[40]

Furthermore, since the start of the NTA process – which was beefed up in 1998 in the form of the Transatlantic Economic Partnership (TEP) – the partners did manage to create a number of conflict-

---

[37] Cited in 'The European Commission and the American Administration are Reviewing Means to Strengthen Coordination in a Large Series of Fields', *Agence Europe*, 18/19 December 1989, p.10.

[38] *The New Transatlantic Agenda and the Joint EU/US Action Plan* (Brussels, Council of the European Union Press Release 12296/95, 3 December 1995), p.33.

[39] 'Testimony of Under Secretary Aaron on US-EU Trade Relations', *USA Text* (US Mission to the EU), 28 July 1998, p.3. See also 'Statement of Ambassador David Aaron before the House of Representatives Committee on International Relations', *USA Text* (US Mission to the EU), 15 June 1999, pp.9-11.

[40] *Declaration on EU-US Early Warning and Problem Prevention – Principles and Mechanisms*, Bonn, 21 June 1999.

preventing instruments such as a Mutual Recognition Agreement, eliminating or substantially reducing testing and certification requirements on such items as computers and telecommunications equipment, pharmaceuticals, medical devices and electrical equipment, and a Veterinary Equivalence Agreement that should facilitate trade in live animals and animal products. At the same time, the transatlantic trade relationship is by no means free from disputes. Most of the remaining conflicts involve basic policy choices in such areas as health of consumers (hormones), culture (market access in the audiovisual sector) and relations with developing countries (bananas) that can hardly be avoided through procedural improvements.

The 'Exploitation of European Weakness Track'

In spite of mutual attempts to pre-empt trade disputes, EC-US trade relations have also been characterized by a series of trade conflicts. In several of these conflictual episodes, Europe's own internal divisions have permitted the US to devise negotiation tactics aimed at benefiting from the EC's remaining weaknesses in external representation. The 'open skies' negotiations in the field of airline services are an example. On other occasions, the US has actively tried to break up the common position which has been adopted by the Community. The use of unilateral trade sanctions is often devised to achieve this result.

Taking Advantage of the Lack of European Unity

Perhaps the clearest example of the able use by the US of the lack of European unity can be found in the area of transatlantic aviation relations. As Martin Staniland has explained, the US – while trying to liberalize transatlantic air services through bilateral 'open skies' agreements – 'has openly adopted [...] a "divide-and-rule" tactic in dealing with the EU'.[41] European transport Commissioner Neil Kinnock agrees. In his words, the Clinton Administration's strategy to negotiate air services agreements with individual Member States has been 'deliberately discriminatory and divisive'.[42] In fact, the US merely took advantage of the attitude of the Member States which – for a long time – per-

41 M. Staniland, *Open Skies – Fewer Planes? Public Policy and Corporate Strategy in EU-US Aviation Relations* (Pittsburgh, University of Pittsburgh, Center for West European Studies Policy Paper No. 3, 1996), p.4.

42 N. Kinnock, 'Speech before the European Parliament', 4 April 1995, p.4.

sistently refused to effectively transfer air services negotiations from their national administrations to the Commission. The first bilateral 'open skies' agreement dealing with transatlantic flights was concluded between the US and the Netherlands in 1992. In December 1994, Washington invited six other smaller Member States – Belgium, Denmark, Luxembourg, Austria, Sweden and Finland – to negotiate bilateral 'open skies' deals too. According to Staniland, the US hoped that liberal agreements with the smaller members would put pressure on the bigger Member States. In the highly competitive airline sector, the threat of trade diversion is an effective weapon, which makes it difficult for the bigger members to refuse conditions already accepted by the smaller countries.[43] And, indeed, both Germany (1996) and France (1998) decided to conclude a bilateral 'open skies' agreement with the US too. Negotiations between the US and the United Kingdom were still pending at the time of writing.

Naturally, the Commission objected to the bilateral approach. In a speech before the European Parliament, Commissioner Kinnock, while requesting the Member States not to negotiate bilaterally with the US, argued that 'the interests of each Member State can best be served by combining the authority of all [...] acting through the Community [... T]he real choice [...] is between adopting that mandate in which [the Member States] have direct influence and having their decisions made for them by the actions of others over which they have no influence.'[44] Still, the Commission did not succeed in stopping the bilateral approach. It was only following the conclusion of the bilateral agreements with the six small EU members and Germany that the Council nevertheless agreed to allow the Commission to play a role in the negotiations. The Commission's negotiating mandate of June 1996 was confined, however, to so-called soft issues which had not been covered by the bilateral deals. The more delicate question of the mutual granting of air traffic rights could not be dealt with by the Commission unless it would obtain a new and explicit instruction from the Council.[45] In spite of the Commission's decision of March 1998 to proceed with infringement proce-

43 Staniland, *Open Skies*, p.4.

44 Kinnock, 'Speech', pp.9 and 4.

45 *European Union Approves Draft Mandate to Negotiate a Common Aviation Area with the United States* (Brussels, Commission Press Release IP/96/520), 17 June 1996.

dures against the bilateral 'open skies' deals before the European Court of Justice,[46] the Member States continued to refuse a united European stance in aviation diplomacy.

Breaking up Europe's Common Position

In periods of trade conflict, the US has been confronted with the difficulty of changing the Community's policy once an internal compromise among the Member States has been worked out. To make the Community more prone to change, Washington has frequently resorted to the targeted use of unilateral sanctions. The purpose of the sanctions is to render the cost of maintaining the common position prohibitively high. In those instances where the US strategy was successful, the sanctions either caused a change in the Community's common position or the defection from the common position by an important Member State. Two cases will illustrate this strategy.

The first case concerned the agricultural consequences of the Community's enlargement with Spain and Portugal on 1 January 1986. The US feared that the application of the Common Agricultural Policy (CAP) by Spain and Portugal would endanger its traditional exports of corn, sorghum and oilseeds to these countries. The Community's initial proposals for compensation were dismissed by Washington as grossly inadequate. On 30 December 1986, President Reagan announced that retaliatory duties of two hundred per cent on a range of Community products would become effective by 31 January 1987. The sanctions were expected to radically interrupt the import in the US of about 400 million dollars in European products. Since the sanctions were specifically aimed at cognac, white wine and cheeses, about half of the sanctions would particularly affect France.[47] During the compensatory adjustment negotiations following the enlargement, the French government had been vigorously opposed to any further agricultural concessions for the US. France expected to gain relatively more than the EC's other Member States from the opening of the Iberian agricultural markets for Community products. By threatening with retaliation against products of special importance to France, however, Washington effec-

---

46 *Commission Takes Further Legal Action against Member States' 'Open Skies' Agreements with the United States* (Brussels, Commission Press Release IP/98/231), 11 March 1998.

47 'The American Measures Affect all Member States, but in Very Unequal Proportions', *Agence Europe*, 5/6 January 1987, pp.7-8.

tively stimulated Paris to become more interested in solving the dispute through a process of mutual concessions. In the end, France did accept a change in the accession regime as well as specific compensation for US farmers in the agricultural sector.[48] Given France's large export interests in cognac and white wine, the French Minister of Foreign Trade admitted it simply 'could not enter into a trade war' with the US.[49]

The second case concerned telecom procurement following the adoption – on 17 September 1990 – of the so-called utilities directive.[50] The directive was intended to establish Community-wide, transparent and non-discriminatory procedures for procurement by entities operating in the water, energy, transport and telecommunications sectors. The directive was scheduled to come into force by 1 January 1993 in nine Member States, Spain (1 January 1996), Greece and Portugal (1 January 1998) having longer implementation periods. In the US, the directive's Article 29 caused considerable concern.[51] This Article contained two controversial paragraphs. Under Article 29.2, any tender made for the awarding of a supply contract *could* be rejected if the non-EC content of the products concerned exceeded fifty per cent. Under Article 29.3, in the eventuality of equivalent tenders, preference *would have to* be given to tenders with an EC content of at least fifty per cent if the price difference did not exceed three per cent. This, in fact granted a three per cent price preference to offers of EC producers over non-EC producers. Article 29 was intended as an instrument for reciprocal market-opening in the public procurement sector and would apply only with regard to those third countries with which the Community had 'not concluded, multilaterally or bilaterally, an agreement ensuring comparable and effective access for Community undertakings'.

---

48 'Statements, Positions, Initiatives', *Agence Europe*, 5/6 January 1987, p. 8.

49 French Minister of Foreign Trade Michel Noir cited in 'EEC/United States', *Agence Europe*, 31 January 1987, p.6.

50 'Council Directive 90/531/EEC of 17 September 1990 on the Procurement of Entities Operating in the Water, Energy, Transport and Telecommunications Sectors', *O.J.*, 29 October 1990, L 297, p.1.

51 *European Single Market. Issues of Concern to US Exporters* (Washington D.C., US General Accounting Office, February 1990), pp.39-45; *EC 1992: A Commerce Department Analysis of European Community Directives* (Washington D.C., US Department of Commerce, Volume 3, March 1990), pp.111-18; *1991 National Trade Estimate Report on Foreign Trade Barriers* (Washington D.C., Office of the US Trade Representative, 1991), pp.72-3.

Although the EC and the US did reach important partial agreements on public procurement in 1993 and 1994, they failed to agree on the strategic telecommunications market. To increase the pressure on the Community, US Trade Representative Mickey Kantor announced on 21 April 1993 that he would impose sanctions prohibiting certain Federal Government purchases of EC goods and services for an annual value of 20 million dollars.[52] Although some Member States had doubts about the wisdom of entering into a tit-for-tat game, the Council decided on 8 June 1993 to counter-retaliate against US suppliers, contractors and service providers in a number of public procurement areas.[53] Soon after the Council's counter-retaliation decision was taken, Germany – which had been involved in bilateral talks with the US on the subject – surprised the Community by announcing that it would not apply Article 29 of the utilities directive with regard to the US. During their bilateral talks, the US had exempted Germany from the unilateral sanctions if it would refrain from applying Article 29 to US suppliers. Consequently, Germany also saw no need to apply counter-retaliation against the US. Germany justified its announcement on the basis of the bilateral German-US Treaty of Friendship, Commerce and Navigation of 1954 and on Article 29.1 itself. According to Article 29.1, its provisions were 'without prejudice to the obligations of the Community or its Member States in respect of third countries'. While invoking this provision, Germany claimed that its 1954 bilateral treaty with the US prevented it from discriminating against US companies. Germany also argued that the Community had routinely endorsed the renewal of friendship, commerce and navigation treaties.[54] The fact that Germany had never raised its position during the Council debate on counter-retaliation, but had negotiated bilaterally with the US to avoid the sanctions, shocked the

52 'Statement by USTR Kantor on Government Procurement Agreement', *USA Text* (US Mission to the EC), 21 April 1993, pp.1-2.

53 'Council Regulation 1461/93 of 8 June 1993 Concerning Access to Public Contracts for Tenderers from the United States of America', *O.J.*, 17 June 1993, L 146, pp.1-23.

54 Germany notably referred to 'Council Decision 69/494/EEC of 16 December 1969 on the Progressive Standardization of Agreements Concerning Commercial Relations between Member States and Third Countries and on the Negotiation of Community Agreements', *O.J.*, 29 December 1969, L 326, p.39. See J. M. Grimes, 'Conflicts between EC Law and International Treaty Obligations: A Case Study of the German Telecommunications Dispute', *Harvard International Law Journal*, 35:2 (1994) 535-64.

other Member States. The Community reacted by adopting, on 6 December 1993, a Council decision specifying that the Member States' bilateral friendship, trade and navigation treaties and trade agreements could only be renewed 'as regards those areas not covered by agreements between the Community and the third countries concerned insofar as their provisions are not contrary to existing common policies'.[55] While the Community's counter-sanction decision in the telecom procurement dispute had initially given an impression of unity and strength, the German defection proved the fragility of the European arrangements in international trade as well as the impact of US representations.

The 'Support for Integration Track'

While resorting to the 'exploitation of European weakness track' to tilt the balance of power in its favor during trade conflicts, the US has simultaneously supported Community unity as a means of facilitating cooperative international trade deals.

US Support for the Community as the Guarantor of European Trade Commitments

The most visible sign of US support for the Community came during a quasi-constitutional crisis between the Commission and France at the GATT Council meeting in Geneva. It was the only case in GATT/WTO history where an EC Member State openly contested the authority of the Commission in front of the other GATT/WTO contracting parties. The crisis was caused by a US request for a dispute settlement panel against the Community's subsidies to oilseeds producers. On 13 June 1988, following months of internal discussion and negotiations with the US, the Community's Agriculture Council had approved the establishment of a panel in the oilseeds case. French opposition had not prevented the Council from reaching a qualified majority.[56] In line with the mandate of the Council, the Commission representative to the GATT Council expressed the Community's agreement with the establishment of the

---

[55] 'Council Decision 93/679/EC of 6 December 1993 Authorizing the Automatic Renewal or Maintenance in Force of Provisions Governing Matters Covered by the Common Commercial Policy Contained in the Friendship, Trade and Navigation Treaties and in Trade Agreements Concluded between Member States and Third Countries', *O.J.*, 18 December 1993, L 317, pp.61-74.

[56] 'The Community Gives Up Opposition to the Creation of a GATT Panel on Aid to Soya Production', *Agence Europe*, 18 June 1988, p.6.

panel. At the same time, he also asked the Chairman of the GATT Council, 'exceptionally and in view of the fundamental importance of this matter, to allow a Member State, France, to express its view'.[57]

On two occasions during the GATT Council meeting, the representative of France asked that note be taken of the fact that his country was a contracting party to the GATT of 1947, and was taking the floor in that capacity. Since France could not agree to the establishment of a panel, the French representative concluded that the Chairman would have no choice but to establish that there was no consensus with regard to the panel request by the United States. Under the pre-WTO dispute settlement system in the old GATT, panels could only be established by consensus among the contracting parties. As a result of this French move, an interesting debate took place in the GATT Council concerning the position of the Community and its Member States in GATT bodies. It must be recalled that although the Commission had been speaking in the GATT meeting in the name of the Community, the Member States had formally remained GATT contracting parties. The Community had never formally gained the status of a GATT contracting party.[58] While the representative of the European Commission agreed that France was clearly a contracting party, he emphasized that it was equally clear that France no longer had competence on matters of trade policy. The Commission representative said that commercial policy was the exclusive competence of the Community, which – in the GATT Council – was represented by the Commission and that France could not raise an objection concerning something which no longer belonged to its competence. The Commission representative also stressed that Community responsibility for trade policy served as a guarantee and security for the other contracting parties. To take French views into consideration would put into question all existing Community obligations and rights. For these reasons, the Commission official concluded that, even when

---

57 GATT Council, *Minutes of Meeting held on 16 June 1988*, C/M/222, p.10.

58 On the Community's *ad hoc* status in the old GATT of 1947 see E.-U. Petersmann, 'Participation of the European Communities in the GATT: International Law and Community Law Aspects', in O'Keeffe and Schermers (eds.), *Mixed Agreements*, pp.167-98; E.-U. Petersmann, 'The EEC as a GATT Member – Legal Conflicts between GATT Law and European Community Law', in M. Hilf, F. G. Jacobs and E.-U. Petersmann, *The European Community and GATT* (Deventer, Kluwer, 1986), pp.23-71.

France spoke as a contracting party, its views as to trade policy were to be considered as null and void.[59]

Interestingly, the representative of the United States took the floor to support the Commission's point of view. Contracting parties had to know with whom they were negotiating and dealing in normal GATT affairs, he said. The Delegation of the United States, he continued, had been instructed by the European Community itself to negotiate and to deal with the Commission. 'Was that process going to change to one in which dealing with the [...] Member States would mean dealing with each one separately and with the thirteenth, the Commission?', he asked. 'Was the word of the spokesman for the Communities not the word of the Communities? If that were the case, it would mean a major change in how everyone operated under the GATT. It meant that at any time, on any issue, when one had an agreement of any sort with the representative of the European Communities, it would be possible that subsequently one of the Member States might void that agreement.' The United States delegate hoped that this was not the case.[60] After some discussion, the Chairman of the GATT Council decided that the panel would be rightfully established, in spite of France's objections. With active US support, the GATT Council thereby confirmed the Commission representative in its role as the Community's sole spokesman whose words bind the Community in the GATT.[61] By helping to protect the Community's status in the GATT, the US in fact was trying to protect the solidity of the EC's trade commitments.

The Community as Facilitator to Reach Trade Agreements

That the US supported the Community during the quasi-constitutional GATT crisis mentioned above should also be seen against the background of the internal compromise-building functions that have been gradually developed by the EC and have facilitated the conclusion of external trade agreements. According to Stuart E. Eizenstat, then US Under Secretary of Commerce for International Trade, 'it is a good bet that the Uruguay Round would not have succeeded in covering agriculture, intellectual property, or services if the United States had been re-

---

59 GATT Council, *Minutes of Meeting held on 16 June 1988*, C/M/222, p.14.

60 GATT Council, *Minutes 16 June 1988*, p.13.

61 GATT Council, *Minutes 16 June 1988*, p.15.

quired to negotiate independently with each Member State.'[62] That the agreement was reached at the multilateral level can be attributed in large measure to two internal functions performed by the Community. Firstly, it allowed the reluctant Member States to voice their objections at a level which did not directly endanger the Round. The inclusive Community process made it possible to avoid the isolation of reluctant members by giving them the occasion to express themselves in the Council of Ministers. At the same time, the Commission – as the Community's negotiator – was able to translate the objections formulated during Council sessions into a negotiating language which did not cause the multilateral Round to go down with a bump. Secondly, the Community served as the framework for solidarity for those economic sectors or Member States which faced particular difficulties as a result of the Round's outcome. Without the necessary promises for internal compensatory adjustment, several Member States would not have been able to give their approval to the successful outcome of the Round.[63]

The Community's Inclusive Political Process [64]

The way in which the Community process kept the French government on board during the Uruguay Round is a perfect example of the Community's inclusive function. After France's rejection of the pre-agreement on agriculture concluded between the US and the Commission at Blair House on 20 November 1992, a positive outcome of the Round was far from certain. The French government was working under severe domestic pressure. French farm organizations were constantly mobilizing forces against the presumed agricultural sacrifices of a

---

[62] S. E. Eizenstat, 'A Strong European Union is in the US Interest', *USA Text* (US Mission to the EU), 24 May 1996, p.2.

[63] As Sophie Meunier has correctly underlined, the Community was also able to use the difficult internal decision-making process, and in particular the need for unanimity among the Member States, as an argument to limit the scope of the concessions which it could make during the multilateral negotiations. See S. Meunier, 'Divided but United: European Trade Policy Integration and EC-US Agricultural Negotiations in the Uruguay Round', in C. Rhodes (ed.), *The European Union in the World Community* (Boulder, Lynne Rienner, 1998), pp.193-211; J. Jupille, 'The European Union and International Outcomes', *International Organization* , 53:2 (1999) 409-25.

[64] This section is based on Y. Devuyst, 'The European Community and the Conclusion of the Uruguay Round', in C. Rhodes and S. Mazey (eds.), *The State of the European Union. Vol.3: Building a European Polity?* (Boulder, Lynne Rienner, 1995), pp.449-67.

Uruguay Round agreement. French intellectuals seemed inclined to look upon the Round's negotiations on audiovisual services as a threat to France's glorious culture. Even French economists, such as Nobel Prize winner Maurice Allais, persistently attacked the Uruguay Round as *'l'intolérable diktat américain'*.[65]

For the Belgian Presidency of the Council, it was clear that an isolated France presented a danger to the Round and would not hesitate to use its 'veto power' to block the approval of the Round's results. To get France out of its corner, the Presidency decided to use the Community's inclusive processes to the full by agreeing to organize a formal and highly visible Jumbo Council of Ministers of Foreign Affairs and Agriculture. This meeting took place on 20 September 1993. Once again in the history of the Community, a positive Franco-German dynamic, actively supported by the Presidency, helped to bridge the cleavage between the more protectionist and more free trade oriented members, while preventing France's isolation. To France, the Jumbo Council proved that working within the European framework could actually Europeanize, and thus strengthen, the essence of its substantive demands. To Germany, the Council seemed an appropriate framework for turning the damaging parts of France's proposals into acceptable compromises that would not endanger the Uruguay Round itself. Germany was thus ready to meet some of France's demands if this meant that the Round as such could be saved. In accordance with France's objectives, one of the results of the Jumbo was that the Commission was assigned to request 'interpretations, amplifications, and additions' to the Blair House pre-agreement. While the Jumbo thus allowed France to claim victory, the Council's conclusions avoided a direct attack on the United States that could have lead to the immediate collapse of the Round. On the contrary, the Jumbo explicitly reaffirmed the Council's 'conviction that the conclusion of the Uruguay Round before 15 December 1993 on satisfactory terms for all the partners' was essential.[66] Furthermore, the Commission remained in charge of the conduct of the multilateral negotiations and was therefore able to translate the Council's conclusions into appropriate negotiating language.

---

65 M. Allais, 'L'intolérable diktat américain', *Le Figaro*, 4 March 1993.

66 *Press Release of the 1685th Meeting of the Joint Council General Affairs/Agriculture* (Brussels, Council of the European Communities, 20-21 September 1993).

The Community's Solidarity Function

Although the Uruguay Round in general was expected to benefit the Community as a whole, obtaining unanimous Member State support proved far from simple. Both during the agricultural and textiles negotiations, the EC needed to come up with substantial internal financial promises to compensate specific economic sectors or particular Member States that claimed damage as a result of the multilateral deal.[67]

As far as agriculture was concerned, France was able to accept the Round's compromise in large measure thanks to the financial compensation that French farmers had received just before the Round's conclusion, in the Fall of 1993, as a result of the EC's internal CAP reform. Furthermore, France obtained the additional internal promise from the Brussels European Council (10-11 December 1993) that extra financial resources would be made available to French farmers, whenever the Uruguay Round agreement would cause 'sacrifices' going beyond those foreseen by the reformed CAP.

With regard to the negotiations on textiles, Portuguese objections had to be overcome. Portugal's sensitivity for the EC's concessions in the textiles sector was not a surprise. About twenty-five per cent of Portugal's industrial employment depended on the textiles sector. Moreover, the sector was concentrated in a few areas that relied entirely on the textiles industry. Since its vital interests were at stake, Portugal informed the other Member States, on the eve of the Brussels European Council, that it could not accept the textiles part of the Uruguay Round. Portugal claimed that the results of the textiles negotiations were unbalanced in terms of the burden sharing of sacrifices within the Community. While the EC as a whole – and more specifically the northern Member States – would obtain important gains from the conclusion of the Round, the poor Portuguese textiles industry would be obliged to bear a disproportionate and untenable market opening cost. It was only on 15 December 1993, after the General Affairs Council had approved a special Community action of 400 million ECU to help modernize the Portuguese textiles industry, that Portugal decided not to prevent a consensus on the approval of the Round's Final Act.

Both in the French and Portuguese case, the internal compensatory deals were essential to sell the agreement to the domestic constituency.

---

67 For more details, see Devuyst, 'The European Community and the Conclusion', pp.456-57 (for the French problem) and pp.459-60 (for the Portuguese problem).

Without the Community acting at the intermediate bargaining level, the positive outcome of the Round would have been extremely doubtful. The Community served as an essential step towards effective European participation in the multilateral trade system – also from the perspective of the United States.

The Impact of the WTO

The issue of the Community's unity in commercial diplomacy has been posed again on the occasion of the establishment of the WTO which started functioning on 1 January 1995. In contrast with its *ad hoc* status in the old GATT of 1947, the Community became a formal member of the WTO. As has already been explained, the European Court of Justice ruled that the new trade fields covered by GATS and TRIPs did not fall exclusively under the Community's common commercial powers, but had to be treated as areas of mixed competence involving both the Member States and the Community. To the Commission, the confirmation of the mixed character of the Uruguay Round Final Act risked harming the Community in future WTO negotiations. The Commission notably recalled the 'disastrous' experience within the Food and Agriculture Organization (FAO), where Community and Member States are to agree before each meeting on a declaration of competence addressed to the other FAO partners regarding every single item on the agenda. This practice has obliged the Community to enter into difficult and lengthy internal discussions before every FAO meeting; moreover, according to the Commission, third countries quickly learned how to take advantage of the situation in trying to divide the Member States.[68] In response to this concern, the Court merely recalled the obligation to ensure close cooperation between members and Community institutions in the areas of mixed competence. Although the Member States and the Commission tried to formalize their duty to cooperate in the form of a broad Code of Conduct regulating the representation of the Community in the WTO, no agreement could be reached. For the Commission, the essence was to maintain the unity of the Community's representation through its monopoly of taking the floor in the WTO. Since a number of Member States continued to insist on their own right to speak in the

68 *Community Participation in United Nations Organs and Conferences* (Brussels, EC Commission, 3 March 1993), p.8.

areas under their competence in the absence of a consensus position, the negotiations did not succeed.

In practice, the Community has nevertheless managed to maintain the unity of representation in the WTO. In areas of mixed competence, the coordination between the Community and its Member States is guided by a short Code of Conduct agreed in May 1994 between the Council, the Member States and the Commission on the post-Uruguay Round negotiations on services. This Code, which predates the Court's Opinion 1/94 of November 1994, stipulates that the Commission should continue – as during the Uruguay Round – to negotiate on behalf of the Community and the Member States. The Community's position is discussed regularly with the Member States in the 133 Committee where the Commission needs to gather a consensus behind its policy lines.[69]

US attempts to divide the Member States in the WTO have, so far, not been successful. Rather than calling upon the Commission, the US has tried to initiate consultations on GATS and TRIPs issues with individual Member States such as Belgium (concerning telephone directory services), Ireland (concerning copyright and neighboring rights) and Denmark and Sweden (concerning the enforcement of intellectual property rights). In each of these cases, it was nevertheless the Commission – in cooperation with the Member States concerned – that was present during the consultations.[70] The US has even requested a dispute settlement panel against two individual Member States (Ireland and the United Kingdom) in an area of exclusive Community competence: the customs classification of certain computer equipment. The WTO Appellate Body explicitly disagreed with this practice. It recalled that the Community is a customs union and that the export market for US computer equipment is therefore the EC and not an individual Member State.[71]

---

69 *Press Release of the 1756th Council Meeting General Affairs* (Brussels: Council of the European Union, 16 and 17 May 1994), p.11. See also *Press Release of the 1830th Council Meeting General Affairs* (Brussels, Council of the European Union, 6 March 1995), p.1.

70 A. Rosas, 'The External Relations of the European Union: Problems and Challenges', in *The Forum for US-EU Legal-Economic Affairs* (Helsinki, The Mentor Group, 1998), pp.65-6.

71 WTO Appellate Body, *European Communities – Customs Classification of Certain Computer Equipment*, 5 June 1998, para. 96.

The US has also continued targeting retaliatory measures against those Member States that have blocked essential concessions during trade conflicts. In contrast with the old GATT, such retaliatory measures have now been formally approved by the WTO Dispute Settlement Body. The banana case serves as an example.[72] In December 1998, US Trade Representative Charlene Barshefsky announced a list of European products on which the US was planning to impose a prohibitive hundred per cent duty because of the EC's alleged refusal to comply with WTO panel rulings against its banana regime. This regime was favoring imports from overseas Community producers and from African and Caribbean countries to the detriment of dollar banana imports from US companies in Central America. Barshefsky's list was targeted mainly at products from the United Kingdom, Italy and France.[73] The United Kingdom and France were the main proponents of the EC's bananas regime designed to help their overseas territories and former colonies. Denmark and the Netherlands, on the other hand, were excluded from the US sanctions threat by virtue of the fact that they voted against the application of the EC's banana regime. While the WTO's arbitrators in April 1999 obliged the US to cut back the sanctions from the originally announced amount of Euro 431 million ($520 million) to Euro 178 million ($191 million), the final sanctions list still focused mainly on products from the United Kingdom and France, while exempting Denmark and the Netherlands because of their voting record in favor of the US position.[74]

While the US continues its policy of trying to weaken the Community during trade disputes by attempting to divide the Member States as it did prior to the creation of the WTO, the new multilateral trade regime did change the environment of transatlantic commercial diplomacy quite drastically. The Uruguay Round's Dispute Settlement Understanding

---

72 WTO Decision by the Arbitrators, *European Communities – Regime for the Importation, Sale and Distribution of Bananas – Recourse to Arbitration by the European Communities under Article 22.6 of the DSU*, 9 April 1999.

73 'USTR Lists European Products Subject to Increased Tariffs', *USA Text* (US Mission to the EU), 21 December 1998; 'EU/United States/WTO: Prohibitive Duties Announced by Americans Would Affect European Exports Worth ECU 501 Million a Year – United Kingdom, Italy and France would be Most Affected', *Agence Europe*, 23 December 1998, pp.9-10.

74 'USTR Announces Final Product List in Bananas Dispute', *USA Text* (US Mission to the EU), 9 April 1999; 'EU/US: EU to Try Revising Banana Regime by Year's End', *European Report*, 21 April 1999, pp. V 7-8.

(DSU) in particular offers both sides new arms during their commercial disputes.[75] The DSU provides for an effective mechanism to help resolve trade conflicts in a rule-based manner via panels, appellate review and arbitration. In case of non-compliance with a WTO ruling, retaliation is automatically authorized. Under the old GATT, the EC was able to block the adoption of panel reports that criticized the Community's commercial policies. The EC made use of this opportunity in several agricultural policy cases to safeguard as much as possible the often delicate internal compromises that form the basis of the Community's legislation.[76] As the banana and hormones cases have shown, the current WTO system no longer allows the Community to stop the multilateral dispute settlement system from functioning properly. But the Community has also learned to take advantage of the WTO's dispute settlement regime. Of the twenty-one completed WTO dispute settlement cases (by April 1999), the EC was involved as a complainant in four cases, all of which it won. The EC participated as a third party in nine cases. It was defendant in four other cases, of which it won two and lost two (bananas and hormones). In other words, the EC was actively involved in eighty-one per cent of all completed WTO cases and was on the winning side much more frequently than it lost.[77] As an additional benefit to the Community, WTO rules have severely restricted the US administration's liberty to resort to unilateral sanctions. The US learned this when the WTO's arbitrators decided to scale back substantially the amount of sanctions it wanted to impose on the EC in the banana case. As the world's largest trading bloc and essentially 'civilian power', the Community has a strong interest in a rule-based rather than a power-

---

75 For an overview of the WTO's dispute settlement system and the adaptations which it required on both sides of the Atlantic, see J. H. Jackson, *The World Trading System. Law and Policy of International Economic Relations* (Cambridge, Mass, MIT Press, 1997), pp.107-37; P. J. Kuyper, 'The New Dipute Settlement System: The Impact on the Community', in J. H. J. Bourgeois, F. Berrod and E. Gippinin Fournier (eds.), *The Uruguay Round Results* (Bruges, College of Europe, 1995), pp.87-114.

76 See R. E. Hudec, 'Legal Issues in US-EC Trade Policy: GATT Litigation 1960-1985', in R. E. Baldwin, C. B. Hamilton and A. Sapir (eds.), *Issues in US-EC Trade Relations* (Chicago, University of Chicago Press, 1988), pp.17-58. It must be noted that the US too has been blocking the old GATT dispute settlement procedures. For instance, in the case of 1983 brought by the US against the EC's export subsidies on wheat flour, the US blocked the panel report because it failed to find against the EC.

77 For an overview of the WTO's dispute settlement panels, see the WTO's website http://www.wto.org.

based international trade system in which disputes are settled in accordance with international law rather than political, military or economic pressures.

Conclusions

The US attitude towards the EC continues to be characterized by ambivalence. While supportive of European integration when serving its interests, the US still attempts to divide the Member States during times of commercial friction. The degree to which the US is successful in dividing the Member States is, of course, only a function of the Community's own level of cohesion. While the Community's founding fathers succeeded in creating a streamlined institutional framework for a common commercial policy, the Member States have shown a profound unwillingness to adapt the scope of this common policy to the realities of today's international economic transactions. Instead, they have insisted on their own external competences in such areas as trade in services, trade-related protection of intellectual property rights and foreign investment. While the EC and its Member States have in practice been able to maintain the unity of their external representation in an important multilateral forum such as the WTO, this has not been possible, for instance, in civil aviation negotiations with the US.

While struggling with the external competencies question, the Community has nevertheless made significant progress in gaining the status of equal partner with the US in commercial policy negotiations. In the WTO, for example, the EC is no longer merely the subject of US attacks in the dispute settlement system. On the contrary, the Community itself uses the new dispute settlement procedures in an offensive and successful way. Equally significant is the evolution under the NTA where the EC and the US operate on equal footing. While the pre-emptive and interventionist strategy set up by the US during the creation of the Internal Market was still a largely one-way street, the early warning procedures established under the NTA at the Bonn Summit of June 1999 illustrate that the transatlantic economic relationship has undergone an institutionalization based on reciprocity and mutual benefit.

CHAPTER 10

Processes and Procedures in EU-US Foreign Policy Cooperation: From the Transatlantic Declaration to the New Transatlantic Agenda

Thomas FRELLESEN *

European Commission, DG External Relations

Introduction

'In the last few years, some have said that the United States and Europe would inevitably drift apart. We have proved them wrong. Our common action in Bosnia has dramatically reinforced the transatlantic alliance and has opened new prospects for lasting European security cooperation. And the New Transatlantic Agenda agreed by the United States and the European Union in Madrid last month will not only expand our economic ties but enhance coordination on political and security challenges around the world.'[1]

US Secretary of State Warren Christopher's remarks in January 1996 were illustrative of a new mood in EU-US relations in official circles at that time.[2] With a feeling that the Bosnian hurdle had been partly over-

* The views expressed here are personal and should not in any way be attributed to the European Commission.

1 Speech by US Secretary of State Warren Christopher, 'Leadership for the Next American Century' at the John F. Kennedy School of Government at Harvard University, *Wireless File,* 18 January 1996.

2 See also the speeches on transatlantic relations by Commission President Jacques Santer at the Transatlantic Policy Network (TPN), Brussels, 30 November 1995 and Commission Vice-President Sir Leon Brittan at the Centre for European Policy Studies (CEPS), Brussels 5 March 1996. See also Commissioner Hans van den Broek's speech on the Common Foreign and Security Policy at the Europees Instituut voor Bestuurskunde, Maastricht, 19 October 1995. Needless to say, this optimistic mood was not shared by everyone and nervousness about future European-American relations continued to characterise some of the debate on both sides of the Atlantic. See, for example, L. Barber, G. De Jonquières, 'US and Europe Eye Each Other up', *Financial*

come, in the light of the Dayton Agreement, and the New Transatlantic Agenda outlining concrete priorities for EU-US relations for the years ahead the outlook seemed promising in terms of the prospects for strengthening cooperation.

The optimism reflected in Christopher's speech remains, to a great extent, valid. The main reason for optimism is the fact that EU-US cooperation has continued to develop and intensify over the past years, and this is also the case for the field of foreign policy. This chapter will focus on EU-US foreign policy cooperation. It will argue that this component of transatlantic relations has developed significantly since the end of the Cold War.[3] As the EU has begun to build its own structures for a Common Foreign and Security Policy, the links between the EU and the US have been strengthened in the area of foreign policy cooperation. A wide range of common interests constitute the basis for an increasing degree of pragmatic cooperation.

It should be said at the outset that while cooperation across the Atlantic is crucial for serving mutual, and wider interests, EU-US relations should not be seen as a panacea for all international problems.

In fact, it could be counterproductive to create the expectation that a somehow perfectly functioning transatlantic relationship could prevent all major tragic events, like the ones we have seen in Rwanda or Bosnia, from happening.[4] Indeed, disappointed hopes could undermine public confidence in and support for the relationship. And public support is much needed for continuing the process of developing relations at a time when world affairs continue to appear to be in a state of flux.

Transatlantic relations are complex. In addition to the EU-US component, bilateral relations between the US and individual EU Member

---

Times, 12 May 1995; E. Mortimer, 'No end in sight to uncertainty', *Financial Times*, 14 June 1995 and W. Pfaff, 'Western Europe Missed Its Chance to Take Charge', *IHT*, 5 December 1995.

3 T. Frellesen, R. Ginsberg, 'EU-US Foreign Policy Cooperation in the 1990s, Elements of Partnership', *CEPS*, Paper No.58, Brussels, 1994.

4 In analysing the European Community (now European Union) as an external actor, Christopher Hill has noted that 'sometimes the language of politics can run ahead of the realities' and that 'the Community's capabilities have been talked up, to the point where a significant *capability-expectations gap* exists'. A similar argument could be made for the EU-US partnership. See C. Hill, 'The Capability-Expectations Gap, or Conceptualizing Europe's International Role', *Journal of Common Market Studies*, 31:3 (1993) 305-28.

States remain very important. Furthermore, Europeans and Americans also interact intimately in a large number of international fora such as NATO, the UN, the OSCE or the G8. In fact, the transatlantic relationship is probably the most interlinked and crucial relationship for both partners. The EU component in this relationship is growing, however, and will be the focus of this chapter.

The EU and the US have in many ways been in a learning phase since the end of the Cold War in terms of managing their relations and finding new ways of cooperating to meet a new range of common challenges. The end of the Cold War brought with it changing outlooks on both sides of the Atlantic with uncertainty in Europe about its own arrangements for cooperation and the continued commitment of the US to European security. On the other side of the Atlantic, there were uncertainties about how best to promote American interests in a new Europe, which new levers to use and how to mobilise the necessary support and resources at home for a continued engagement abroad.

The two parties have been forced to reassess how to deal with each other. Developments over the past years should lead to a positive assessment of the results so far. The 1990 Transatlantic Declaration established a formal framework for dialogue between what was then the European Community and the US and gave an important impetus for furthering what now amounts to an almost automatic habit of consultation.

The signing of the NTA took the relationship a step further by outlining priorities for cooperation and fleshing out specific projects where the EU and the US wanted to be seen acting together. In terms of the foreign policy aspects of these efforts, a main motivation for the US side was to establish stronger links with the new and somehow more political 'animal' that the EU became with the Maastricht Treaty and the emergence of Pillars II and III, that is a Common Foreign and Security Policy and cooperation on Justice and Home Affairs issues. The US aim was in many ways to support the establishment and implementation of an effective CFSP.[5] But it was also to ensure that whatever kind of EU foreign policy emerged it would be one that took US views duly into account and which worked for rather than against US interests. This US

5 See, for example, A. Gardner, *A New Era in US-EU Relations: The Clinton Administration and the New Transatlantic Agenda* (Aldershot, Avebury, 1997), p.65.

aim of being heard was nothing new, or even surprising, and echoed US aims since the first US-EU foreign policy frictions in the early 1970s over Middle East policy.

For the EU – Commission and Member States alike – the NTA was a way of achieving the widely perceived need for reinforced relations: a strengthening of the Transatlantic Declaration without entering into a complicated exercise of trying to flesh out a comprehensive Transatlantic Treaty shortly before the EU would enter into yet another Intergovernmental Conference which would again change internal EU workings. For the EU, the question was therefore partly to see how to make use of the new pillars established by the Maastricht Treaty and to give the Union a stronger profile in the foreign policy field. The Commission had already indicated the need for a comprehensive initiative to further develop EU-US relations, including CFSP, in its Communication to the Council on EU-US relations in July 1995.[6] In addition, EU Member States – including those traditionally identified as being less 'transatlantic' than others – were not shy in continuously calling for a beefier foreign policy section in the NTA when draft texts were discussed in the Council.

Indeed, there seem to be two main reasons for increased EU-US foreign policy cooperation in recent years: moves towards greater European integration and the changing nature of foreign policy and security issues in the post-Cold War world.

First, the Maastricht Treaty represented an important new step in the European integration process which also increased the momentum towards strengthening EU-US ties, especially in the new areas of Pillars II and III. The reason was partly that the US has traditionally sought to fortify its ties with the EU whenever steps have been taken towards further integration. Also greater European integration on Pillar III issues, such as international organised crime – a major US foreign policy concern – opened up the perspective for increased cooperation between the EU and the US. The same can be said for Pillar II, the CFSP, where a greater degree of European integration in the long term promised the US a better European interlocutor in foreign affairs.

With respect to the second main reason for increased EU-US foreign policy cooperation – the changing nature of foreign and security issues –

6 European Commission, 'Europe and the US: The Way Forward', Brussels 26 July 1995.

the Union's external actions under the Community framework, which have always had important political ramifications, have also become more interesting and important for the US. Many of our common security interests are now more often met by civil and economic rather than military means.[7] In other words, in the post-Cold War era, the definition of 'security' has become increasingly blurred and one could argue that many aspects of EU-US foreign policy cooperation, and, indeed also, EU-US cooperation within the Community framework (Pillar I) have significant security implications. US officials have stressed again and again this new dimension of security in outlining US policy towards Europe over the past years. In his *Hôtel de Ville* speech in Brussels in January 1994 President Clinton said:

> During this past half-century, transatlantic security depended primarily on the deterrents provided by our military forces. Now the immediate threat to our East is not of advancing armies, but of creeping instability. Countering that threat requires not only military security, but also the promotion of democratic and economic renewal. Combined, these forces are the strongest bulwark against Europe's current dangers – against ethnic conflict, the abuse of human rights, the destabilizing refugee flows, the rise of aggressive regimes and the spread of weapons of mass destruction.[8]

Similarly, in a statement on European security to Congress in April 1995, Assistant Secretary of State for European and Canadian Affairs Richard Holbrooke said:

> Disappearance of Cold War structures has left important parts of Europe without a sense of security provided by a credible framework. This sense of insecurity is related less to the perception of a new threat than it is to the need to generate a climate of confidence [...]. In this context, building a new security architecture for Europe means providing a framework to build democracy, market economies, stable societies, and ultimately a stable and just peace across the continent.[9]

In short, the action of the EU in its traditional framework of Pillar I (through which, it channels via the Commission massive resources for reform assistance and provides for market access via association agreements and other accords, for example) has gained in political importance. Pillar I has also raised the political profile of the EU, including its

---

7 This chapter focuses on foreign policy co-operation and will not cover security and defense relations (Article J.4 of the Maastricht Treaty).

8 *USA Text,* 9 January 1994 (USAT PL 2).

9 *Wireless File,* 5 April 1995.

profile as regards cooperation with the US in these areas, not least in the light of severe budget cuts in the US. The former US Ambassador to the EU, Stuart Eizenstat, a driving force behind the NTA, has noted:

> To the degree that foreign assistance and trade are the currency of a foreign and security policy, the EU for many years has used them effectively. Its large humanitarian and development assistance budget – coming at a time when ours is shrinking – provides the EU and its Member States with political influence in the Middle East, Africa, Bosnia, and elsewhere. Its creative packaging of policy in the Euro-Mediterranean initiative, its outreach to Mexico and the Mercosur countries, partnership and cooperation agreements with Russia, the Ukraine and the NIS, its Lomé Convention with its grants and trade preferences – all give it a seat at the foreign policy table.[10]

Needless to say, Eizenstat's generous assessment was not, is not, and probably will never be shared by the entire US administration. 'NATO-firsters' remain a considerable force who have tended to play down the significance of the EU on security related issues and would instead like to focus relations with Europe on bilateral ties with EU Member States. It is important to note, however, that key US decision-makers took a more forthcoming view of the EU's existing role and future potential in the NTA context. Moves to strengthen ties between the EU and NATO certainly indicate that this position is likely to have been the more forward-looking one.

---

[10] Farewell remarks to the EU Committee of the American Chamber of Commerce in Brussels on 8 February 1996, *Wireless File* 9 February 1996. With respect to budget cuts the administrator of the US Agency for International Development (USAID) Brian Atwood said in a testimony to the House Appropriations Subcommittee on Foreign Operations, Export Financing and Related Programs on 24 April 1996: 'USAID will enter Fiscal Year 1997 still adjusting to the severe cuts imposed during Fiscal Year 1996. These cuts have had a significant impact on our programme. In FY 1996 alone, Development Assistance was cut 23.1% from the year before. Support for Eastern European Democracy was cut 9.7%; aid to the New Independent States of the Former Soviet Union was cut 24.6%. In dollar terms, these cuts totaled $807,000,000.', *Wireless File* 24 April 1996. A US Fact Sheet on relations with the EU issued on 5 September 1997 noted that 'The EU also has taken on an increasingly important role in foreign affairs, especially in the area of humanitarian and development assistance. The EU's foreign aid budget for 1995-98 exceeds $36 billion. This assistance reinforces many important US interests. For example, the EU is the largest donor of grant assistance to the countries of central and eastern Europe – $7.3 billion during the period 1990-94 – and has a similarly large assistance program for the former Soviet Union to help promote democracy and free market reforms. EU aid also supports US efforts to bring stability and prosperity to the Middle East, the former Yugoslavia, Albania, and Central Africa'. USIA (Washington File) 5 December 1997.

Mechanisms of EU-US Foreign Policy Cooperation

Objectives

European foreign policy cooperation of course has a longer history than the Maastricht Treaty. It goes back to the early 1970s and what was then called European Political Cooperation (EPC). The US soon wanted to establish a dialogue in this area. *Ad hoc* talks began in 1974 and were developed further in the course of the 1980s with regular talks between Political Directors and Foreign Ministers of EC Member States and their US counterparts.[11]

The tumultuous events in Central and Eastern Europe in the late 1980s and the steps taken to continue the integration process in the EC with the Single Market program prompted calls for setting transatlantic relations on a more secure and predictable footing. Most prominent among these was Secretary of State James Baker's Berlin speech in December 1989.

These calls eventually led to an EC-US agreement – the Transatlantic Declaration of November 1990 – which, for the first time, provided a formal outline for EC-US talks and spelled out common objectives.

The Transatlantic Declaration was a result of the need to reinforce the relationship between the two sides following the dramatic changes taking place in Europe. Not least important in this respect was the need to co-ordinate approaches towards supporting reform in Central and Eastern Europe. The Bush administration realised that the European Community, invigorated and strengthened by the Single Market programme, would play an important role in this transformation process and that the traditional forum for transatlantic consultations in NATO would benefit from complementary economic and political discussions between the US and the Community.

The objectives of the Transatlantic Declaration reflected the commonality of interests. In terms of EU and US aims and interests, it is remarkable to note how similar the common objectives, as delineated in the Transatlantic Declaration, were with those of the Union within the CFSP

---

[11] On this early period see, for example, R. Ginsberg, *Foreign Policy Actions of the European Community – The Politics of Scale* (Boulder, Lynne Rienner, 1989) and R. Ginsberg and K. Featherstone, *The United States and the European Union in the 1990s* (New York, St. Martin's Press, 1996). Among other interesting references, see such classics as S. J. Nuttal, *European Political Cooperation* (Oxford, OUP, 1992); P. de Schoutheete, *La Coopération Politique Européenne* (Brussels, Labor, 1986); P. Ifestos, *European Political Cooperation* (Aldershot, 1987).

even though the Declaration predated the Maastricht Treaty.[12] The objectives of the Declaration remain at the core of most EU-US cooperative efforts.

Mechanics

The mechanics by which the EU and the US carry out their foreign policy dialogue and cooperation were in part laid down formally in the Transatlantic Declaration. The Declaration did not, however, include all foreign policy-type consultative arrangements agreed upon given sensitivities in several Member States. There was thus no reference to meetings of Political Directors and foreign policy experts.[13] Furthermore, since the issuing of the Transatlantic Declaration in 1990, further efforts were made to add to the basic framework for dialogue. The Declaration itself contained an 'evolutionary clause' stating that 'both sides are resolved to develop and deepen these procedures for consultation so as to reflect the evolution of the European Community and of its relationship with the United States'. For instance, it was agreed in 1991 to institutionalise consultations in certain third country capitals where a regular dialogue now exists between Troika[14] Heads of Mission (HOM) and US Ambassadors.

---

12 The objectives of the Transatlantic Declaration were to: 'support democracy, the rule of law and respect for human rights and individual liberty; safeguard peace and promote international security, by co-operating with other nations against aggression and coercion, by contributing to the settlement of conflicts in the world and by reinforcing the role of the United Nations and other international organisations; promote market principles and to strengthen and further open the multilateral trading system'. The objectives of the CFSP as they were spelled out in the Maastricht Treaty were to: 'safeguard the common values, fundamental interests and independence of the Union; strengthen the security of the Union and its Member States in all ways; to preserve peace and strengthen international security, in accordance with the principles of the United Nations Charter as well as the principles of the Helsinki Final Act and the objectives of the Paris Charter; to promote international co-operation; to develop and consolidate democracy and the rule of law, and respect for human rights and fundamental freedoms'.

13 The areas for which meetings of 'experts' at working level are organised usually include: Africa, Asia, Central Europe, Consular Affairs, Counter-terrorism, Former Yugoslavia, Human Rights, Latin America, Mashrek/Maghreb, Non-proliferation (arms exports/disarmament/chemical and biological arms/nuclear non-proliferation), OSCE, and UN Affairs.

14 In EU external relations the term 'troika' traditionally referred to the EU Presidency, its immediate predecessor and successor, and the Commission. The Amsterdam Treaty brought with it changes and although the formula remained flexible the 'new' Troika

The NTA added yet another mechanism, that of the Senior Level Group (SLG), which was to monitor the implementation of the NTA, including foreign policy aspects. The SLG was aided in this by the NTA Task Force which, at Director level, was to prepare SLG meetings and deal with all NTA related issues (including foreign policy issues) which could be handled without involving higher levels.

Taking the Transatlantic Declaration and other arrangements for political consultations, including the NTA, into account, the framework for the EU-US dialogue on foreign policy issues presently looks as illustrated in the following graph.

---

was to be composed of the Presidency, the Commission and the new High Representative for CFSP and, if need be, the next Member State to hold the Presidency.

EU-US Political Dialogue

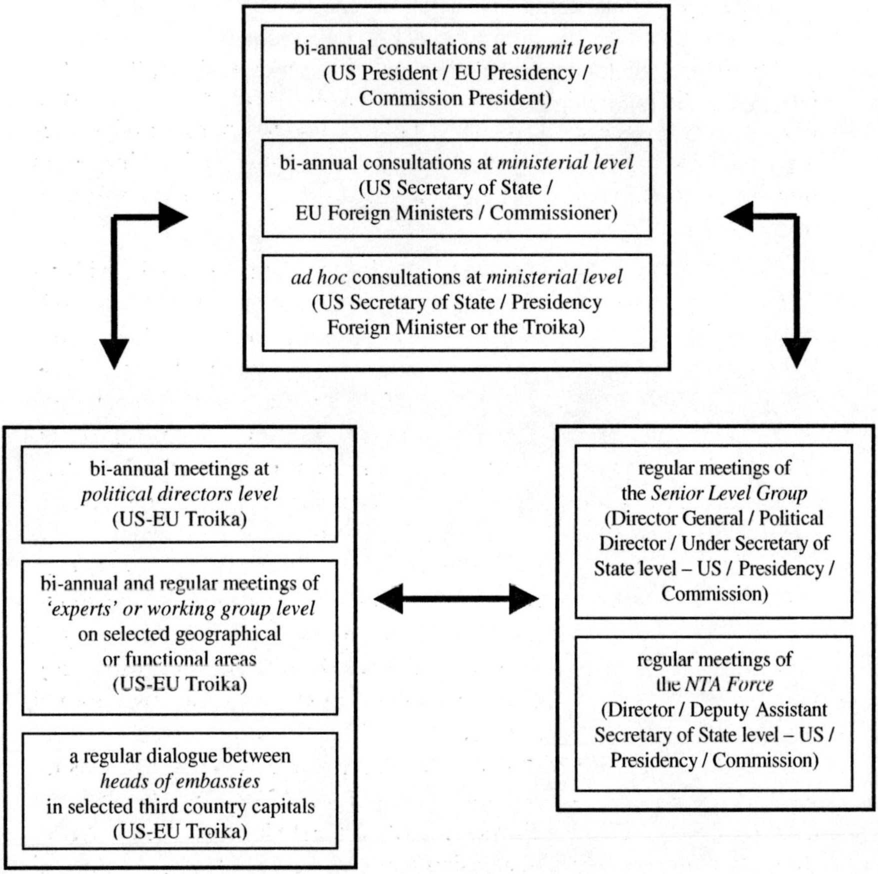
bi-annual consultations at *summit level* (US President / EU Presidency / Commission President)
bi-annual consultations at *ministerial level* (US Secretary of State / EU Foreign Ministers / Commissioner)
ad hoc consultations at *ministerial level* (US Secretary of State / Presidency Foreign Minister or the Troika)
bi-annual meetings at *political directors level* (US-EU Troika)
bi-annual and regular meetings of *'experts' or working group level* on selected geographical or functional areas (US-EU Troika)
a regular dialogue between *heads of embassies* in selected third country capitals (US-EU Troika)
regular meetings of the *Senior Level Group* (Director General / Political Director / Under Secretary of State level – US / Presidency / Commission)
regular meetings of the *NTA Force* (Director / Deputy Assistant Secretary of State level – US / Presidency / Commission)

A slight differentiation is made above between the NTA mechanisms and the 'traditional' dialogue mechanisms. What emerges is a kind of triangular structure with the EU-US Summit at the top. This is done to distinguish between the traditional political dialogue mechanisms, which mirror the internal EU set-up for CFSP, and the NTA mechanisms (SLG and Task Force) which do not.

The Senior Level Group

The SLG was a unique invention in that it was a cross-pillar body, covering CFSP and other issues in a horizontal manner. It is important to keep in mind that it was created with the specific purpose of preparing more thoroughly Summit level discussions. It thus had the important function of pulling together the threads and giving greater coherence to overall EU-US discussions.

The SLG was an informal and flexible mechanism which, with its composition, was given the task of covering economic as well as political issues in order to be as comprehensive as possible. For this reason, EU representation was ensured by the Presidency (leading for the EU on CFSP and Third Pillar issues) and the Commission (leading for the EU on economic and other Pillar I issues). On the US side, under the Clinton administration, the two SLG members were the Under-Secretary for Political Affairs (first Peter Tarnoff, later Thomas Pickering) and the Under-Secretary for Economic Affairs (first Joan Spero, later Stuart Eizenstat). On the European side, the Presidency was represented by two senior political and economic officials which, at times, included the Presidency Political Director or the Secretary General of the Ministry of Foreign Affairs (depending on the Member State acting as Presidency). For the Commission, under the Santer Commission, the two formal members were the Director General of DGI – External Relations: Commercial Policy and Relations with North America, the Far East, Australia and New Zealand – (first Horst Krenzler, later Hans Beseler) and the Chef de Cabinet of Vice-President Brittan (first Colin Budd, later Ivan Rogers). However, the Commission team in the SLG was strengthened by the regular participation of the Director General of DGIA (External Relations: Europe and the New Independent States, CFSP and External Missions), Günther Burghardt, who was at the same time, and had been for many years, the Commission's Political Director and representative in the Political Committee. This was due to both the significance of the issues discussed – CFSP aspects and key foreign policy issues concerning Central and Eastern Europe, the Balkans, the NIS and Russia – and the fact that responsibilities for external relations within the Commission had been divided among four Commissioners.

No formal decision was taken on the frequency of SLG meetings but in practice the group ended up meeting twice per Presidency, with locations alternating between Washington, Brussels and the Presidency capital. The SLG met once early on in a new Presidency, in order to identify possible 'deliverables' for the EU-US Summit, and once later, close to the Summit date, in order to 'harvest' these deliverables and give where necessary the final political push to remaining obstacles. The Task Force met somewhat more frequently, up to four times during a Presidency, including occasional video-conferences, and usually in advance of SLG meetings in order to prepare discussions. For both SLG and Task Force meetings it became habit to involve a broad range of experts in discussions in order to get regular and precise updates on the state of play on various dossiers and to give these experts a dose of 'transatlanticism' and encourage them increasingly to include the EU-US angle in their deliberations. The US side was particular adept at involving a wide range of officials and it was not unusual for the list of US participants at Task Force meetings held in Washington to number more than forty people (with rotating chairs naturally, so that the group could remain relatively small and informal).

CFSP

As suggested above, the set-up for the EU-US foreign policy dialogue closely follows internal arrangements for EU foreign policy cooperation within the framework of CFSP as established by the Maastricht Treaty in 1991. As I will explain below, this is no coincidence and it is important to understand CFSP structures in order to understand fully the process of EU-US foreign policy cooperation and the opportunities and obstacles involved. The arrangements for the CFSP roughly consist of:

- The European Council (Head of State and Government and Commission President meeting at least once every six months to set priorities and give broad guidelines for EU policies, including the CFSP).
- The Council of Ministers (EU Foreign Ministers and Commission External Relations Commissioners meeting as the General Affairs Council at least once a month to decide on external relations issues, including CFSP policies).

- The Committee of Permanent Representatives (known as 'Coreper' – Ambassadors of EU Member States to the EU and the Commission Deputy Secretary General meeting once a week to prepare Council meetings and decisions, including those related to the General Affairs Council and CFSP).
- The Political Committee (Political Directors of EU Member States and the Commission meeting about twice a month to monitor international affairs and the implementation of CFSP decisions and to contribute to the definition of CFSP policies by submitting opinions to the General Affairs Council).
- European Correspondents of EU Member States and the Commission assist the Political Directors, coordinate daily CFSP communications, and prepare the meetings of the Political Committee.
- CFSP Working Groups, composed of experts from EU Member States and the Commission, meet along geographical and horizontal lines to elaborate policy documents and options for the consideration of the Political Committee.

In addition, the European Parliament has a consultative role and the functions of the Council Secretariat have been reinforced in terms of its role in assisting the Presidency. Furthermore, day-to-day contact on CFSP issues is maintained via the Coreu (Correspondance européenne) telex network which allows for an ongoing exchange of enciphered messages among Member States and the Commission. The network is used to exchange confidential information and to finalise reports and declarations as well as for decision-making by written procedure.

In terms of CFSP in general, the Maastricht Treaty foresaw two ways in which the objectives of the Treaty could be achieved. First, through systematic political cooperation (information exchange, coordination, convergence of national action) on all foreign and security policy questions when the Council thought that it was needed. This could be done via what was called a 'common position'. If such a common position was defined, Member States were to ensure that their national policies conformed to the common position. The second way to achieve the objectives was by making use of the concept of 'joint actions' established by the Maastricht Treaty. This meant laying down rules which legally bound the Member States.

One may ask why the mechanisms for the CFSP and EU-US political dialogue mirror each other to a great extent. The answer to this should not come as a surprise. As should be evident from the above CFSP is a very formal framework. Foreign policy cooperation remains one of the most sensitive areas for cooperation among EU Member States who are keen to maintain autonomous individual foreign policies. They are much less eager to create a foreign policy at EU level although they realise that some kind of EU-level policy is necessary in order for the Union to act effectively internationally and, indeed, for the Member States to achieve their foreign policy objectives which are, to a large extent, and increasingly so, similar. These are thus parallel processes – CFSP complements the foreign policies of Member States – and are likely to be so for a long time to come. The formality of the CFSP processes means that the mechanisms for dialogue with third countries are defined very clearly. The Treaty spells out that the Presidency represents the Union in CFSP, assisted where necessary by the Troika and with the Commission fully associated, and that political dialogue meetings can take place at the levels of heads of state, ministers, senior officials and experts. These are natural interlocutors for third countries since each of these groups, as explained above, meet among themselves and discuss and decide EU policy. What makes the political dialogue with the US differ from any other third country is the fact that it is the oldest and most developed dialogue and makes full use of all the possibilities offered by the Treaty provisions. No other third country has such an intensive and broad political dialogue with the EU.

The NTA, along with the SLG process, added yet another mechanism which filled a gap between the multitudes of EU-US talks in the framework of the different pillars. In this sense, the SLG was a very useful invention, but it was also a very time-consuming process which was not likely to be copied with any other third country. Whatever one may think of the EU's capacity to conduct a political dialogue the fact remains that countries have lined up over recent years to intensify their political dialogue with the Union and many voices in the EU (Member States and the Commission alike) have called for the need to avoid overloading responsibilities further. In terms of the SLG, it should also be noted that since it does not conform with the traditional pattern of the EU's external dialogue, Member States have at times felt that this was a process which was difficult to control. This was also reflected in the establishment in the Council of a Transatlantic Working Group in 1995. This group, with representatives from each Member State, the Presidency and the Commission, meets for regular sessions at which the Presidency and the Commission keep Member States informed of the NTA process and meetings held in that context.

The Amsterdam Treaty

The Amsterdam Treaty, which entered into force on 1 May 1999, sought to improve the CFSP in a number of ways which were unlikely to affect transatlantic cooperation greatly but which could nevertheless have some impact. As regards the CFSP, the Treaty stated that: overall consistency was to be improved by strengthening the role of the European Council in defining what was called 'common strategies' for the Union's foreign policy; a High Representative for the CFSP, who would be the Secretary-General of the Council, would assist the Council and the Presidency in CFSP matters. The High Representative would also head a Policy Planning and Early Warning Unit which would be established to provide policy assessments and more focused input into policy formulation.

The Treaty aimed to improve CFSP decision-making procedures by providing for a constructive abstention procedure in order to reduce the risk of deadlock by allowing a Member State not to be obliged to apply a certain decision. Furthermore, qualified majority voting was to be the rule for decisions under the CFSP which implemented any 'common strategies' agreed unanimously by the European Council, or which implemented joint actions or common positions which had already been adopted. An 'emergency brake' was provided for which allowed any Member State to oppose the adoption of a decision for important reasons on national policy. In such cases, those Member States which considered it important for the Union to act could, if they represented a qualified majority, refer the matter to the European Council for decision by unanimity.[15]

---

15 The Union's security and defence objectives were reformulated to take account of developments in this area since the negotiation of the Maastricht Treaty. The so-called Petersberg tasks (*i.e.* humanitarian and rescue tasks, peacekeeping and crisis management) were explicitly mentioned in the Amsterdam Treaty as aspects of the Union's security policy thereby underlining the Union's desire to develop its action in these areas more effectively, while ensuring that all Member States were involved as far as possible in their implementation. The Treaty provisions were to enhance co-operation between the EU and the Western European Union (WEU) and the possibility of the Union's CFSP evolving into a common defence, along with the integration of the WEU into the Union, was envisaged.

The advances made by the Amsterdam Treaty in the field of CFSP were limited.[16] The CFSP, the Pillar II framework, remained very much an intergovernmental process. In terms of transatlantic foreign policy cooperation the Treaty was therefore unlikely to lead to significant qualitative changes although some improvements were likely, such as an 'improved' new EU troika consisting of the Presidency, the Commission and the High Representative (as well as the next Member State to hold the Presidency if need be) which promised more continuity in talks than the 'old' Troika system with former, present and future Presidencies.

What will ultimately happen with the CFSP as a result of the Amsterdam Treaty remains to be seen, however, and will depend much on how the Treaty will be implemented and how the CFSP provisions will be made use of. This, in turn, will determine the impact of the Treaty on relations with the US.

Pillars I and II and the Commission

The Presidential and Ministerial level EU-US meetings referred to earlier are of course not limited to external political issues. They also cover external economic matters, that is to say matters falling under the traditional Community framework (Pillar I) where the Commission acts as the executive body on the basis of policies and mandates agreed upon by the Council. To the extent that Pillar I issues are of interest to the US in terms of foreign policy, such as assistance to the reform process in Central and Eastern Europe, one should note that the Commission has an extensive and ongoing *ad hoc* dialogue with the US which includes on-the-ground talks in recipient countries. This dialogue is so extensive that it is almost impossible to quantify. Moeover, it is partly the result of the fact that the Commission to a great extent acts autonomously on these issues and can make its own arrangements for talks with the US.

The procedures in Pillar I are simply less cumbersome than those under Pillar II where a rotating Presidency and troika as dialogue partners often do not provide sufficient continuity. Development aid and humanitarian assistance are other areas where the Commission's prerogatives allow for a broad dialogue with the US.

---

16 On this see, for example, the speech by Dr. Günter Burghardt, Director General of DGIA (Europe and the New Independent States, Common Foreign and Security Policy and External Services) of the European Commission, 'Perspektiven der Gemeinsamen Aussen- und Sicherheitspolitik nach Amsterdam',Vienna, 3 October 1997.

This was well-illustrated by the Third Annual High-Level Consultations between the Commission and USAID which were held in Brussels on 23-24 October 1997 with around sixty Commission participants and thirty USAID representatives, including Commissioners Bonino and Pinheiro and USAID Director Atwood. Discussions were held in different working groups (Food Security, Latin America, Asia and the Mediterranean, Humanitarian Assistance, NIS) and new elements included talks on best practice in linking relief, rehabilitation and development, and exchanges on approaches to conflict prevention and disaster preparedness. The conclusions included references to the Joint USAID/EC Benin Good Governance Assessment, complementary approaches to fighting drug-trafficking and abuse in Southern Africa, mutual support for justice sector reform in Haiti, joint missions to Bolivia in support of civil society projects, parallel financing of projects in Bangladesh, joint interest in environmental protection schemes in Egypt, and closer coordination of assistance to NIS countries, notably Ukraine.[17]

Ad hoc *Dialogue*

It would be a fallacy to assume that the specifically political dialogue is limited to the more or less bi-annual mechanisms mentioned above. The Presidency of the EU (with the Commission associated) is responsible for the day-to-day management of the CFSP. As such it is in touch with the US whenever the need arises and keeps EU partners informed of such contacts. These informal contacts and the formal meetings, especially the working group meetings, can lead to suggestions for coordinated or complementary action with the US on foreign policy issues. A practical recommendation would be to coordinate démarches with the US in order to put maximum pressure on a third country in human rights or other political reform issues (as has happened regularly over the past years concerning Slovakia).

This *ad hoc* dialogue often takes place in the wings of multilateral fora and gives a certain degree of flexibility to the cooperation process. With respect to cooperation within the UN framework, for example, there can be *ad hoc* meetings between the EU Troika and the US in advance of UN events, if contacts are considered necessary for specific purposes. Examples over the past years include the Social Summit and

---

[17] 'Conclusions', *Third Annual High-Level US/EC Assistance Consultations*, 23-24 October 1997, European Commission Document, Brussels 19 November 1997.

the World Conference on Women. Likewise, informal contacts are extensive in the General Assembly and the UN Commission on Human Rights on human rights issues. A further example is the OSCE where there are regular contacts in Vienna and at other OSCE events.

In a certain sense, therefore, the formal framework for talks should be seen as a structure for giving a certain degree of regularity to the dialogue and providing stimulus for cooperation on a day-to-day basis at working level.

Assessing the Mechanisms

Various assessments of the mechanisms for political dialogue were carried out on both sides of the Atlantic in the course of 1993 and 1994 and there was a basic agreement that the existing framework was sufficient. There was also an agreement, however, to get more 'mileage' out of existing talks and the priority given to transatlantic relations during the German EU Presidency in 1994 in part led to the establishment of three *ad hoc* study groups at the Berlin EU-US Summit in June 1994. These groups, focusing on EU-US cooperation concerning Central and Eastern Europe, foreign policy issues in general (Pillar II), and international organised crime (Pillar III) were intended to produce operational recommendations to inject additional substance into ongoing talks.[18]

The conclusions of the *ad hoc* study groups were submitted to the Washington EU-US Summit on 14 June 1995 although the results were perhaps not as ambitious as had been expected. The Pillar III study group was particularly disappointing for the US side. US frustration was perhaps predictable given the degree of intergovernmentalism prevailing in this area of EU cooperation.

The CFSP group did produce a number of useful recommendations, however. As mentioned earlier, there was general agreement that the number of meetings and opportunities for dialogue sufficed. The recommendations of the group were therefore more a question of fine-tuning than structural change. They included suggestions such as ensuring a better preparation of Summit discussions and making the latter more focused as well as assuring a better link between the various levels of dialogue in general with emphasis on priority setting and follow-up being.

---

[18] See the chapter by Anthony Gardner in this book.

Perhaps the most important result of the study group exercise was that the Washington EU-US Summit, which adopted the conclusions, also set up what was called a Senior Level Group (SLG). The group was made up of personal representatives of the Summit leaders who were charged with preparing the following Summit in Madrid by generating ideas for EU-US cooperation. The study group exercise thus set a precedent: subsequent EU-US Summits would now have to be properly prepared. In addition, the gathering of EU and US leaders every six months would be used to the full in order to create additional political impetus for EU-US cooperation in operational terms and to contribute to an overall strengthening of the relationship.

The New Transatlantic Agenda

The Washington Summit to some extent represented a culmination of reflections on the mechanics of EU-US consultations. It confirmed that the basic framework for dialogue was sufficient. The issue now was how to better use the framework and flesh out the dialogue.

As already mentioned in previous chapter, various Commission and US proposals for a new initiative circulated in 1995. They were strongly supported in the Council, the EU decision-making body, where transatlantic relations continued to be considered a major priority, not least during the Spanish Presidency.

Spain's ambitions concerning transatlantic relations had been set out early in a non-paper for informal discussion among EU planners during the first weeks of the Spanish Presidency in July 1995. The Spanish paper began by noting a favourable US attitude to calls for initiatives to develop transatlantic relations and denoting possible US frustration if the EU did not respond to these calls. It noted historical links, trade ties and polls in the US indicating public preference for US relations with Europe as compared to relations with Asia. The paper argued that this priority was reinforced by the new Republican majority in Congress (with NATO focus). A number of reasons were listed which demonstrated the need for an initiative: the absence of a common threat could cause drifting apart; introspectivity on both sides; the danger of aggressive unilateralism in the US; growing regionalism; the growing capacity of the EU to act; growing economic competition; tensions within NATO; the need for coordination on adapting international economic structures; the needs of global monetary conditions; the need for responses to links between economic, political and security aspects of relations; the possible impact of the cumulative effect of minor disputes, not least in light of an increasingly volatile American foreign policy; the lack of knowledge in the US of the EU and demographic changes in the US; US frustration at the absence of a single EU interlocutor.

The Spanish paper echoed general feelings among EU Member States and the Commission. It was not surprising therefore that the Council gave a very favourable view of the communication on EU-US relations adopted by the Commission in July 1995. The Communication covered economic as well as political and security issues and many elements were drawn from it for the EU input tabled when the subsequent NTA and Action Plan were elaborated in conjunction with the US. The Commission notably called for a closer dialogue on EU and NATO enlargements and a greater degree of cooperation on non-proliferation issues, export controls, preventive diplomacy, human rights and minority problems and humanitarian and development assistance. The Communication also lent support to the call by the 14 June 1995 EU-US Summit for closer cooperation on Bosnia and Croatia, assistance to the Palestinians and environmental issues in Central and Eastern Europe, and it proposed that concrete projects for joint action should be developed in these areas.[19]

Efforts for a new transatlantic initiative gained crucial momentum during the Spanish Presidency notably because thoughts had crystallised and expectations had been raised. The experience with the three working groups had left much to be desired and little progress had been made during the French Presidency which preceded that of Spain. The Spanish Presidency thus plucked an apple that was more than ripe and which promised a high profile success for the Presidency. In connection to this, one should not underestimate the significance attached by EU Presidencies to Summit meetings with the US. They are THE most important Summit meetings for the EU with any third country and meeting the US President is still a very exciting and important event for any EU leader. In addition, the US has always been good at holding out the Summit meeting as a kind of 'carrot' for which 'deliverables' are needed in terms of substantive and well-prepared issues for discussion and possible agreement. The NTA was in part created to serve this purpose.

---

[19] 'Europe and the US: The Way Forward', Communication from the Commission to the Council, Brussels: European Commission, 26.07.1995.

The process of fleshing out a common agenda was set into motion following the EU-US Ministerial meeting on 24 July 1995 in Washington. The process was conducted by the SLG, assisted by lower working levels, and involved a wide range of bureaucracies on both sides of the Atlantic. It led to a political declaration, the NTA, and an accompanying Joint EU-US Action Plan with 120 proposals for cooperative actions.

The NTA re-affirmed the continuity of relations and emphasised the need to 'strengthen and adapt' the partnership to meet the 'new challenges at home and abroad'. It made explicit reference to the 'common strategic vision of Europe's future security' and stressed the 'complementary and mutually reinforcing roles' played by NATO, the EU, the WEU, the OSCE and the Council of Europe. It also noted how the development of the emerging European Security and Defence Identity would strengthen the European pillar of the Alliance and the complementarity of NATO and EU enlargements. It said that 'increasingly, our common security is further enhanced by strengthening and reaffirming the ties between the European Union and the United States within the existing network of relationships which join us together'.

The NTA noted further that the 'economic relationship sustains our security' and said that the two sides were determined to reinforce the political and economic partnership as a 'powerful force for good in the world' and that 'to this end, we will build on the extensive consultations established by the 1990 Transatlantic Declaration and the conclusions of our June 1995 Summit and move to common action'.

The political tone of the NTA was remarkable. Never before had the EU and the US expressed themselves so explicitly about the security aspects of their relations in a joint document. In this sense the NTA marked a major new step in expanding and deepening the scope of relations.[20] This new dimension was also reflected in the fact that the NTA exercise led to the first meeting of the CFSP Security Working Group with the US in Washington on 10 April 1996.[21]

---

20 Ambassador Eizenstat, who in his farewell address considered the NTA 'a quantum leap forward' in EU-US relations also said that the NTA 'marks the first time we have dealt comprehensively with the EU, not simply as a trade and economic organization, but as a partner in a whole array of foreign policy and diplomatic initiatives', *Wireless File,* 9 February 1996.

21 *Reuter*, Washington, 10 April 1996.

Drawing on the more detailed Action Plan, the NTA set out general goals which echoed the objectives of the Transatlantic Declaration. The NTA was in many ways a natural continuation of the Declaration. Where the latter mainly focused on structures for dialogue the emphasis of the NTA was on substance, on giving a certain degree of specificity to ongoing cooperation, not least with a view to rendering cooperation more visible to the public at large.

In terms of foreign policy cooperation, the approach of the NTA and the Action Plan was global and, in addition to fighting international crime, drug-trafficking and terrorism, included efforts to: assist in reconstruction in the Former Yugoslavia; support democracy and reform in Central and Eastern Europe as well as in Russia, Ukraine and other New Independent States; secure peace in the Middle East; advance human rights; promote non-proliferation; and cooperate on development and humanitarian assistance in Africa.

Former Yugoslavia remained on top of the agenda of EU-US cooperation and the Action Plan emphasised specific areas where working together would be particularly important. These included issues such as the establishment of a framework for free and fair elections in Bosnia-Herzegovina and the implementation of the agreed process for arms control, disarmament and confidence-building measures in addition to providing humanitarian assistance and contributing financially to the reconstruction effort. This last point was particularly important and it should be emphasised that the EU and the US basically had permanent consultations on the question of the reconstruction of Bosnia.

The first donors' conference was jointly organised by the European Commission and the World Bank in Brussels on 20-21 December 1995. Since this date, the EU and the US have closely coordinated their policies with respect to the implementation of reconstruction projects and were in permanent contact in advance of the second donors' conference held at Ministerial level on 12-13 April 1996 in Brussels. One element of the success of this and subsequent conferences was indeed the close cooperation between the EU and the US in particular. This was also reflected in the Fact Sheet on EU and US Assistance to Bosnia which was published in the margins of the EU-US Summit in December 1996. The Fact Sheet stated that:

> The United States and the European Union have been leading partners in helping rebuild and bring long-term peace to Bosnia-Herzegovina. The US and EU are the major donor countries to the reconstruction effort and coordinate closely to ensure that assistance reaches those who need it. In late

> 1995 and early 1996, the US participated in two successful donor coordination meetings hosted by the EU and the World Bank. At those meetings, donors pledged over $1.9 billion for reconstruction costs for 1996, including approximately $282 million from the US and $718 million from the EU. The US supports the EU and World Bank plans to host a donors' conference in late February or early March to raise funds for 1997. We expect the US and the EU to be leading donors in 1997 as well. In addition to assistance for reconstruction, the US and EU countries have been working together for long-term peace in Bosnia in other ways as well, including helping the OSCE to organize Bosnia's first democratic elections, contributing international police monitors to the International Police Task Force, jointly pressing the parties to live up to their Dayton commitments, and serving as the leading troop contributors to IFOR.[22]

In the same vein the SLG report to the EU-US Summit in December 1997 concluded that 'in Bosnia, we worked together to support successful municipal elections and Assembly elections in Republika Srpska, and have agreed on a joint strategy to promote human rights and democratisation' and that 'we have successfully coordinated to bring about Croatia's transfer of war crimes indictees to the International Tribunal in The Hague'.[23] The Joint EU-US Democratisation Plan for Bosnia-Herzegovina referred to was finalised at the EU-US Summit on 5 December 1997. The document reflected EU-US agreement on a long-term strategy to address human rights and democratisation issues in Bosnia. It emphasised that human rights and democratisation were essential to civilian implementation of the Dayton Agreement and stressed the importance of securing cooperation and support for the International Criminal Tribunal for the Former Yugoslavia, construction of an independent media, supporting Bosnian capacity to hold elections, reforming property laws, and building respect for the rule of law.[24]

In terms of Former Yugoslavia, the establishment of the Contact Group created some misgivings among Member States excluded from the process. It was to some extent an example of how US frustration with the EU decision-making process could lead the Americans to seek alternative venues and opt for bilateral cooperation with selected EU Member States. This was understandable but did, at the same time, undermine the coherence and further development of the CFSP and, one

---

22 *USIA Washington File*, European Edition, 16 December 1996.

23 *Senior Level Group (SLG) Report to the EU-US Summit*, 5 December 1997.

24 'Joint US-EU Statement on Democratization Plan for Bosnia', *USIA – Washington File*, 5 December 1997.

might say, long term EU and US interests in seeing the European integration process consolidate. In the end, however, as far as Former Yugoslavia was concerned, regular participation by the Presidency and the Commission was ensured, setting a precedent for how the EU wanted to participate in similar bodies that might be established concerning other events.

With respect to Russia, Ukraine and the other NIS, the Action Plan spelled out that activities would be coordinated in support of the integration of these countries into the global economy. It also stipulated that the existing EU-US relationship on assistance coordination would be reinforced and that coordination on food assistance would continue to be improved, using the successful coordination experience in the Caucasus as an example to follow.

One of the most important issues which emerged from this commitment to cooperate more closely as regards the NIS was the case of Ukraine. Promoting reform in and securing the independence of Ukraine was a top priority for both the Union and the US. At technical level, Commission and USAID officials had been working well together all along, notably on the ground in Kiev, where much of the international assistance coordination was taking place. However, the point was to give greater visibility to this cooperation and to make a joint push for the reform process which threatened to stall. This commitment led to a number of initiatives which were published in a joint statement on Ukraine released at the EU-US Summit on 5 December 1997. The two-page statement affirmed the mutual EU-US support for Ukraine and recalled that the EU and the US had been the leading contributors to support the transition process in Ukraine (EU: $US 4.6 billion since independence, US: $US 2.18 billion). In a message to Ukraine the statement stressed the importance of structural reforms and stated that the EU and the US would: jointly support Ukrainian restructuring plans in the energy sector; coordinate programmes in support of public administration reform; coordinate programmes in areas such as small business development, fiscal reform, civil society and civic education; and cooperate on practical steps to assist Ukraine in its efforts to build grass-roots momentum for reform through work on the ground in Ukraine's regions and municipalities. The statement also addressed the important nuclear safety chapter and confirmed the commitment to assist Ukraine in its efforts to close the Chernobyl Nuclear Power Plant by 2000 on the basis of the G7 Memorandum of Understanding (different interpretations of this memorandum had earlier led to strained EU-US exchanges but close consultations ultimately brought about similar positions).[25]

Cooperation regarding Ukraine strengthened, particularly in the area of civil society issues. A Transatlantic Civil Society Support Programme was established on the basis of several joint missions to Ukraine in spring 1998. The programme was financed through an EC grant of 2.3 MECU and a US grant of $US 2.5 million and targeted projects in the areas of civil society, civic education, public administration and strengthening legislative institutions.

Another important cooperative project concerning the NIS were the New Regional Environmental Centres to which the EU and the US were leading contributors. These centres were to support NGOs, central and local governments and business communities in improving environmental practices and actions both nationally and regionally. Following the Environmental Ministerial Conference in Aarhus, Denmark, in June 1998, four such centres were to be established first in Georgia, Moldova, Russia and Ukraine, and the project was expected to be extended to cover Central Asia as well.

Nuclear safety was another major concern and joint reflections were intensified in spring 1998 to advance this issue notably in Northwest Russia. This led to a joint non-paper by EU and US experts to the SLG. The initial focus was to deal with submarine and icebreaker fuel and waste and American and EU experts met with Russian counterparts to seek agreement on how to handle the most urgent nuclear waste problems. The SLG report to the EU-US Summit in May 1998 could therefore recount: 'we have drawn up a five-point agenda for a common approach with the Russian Federation and all interested parties to the problem of nuclear waste management in North West Russia'.[26] The matter will remain a priority for a long time to come.

With regard to the Middle East Peace Process the Action Plan stipulated that the EU and the US would continue their support for Palestinian self-government and economic development, that they would encourage regional economic cooperation and also support regional efforts to establish road links, electricity grids, gas pipelines and other joint infrastructure necessary to foster regional trade and investment. The plan also stated that the EU and the US would continue their efforts

25 'EU-US Joint Statement on Ukraine', *USIA – Washington File*, 5 December 1997.

26 *SLG Report to the EU-US Summit*, 18 May 1998.

to promote peace between Israel, Lebanon and Syria. Efforts to strengthen cooperation in relation to the Middle East Peace Process also led to intensified contacts with senior officials meeting in Washington in March 1996 to maintain an 'active open channel of communication on the Middle East Peace Process'. Much has been made of the proliferation and possible divergent EU and US peace efforts following events in Lebanon in mid-April. Suffice to say here that the EU in a declaration on 22 April 1996 reiterated the commonality of their aims and expressed support for US efforts:

> The European Union reaffirms its support for all the parties involved in peace negotiations. It confirms its willingness to contribute actively to the search in progress for an immediate halt to hostilities and a lasting peace in the region. In this regard it supports the action undertaken by the Presidency, the Troika and Member States, notably France, who have been in the region or made representations in recent days. It supports all the efforts, notably those of the USA, currently being undertaken with the same purpose.[27]

EU-US cooperation with regard to the Middle East has always been, and continues to be, difficult. The EU, as the main paymaster, wants to carve out a more significant political role for itself. This ambition is not an easy one for the EU to achieve despite Arab encouragement. Reluctance by Israel, and some would say the US, has so far prevented the EU from contributing more politically to achieving a settlement in the region. Nevertheless, the EU supports US efforts and there is much cooperation on an ongoing basis. The SLG report to the 12 June 1996 EU-US Summit in Washington could therefore note that 'the US and the EU worked in partnership at the Sharm el-Sheik Summit in March 1996 and its follow-up meeting in Washington. We have also worked together in the *Ad Hoc* Liaison Committee; in the Regional Economic Development Working Group (REDWG) and the other working groups of the multi-

---

27 The text of the press statement released in Washington on 8 March 1996 reads as follows: 'This morning Middle East Coordinator Dennis Ross, Assistant Secretary Robert Pelletreau and Deputy Assistant Secretary Tone G. Verstandig met with European Union Troika Senior Officials responsible for the Middle East. They agreed that the United States and the European Union would intensify their active consultations and coordination. They committed to maintaining an active open channel of communication on the Middle East Peace Process. They agreed on the importance of the Summit of Peacemakers scheduled for 13 March, and focused on how the European Union and the United States can work together at this time to enhance peace, promote security and combat terrorism.'

lateral track; in the preparations for the Cairo Economic Summit in November 1996; and in other appropriate economic institutions.'[28]

In the field of development and humanitarian assistance, the Action Plan highlighted the establishment of a High-Level Consultative Group which was to assess policies and priorities and identify projects and regions for strengthening cooperation. On development cooperation, specific proposals included coordinating policies on democracy and civil society, health and population, and development cooperation within the framework of international institutions and organisations and on food security. In the field of humanitarian assistance, the Plan specified that the two sides would seek greater complementarity in their programmes by extending operational coordination to include the planning phase in addition to cooperating to improve the effectiveness of international humanitarian relief agencies. Moreover, the EU and the US were to consider joint assessment missions.

This last commitment led to the Great Lakes Joint Assessment Mission – 1-3 April 1996 – undertaken by Commissioner Emma Bonino and USAID Administrator Brian Atwood. The aim of the mission was to evaluate the prospects for humanitarian assistance to the region and the regional political impact of the refugee crisis. The joint statement issued after the mission explained: 'the mission to Rwanda, Burundi, and Tanzania demonstrates a new level of coordination between the region's two largest donors, and is the first joint assessment completed as part of the New Transatlantic Agenda.'

The joint statement went on to say that the mission also reflected 'the common concerns over the deteriorating security situation in the region' and that, in Burundi, Bonino and Atwood 'urged the government and all parties to commit themselves to meaningful national dialogue and reconciliation'. In Rwanda they expressed 'their support for the progress the Government has made in restoring stability in the country' while still being concerned by the fact 'that a properly functioning judiciary system was not yet in place'.

More generally, cooperation on assistance issues was strengthened in a wide range of areas. The SLG report to the EU-US Summit on 16 December 1996 could thus note that:

> We have improved our coordination of humanitarian and development assistance by holding a further round of high-level assistance consultations in

---

28 *Senior Level Group Report to the US-EU Summit*, 12 June 1996.

> October. By way of example, we have agreed to work together on strengthening civil society in some Latin American and South Asian countries and are supporting democracy in Nicaragua and Benin. Programs on the environment are moving forward for the Congo Basin, and we are working with the new democratic government in Haiti on judicial reform. We are helping ensure food security in Ethiopia and Malawi and are cooperating on an immunization programme in nine West African countries.[29]

The Action Plan also contained a number of proposals in the field of non-proliferation, international disarmament and arms transfers. These included the commitment to promote Nuclear Non-Proliferation Treaty adherence by non-parties to the Treaty and coordinated action *vis-à-vis* non-adherents. The two parties also committed themselves to combine efforts to conclude in the Geneva Conference on Disarmament an effective, verifiable and universally applicable Comprehensive Test Ban Treaty as well as undertaking joint efforts for immediate negotiations on a Fissile Material Cut-Off Treaty. Proposals also included commitments to support international efforts to curtail the use and proliferation of anti-personnel landmines and to provide support to the Korean Peninsula Energy Development Organisation (KEDO) as a way of underlying the shared interest in solving proliferation challenges.

With respect to KEDO, the EU manifested its commitment of support in February 1996 by adopting a CFSP Joint Action which included an immediate financial contribution of ECU 5 million. At the initiative of the Commission, the scope for further regular EU contributions and membership of KEDO was also being considered insidc thc EU.[30] Subsequently, the EU agreed to provide ECU 75 million over a five year period and an agreement for the EU (Euratom) to join KEDO entered into force on 19 September 1997. The complemcntarity of EU and US views and interests in Asian security questions was similarly manifest in the EU's support for the US-South Korean initiative on Four Party Peace Talks (South Korea, North Korea, China, USA) concerning the situation on the Korean peninsula.

As regards non-proliferation issues in general, a joint statement was issued at the EU-US Summit in London on 18 May 1998. A US Fact Sheet concerning the declaration explained that 'building on the already high level of cooperation between the United States and the European

---

[29] *Senior Level Group Report to the EU-US Summit*, 16 December 1996.

[30] See *Commission Press Release*, 24 April 1996.

Union through multilateral fora, such as the Missile Technology Control Regime (MTCR), Nuclear Suppliers Group, Zangger Committee, Australia Group, and the Wassenaar arrangement' the EU and the US would: increase cooperation, notably to prevent dual use technology transfers with risk of diversion to Weapons of Mass Destruction purposes; strengthen information-sharing on non-proliferation issues; pursue the development of new and better controls on 'intangible' technology transfers; and coordinate more closely on export control assistance to third countries; and on diplomatic efforts to stem technology exports by other countries to proliferators.[31]

The joint declaration was implicitly part of a Summit 'package' to agree on settling a dispute concerning the US Helms-Burton Act. It provided the US administration with an opportunity to demonstrate to Congress that the EU and the US were cooperating closely on issues of importance to the US concerning Cuba and Iran, and that 'waivers' could therefore be given to the EU on certain trade restrictive aspects of the Helms-Burton legislation.[32] Similarly, the Summit agreed a two-page document entitled 'Transatlantic Partnership on Political Cooperation'. This agrement spelled out a commitment to early political consultations on threats to international stability and security, using the existing consultative framework as well as a commitment to work for multilateral (instead of unilateral) sanctions where necessary.

Cooperation concerning terrorism was likewise on the agenda of the London Summit which issued a joint declaration, parts of which explained that: 'The EU and the US cooperate in the United Nations framework to elaborate the necessary international legal instruments for the fight against terrorism. They work in tandem to promote universal adherence to the eleven international counter-terrorism conventions. EU partners contributed to the rapid and successful negotiation of the most recent UN Convention (for the Suppression of Terrorist Bombings) based on a draft proposed by the US.'

The statement highlighted current areas of common concern and efforts, including joint initiatives against terrorist funding. It also affirmed a commitment 'to strengthen further their close ties in the field of coun-

---

31 *USIA*, Washington File, 18 May 1998.

32 The May 1998 Summit agreed an Understanding on Disciplines on Investment in Expropriated Properties (this included the US commitments on waivers under Titles III and IV of the Helms-Burton Act).

ter-terrorism' by 'additional information-sharing at their regular Troika meetings, enhanced bilateral intelligence exchanges, and sustained co-operation at the United Nations and in other fora to advance their common objectives'.[33]

The Action Plan also foresaw closer cooperation on anti-personnel landmines and much has happened over recent years. Consultations were stepped up and at the Washington Conference on Global Humanitarian Demining on 20-22 May 1998, the US and the Commission presented three cooperative proposals to be considered by the broader international community. These proposals called for: the creation of internationally accepted standards to describe the types of mine action technology needed to help solve this problem; the identification of a worldwide network of test and evaluation facilities which would assess promising mine action technology, and aid in the creation of new or improved systems; the development of international technology demonstrator projects – these 'demonstration projects' would apply advanced technologies to the demining of critical areas, create a visible product, establish a programme for action, and provide a platform for cooperation and new investment. These proposals were well received at the conference and were developed further at an international conference hosted by the Commission in Ispra, Italy, from 29 September to 1 October 1998.[34]

On human rights, the Action Plan included a commitment to consult bilaterally (and within the framework of the relevant bodies of the UN, particularly the UN Commission on Human Rights) on countries where serious violation of human rights occurred. This was with a view to coordinating policies and, where appropriate, developing joint initiatives. This commitment led not only to intense EU-US cooperation on a human rights resolution concerning China within the framework of the UN Human Rights Commission, it also facilitated the decision not to table a resolution in 1997. The SLG report to the EU-US Summit in December 1997 noted that 'underscoring our strong commitment to respect for human rights and democratic practices, we have continued to

---

33 *USIA*, Washington File, 18 May 1998.

34 Washington Conference on Global Humanitarian Demining, Chairman's Report, 22 May 1998, and Joint Press Statement by Commissioner Edith Cresson and Ambassador Rick Inderfurth, The President's Special Representative for Global Humanitarian Demining, and Ambassador Miyet, Under-Secretary General of the United Nations, UN Mine Action Services.

seek out new opportunities to support these principles in the Great Lakes region of Africa, Nigeria, Burma, Cuba and elsewhere'.

A more concrete expression of cooperation in this area were the awards given by the May 1998 EU-US Summit to fifty individuals and organisations in Central and Eastern Europe and the New Independent States who had promoted democratic values and civil society in their countries. The prize-scheme, a US initiative, had come about in order to commemorate the 50th anniversary of the Marshall Plan and the 40th anniversary of the Treaty of Rome. Awards of $US 20.000 were given to outstanding individuals, communities and local non-governmental organisations whose activities had promoted good governance and rule of law, strengthened civil society, increased women's political participation, or boosted labour and business support for democracy.[35]

Conclusion

EU-US foreign policy cooperation has developed significantly since the end of the Cold War mainly as a result of largely common interests, a realisation among policy-makers on both sides of the commonality of these interests and the need for maintaining close ties, and the development of a Common Foreign and Security Policy in the EU. It would seem appropriate to stress yet again that we are only at the very beginning of the CFSP. Former Yugoslavia is, of course, a case in point which has frequently been used as an example of how the CFSP has been a failure. The EU record during the early part of this crisis was indeed not impressive, but to place the blame for the failings of the West squarely on the EU is simply out of place, a point on which even outspoken critics of EU efforts appear to agree increasingly. Speaking as a private citizen, Ambassador Richard Holbrooke, former Assistant Secretary of State for Europe and Canadian Affairs and President Clinton's chief negotiator for the Dayton Agreement, said in a speech in Oslo on 5 September 1996:

> We have to be frank. The former Yugoslavia was a failure of the West. I've said this before, and I cannot help but say it again. At the exact moment that the Cold War ended Yugoslavia fell apart and Iraq invaded Kuwait. The United States focused on the Iraqi problem and when Desert Storm was over, the administration turned away from Europe very rapidly to confront the 1992 presidential election. At that point, the United States and Europe made what I believe a fatal mistake. It is one that both sides of the Atlantic

35 *Senior Level Group Report to the EU-US Summit*, 18 May 1998.

> bear equal responsibility for. In Europe, the European Community as it was then called, stated that the hour of Europe has dawned and told Washington officials [...] that they would take care of Yugoslavia. And the United States said, 'Fine, you take care of it'. And it was then turned over to the EC instead of to NATO [...].
>
> This tragic mistake on the part of the United States and Europe, which seems to me to deny the lesson we learned in history – that together the United States and Europe have a common interest in pursuing peace and stability – led to the collapse of Yugoslavia. Europe was not able to deal with the problem alone, and the United States disappeared from the scene at just the moment when I believe a strong warning from the United Atlantic Alliance might have deterred the leaders in the Balkans from the insane course that they set their country upon'.[36]

There can be no doubt that the CFSP has not yet developed its potential and needs to be pushed further in order for the Union to act effectively internationally. But the complex nature of the conflict in Former Yugoslavia went beyond what anyone could have anticipated and we are far from having a CFSP that would be able to deal with such a crisis, not least if military means should be required as turned out to be the case. However, this is not an argument against the CFSP but rather one for developing it further in order for the EU to take on more responsibilities in support of international stability.

But while the EU needs to provide greater leadership to create a 'real' CFSP, the US also needs to continue lending its support to such a development. The Clinton Administration has indeed been very supportive of European integration in general. But as a speech by Commission Vice-President Brittan in September 1998 indicated, the US should continuously take the complex way in which the EU works seriously:

> There should be a clearer recognition in Washington that cooperation with the European Union does not mean simply signing up the European Union to endorse, execute, and sometimes finance, United States policy. This is not good enough. We need a genuine discussion of the issues, and a readiness for give and take in policy formulation on both sides. The process is complex and can be frustrating, because there are fifteen sovereign nation states involved in discussions between the European Union and the United States, as well as the European Commission with its own powers and competences. But it is the only way forward.[37]

---

36 *US Wireless File*, 6 September 1996.

37 'Europe and the United States: New Challenges, New Opportunities', address by Leon Brittan, to the Foreign Policy Association, New York, 23 September 1998.

It is important that the US works through the EU and its institutional structures, no matter how complex and slow these may seem. In short, US support is crucial for nurturing the 'enabling' partner which the US seeks in its cooperation with the EU.

Despite its embryonic nature the CFSP has already opened up new perspectives for EU-US cooperation and given an important impetus for strengthening ties and coordinated action on a wide range of issues. The Transatlantic Declaration of November 1990 provided the formal framework for dialogue which, with later additions, gave regularity to talks, familiarised officials, and contributed to creating a certain habit of consultation, also outside the formal framework. The NTA took the relationship further by literally setting an agenda for EU-US cooperation and setting up a horizontal coordinating fora, the SLG, in order to energise the existing consultative mechanisms.

In terms of foreign policy cooperation, the NTA has been significant for at least four reasons which are more or less linked. First, it set a number of priorities within the various areas of cooperation concerning foreign policy issues. These priorities have been important for giving greater focus and coherence to talks, making these more operational and ensuring that the various levels of dialogue maintained largely similar agendas. The NTA listed a panoply of priorities but it goes without saying that these priorities were to give a general sense of where the EU and the US wanted to go and that they were adjusted regularly according to how events evolved. The half-yearly SLG report to the EU-US Summit therefore included a condensed priorities section which set the agenda for cooperation for the following six months and the next EU Presidency.

The second important aspect of the NTA is visibility because it serves to give a certain degree of reassurance. This is important not least because the fear in the post-Cold War years has often been that, despite a commitment to transatlantic relations among decision-makers on both sides, a public perception of drift could undermine the stability of relations in the long run. The need has therefore been, and will continue to be, to demonstrate what is at stake and what is in it for both the EU and the US. Transparency can, however, be problematic. For foreign policy cooperation is indeed traditionally a very sensitive area where cooperative actions cannot always be made public because of concerns about relations with third parties or because public action would otherwise undermine the objective. Some visibility is nevertheless important for promoting public confidence in the relationship, not least in the light of the major headlines trade or other frictions are given. As I have tried to illustrate in this chapter the EU and the US have indeed over the past years increasingly taken joint public positions on a number of important issues of common concern.

Third, as suggested above there is a more or less permanent dialogue between the EU and the US in many areas. But the NTA has led to an intensification of talks given the specific priorities it sets and the regularity of high-level meetings for which visible progress is often required. In this sense, the NTA has brought with it a reinforcement of the framework for dialogue. It has also given it a greater sense of purpose and added substance to talks which now increasingly focus on ways and means to develop concrete actions.

Fourth, and this point relates to the above, the NTA exercise, with the Senior Level Group arrangement, has led to a better preparation of EU-US Summit meetings. These are thus also becoming more and more operational and increasingly give the necessary political impetus needed at lower working levels.

While EU-US foreign policy cooperation has developed significantly over recent years, there are also, of course, differences between the EU and the US on important issues such as recent policy towards Cuba and Iran or occasional public spats over responsibilities for set-backs in crisis areas such as Former Yugoslavia. From the perspective of the EU, many of the transatlantic tensions which have emerged were caused by extraterritorial legislation passed by Congress (notably the Helms-Burton and Iran-Libya Sanctions Act). Such legislation often prevents the EU and the US from developing joint or complementary approaches on issues where there may be a great commonality of interests. As Commission Vice-President Brittan asked in New York in September 1998: 'What on earth is the point, when you are trying to deal with a country like Iran or Libya or Burma, of passing a law which creates a confrontation with precisely those partners who are your closest allies in dealing with countries of that sort, even if they do not always agree hundred per cent with your policy prescription?'[38]

Differences over such legislation are serious and are never taken lightly. Nevertheless, such problems are discussed extensively and do

---

38 'Europe and the United States', address by Leon Brittan, to the Foreign Policy Association, New York, 23 September 1998.

not prevent the EU and the US from seeing eye-to-eye and pursuing complementary policies on most other major foreign policy issues. In fact, frictions are often dealt with successfully by the intricate web of consultations and the realisation that no one gains from ongoing disputes. The agreement to settle the dispute over the US Helms-Burton and ILSA Acts in May 1998 should be seen in this light.

The present approach in developing EU-US cooperation is a pragmatic one, reflecting both the fact that the existing framework is considered sufficient and the realisation that future developments will depend very much on how the EU decides to organise itself in the area of CFSP. The future of EU-US relations in the field of foreign policy will thus depend to a great extent on the future of the CFSP. The consolidation of European integration in the mid-to-late 1980s contributed to the reinforcement of transatlantic relations with the Declaration in 1990. Similarly, the continuation of the European integration process with the Maastricht Treaty contributed to the efforts to strengthen relations with the NTA. The next steps towards further European integration with the Amsterdam Treaty can thus also be expected to lead to further adjustments in the arrangements for EU-US cooperation. Whether this will eventually lead to a formal Transatlantic Treaty, called for regularly by various parties, remains to be seen. But there can be no doubt that ties will continue to be consolidated.

PART III

TAKING STOCK OF US-EU RELATIONS

CHAPTER 11

EU-US Relations after Amsterdam: 'Finishing Europe'

ROY H. GINSBERG

Skidmore College, Saratoga Springs

This volume reveals the scope of change in EU-US relations in the post-Cold War period. It highlights the depth, breadth, complexity, and maturity of EU-US relations following adoption in 1995 of the New Transatlantic Agenda and it embeds our understanding of those relations in historical and analytical frameworks enriched by their links to the theoretical literatures in international politics. The book's theoretical and empirical chapters inspire analysts to move beyond identifying the objectives of the NTA to conceptualizing and evaluating its outputs and identifying what shapes the evolution of EU-US structures and processes. Outputs are the outcomes or 'deliverables' of bilateral consultation and coordination with which the EU and the US justify the human and time resources invested in arranging and participating in NTA mechanisms. Whether in presentation of joint demarches in third country capitals, coordination of humanitarian aid in war-ravaged lands, or joint accords on drug interdiction, non-proliferation of weapons of mass destruction (WMD), and early warning systems to reduce bilateral frictions, the EU and US are moving beyond the promise of consultations provided for in the 1990 Transatlantic Declaration to the practice of international coordination and to joint action provided for in the NTA.

Trade and Investment: The Bread and Butter of Bilateral Relations

The bread and butter of the EU-US relationship is commerce, defined here as two-way trade and investment. The US and EU are not only each other's largest trade and investment partners but they together dominate the global political economy. Nearly all commerce flows smoothly across the Atlantic. Disputes over restrictions on EU imports of bananas from Central America, the EU ban on hormone-treated beef from the US, and the extraterritoriality of certain US laws are serious and do adversely affect other industries when they are targeted for retaliation in the course of WTO dispute settlement procedures. However friction-filled these disputes are, two-way commerce is too large and mutually beneficial for them to disrupt overall relations; when disputes do break out, the two sides are generally respectful of WTO dispute settlement adjudication.[1]

A new generation of commercial disputes – *e.g.* electronic commerce, open skies, aircraft hush-kits, and genetically-modified crops – looms on the horizon and will require early warning efforts by both sides to avoid restrictive action/reaction. A new mechanism designed to avoid trade disputes and reduce trade barriers is the Transatlantic Business Dialogue about which Maria Green Cowles has written in this volume. Private US and EU firms and business associations advise policymakers on eliminating trade barriers, participate in EU-US negotiations and thus in 'industrial diplomacy', and generate political momentum to reduce and eliminate trade barriers. The TABD and other non-governmental dialogues that are forming under the NTA rubric lend an extraordinarily useful, people-to-people quality to the NTA.

---

1 For example, the WTO ruled in 1999 on the complaints against EU import restrictions on bananas and hormone-treated beef and the partners are resigned, however disappointed they are, to end and move beyond these disputes. A WTO dispute settlement panel ruled that the EU preferential regime for banana imports is not WTO-compliant. In April 1999 the World Trade Organization authorized the United States to impose trade sanctions against the EU on $191.4 million of EU imports in retaliation for the EU's failure to comply with WTO judgements against its banana import regime. US sanctions will continue until the EU alters its banana import regime to comply with the WTO. A WTO dispute settlement panel ruled the EU ban on hormone treated beef is inconsistent with the WTO rules. In July 1999, the WTO authorized the US to impose trade sanctions on EU imports to compensate the United States for the EU ban on hormone-treated beef after which the US imposed hundred percent duties on imports of selected EU goods covering $116.8 million in annual imports on 29 July. Examples of dispute settlement reached bilaterally include the 1998 accord by which the US Administration agreed to waive the application of the provisions of the Iran-Libya Sanctions Act and the Helms-Burton Act on EU firms and the 1999 EU-US Veterinary Equivalency Agreement that provides for mutual recognition of animal health and meat product inspection rules.

Foreign Policy Cooperation: Growth Area of EU-US Relations

The commercial relationship is complemented by the world's most dense set of bilateral foreign policy consultations aimed at joint or complementary problem-solving cooperation and/or joint action in multilateral and other fora. Once a commercial relationship overshadowed by its NATO cousin during the Cold War, the EU and the US are developing a political partnership on a global scale after the Cold War. The US sees in the EU the real and potential value of a partner of scale able to work with it to solve global problems too big for any one actor to tackle alone (*e.g.* cross-border crime, humanitarian disasters, and proliferation of WMD). The EU sees the need to continue to engage the Americans in Europe absent the Soviet threat. As demonstrated by Anthony Gardner and Thomas Frellesen in their contributions to this volume, the EU-US bilateral partnership is characterized by an intensity and frequency of consultations on a wide range of transatlantic and multilateral issues unprecedented in the diplomatic relations of either partner and in the history of diplomacy writ large. The NTA provides a mosaic of consultations from working groups to political directors, and from senior-level task forces to government ministers, capped by twice-yearly Presidential Summits focused on producing tangible outcomes of cooperation.

The quality of spillover from commercial to diplomatic cooperation, the dense multiple linkages among the Atlantic civil societies, and the emergence of a security community of like-minded states that increasingly serves as a forum for global problem-solving in multilateral settings are reflective of the 'ideal type' of complex interdependence introduced by Keohane and Nye and tested for salience in EU-US relations by Featherstone and Ginsberg.[2]

Three major end-of-century developments affect the future of the EU as an international political actor and, as a consequence, the ability of the EU-US partnership to develop more fully and evenly: the 1st May 1999 entry into force of the Treaty of Amsterdam; the March-June 1999 NATO intervention in Kosovo; and the conclusion of the 3-4 June 1999 Cologne EU Council Summit.

---

2 R. Keohane and J. S. Nye, Jr., *Power and Interdependence* (Boston, Little Brown [1977] 1987); K. Featherstone and R. H. Ginsberg, *The United States and the European Union in the 1990s: Partners in Transition* (London, Macmillan, 1996).

EU-US Relations after Amsterdam: 'Finishing Europe'[3]

Will the Amsterdam Treaty have an impact on EU-US relations? The answer is affirmative *if* the next US Administration takes the EU seriously as a foreign policy partner[4], *if* the EU makes use of the new CFSP instruments Amsterdam provides, and *if* the EU succeeds in making long-overdue institutional and decisionmaking reforms ahead of eastern enlargement at its Intergovernmental Conference (IGC) in 2000. A European Union better able to ease and rationalize internal decision-making[5] in advance of enlargement – a specter that will strain an institutional structure that still resembles the European Community of the 1950s – will give the EU the internal confidence required for outward confidence. Such improvements would in turn empower the EU to work with the United States in a partnership of scale in tackling global problems, preventing conflict, and responding to threats to peace and to crimes against humanity. In the areas of most concern to the EU-US relationship, the Treaty of Amsterdam:

- incorporates into the EU Treaty structure the WEU's Petersberg Tasks (humanitarian and rescue tasks, peacekeeping tasks and tasks of combat forces including peacemaking);
- provides for the possible integration of the WEU into the EU if the European Council so decides;
- permits members to abstain from a future EU security action without blocking the will of the majority;[6]
- permits more opportunities for use of qualified majority voting in the implementation of CFSP instruments (but retains members' right to veto actions when vital national interests are adversely affected);
- introduces a new CFSP instrument – common strategies – which will be Council recommendations to the European Council and

---

3 The notion of 'finishing' Europe was given to the author by Dr. Donald Puchala in a conversation at the ECSA World Conference, Pittsburgh, June 1999.

4 The quality of the Clinton Administration's rhetorical support for the NTA and the ESDI may not necessarily be embraced by its successor.

5 For examples, reduce number of Commissioners and reweigh and extend usage of qualified majority voting.

6 Unless members qualifying their abstention represent more than one third of the votes weighted (members will enjoy 'veto' power if vital national interests are at stake.

will be implemented by the adoption of joint actions and common positions; and
- establishes the position of the CFSP High Representative who will also be a member of the newly reconfigured EU troika and sets up a new policy planning and early warning unit.

Are these merely changes at the margins or will they be employed to finish the tasks of 'finishing' CFSP and ESDI? It will now be up to the Europeans themselves to make use of these changes.

The new European Parliament and European Commission instituted in 1999 provide fresh impetus for change, hold out prospects for more democratic accountability and legitimacy (both of which in the end must underpin foreign policy initiatives), and are critical links in the CFSP/ESDI decision-making chain.

The introduction of the last phase of the EMU in 1999, the opening of the European Central Bank, and the phased introduction of the Euro allow the EU to 'finish' the process of regional economic integration begun in 1952. Over time EMU will increase global expectations of the EU to act as a unit in international affairs and will focus attention on 'finishing' the political union aspects of integration – CFSP and ESDI. Finally, a new sense of urgency following the EU's impotence as a security actor during the NATO bombardment of Kosovo and Serbia has permeated the leadership of the EU members, particularly the large member governments, focusing their attention on empowering the EU to make contributions to multilateral security operations.

In Kosovo, the EU demonstrated a collective diplomacy it did not have in Bosnia. The tragic conflict in Croatia and Bosnia was made worse, in retrospect, by a disastrous EC policy of offering diplomatic recognition to former Yugoslav republics in the absence of guarantees for minority rights. Serious divisions among EU member governments denied the EU a common policy. However, in the subsequent conflict in Kosovo, the EU and its member governments generally followed a collective diplomatic course from Rambouillet through the NATO action and the EU-NATO-Russian diplomatic activity that finally led to Milosevic's withdrawal from Kosovo.

Put in geological terms, Amsterdam is another stepping stone the EU must pass across a wide stony creek between two shores. On the shore behind is a Europe overly dependent on the US in times of crisis management and in terms of multilateral force deployment – and the technology, assets, and resources that make deployment possible. On the shore ahead is a European Union with an operational ESDI, able to implement the Petersberg Tasks on its own or as a Combined Joint Task Force (CJTF) with NATO.

Amsterdam introduces changes that could enhance the EU's international capabilities if there is the political will[7] to make the EU face up to its global responsibilities. The more the EU takes charge of crisis prevention and management and organizes and deploys troops for Petersberg Tasks, the more the EU and US will develop a partnership of scale and equality that better reflects common needs and relative strengths.

EU-US Relations during and after the Kosovo Crisis: Old Rhetoric or New Trajectory?

The Serbian-sponsored ethnic cleansing of Albanians in Kosovo – which went against all EU and western norms and horrified Europeans in 1998 and 1999 – was met with NATO air bombardment of Serbian military targets in ex-Yugoslavia in March-June 1999 after European-led diplomatic efforts to end the atrocities failed. The punitive strikes were designed to put an end to Serbian atrocities and force Serbian withdrawal from Kosovo. Marginalized by its own underdeveloped security structures and held prostrate by an inadequate political will to operationalize its own ESDI, the EU again did not back its own values and formidable civilian diplomacy with a contribution to multilateral intervention in Kosovo (although individual EU NATO members contributed, especially the UK, France, Germany, and Italy). Thus NATO's Kosovo action spearheaded by US leadership reopened an old debate within the EU over how to provide for common security needs without an over-dependence on the North American NATO allies. As in Bosnia, the EU was incapable of mounting (or unwilling to mount) a concerted and coherent response to a European crisis of mammoth proportions – however well-intentioned it was – and the US was unable to engage the allies on an equal footing. The EU remains caught between a rock and a hard place: diplomatic inaction brings in American leadership – even US unilateralism – which the Europeans resist, yet in the absence of a credible ESDI, the US has to fill the vacuum of leadership.

---

7 Here political will refers to the interest to articulate, implement, and sustain an EU policy initiative supported by the EU member governments and their common institutions.

Kosovo exposed again painful but truthful clichés: the EU is a 'payer not a player'; the EU is an 'economic superpower' and a 'political dwarf'; and the EU cannot take military action because it is a 'civilian power'.

These clichés will not go away until the EU develops the necessary military capabilities and appropriate structures for decision-making in crisis management/prevention for the Petersberg Tasks. Proponents of an EU security capability speak of the need to bring the defense industry inside the 'common market', develop joint research and development projects, and merge members' defense manufacturers into European ones capable of reaping economies of scale, competing globally, and providing the putative ESDI with standardised military equipment and materiel. However, one would be hard pressed to find any one in the US military-industrial complex who would welcome increased European competition for foreign markets. Thus there will always be a gap between the rhetoric of official US support for the ESDI and the resistance to that rhetoric from US manufacturers unwilling to face new competition. Others argue that the EU need not wait until it achieves defense integration before beginning to operationalize the Petersberg Tasks.

Kosovo catalysed the Europeans into a new sense of sobriety and urgency about their security predicament. The leadership of the large EU countries are now professing the need for the EU to integrate defense policies and acquire security assets and capabilities of its own. The rhetoric of change was reflected in the Franco-British St. Malo (1998) and Anglo-Italian (1999) initiatives designed to break the impasse over the development of the ESDI. The unprecedented EU-NATO consultations that began under the Austrian and German EU Presidencies and continued through Finland's was more than a sign of rhetorical change. For all its inadequacies exposed by the US-led military action in Kosovo, the EU did do what the EU traditionally does well: it contributed to the last minute diplomacy that led Milosevic to cease hostilities and it took international leadership of the stabilization of the countries of the western Balkans and of the post-war reconstruction plan for Kosovo.

Has the rhetoric of St. Malo and Cologne moved too far ahead of substance or is the EU placing security on a new trajectory? There is certainly room for pessimism given the many decades which the Europeans have spent discussing the efficacy or modalities of the ESDI. The obstacles to ESDI are still formidable. Yet, separating rhetoric from action, one is still left with the impression that, at the turn of the century, the EU states are making more political headway in embracing a security identity now than at any time since the 1954 collapse of the EDC. The EU's political environment is conducive to ratcheting the ESDI up to its next stage of development. What makes the post-Kosovo hand-wringing in the EU over its putative security policy any different from that which occurred after Bosnia?

A confluence of personalities, perceptions, and events occurred in 1998-99 that raises the level of rhetoric on 'finishing' the CFSP/ESDI to a new high. The French, at least for now, no longer oppose ESDI as a strengthened European pillar of NATO and appear to have suppressed their hope for an independent ESDI expressed through the WEU. However, some suggest that France now wishes to develop an independent ESDI through the EU despite having little if no support for that from the other member governments. Those Americans who feared that the WEU/ESDI would compete with NATO no longer oppose the WEU (or possibly the EU) as a strengthened European pillar of NATO, but would still not support the EU's usage of NATO/US assets in a CJFT without NATO (read US) approval. The British have dropped their long standing opposition to the merger of the WEU into the EU and the Germans have overcome domestic opposition to the commitment of their troops to multilateral peacemaking in Kosovo. There seems to be a convergence of perceptions based on the dire need for the EU to 'finish' ESDI and CFSP.

Was the EU a failure in response to Kosovo? The EU is better at helping end conflict than it is in preventing conflict or organizing multilateral forces to end conflict. As an organization founded on a pacific/integrationist ethos born out of effects of totalitarianism, the EU did not develop a common security policy; instead it depended on the security provided for by NATO. The diplomacy surrounding the end of the war in Kosovo, however, exposes the EU's role, in conjunction with NATO, in ending conflict. Following the suggestions of US Secretary of State Madeline Albright, the German EU Council Presidency appointed Finnish President Martti Ahtisaari – a member of the EU troika – EU emissary to Belgrade. He was selected to engage the Russians in an agreement by which Serbia would cease hostilities in and withdraw from Kosovo. Ahtisaari was able to bring Russia back into the stream of negotiations and to bridge NATO-Russian positions – critical factors that led Milosevic to settle for peace. Ahtisaari and Russian emissary Chernomyrdin flew to Belgrade to present Milosevic with a take-it-or-leave-it offer. On 3 June 1999 Ahtisaari told the EU leaders gathered at Cologne that the Serbs agreed unconditionally to the peace plan.

The final document accepted by the Serbs incorporates the main points of the peace plan submitted by EU Council President Foreign Minister Fischer. But when it came to the EU as a lead forum for engaging allied states in crisis management, the EU took a back seat to NATO. Only time will tell if the Kosovo inspired rhetoric behind the new push to make ESDI operational will translate into constructive change but, as the sections below discuss, chances are better than even that there will be progress.

EU-US Relations after Cologne: The Limits and Possibilities of the NTA

The Cologne Summit called for the acceleration of the development of ESDI. The EU Finnish Presidency was charged with reporting back on progress at the December 1999 Helsinki European Council Summit. The EU leaders appointed NATO Secretary-General Javier Solana as the new High Representative of CFSP and Secretary-General of the European Council – a boon to the ESDI and EU-US relations given Solana's international stature and the high regard in which he is held in NATO capitals. Breaking with past taboos, EU leaders agreed to bring security issues into the framework of EU institutions; consider a capacity for analysis of security risks and relevant strategic planning; approve a plan for combined, although limited, EU military operations in future emergencies in Europe; consider participation of members' defense ministers in the meetings of the Council of Foreign Ministers; consider creation of an EU military committee composed of military personnel that would make recommendations to a new, permanent political and security committee in Brussels; request that the WEU audit the EU members' military capacities and assets; undertake sustained efforts to strengthen the industrial and technological defense base of the EU through closer and more efficient defense industry collaboration; and develop an effective EU-led crisis management capacity in which NATO members and neutral/nonallied EU members participate in EU operations. The leaders also asked the General Affairs Council to prepare the conditions and measures necessary to achieve the above objectives including the definition of the modalities for the inclusion of those functions of the WEU necessary for the EU to fulfill its new responsibility in Petersberg Tasks.

There is reason for scepticism if not at the EU's ability to carry through the rhetoric of Cologne then at the time horizon for intra-EU military cooperation. Some claim that it could take at least five years for the Europeans to husband the resources and perhaps another five to actually increase their collective capacity to deploy forces. Still the spirit of Cologne reflected the extent to which the Europeans felt a deep sense of impotence relative to the US and NATO during the Kosovo crisis, and since the development of the EU as an international political actor has been shaped by external stimuli, the Cologne Summit conclusions have a fighting chance of finally ratcheting up the development of ESDI/CFSP. The EU-US political relationship would be strengthened in turn so long as the ESDI/CFSP is, from a US perspective, not a competitor to NATO – which does not seem a likely scenario for the foreseeable future. A word of warning is warranted. The issue of NATO/US approval of all European-led CJTFs is a time bomb because the issue of who decides when the Europeans employ NATO assets for a European-only operation cuts deeply into NATO's command structure and into entrenched national prerogatives. There may be an assumption, largely a French one, that the European pillar of NATO will be able to draw on NATO assets in a CJTF without NATO/US approval. One would be hard pressed to find anyone in the US military, executive branch, or Congress who would agree to such a scenario. Until this issue is clarified, a degree of uncertainty hovers over how the EU will develop into an independent security actor if it does not develop, own, and control its own assets and instead depends on the integrated command structure, resources, intelligence, lift power, and air power of NATO.

What does the near future hold for the EU-US relationship? As much as the NTA now reaches in to many areas of bilateral cooperation, the EU-US relationship is actually larger than the NTA: farm trade, monetary affairs, and defense, for examples, fall outside the NTA mainstream, a reminder that the EU-US relationship intersects frequently with many other actors and issues. Neither the NTA nor any other umbrella of EU-US relations are ever likely to be large enough to cover the scope of bilateral relations. It is perhaps because the scope of relations is so large and pervasive that the NTA lacks concrete visibility. Indeed a recent Council on Foreign Relations publication on the future of Transatlantic relations barely made mention of the NTA, which suggests how few in the US foreign policy establishment know about it.[8]

The partnership is an active and relatively equal one in terms of the capabilities of each side in the areas of commercial, diplomatic, humanitarian, and development cooperation but remains uneven in areas where the EU itself is not capable of playing a role as a coherent and effective actor, such as the deployment of troops for the purposes of peacekeeping and crisis management.

Another critical opportunity for – and constraint on – the NTA is the abundance or absence of individual transatlantic leadership. Leadership is a critical variable in EU-US relations. Individual leaders catalyzed EU-US cooperation in the 1990s (Robert Zoellick, Jacques Delors, Stuart Eizenstat, and Sir Leon Brittan) because they invested political capital in EU-US relations first through the 1990 Transatlantic Declaration and then through the NTA. The NTA, as a young regime, depends not only on the commitment of foreign service bureaucracies to operationalize it on a year to year basis but on robust leadership to make tangible the time and money invested in the vast machinery of consultations. With the US presidential election in 2000 and the EU absorbed in internal reforms and eastern enlargement, it will take concerted leadership efforts to keep the NTA from losing its momentum. However, with the start of a new session of the European Parliament coupled with the arrival of a new reformed-minded EU Commission in 1999 and a new sense of urgency among EU members that progress in CFSP/ESDI is needed, there are opportunities for the Europeans to reactivate their decades-old goal of better providing for their own security and the defense of their own values. This piece has stressed the importance to the NTA of the EU's success in taking CFSP/ESDI to its next stage of development.

Neither a panacea nor a terminus for all the fixes necessary to manage the EU-US relations, the NTA is still a work-in-progress. It is still not larger than the sum of its parts. But it represents value added over its less ambitious antecedent, the Transatlantic Declaration, and it is likely to be reformed and improved in the years ahead given the depth of EU-US complex interdependence. Absent the NTA, the EU-US relationship would appear anachronistic in that it would be defined in largely com-

---

8 R. D. Blackwill, *The Future of Transatlantic Relations* (New York, Council on Foreign Relations, 1999).

mercial/apolitical terms – lacking a political context to achieve broader common goals. The end of the Cold War catapulted the EU into a leading role in European international politics and in the wider international political economy. The NTA helps to drive the foreign and security policy integration of the EU. It offers the US a partnership, however imperfect and incomplete, with a group of important like-minded states with comparable scale of resources and population increasingly able to work with the US to solve bilateral, multilateral, and global problems shared by the advanced industrialized democracies at the dawn of a new millenium.

CHAPTER 12

Drifting apart? Dissociative and Associative Approaches[1]

René SCHWOK

Université de Genève, Institut Européen

There is no consensus in the scientific community about the main characteristics of the relationship between the European Union and the United States. Analyses about EU-US relations are strongly dichotomic and often antithetic. In order to analyse and conceptualise the debate, I have resorted to neologisms and will distinguish between a dissociative approach and an associative approach.

Analysts belonging to the dissociative approach diagnose a deterioration of the transatlantic link. For these researchers, relations between the EU and the US – always tense – have been aggravated by the end of Cold War. Of course, this approach does not overlook the fact that certain relations between the two rims of the Atlantic Ocean may be positive, but the few positive aspects are minimised. For dissociative analysts, today's situation is characterised by the disappearance of the common communist enemy and by a growth of conflicts between the commercial blocs. In such circumstances, the relations between the US and the EU can only deteriorate further.

The associative approach, on the other hand, underlines the depth of the transatlantic link. Researchers adhering to this approach point out the numerous elements of convergence between Europe and America. Relations between the EU and the US are good and there is so far no indication that this should change. Naturally, the associative approach does not ignore that there have been some clashes between the two actors, but it considers them of relatively minor importance. For associative analysts, the post-Cold War era has not radically altered the relations between the EU and the US.

---

1 Parts of the material used in this article have been published in R. Schwok, 'Les relations entre l'Union européenne et les États-Unis: analyse critique de l'approche "dissociative"', *Relations internationales*, 29:1 (1998) 107-26.

The main theme of this chapter is precisely to conceptualise this dichotomy between dissociative and associative approaches. I am, of course, aware that such a didactic approach contains risks: (1) reality is not as Manichean as is indicated here; (2) one analyst can be at the same time dissociative and associative. One has then to understand this conceptualisation as ideal-types in the Weberian way. My typology does not aim to reify thoughts or to attribute to authors ideas they have not expressed. It aims only at extracting the main articulations of a certain way of analysing EU-US relations.

In the first part of this article, I will deal with the political aspects. I will analyse a limited number of issues such as the end of the Cold War and hegemonic competition and show how dissociative and associative approaches treat these issues. I will then use a similar method with regard to the second part which includes the economic aspects. I will also seek to study the manner in which the dissociative and associative approaches may be compared to concepts such as a self-centred Europe, the Economic and Monetary Union, protectionism and multilateralism.

Hypotheses on EU-US Political Issues

The End of the Cold War

Dissociative Approach

For the dissociative approach, the end of Cold War represents a turning point in human history and a breakdown in European-American relations. Events such as the collapse of the Soviet Union, the crumbing of communism in Central and Eastern Europe, German unification and the end of the East-West rivalry in the Third Word have deeply altered the transatlantic alliance.

Accordingly, Europeans and Americans have lost the main cement of their unity since an alliance as heterogeneous as the one unifying Western Europe and the United States can be based only on the functionalisation of a common enemy.[2] There is no longer the necessity to fight to promote democracy, pluralism, the respect of minorities, human rights,

---

2 J. Mearsheimer, 'Back to the Future: Instability in Europe after the Cold War', *International Security*, 15:1 (1990) 47.

market economy and all those values which marked the difference between the Western and the communist world during the Cold War era.[3]

Some dissociative analysts are even more radical. They argue that, with the end of Cold War, the main cultural areas will demand much greater independence from the American influence. These researchers claim, for instance, that neither the Europeans nor the Japanese have ever believed in the values of a Western civilisation led by the Americans: now they do have a choice, however, and that is 'to go their own ways and assert their own culture-area'.[4] Some authors also claim that there is a 'notable general decline' of pro-American attitudes.[5]

According to dissociative researchers, dangers for future EU-US relations come from both Europe and America. First, argue the researchers, fewer and fewer Europeans feel they have a debt to the US in strategic matters. The Old Continent fears external dangers less and thus minimises the risks of staying outside the American shield.[6]

As for the Americans, their motivation to stay in Europe is declining. Galvanised by growing isolationist feelings, they increasingly question their own motives to maintain a heavy and expensive military presence, as well as to continue to spend money in support of Europeans rich enough to pay for the burden of their own defence.[7] It is, incidentally, interesting to observe that, on a regular basis, before every US election, some Europeans sound the alarm and mention the risks of a return to American isolationism. In the post-Cold War era, similar complaints were expressed again; the candidate Bill Clinton was labelled an isolationist at the beginning of his mandate.[8]

---

3 S. D. Krasner, 'Power, Polarity and the Challenge of Disintegration' in H. Haftendorn and C. Tuschhoff (eds.), *America and Europe in an Era of Change* (Boulder, Westview Press, 1993), p.23.

4 M. Vlahos, 'Culture and Foreign Policy', *Foreign Policy*, 82 (1991) 68.

5 R. Ingelhart, *Cultural Shifts in Advanced Industrial Society* (Princeton, Princeton University Press, 1990), p.408.

6 Mearsheimer, 'Back to the Future', p.7.

7 D. Calleo, *Beyond American Hegemony: The Future of the Western Alliance* (New York, Basic, 1987).

8 M. Smith, 'Clinton and the EC: How much of a New Agenda?', *World Today*, 49:4 (1993) 70.

With regard to the important issue of NATO, dissociative researchers claim that this organisation long since lost its *raison d'être*.[9] This institution is doomed to disappear in the long term.[10] In this perspective, each incident is interpreted as proof of an incurable illness which has permeated this organisation. Thus, it has been said that the Europeans wish for the disappearance of NATO, or, at least, its transformation into an organisation dominated by the Europeans. The 'negative' role of France has been underlined, in particular its attempts to use the European Union and Western European Union (WEU) in an effort to replace the American leadership.[11] According to this interpretation, the Maastricht Treaty contains infectious germs which will lead to the crumbling of the Atlantic Alliance. Notions such as the Common and Foreign Security Policy (CFSP) are simply the product of an obvious attempt to be emancipated from the United States.[12] In other words, this concept of a European identity in security matters would simply be the latest French attempt to get rid of the Americans.[13]

The creation of a Franco-German brigade, and then of a European Corps have also been interpreted as another manifestation of those attempts to expel NATO, *i.e.* the US, from the Old Continent. The European Union, using a revitalised Western European Union, is looking to regain a hegemonic power based on the Franco-German axis. In the long run, if the European Union becomes a military alliance, either directly or by absorbing the WEU, this would lead to the dissolution of the Atlantic Alliance and, consequently, to the disappearance of the American strategic guarantee over Europe.[14]

The December 1998 Saint-Malo declaration between France and the UK, together with the introduction of the Euro, has also been interpreted

---

9 S. Gill (ed.), *Atlantic Relations: Beyond the Reagan Era* (New York, St Martin's, 1989).

10 J. Lepgold, *The Declining Hegemon: The United States and European Defense, 1960-90* (New York, Greenwood, 1990).

11 Analysed by P. H. Gordon, *A Certain Idea of France: French Security Policy and the Gaullist Legacy* (Princeton, Princeton University Press, 1993), pp.174-6.

12 Krasner, 'Power, Polarity and the Challenge of Disintegration' in Haftendorn and Tuschhoff (eds.), *America and Europe*, pp.36-7.

13 A. Menon, 'From Independence to Cooperation: France, NATO and European Security', *International Affairs*, 71: 11 (1995) 22-3.

14 Krasner, 'Power', p.67.

as a manifestation of European rejection of US hegemony. According to this theory, as the development of credible and autonomous EU military forces capable of acting without any American support was considered intolerable for Washington, the US deliberately provoked a *casus belli* with Belgrade by imposing impossible conditions during the Rambouillet talks in order to supplant the embryonic European leadership.[15]

Associative Approach

Researchers belonging to the associative framework claim, on the contrary, that the end of the Cold War has not changed anything fundamental in the relations between the US and the EU. Contrary to the Cassandras who have predicted the crumbling of the transatlantic link and mainly of NATO, these analysts observe that NATO is capable of finding a new *raison d'être* following the disappearance of the Soviet Union and that it remains a very attractive organisation, given that practically all former Eastern European countries want to join.

They also claim that European feelings towards the United States, far from being weaker, were strengthened by the end of Cold War.[16] They remark that fears concerning American isolationism are nothing new: they have regularly surfaced since the end of the Second World War. The West European psychosis could be explained by the memory of the American withdrawal in the interwar period which was a factor of instability having led to the rise of authoritarian and expansionist regimes, and finally to the Second Word War. Traumatised by such an historical memory, numerous Europeans remain vigilant about any American isolationist trend.

The associative analysts observe that the Americans have also learned something from their mistakes of the 1920s and that they will maintain their presence on the Old Continent. Moreover, they underline the fact that President Bill Clinton, who has been accused of being indifferent to world affairs, has strongly reiterated his support for strong

---

15 B. Guetta, 'Cette guerre peut en cacher une autre', *Le Temps*, 30 March 1999.

16 K. S. Smith, D. A. Wertman, 'Redefining US-West European Relations in the 1990s: West European Public Opinion in the Post-Cold War Era', *PS: Political Science & Politics* (June 1992) 188-9.

American involvement on the Old Continent[17] and has never taken any concrete isolationist steps.

They point out that the United States remains not only firmly involved in Western European affairs, but that moreover it invented the concept of Partnership for Peace among the NATO countries and almost all European States which do not belong to it. More discreetly, but even more efficiently, the US has introduced programmes of military cooperation with most Central and Oriental countries and has even been successful in establishing military bases (in Hungary, Albania, Macedonia etc.).

Finally, far from abandoning the Old Continent, the United States has taken diplomatic initiatives, sometimes militarily guaranteed in the Irish, Greco-Turkish, Cypriot, Macedonian and Bosnian conflicts (Dayton agreements). The latest example is the close cooperation the US had with the EU in developing coherent and consistent economic sanctions on Yugoslavia during the 1999 Kosovo crisis. The EU adopted an oil embargo and a financial assets freeze legislation complementary to that of the US. Both also cooperated at a donor's conference (Sarajevo, July 1999) to help rebuilding in the region.

On US-EU relations *stricto sensu*, emphasis is put on three key elements. First, the United States does not oppose, and, on the whole, even supports any attempt by the European Union to establish its identity in security and defence matters. Washington thus welcomed the Maastricht Treaty which mentions the evolution of the EU towards a Common Foreign and Security Policy.[18] Second, the United States has accepted the principle that NATO's infrastructure in transportation and communication may be used by the Western European Union, (mandated or not by the European Union), without American involvement. This is the concept of Combined Joined Task Forces (CJTF). This procedure will allow any combination of European countries linked to the WEU to borrow NATO's capabilities if the US does not want to or cannot take part in a European mission. In other words, this allows the European Union to use NATO infrastructure without American participation.[19]

---

17 J. Peterson, 'Europe and America in the Clinton Era', *Journal of Common Market Studies*, 32:3 (1994) 411-26.

18 R. Schwok, *US-EC Relations in the Post Cold War Era. Conflict or Partnership?* (Boulder, Westview Press, 1991), pp.185-6.

19 R. Smith, 'A Changing NATO', *Nato Review*, 45:3 (1997) 10-1.

Third, in Cologne in June 1999, EU leaders went even further by agreeing that the Union should have its own military capacity to tackle regional crises in Europe, backed by sources of intelligence and capabilities for analysis and strategic planning. It means that Washington has accepted that EU countries wich are members of NATO but also that neutral and non-allied members of the Union may participate in crisis management operations using NATO resources.[20]

Hegemonic Competition

Dissociative Approach

According to this interpretation, the end of Cold War leads to new rivalries in the world between the main blocs, and, in so doing, between the EU and the US. As these two partners no longer face a common enemy, they revert to their true imperialistic impulse. Today's epoch is that of a quest for a hegemonic position everywhere in the world. The EU and the US are mainly in competition in Eastern Europe. Washington is looking to extend its economic, political and cultural influence over this former Soviet sphere of influence, while Western Europe, where Germany 'might soon be the most important military factor',[21] is attempting to follow the same policy.

As a consequence, some American lobbies are pressing Washington to exchange the American military presence on the Old Continent for more European docility in other areas of the world. Dissociative proponents frequently quote a report by the Defense Planning Guidance (DGP) of the Pentagon suggesting that the American Ministry of Defence wants to avoid the emergence of any rival superpower in Western Europe, in Asia or on the territory of the former Soviet Union. According to this document, Washington should 'convince potential competitors that they need not aspire to a greater role or pursue a more aggressive posture to protect their legitimate interests' and that the US 'must sufficiently account for the interests of the advanced industrial nations to

20 P. Norman, 'Defence: Europe to Share Resources', *Financial Times*, 4 June 1999.

21 S. Hoffmann, 'America and Europe in an Era of Revolutionary Change' in Haftendorn, Tuschhoff (eds.), *America and Europe*, p.63.

discourage them from challenging our leadership or seeking to overturn the established political and economic order'.[22]

Divergence between the EU and the US in ex-Yugoslavia is presented as a particularly clear illustration of the growing rivalries between those two superpowers.[23] Dissociative researchers insist that the United States did not support the first European plan to cantonalise Bosnia and that Washington's support to the Bosnian Croats and the Bosnian Moslems was much stronger than that of Paris and London. Some Americans have also strongly criticised the German position on Croatia and Slovenia's recognition of independence. Its unilateral action has been seen by some Americans as a clear expression of a rejuvenated German imperialistic comeback on the international stage. Finally, in the last phase of the conflict, one heard (mostly European) voices expressing criticism about the so-called American Dictate, *i.e.* that the US has imposed throughout the Dayton agreements its own solution to the conflict. All the above examples are interpreted by dissociative researchers as yet further proof of the growing divergence between the EU and the US.

The same types of arguments also circulated during the 1999 Kosovo crisis. A couple of experts even accused the US of having deliberately started the war against Yugoslavia in order to reassert American hegemony, initiate a new 'Cold War' with China and convert the Europeans into obedient servers.[24]

Associative Approach

Associative scholars maintain that there is much more convergence than rivalry in the world between the EU and the US. They observe that the 1990s consecrate the establishment of a kind of burden-sharing pact for the management of world affairs. They mention particularly the 1995 New Transatlantic Agenda and its Joint Action Plan[25] presented as the

22 M. Ougaard, 'Dealing with the Community: The Bush Administration's Response to Western European Integration', in O. Noorgaard, T. Pedersen, N. Petersen (eds.), *The European Community in World Politics* (London, Pinter, 1993), p.199.

23 Analysed by J. Peterson, *Europe and America in the 1990s. The Prospects for Partnership* (Aldershot, Edward Elgar, 1993), pp.78-80.

24 B. Guetta, 'Cette guerre peut en cacher une autre'; N. Birnbaum, 'De Pristina à Pékin', *Le Monde*, 17 June 1999.

25 W. Weidenfeld, 'The New Transatlantic Agenda: A New Basis for Euro-American Co-operation?', *European Access*, 2 (1996) 10-2.

most significant and substantial step in the relationship between the US and the EU, since its establishment in 1958.

For Washington, this document means that the US now considers the EU not only as an economic and commercial partner but also as a political force capable of acting with the United States as an almost equal partner. This declaration of objectives and of about 120 themes of specific action represents a greater degree of consensus than the US would have been capable of achieving with any other region, with any other group of countries, or – with the possible exception of Canada – with any country taken individually.[26]

Now, specifically regarding the ex-Yugoslavia issue, associative analysts consider that the EU and the US have acted, generally speaking, in a complementary way.[27] There have been of course some misunderstandings, but regarding the main issues, Europeans and Americans have shared the same political and military objectives *vis-à-vis* former Yugoslavia. For instance, the fact that Washington wanted the EU to be the main intercessor was a sign of confidence, not of mistrust. There were subsequently other misunderstandings on numerous points but those relatively minor clashes did not concern fundamental issues. Moreover, the 'associativists' observe that these transatlantic clashes were often less severe than those between the Administration and the Congress in Washington, or than those between France and Germany in Europe, without mentioning the open conflicts between the fourteen members of the EU and Greece on the issue of Macedonia.

The Yugoslav crisis (in Bosnia and Kosovo) finally led to the strengthening of the transatlantic link because the Europeans, and especially the French, had to admit that they cannot solve any major crisis of this type alone. Paris needed to ask the Americans to intervene under the NATO umbrella in order to give some credibility to the European diplomatic pressure.[28] As a consequence, the American leadership over the both Western alliance and NATO was strengthened.

---

26 Weidenfeld, 'The New Transatlantic Agenda'.

27 T. Frellesen and R. H. Ginsberg, *EU-US Foreign Policy Cooperation in the 1990s. Elements of Partnership* (Brussels, Centre for European Policy Studies, 1994), pp.31-6.

28 A. Menon, 'From Independence', p.22. See also A. Frachon, 'L'Amérique et le besoin d'Europe', *Le Monde*, 25 March 1999.

Theoretical Underpinnings

Dissociative Approach

The dissociative interpretation is deeply influenced by the so-called realist theory, a very important approach in the study of international relations. According to this theory, international relations are characterised by continuing rivalry among those States who are the main actors in the international system. There is no monopoly of the legitimated violence in the international society, where these States are perpetually in conflict. It is therefore an illusion to argue that they could durably become allies. 'States are the units whose interactions form the structure of international political systems' and 'they will long remain so'.[29] Kenneth Waltz, the main theoretician of neo-realism, dismisses the role of international organisations. Either international organisations behave as new states or they remain so weak that the power of the individual states within them shines through.[30]

Due to this conceptual and ideological underlying way of thinking, realists strongly doubt that the European countries can be united. They believe that the EU is closer to a classical international organisation than to a federal State such as Germany, the United States or Switzerland. They find it difficult to admit that the EU has a kind of international personality. *A fortiori*, realists generally study the transatlantic relations as relations between each individual Member State of the EU, and the US.

As the realist paradigm cannot accept that relations between European States may be peaceful, it has even more difficulty accepting the fact that the relations between the EU and the US could be non-conflictual.

Associative Approach

Associative researchers belong to the so-called pluralist trend in the study of international relations. In other words, they accept the idea of a plurality of explanations. They are sceptical about explanatory, systematic and predictive theories. Their framework is called complex inter-

---

29 K. Waltz in R. O. Keohane (ed.), *Neorealism and its Critics* (New York, Columbia University Press, 1986), p.81.

30 K. Waltz in Keohane (ed.), *Neorealism*, p.81.

dependence.[31] Generally speaking, this approach claims that international relations – EU-US relations included – have three main features: (1) the societies are linked by numerous channels of different types; (2) the agenda of international relations is made of numerous issues which cannot be fixed in an intangible and clear hierarchy; (3) military power is not used by governments against other governments when interdependence is well developed.

According to associative analysts, complex interdependence applies well to the relations between the EU and the US.[32] Numerous channels are used to connect the American and the European actors. The agenda of the relations between the EU and the US is composed of numerous issues which are not fixed in a consistent and hierarchical manner. The use of force by either the EU or the US seems to be inconceivable.

It is important to underline that associative analysts (influenced by the complex interdependence framework) do not refrain from sometimes using a realist or a mercantilist approach when necessary.[33] They also admit that the State is the main actor in international relations, that it usually acts in a rational way (or at least aims at doing it this way), and that the EU, as well as the US, may use protectionist devices according to circumstances.

The complex interdependence analysts, however, do want to maintain a pluralist approach. They also observe that the states are not the only actors in the international system, that they do not always act in a rational way (in the game theory's acceptation, with perfect information and with fixed preferences and objectives), and they doubt that the quest for power constitutes the sole aim of any foreign policy.

---

[31] R. O. Keohane and J. S. Nye, *Power and Interdependence* (Boston, Little Brown, 1987, 2nd revised edition).

[32] K. Featherstone and R. H. Ginsberg, *The United States and the European Community in the 1990s. Partners in Transition* (London, Macmillan, 1996, 2nd edition), p.65.

[33] Peterson, 'Europe and America', pp.217-18

Hypotheses on EU-US Economic Issues

An 'Isolationist, Introvert and Self-Centred' Europe

Dissociative Approach

According to the dissociative approach, Europe is no longer interested in the rest of the world. Looking inward to its own problems, the Union is losing interest in international relations, as well as in its former colonies. Entangled in its problems of unification – completing its Single Market, creating its Economic and Monetary Union and enlarging to Eastern Europe – the EU's sole aim is to strengthen integration around a Western European core. Far from having an international dimension which fits its economic power, the Union is increasingly concentrating on its own problems, forgetting its economic, political and cultural importance.

Thus, according to dissociative analysts, the 1992 Single Market was equated by most Americans with an unacceptable 'Fortress Europe'.[34] Many Americans complain that the European committees of standardisation shape norms differently to the American ones. This could discriminate against some American firms and exclude them from the European market. As regards tests and certifications, some similar fears have been expressed in the US; this concerns the extension of the principle of mutual recognition for American products as well as the conformity of some American laboratories for proceeding to certifications that are valid in the EU. Regarding public procurements, the Union's directive on the so-called excluded sectors also creates some uneasiness. It contains a 'Buy European' clause which authorises the Union to reject bids containing less than fifty percent EU content.

Dissociative analysts also add that the European economic situation is getting worse. Levels of unemployment have reached their peaks and are not going down. Public deficits are still huge. Debts have accumulated. Public opinion refuses to make any economic sacrifice, for instance in order to comply with the so-called Maastricht criteria.[35] Every indi-

---

34 J. Van Scherpenberg, 'Wirtschaftlicher Aufbruch nach Europa? Die innere und äussere Dynamik des EG-Binnenmarktes' in B. W. Kubbig (ed.), *Transatlantische Unsicherheit* (Frankfurt/Main, Fischer Taschenbuch Verlag, 1991), p.93.

35 D. R. Cameron, 'From Barre to Balladur: Economic Policy in the Era of the EMS' in G. Flynn (ed.), *Remaking the Hexagon. The New France in the New Europe* (Boulder, Westview Press, 1995), p.149.

cator shows that Europe is not recovering from the economic crisis and that protectionist pressure will continue to grow, which, in turn, according to this analytical framework, will feed anti-American attitudes.

Associative Approach

According to the associative researchers, there is no credible sign that the EU is characterised by protectionist tendencies. On the contrary, the Single Market has proven to be much more free trade oriented than was originally predicted by most experts. The Common Agricultural Policy (symbol of EU protectionism and dirigism) is on the way to fundamental reform. Moreover the establishment of an Economic and Monetary Union is another indication of a general trend towards more economic liberalism and less State controls.

With regard to, more specifically, the 1992 Single Market, it is wrong to claim that it has been seen by most Americans as the equivalent of a 'Fortress Europe'. On the contrary, American business circles, as well as the Bush and Clinton administrations, have supported this objective. This endorsement was motivated by the following reasons: (1) EC-1992 enhances free trade; (2) it offers opportunities for commercial development; (3) it creates economic growth; (4) the whole world will profit from more economic and monetary stabilisation; (5) Eastern Europe will be developed and strengthened by a stronger Western Europe; (6) the US will benefit from a more reliable partner to keep the world order.[36]

More concretely, there has been, in the meantime, no statement by any political or economic American leader arguing that the EU is a fortress. Most problems have been solved or are on the right path. This is the case of the American companies which are now informed well in advance, and sometimes even consulted, on the new norms shaped by the European bodies of standardisation. There have been successful negotiations between the EU and the US in order to reach the largest level of mutual recognition between the European and American standards. The same is true about tests and certifications.[37] Finally, on public procurements, most of the problems have been solved by the agreements made – in the margins of the Uruguay Round negotiations –

36 Schwok, *US-EU Relations*, pp.227-8.

37 EU & US, *Mutual Recognition Agreements on Conformity Assessment* (Brussels, 20 June 1997), http://europa.eu.int/en/comm/dg01/mra01.htm.

between the EU, the US, and most industrialised countries, Japan included.[38]

Associative approach observers reject the claim that the completion of the Single Market, association agreements with EFTA, Central and Eastern European and Mediterranean countries, as well as the enlargement of the EU to include thirteen new members constitute any proof of an inward looking orientation. These aspects show, on the contrary, that the Union is open to foreign countries despite its budgetary constraints and the risk of political dilution. Moreover, associative researchers underline the fact that all European projects of integration follow a free trade philosophy and are relatively non-discriminatory towards third countries. In order to support their argument, they show that the United States has always supported all efforts towards deepening and enlarging the Union, albeit on the condition that some compensation be provided.

The Economic and Monetary Union (EMU)

Dissociative Approach

The completion of the EMU by the year 2002 with the fixing of irrevocable exchange rates in 1999 between many key EU countries generated a great deal of analyses related to Euro-American relations. For dissociative analysts, the US supports neither the economic, nor the financial, nor the political objectives of the Single Currency.

Dissociative analysts such as the MIT Professor Rudi Dornbush are convinced that the US is fearful of the EMU as the Single Currency will contribute to recession and political trouble which have always been expensive for the Europeans as well as for the Americans.[39] Martin Feldstein even argues that 'EMU [...] will change the political character of Europe in ways that could lead to [...] confrontations with the United States'.[40]

They also underline that one of the main arguments in support of the Single Currency – often openly expressed by the French – is that the dollar will be replaced as the main international currency and that the economic, commercial and political power of the US will be challenged

---

38 J. Croome, *Reshaping the World Trade System. A History of the Uruguay Round* (Geneva, World Trade Organization, 1995), p.92.

39 R. Dornbush, 'Euro Fantasies', *Foreign Affairs*, 75:5 (1996) 123-4.

40 M. Feldstein, 'EMU and International Conflict', *Foreign Affairs*, 76:6 (1997) 63.

by a much more assertive Europe.[41] Moreover, the European Single Currency could reduce the autonomy of the American monetary policy by limiting its political options. Clearly, confronted with such a discourse, dissociative researchers have no difficulty in claiming that the Americans have every reason to fear a European Single Currency and thus will do everything to torpedo it.

Associative Approach

Associative analysts maintain that the United States welcomes the perspective of the EMU. They quote numerous statements made by American officials and business leaders. They of course do not ignore the fact that some American speculators are keeping their eyes open for a European monetary mistake, but this is only true in some circles, and is not the case for the entire American administration.

The support of the Single Currency by America and most business leaders can be explained by the six following motives:

- First, the Euro will contribute to the creation of wealth (static and dynamic effects), which will benefit everyone, *i.e.* Americans included.[42]
- Second, American firms (Ford, GM) are very well established in Europe, even better than European ones. They will be the first to benefit from the abolition of monetary protectionism which penalises them more than it does the national European companies.[43]
- Third, if the creation of the Euro leads to more growth thanks to sounder public finance (Maastricht criteria on budgetary deficit and public debt), this process can only strengthen political and social stability in Europe.
- Fourth, the establishment of the European Central Bank will be at the expense of the German Bundesbank; Washington generally supports any measure which could counterbalance the hegemony of one single state.

---

41 M. Nelson, J. G. Ikenberry, *Atlantic Frontiers. A New Agenda for US-EC Relations* (Washington D.C., Carnegie Endowment for International Peace, 1993), p.26.

42 R. Mundell, 'The Case for the Euro', *The Wall Street Journal*, 24 March 1998.

43 E. Thiel, 'Dollar-EMU-Yen: An Evolving G-3 Relationship', *Paper presented at Biennial Conference of the European Community Studies Association* (George Mason University, 22-24 May 1991), p.10.

- Fifth, the Euro will help to insulate the European economy from fluctuations in the US dollar and thus reduce the costs of transatlantic monetary conflict for Europe.[44]
- Sixth, the passage to the Single Currency will have political consequences by deepening the EU. For a United States which does not want a weak Europe, the political functionality of the EMU plays an important role.[45]

Protectionism and Multilateralism

Dissociative Approach

The dissociative approach assumes that the world is leaning towards the constitution of protectionist commercial blocs. The EU is deepening its integration through the Single Market and the Single Currency, while consolidating its links with EFTA countries through the European Economic Area (EEA) and with Eastern and Mediterranean countries through all kinds of association agreements. In the meantime, the United States has established NAFTA and is active in APEC and other free trade areas in Central and South America. According to this approach, these developments are bound to lead to a series of trade clashes. Pushing the argument a bit further, one theory even argues that, by the end of the Cold War, conflicts will be increasingly economic.

Throughout the Uruguay negotiations (1986-93), analysts belonging to the dissociative school predicted their failure. Almost all points on the EU-US negotiation agenda were labelled as wars (cf. wars on civil aviation, bovine hormones, soybean, tropical wood, textile, anti-dumping measures, public procurements, financial services, maritime rights, cultural area etc).[46] The prediction of the Uruguay Round's failure was derived from an analysis of the American evolution. The most famous Cassandra – who exerted quite an important influence on public opinion – is Professor Lester Thurow, then Dean of the Sloan School of

---

44 C. R. Henning, 'Europe's Monetary Union and the United States', *Foreign Policy*, 7:102 (1996) p.94.

45 Peterson, 'Europe and America', p.122.

46 The EC Common Agricultural Policy was their prime target, presented as the archetype for the entire European commercial policy – see A. Stoeckel, D. Pearce, G. Banks (eds.), *Western Trade Blocs* (Canberra, Centre for International Economics, 1990), p.39. It has to be said that the CAP was indeed designed as a protectionist and state run system.

Management at the Massachusetts Institute of Technology (MIT). Author of expressions such as: 'The GATT-Bretton Woods trading system is dead',[47] Thurow was convinced that the European Community would just about finish it off.[48]

Another influential professor, Robert Gilpin from Princeton University, also prophesied the collapse of the multilateral trade system, attributing its likely failure to the conjunction of four interdependent factors:

- Sectoral protectionism such as the multifibre agreement will develop and replace GATT multilateralism by 'minilateralism'. 'In this new environment, bilateralism or minilateralism has largely displaced the multilateralism of the GATT'.[49]
- Multilateralism will be replaced by economic regionalism (NAFTA, EC internal market, see *supra*).
- Mercantilist competition (economic nationalism) will develop, especially after the end of Cold War. The EU is becoming more and more a fortress, abusing anti-dumping measures, while the US uses excessively protectionist instruments such as the sections 301-310 of the 1988 Omnibus Trade and Competitiveness Act. 'Super 301', as it is called, became a device of export-protectionism and the behaviour of the US bordered on predation.
- The trend induced by the three previous factors is strengthened by the assumption that the US is losing its capacity to guarantee economic liberalism (see *infra*, 'theory of Hegemonic Stability).

As Robert Gilpin concisely puts it: 'A mixed system of nationalism, regionalism, and sectoral protectionism is replacing the Bretton Woods system of multilateral liberalization'.[50] Most media have reflected, or sometimes anticipated, such predictions. The list of such affirmations is endless. Even a reliable, influential and pro-GATT magazine, *The*

---

47 L. Thurow, *Head to Head. The Coming Economic Battle Among Japan, Europe and America* (New York, William Morrow & Company, 1992), p.65.

48 Thurow, *Head to Head,* p.76, 'GATT bled to death from the wounds described in the previous chapter, but European integration will provide the official death certificate'.

49 R. Gilpin, *The Political Economy of International Relations* (Princeton, Princeton University Press, 1987), p.408.

50 Gilpin, *The Political Economy*, p.394.

Economist, has predicted that the GATT itself would collapse because of the American hegemonic decline.[51]

Associative Approach

Associative analysts do not accept the expression 'trade bloc'. They claim that neither the European Union, nor the EEA, nor the Europe Agreements, nor NAFTA, nor APEC constitute proper 'trade blocs'. As a matter of fact, these agreements are not protectionist and directed consciously in a discriminatory way against third countries. All those agreements are based on the principle of free trade and comply with GATT and WTO criteria on the constitution of free trade agreements (especially article XXIV).

The non discriminatory nature of these forms of integration is implicitly acknowledged by the fact that the US has not criticised, and has by and large welcomed, all steps towards further integration and enlargement of the EU. The same is true for the EU which has never expressed any reservation about the US free trade agreement with Canada, or about NAFTA or APEC.

As far as the Uruguray Round is concerned, associative analysts insist that what matters is the result and, in the present case, this was positive: it led to the most important multilateral trade agreement in the entire history of commerce and to the creation of the WTO. Analysists finally recall that its success can be attributed mainly to the EU and the US.[52]

For associative analysts, the success of the Uruguay Round, and especially the desire of both the EU and the US to find workable agreements, can be explained by the fact that these two actors share a common economic interest in freer trade and that they do not want to strain their political and military relations with trade and agricultural conflicts.

---

51 A selection of a few titles speaks for itself: 'GATT in Peril', 23 November 1990; 'Dancing from Bad to Worse', 23 November 1990; 'GATT's Last Gasp', 7 December 1990; 'A Lifeboat for Trade', 14 December 1990; 'Rocking a Lifeboat is Dangerous', 14 December 1990, 'So Close, and Yet so Far', 4 January 1992, 'Free Trade's Fading Champion', 11 April 1992, 'Poor Odds, High Stakes', 27 June, 1992, 'The Uruguay Round ... and Round', 23 January 1993, 'Bye-Bye, Uruguay', 30 January 1993, 'Going Bananas, America and Europe Are at War', 6 March 1999.

52 J. Croome, *Reshaping the World Trade System. A History of the Uruguay Round* (Geneva, World Trade Organization, 1995), pp.351-64.

This means that for analysts belonging to the associative approach, the Cassandras who predicted 'the end of GATT' were simply wrong. The Uruguay Round success is, on the contrary, symbolic of the EU-US dominance on international trade rules. Those two blocs have indeed simply imposed their bilateral compromise on the hundred other GATT Member States; this is the best proof of Euro-American cooperative leadership in the world.

Theoretical Underpinnings

Dissociative Approach

Neomercantilism is the theory which had the greatest influence on the dissociative approach.[53] It is a variance of the realist theory applied to economic aspects of international relations insofar as it assumes the primacy of the State in international relations and has sceptical views on the positive contribution of free trade. In other words, neomercantilists doubt that the so-called virtues of free trade are well understood by the States, that they accept to give up their national protection and expose themselves to foreign competition for its potential benefits.

Along these premises, neomercantilist researchers focus on the growth of protectionist barriers. They want to demonstrate that the end of the Cold War opens opportunities for numerous hidden economic protectionist conflicts. They particularly see, as already mentioned, the constitution of economic blocs as the most manifest illustration of the transformation of national protectionism into bloc protectionism.

The theory of hegemonic stability has grown within this neomercantilist theoretical framework. This theory's key element is the view that stability in international relations stems from the presence of hegemony or dominance.[54] The absence of hegemons implies a lack of order in the relations among States whether in commercial activities (trade, money), social issues, or security concerns. Its main axiom is to establish a correlation between hegemonic power and stability of international regimes (such as GATT). As long as the hegemon (the United Kingdom in the 19th century or the United States after the Second World War) can bear the costs of its supremacy, international regimes remain credible. When

---

53 Analysed by O. R. Keohane *After Hegemony. Cooperation and Discord in the World Political Economy* (Princeton, Princeton University Press, 1984), p.22.

54 R. Gilpin, *The Political Economy of International Relations* (Princeton, Princeton University Press, 1987).

a hegemon declines or abdicates (*i.e.* through isolationism), instances of defection rise sharply among its followers (Japan, Europe etc). Applied to international trade, the logical conclusion of the theory of hegemonic stability is that we are aiming for a reorganisation of the system towards insular and conflictual trade blocs.

The main assumption underlying this scenario, *i.e.* the decline of the United States, is one of the most popular themes in American academic literature of the late 1980s. It was mainly popularised by Professor Paul Kennedy of Yale University.[55] This historian became famous by claiming that the US would collapse, following the path of the Roman Empire, if it did not reduce its public budget, especially military expenses.[56]

It is precisely in the name of these theories that numerous authors have predicted that the US no longer has either the will or the strength to impose its rules within the international organisations and that the liberal economic system (WTO, IMF, World Bank included) will crumble because of a lack of leadership.[57]

---

55 P. Kennedy, *The Rise and Fall of the Great Powers: Economic Change and Military Conflict from 1500 to 2000* (New York, Vintage, 1987).

56 Among the indicators of decline, the main ones were: the weakness of the dollar, the accumulation of debts and public deficits, the loss of competitiveness of the American enterprises with regard to their Japanese and other Asian competitors, especially in key sectors such as automobile or computer industries. 'Declinists' also insist on the high level of illiteracy in the US and the American workforce's relative lack of training.

57 One can apply the conceptualisation I propose to more recent issues. Look, for instance, at the way some dissociative researchers have anticipated serious confrontations, if not war, between the US and the EU when Washington, under pressure from the Congress enacted the US Helms-Burton anti-Cuba law and the Iran-Libya Sanctions Act which ban any foreign company to invest in those hostile countries. The EU rejected what it considered 'extra-territorial' US legislation. Tension reached its climax when Total, the French energy group, signed a $2bn contract to develop an Iranian gas field. See H. Lesguillons, 'Les lois Helms-Burton et D'Amato: réactions de l'Union européenne', *Revue de droit des affaires internationales*, 1 (1997) 95-111; G. Kinka, 'The Transatlantic Rift over Cuba. The Damage is Done', *International Spectator*, 32:2 (1997) 27-52. Similar worries were expressed – only in the press as there was not sufficient time for academics to publish their articles – when the European Commission threatened to ban the merger between Boeing and McDonnell Douglas, two US aircraft manufacturers. E. Tucker, 'Boeing/McDonnell Douglas: EU Commissioners Set to Ban Merger', *Financial Times*, 21 July 1997.

Associative Approach

Critics of the theory of hegemonic stability claim that the theory is wrong on the conditions which motivate a State to exercise its leadership[58] and that it ignores the true motivations of the followers (Japan, Europe) towards the leader (USA).

In other words, the theory of hegemonic stability was misled by a simplistic application of game theory[59] and in particular by the metaphor of prisoner's dilemma which too often leads to analysing international trade relations as a zero-sum game. According to this theory, the EU and Japan would have automatically chosen to defect as soon as the US could not or did not want to uphold the international regimes it created.

This discounts the fact that both Japan and the EU (the so-called 'demand-side of trade regimes') also have an interest in keeping, developing and guaranteeing free trade through international regimes: that they are trying to diminish the costs of transaction and of the diffusion of information, and they are pressurised by their own myopic interest to cooperate and dismantle their protectionist barriers.

One should also finally point out the fundamental role played by the transnational interests in the success of the Uruguay Round. There were as many European and Japanese multinational companies as American firms which had an interest in keeping the GATT system alive. Those multinational companies put tremendous pressure on the European governments (with the support of European-based American companies) in order to force them to play the game of multilateralism.[60]

The theory of American decline has also been sharply criticised by numerous authors.[61] They have shown that the United States is far from being ruined, that military expenses do not represent such a large percentage of US GNP and have anyway been cut thanks to the end of Cold

---

58 Keohane, *After Hegemony*, pp.49-64.

59 Keohane, *After Hegemony*, pp.65-84.

60 Putnam, 'Two-Level Games', in Haftendorn, Tuschhoff (eds.), *America and Europe*, p.77.

61 H. Nau, *The Myth of America's Decline. Leading the World Economy into the 1990s* (New York, Oxford University Press, 1990); J. Nye, *Bound to Lead* (New York, Basic Books, 1990); J. Nye, 'Patrons and Clients: New Roles in the Post-Cold War Order' in Haftendorn and Tuschhoff (eds.), *America and Europe*, pp.87-104.

War, and that they are moreover necessary to preserve American leadership and international stability.

They also argue that a weak dollar is a conjunctural element, and not necessarily the sign of an American decline; that American public deficits and debts are not higher, in percentage, than in Europe; and that American companies have been successful in their very serious phase of restructuration, being now capable of reconquering some sectors commanded by the Japanese and the 'Asian tigers' (cars, computers, microchips etc.).

On Euro-American relations, it is striking to observe that 'associative' and 'anti-decline' analyses[62] are, to a large extent, converging. Anti-declinists are indeed convinced that the United States can continue to dominate the international system (they give the example of the use of the UN framework in both the Gulf and the Yugoslav crises). They claim that NATO can be kept alive, although they would prefer some reforms in order to strengthen the European pillar. Finally, they are convinced that the US, jointly with the EU, can consolidate the WTO and conclude more bilateral trade agreements on non-tariff barriers.[63]

Conclusion

The preceding analysis has deliberately tried to present in a dichotomic way the different interpretations of the relationship between the EU and the US. By pointing out the divergences between the two approaches, I have tried to conceptualise the debate better and to contribute to a clearer understanding of its essence.

I have also tried to expose exaggerations, and sometimes even the objective errors, which have mainly appeared in the dissociative approach. This article indeed questions the theoretical assumptions as well as the empirical observations of those researchers who have predicted a

---

62 R. Keohane, 'The Diplomacy of Structural Change: Multilateral Institutions and State Strategies', in Haftendorn, Tuschhoff (eds.), *America and Europe*, pp.43-62; Nye, 'Patrons and Clients'; Putnam, 'Two-Level Games'.

63 Contrary to some gloomy forecasts, in May 1998, the US and the EU came up with a formula to resolve their serious differences on the Helms-Burton act and on the Iran-Libya Sanctions Act with the United States agreeing to waive the Act's provision for the French company Total for its planned investment in Iran. See US Representative to the European Union, *Letter from Brussels*, Vol.11/2, 20 July 1998, p.1. The issue on the merger between Boeing and McDonnell Douglas was also solved without major difficulties.

dislocation of the transatlantic link after the end of the Cold War. This study mainly analyses the reasoning which led to affirm that NATO was condemned to disappear, that the Uruguay Round agreements would never be concluded, that the EU would be transformed into a protectionist fortress and that the US were committed to torpedo both the European Single Market and the Single Currency.

After this clear reminder of the approximation which characterises social sciences, it is of course risky to embark on predicting. My conviction is that the associative approach is the most valid of the two, with all the limitations which go with ideal-type. This means that the analysis I have developed here, added to what I formulated on the relationship between the European Community and the United States between 1950 and 1990,[64] corroborates my opinion that the EU-US relationship will evolve towards greater partnership rather than conflict.

64 R. Schwok, *US-EU Relations…*

CHAPTER 13

Ever Closer Partnership? Taking Stock of US-EU Relations[1]

Éric PHILIPPART and Pascaline WINAND

Fonds National de la Recherche Scientifique (Belgium),
Université Libre de Bruxelles,
College of Europe (Bruges)

The 1990-2000 period has been an eventful one for transatlantic relations. New US-EU institutional structures and processes were put to the test and higher ambitions, coupled with a wider agenda were assigned to the revamped partnership. At the same time, developments taking place on both sides of the Atlantic and in the world at large either fostered cooperation or created tensions between Europeans and Americans. The aim of the last two chapters of this book is to take stock of the rich and complex US-EU relationship at the beginning of the 21st century.

This chapter looks at the evolution of US-EU structures and processes. In chapter one, we outlined the evolution from WWII to 1990 in terms of how the benefits, costs and dangers of the relationship are perceived. We also considered the formula of cooperation as well as the patterns of tensions, conflicts and parallel strategies. The second part of the book shed a tentative light on the recent developments at these levels, particularly since the watershed of the Transatlantic Declaration. The findings relative to the two periods are compared here. Major enduring features but also discontinuities in the dynamics of policy-shaping and policy-making are then identified and explained.

---

1 Although this chapter is in part the result of joint cogitation, the first section 'Evolution in Terms of How the Benefits, Costs and Dangers of the Relationship Are Perceived' and the last section 'Evolution of the Tensions between Transatlantic Partners and their "Containment" Strategies' were mostly written by Pascaline Winand. Éric Philippart wrote most of the middle section 'The Evolution of the Format of the US-EU Relationship: Strengths and Weaknesses of the New Partnership Formula'. This chapter benefited from interviews with many US and EU officials on a non-attributable basis. The discussions with Wendy Moore were also of great help.

Evolution in Terms of how the Benefits, Costs and Dangers of the Relationship Are Perceived

As we shall see, the comparison of present and past perceptions of US-EC/EU relations generally shows strong enduring features, both on the American and on the European sides, although some would appear to be waning or have disappeared altogether.

Our first chapter posited that American backing of European integration was not just a Cold War-bound affair, but that there were additional cogent reasons for this support. Thus, while the US did support European integration as a way of fostering European prosperity and political stability, thereby reinforcing the Alliance and helping to contain the Soviet Union, other motivations existed prior to the Cold War, some of which continued to warrant American support for European integration after that period. It should thus come as no surprise that some of the Clinton administration's pronouncements appeared to mimic those of earlier periods, including World War II.

This is particularly so if we look at the arguments and the expressions used about market access and the benefits anticipated from an environment of democratic regimes. If World War II planners in Washington hoped that a European Union would help to simplify commercial policy with the United States and circumscribe European protectionism, the Clinton administration similarly placed the emphasis on the advantage of doing business with a single address for American exporters.[2]

Concurrently, we might add that the American perception of the opportunities offered by transatlantic economic cooperation improved thanks to the contrasted economic fortunes of Europe and Asia in the second part of the 1990s. Because of its relative economic vitality and the eventual launch of the Euro (compared to the long stagnation and slow structural adjustments of the Japanese economy), the EU was seen, along with the US, as the other bulwark of world economic growth. For example, the US administration insisted that Europe could and should take more of the exports of those countries shaken by the 1998 Asian crisis.

Let us now turn to the argument of democratic regimes. If US World War II planners anticipated that a European Union would be conducive

---

2 USIS, 'US-European Summit discussed', 15 June 1995.

to greater prosperity and thus to political stability in Europe, which would help support democratic regimes in Europe, the Clinton administration handsomely summed up this very same idea, which also applied beyond a European framework, by using the telling phrase of 'market democracies'.[3] Accordingly, the argument of the special contribution democracy, embedded in prosperous markets, made to a stable and peaceful international environment, and of the no less special role of a prosperous and democratic EU in helping to guarantee such an environment, including in Central and Eastern Europe, would appear to be stronger than ever.

By contrast, the need to 'contain' Germany through European integration, while maintaining its presence, seems to be less pressing than in the past. To be sure, the Clinton administration stated that the EU 'provides a home for Germany to act out its future in an integrated Europe and not independent of it.'[4] Yet the perception of Germany by the United States has also taken an increasingly positive turn with the growing importance in the 1990s of what we might term a 'special relationship' between the new Germany and the United States (which contrasts with the weakness of the US-French relationship and the fluctuations in the US-UK special relationship).

If we now consider American fears of the likely negative consequences of a European Union on American interests (which, to some extent, mirror the reasons for US support of European integration), the fear of a Europe dominated by a power or a group of powers with hostile intentions, would seem to have receded with the momentous changes which occurred in the Soviet Union. This fear has largely been replaced, however, by that of an unstable Europe, especially in Central and Eastern Europe, hence the need, once more, to foster 'market democracies' in these regions.

As to the American fear of a 'Fortress Europe', this fear would seem to have waned since 1992 and the completion of the European Single Market. This is so in spite of the eruption of numerous trade conflicts over the last decade. Indeed, although the EU is viewed in the US as a difficult interlocutor and negotiator, it is at the same time recognized as

---

3 Secretary Christopher, 'Toward a More Integrated World, Statement at the OECD ministerial meeting', Paris, France, 8 June 1998, US Department of State, Bureau of Public Affairs, Office of Public Communication.

4 USIS, 'US-European Summit discussed', 15 June 1995.

being open to dialogue, cooperation or even joint action with the United States, including in attempting to diffuse conflicts or reach common positions ahead of WTO meetings.

The fear of a European regional bloc that would undermine the world organization and trigger the creation of a series of similar blocs acting in unstable equilibrium, is, however, to a certain degree still present. As we have seen, several regional agreements, partnerships, areas or associations have been created over the last decade, some of which were encouraged in part by the competitive efforts of either the US or the EU. If Robert Zoellick hoped that APEC, NAFTA and other such regional endeavors would help to bind US partners closer to the US in the post-Cold War era and to liberalize trade and economics in these regions, the establishment of such frameworks with the prompting of the United States has also been partly motivated by the perceived economic challenge of the EU, and of the partnerships it encouraged on the European side.

Finally, the fear of cultural, political and economic isolation would seem to have lessened to some degree on the American side considering the very central position of the US in today's world order. On the other hand, the European side has been worried by the perceived American turn, especially in the US Congress, towards the South and Asia.

American reactions to the introduction of the Euro not only demonstrated that the fear of an independent and/or unstable Europe is still very much present, but also highlighted the ambiguity of the American position. Now, as in the past, US support for European economic integration seems to be predicated upon continued American access to European markets and the participation of the EU in common tasks with the United States. Thus, inasmuch as the Euro is an instrument of growth which could contribute to more prosperity and to better burden-sharing, it is to be encouraged. Some authors have argued that 'U.S. policy is not hostile toward the monetary union. It is distinctly positive-sum in orientation and, at the rhetorical level, certainly supportive.'[5] On the other hand, however, some American circles are worried about the negative impact the Euro might have on the American economy if the

---

5 Randall C. Henning, 'US-EU Relations after the Inception of the Monetary Union: Cooperation or Rivalry?', in Randall C. Henning and Pier Carlo Padoan, *Transatlantic Perspectives on the Euro* (Washington D.C., Brookings Institution Press, 2000), p.17.

Monetary Union proves unable *inter alia* to prevent extreme variations in interest rates and strong increase of interest rates. Thus, the fear here would seem to be less that of the EU as competitor than as a dangerously unstable entity.

All in all, despite generational changes, we could argue with Joseph Nye that 'large majorities of Americans [still] see Europe as a vital interest' and that, while the EU might not be perfect, they see 'a united Europe as better than the alternatives', in particular as a 'partner in dealing with global challenges'.[6] As Roy Ginsberg states in his chapter, Europe and the EU is still commonly perceived as the only available 'partner of scale'.

If we now turn to the European side, we find a similar blend of continuities and discontinuities.[7] The American involvement to guard against major security threats in Europe and in the world at large is still mostly seen as very important, if not indispensable. The majority of decision-makers are still convinced that the economic prosperity of the EU is dependent to a large extent on continued good relations with the US. Furthermore, some of them see cooperation with the American partner as an effective way of restoring European economic power on the world stage. For these decision-makers, the main fear has been the return to US isolationism, triggered in part by a European Union that would act too independently from the US. This fear was further magnified by a number of measures adopted by the US Congress (for instance on foreign aid, funding for the IMF and the UN, or the Comprehensive Test Ban Treaty) and which were only blocked thanks to the repeated use of the presidential veto.

At the same time, mixed feelings about the consequences of US cultural invasion and political intrusion lingered on, in particular with regard to the development of the EU and its institutions. Beyond that, more and more European leaders displayed discomfort with the sturdy resilience of the US foreign policy's traditional frames of reference.[8]

---

6 Joseph S. Jr. Nye, 'The US and Europe: Continental Drift?', *International Affairs*, 76:1 (2000) 51-59, p.55.

7 Miles Kahler and Werner Link, *Europe and America: A Return to History* (New York, Council on Foreign Relations Press, 1996).

8 See Michael Dunne and his analysis of the Clinton rhetoric on the 'indispensable nation'. M. Dunne, 'US Foreign Relations in the Twentieth Century: From World Power to Global Hegemony', *International Affairs*, 76:1 (2000), p.26.

Patience with the rhetoric of American exceptionalism when it leads to US unilateralism wore significantly thinner. The fear of being kept in a second-rate status in the political and defense fields by an overbearing American tutor is still very much alive, although it has been somewhat tempered by recent progress of the EU towards a Common European Security and Defense Policy.

The Evolution of the Format of the US-EU Relationship: Strengths and Weaknesses of the New Partnership Formula

The Transatlantic Declaration and New Transatlantic Agenda / Joint Action Plan ushered in an era of greater ambition for transatlantic co-operation and a new approach to policy-making: from then on US-EU ambitions were to be defined in a global and adjustable framework, with the involvement of a wider number of actors. These documents first innovated in terms of the regularity, frequency, degree of formality and level of the meetings between US and EU officials (reviewed below under 'New Summitry' and 'New Co-ordination Organs'). In addition, they encouraged the creation or further development of transatlantic fora, some of which were invited to participate in the definition of trans-atlantic and global governance (reviewed below under 'Formal Opening to New Categories of Public Actors' and 'Formal Opening to Private Actors'). Together with the adjustments made in the course of the implementation of the NTA, these institutional features will be compared here with the pre-1990 formula of cooperation. The innovations will then be assessed in turn. The last sub-section will consider the organizational framework as a whole: its general state of development, its nature, its strengths and weaknesses.

New Summitry

When regular summit meetings were established in the mid-1970s, the main objective was to hold one systematic 'get-together' between the US President and the head of state or government chairing the European Community. Good personal relations were generally regarded as an important facilitating factor in the US-EU partnership. These meetings were also seen as an occasion for exchanging views, gathering information, clarifying intentions and informal consultation.

The type of summitry introduced in the 1990s was supposed to carry on with these tasks. Thus, a special emphasis is still placed on socialization through US-EU summits. Such socialization was particularly important for the European Commission and, above all, for smaller EU Member States since these summits are clearly their best opportunity to have a direct and relatively exclusive access to the US President. It is less true for the heads of state or government of the largest Member States of the EU, who have more opportunities than before to socialize with the US President in a number of other small circles (contact groups…), not to mention the 'privileged' bilateral relationship enjoyed by some (UK Germany and France).

Admittedly, the development of cooperative reflexes depends on 'personal chemistry' but also is conditioned by the format of the meetings. As far as the first factor is concerned, the arrival of Bill Clinton at the White House would seem to have changed the transatlantic 'personal' atmosphere dramatically while the personality of Jacques Delors also did much to rekindle dynamism in US-EU relations. The Clinton-Santer relationship failed to spark the same chemistry, probably because of a difference in style and intellectual affinities. More recently, Romano Prodi, in line with his recent past as the prime minister of a large country, opted for a bolder approach and initiatives, which resulted in occasional controversies with the United States – for instance on the Libyan question. George W. Bush's inexperience in foreign policy and the low probability that it might quickly become one of his priorities mean that he will rely for some time on his personal advisers – some of whom like R. Zoellick are transatlantic veterans. His personality is therefore unlikely to have much immediate impact on the summits and, beyond, on the partnership as a whole. At a later stage, the rather casual and 'easy-going' style, but also the coalition-building talent displayed during his relatively short political career will, *a priori*, be an asset for the summits. If we now consider our second factor, the format of the meetings, the formality of the new summitry would appear to leave less room for the development of personal bonds (although some informality was 'officially' reintroduced at the May 2000 US-EU Summit hosted by Portugal in Queluz, with the idea of keeping some time for a 'free' discussion over a particular topic).

The consequences of the variation in personal chemistry and of the relative decline in terms of opportunity to socialize informally seem so far to have been rather limited. The process remained well lubricated throughout: no summit was ever postponed for political reasons; and not only was there no record of major incidents, but most reports insisted on the (very) positive tone of the debates. In addition, every summit ended up with joint conclusions and the announcement of a battery of new agreements and each party showed restraint in point scoring on these occasions. At first sight, this positive attitude indicates that the partnership rests on a solid basis, but also that US-EU relations are largely organized outside the men at the top.

Leaders' socialization and the exchange of views are but one of the many missions assigned to the revamped US-EU summits, and probably no longer constitute the most important one. Contrary to the pre-1990 meetings which were not meant to achieve much and indeed mostly resulted in few concrete achievements, the new format was expected to create diplomatic momentum, provide a general sense of direction, overcome deadlocks, deliver final arbitrations and, last but not least, attract higher media coverage. Yet the record for the 1995 to 2000 period has been a mixed one. The new formula managed to create a new sense of urgency: the obligation of having to deliver 'something' every six months truly kept top officials under constant pressure. The only pauses in relative terms have coincided with the peak of the US presidential electoral cycle (mid-1996 and mid-2000). Serial summitry also brought more stability, continuity and a sense of direction to the US-EU processes. It would nevertheless be exaggerated to claim that it has so far been an effective instrument in restoring political authority over bureaucratic fragmentation. In this respect, summits have so far been more of a place for formal endorsement of initiatives developed from below than the source of new initiatives. Finally, except for the London Summit of May 1998, summits resulted in few major arbitrations.[9]

The fact that so little is actually taking place at summit level seems to run counter to the well-established view that serial summitry is most suited for negotiation.[10] This should, however, come as no surprise since the US-EU format does not correspond to classical meetings of heads of government, each of whom have the power to engage their respective administrations. On the European side, the Council and the Commission presidencies indeed do not have the authority to change

---

9 The package agreed in London included, for the Europeans, the Iran/Libya Sanctions Act waiver for South Pars project and the understanding on expropriated property in Cuba, and, for the Americans, the commitment to launch a new trade expansion initiative as well as the joint statements on non-proliferation and counter-terrorism issues.

10 G.R. Berridge, *Diplomacy – Theory and Practice* (London, Prentice Hall, 1995), p.86.

orientations dramatically or to promise significant concessions. In most cases, the duo works under strict mandates given by the Council to which it has to report and obtain its endorsement. The configuration of power within the EU makes it (very) difficult for US-EU summits to produce on the spot negotiation breakthroughs. Consequently, most of the time the summits are but the place where deals already negotiated and pre-approved are publicly announced. This is nevertheless sufficient to meet their ambition to secure higher media coverage of US-EU co-operative endeavors. How much the summits succeeded in counter-balancing the negative publicity made around trade tensions is, however, difficult to say.

All in all, compared to previous schemes and to the expectations initially placed on the newly designed summitry, the record is globally positive. Yet, whereas the principle of formal serial summitry is now well-established, some rigidities in its current settings raise a number of questions, in particular with respect to its timetable and its periodicity. The US-EU summits timetable is problematic in terms of the European institutional logic. Although the frequency of the summits is more or less dictated by the existence of a six month rotation at the helm of the European Council, the timetable of the summits is in actual fact in flagrant contradiction with one of the fundamental rules of the EU presidency system. Holding the summits in December and in June means that, from a formal point of view, the outgoing EU presidency sets the priorities for the incoming one. This anomaly is certainly not a major problem, provided that the two Member States concerned have good channels of communication and that they are not at odds on the transatlantic agenda. Should it be otherwise (and this is not infrequent as Gardner shows in his chapter), it usually means a period of stagnation for the US-EU relationship or a larger opportunity for the European Commission to take the lead on the European side. The constraints of the US and EU calendars however leave little room for change as far as the summits timetable is concerned.

With regard to the periodicity of US-EU summitry, the obligation to hold two summits per year could appear excessive in a context of increasing overload of the US and EU international agendas. Considering the complexity of many issues, such an interval might in addition be deemed too short to come up systematically with substantive progress worthy of a summit and international headlines. In this respect, provided that partners manage to commit themselves to firm deadlines, the *ad hoc* formula would allow for a better management of scarce resources. A second option would be to switch to one 'fixed' summit per year, plus an optional one. It would, however, be difficult to decrease the frequency of the US-EU summits unless the rotating system for the EU presidency is reformed. As mentioned earlier, summitry remains important for the socialization of the top executives of the smaller Member States. Moreover, few Member States – small or large – are easily likely to accept being deprived of the high symbolic value of a US-EU summit during their presidency. Finally, decreasing the frequency might appear too costly for those eager to project an image of transatlantic vitality: any such move is indeed likely to be interpreted by opinion leaders as a sign of the relationship's weakening. While the possibility of postponing summits when necessary should not be overruled outright, it should be carefully weighed up.

New Coordination Organs

Before the launching of the NTA, consultations at officials' level were basically restricted to a few institutional actors: on the American side, the White House, the Department of State, the Department of Commerce and the Office of the US Trade Representative, and on the European side, the Foreign Ministry holding the EC presidency and the Directorate-General for External Relations of the European Commission. With the inclusion of officials at far lower levels, but also of many other departments and agencies, ensuring coherence and complementarity became a much tougher challenge. New coordinating and monitoring organs were therefore successively added to the US-EU institutional framework.

Established in 1995, the 'Senior Level Group' meets twice or thrice each semester either in Brussels or in Washington at sub-cabinet officials level. It is responsible for the overseeing of all US-EU relations and is therefore, from the EU viewpoint, a cross-pillar body. The group prepares a report for each summit assessing the past six months and proposing 'new priorities' for the coming six months. The fact that it usually gathers at the beginning of each EU presidency in order to identify possible 'deliverables' for the following EU-US Summit gives the Member State taking the helm of the Union a chance to have a direct input in US-EU priorities (and, by the same token, partially solve the timetable problem mentioned above). Over the years, the SLG managed to preserve a significant dose of informality, pragmatism and openness. Each side is, for instance, authorized to add any topic for discussion to the agenda. Another important element of flexibility is that sectoral agencies and administrations are requested to inform the SLG of their initiatives and actions, but do not need to obtain its formal assent to proceed.

Working-level officials help the SLG to fulfil its duties. They initially gathered in an 'NTA Task Force' which mirrored the structure of the SLG. Also created in 1995, the Task Force convened systematically before and after every SLG meeting. Made up of officials from the US mission to the EU and the European Commission's DGI, it identified areas for joint action and prepared texts for the SLG and also played a key role in implementing decisions. With the launch of the Transatlantic Economic Partnership in May 1998, both sides agreed that some refocusing of the organization of US-EU economic relations was necessary. To that effect, the TEP Joint Action Plan of November 1998 established a Steering Group which meets on an *ad hoc* basis to cover primarily trade and investment problems. From then on, the NTA Task Force was asked to concentrate on 'diplomatic, global and other problems'. In their respective domains, the Task Force and the Steering Group have a pivotal role. They identify cooperative objectives on an ongoing basis. They insure that the decisions are carried out, plan activities, set 'appropriate follow-up procedures' (for example, by assigning contact points and timelines for reporting back) and review the progress achieved. They are also entrusted with early warning and conflict prevention. For that purpose, the majority of the Task Force's agenda is made up of checking points: very few items are put on the agenda for closer debate (four per meeting); the remaining points are listed to make sure that the other side has been properly informed of new initiatives. Inasmuch as the Task Force and the Steering Group have different *chefs de file* (respectively, on the European side, the External Relations DG and the Trade DG), a set of common principles in these matters has been codified to help keep their approaches in-line (among other things, the joint statement adopted by the Bonn US-EU Summit of June 1999 defines general rules in terms of transparency, open agenda and commitment to answer any invitation to consult). Finally, the 'TEP Steering Group' receives recommendations issued by the business, labor, consumer and environment dialogues.

The addition of specific intermediary structures have obviously not answered all US-EU problems. Among various things, the imbroglio of the hush kits question is probably the best indication that we have not reached the point where all relevant information is communicated and where the level of 'de-compartimentalization' is satisfactory.[11] More generally, each side continues to see the internal decision-making processes of the other as complicated and inflexible. A more difficult problem also persists at the programming level. Global programming requires institutions capable of aggregating many divergent interests. Some centralization of the processes is often indispensable to succeed in such an endeavor. Unfortunately the new structures contributed very little in this respect. As a consequence, the objectives defined in the NTA Joint Action Plan lack proper prioritization, quantification as well as assessment of their internal consistency. Trade and investment are a partial exception in this respect. The TEP Action Plan (TEPAP) indeed addresses some of these flaws: instead of simply listing areas for dialogue, cooperation or action as in the JAP, the TEPAP includes a timetable with target dates for achieving concrete results. At the same time, by facilitating evaluation, the TEPAP runs the risk of raising public expectations to no avail, thereby increasing political costs, which is precisely what the NTA wanted to avoid. If in the NTA/JAP, trade and economic issues were mostly shrouded in technical clothing it was to make them seem less controversial and to secure a positive outcome. In the same manner, if the NTA/JAP avoided prioritization, it was for the sake of flexibility, *i.e.* to be able to secure agreement in at least one field

[11] EU coordination had been marred in particular under most of the Santer era by intra Commission conflicts and clashes between the Commission and the Member States. This was partially due to the organization of the Santer Commission along regional and thematic lines and to the difficult connections between the EU pillars. Not only were NTA Commissioner Brittan and Common Foreign Security Policy Commissioner Hans Van den Broek vying for power, but so too were the other Commissioners responsible for other parts of EU external relations. One might argue that if Leon Brittan devoted so much energy to the NTA and the NTM, it was in part to enhance his own power *vis-à-vis* the other Commissioners given the then allocation of portfolios in the Commission. Keen to prevent the recurrence of such situations, the Commission, headed by Romano Prodi, decided in 1999 to return to a single DG for 'external relations' under the authority of one Commissioner (Chris Patten), alongside one 'enlargement' DG and one 'development' DG. The same year however saw a new element of fragmentation in external responsibilities, with the inauguration of the first 'Mister PESC' (Javier Solana) at the head of the General Secretariat of the Council. On the American side, there were also various instances of turf battles and foot-dragging mainly between the White House, the US Treasury Department, the Office of the US trade representative, the State Department and the Commerce Department's Foreign Commercial Service, the Department of Justice and the Federal Trade Commission.

should it prove difficult to do so in other fields. Here the transatlantic partners would appear to find themselves in a Catch-22 situation: prioritize, increase pressure for results by making outcome assessments easier, politicize the issues and possibly disappoint the public; or not prioritize, push less for results by making outcome assessments difficult, depoliticize the issues and equally disappoint the public through low visibility and a sense of uselessness of the Action Plan exercise. The only solution of course is to make the Transatlantic Economic Partnership exercise into a success story.

The work of these coordinating organs has nevertheless improved the situation in several respects. It has clearly increased personal contact points between the EU and the US administration, made it easier to identify relevant interlocutors, enhanced the habit of contacting each other and cultivated mutual understanding – EU and US representatives often described their contacts as good or very good. If the system is still clearly short of a kind of 'one stop shop', it contributed a lot to linking one US-EU Summit more closely to the next and managed to tie the various levels of transatlantic consultations together. It provided the close monitoring instrument that the previous structures dramatically lacked.

The efficiency of the process, however, could and should be improved. On the whole, as Frellesen points out, it is very time-consuming. Both sides have been complaining about the frequency of the meetings. With two summits, four SLG meetings and six Task Force meetings on average, plus *ad hoc* meetings of the Steering Group, the number of meetings is well over twelve per year. In many cases, little progress can be achieved within a month. In this respect, US-EU relations might well have reached a state of saturation. Accordingly, these organs should perhaps best focus on their first task, coordination. Some of the other functions of the process could moreover be dealt with differently (for example, more regular updating, and making organizational charts and directories more detailed and more widely available should, in most cases, suffice to identify the relevant interlocutor). Furthermore the US and the EU sides should not hesitate to postpone or regroup their meetings when the agenda is too light. Contrary to US-EU summits, these meetings are not highly publicized. Rescheduling would therefore not damage the image of a thriving relationship.

Even in the absence of such adjustments, the organizational settings chosen for the NTA would remain a better solution than most competing formats used for the conduct of the EU's external relations. Presidential Summits, the SLG, the NTA Task Force and the TEP Steering Group are all restricted to representatives of the US administration, the European Commission and the EU presidency. This trilateral format, or rather its generalisation, clearly breaks away from the options taken by the Transatlantic Declaration. The main concern of many EU Member States at that time was to maintain a strict control over the process in general and to keep Community and foreign policy issues apart as much as possible. It was thus decided to confirm and entrench the coexistence of three additional formats in the US-EC institutional framework: the meetings between the US and all EU Member States accompanied by the Commission; the meetings between the US and the EC Presidency or the Troika; and the meetings restricted to the US and the European Commission. Several reasons, linked with effectiveness and efficiency but also political preferences and constitutional evolution, have since concurred to gain wider acceptance for the trilateral format.

Firstly, functional arguments which pleaded in favor of the trilateral format eventually prevailed thanks to the reappraisal of what is, for EU Member States, an acceptable level of control over the US-EU relationship. The participation of all is of course the most effective means for Member States to control the process, but it is also terribly cumbersome from an operational viewpoint and *in fine* paralyzing. The Troika format offered a lighter yet still very effective means of control. In a Community of nine members, it meant that a country was closely involved in running European affairs for one and half years, followed by three and half years of back bench. The probability of having an 'ally' at all times or at least a sympathetic government on the Troika was, moreover, rather high. In an Union of twenty members, each country will have to spend eight years on the back bench and, with the rise of diversity within the EU,[12] will less often find 'close' partners on the Troika. In other words, the potential of the Troika as an instrument of control over the course of European integration has sharply decreased and will continue to do so.

---

12 Éric Philippart and Monika Sie Dhian Ho, 'From Uniformity to Flexibility. The Management of Diversity and Its Impact on the EU System of Governance', in G. de Búrca and J. Scott (eds.) *Constitutional Change in the EU: From Uniformity to Flexibility* (Oxford, Hart Publishing, 2000), pp.299-336. Éric Philippart and Monika Sie Dhian Ho, *Pedalling against the Wind – Strategies to Strengthen the EU's Capacity to Act in the Context of Enlargement* (The Hague, Scientific Council for Government Policy, 2001).

Most Member States had to admit, at least implicitly, that these formula were not only becoming way too costly or disruptive, but also that their direct involvement or even that of the Troika was not indispensable to securing sufficient control over the process. Imperative mandates defined by the Council on the most sensitive issues, combined with adequate Council comitology (*i.e.* the creation of a NTA-specific working group to which the Commission must report regularly), were effective tools both in terms of output and control. Furthermore, European governments – some of which were still haunted by the scenario of a single-handed presidency espousing the views of the Commission or 'fooled' by the latter's proposals – retained auxiliary means to shape and monitor the process. The (re)establishment of parallel privileged connections with the US bureaucracy in specific areas is one option that is particularly dear to the largest Member States (in 2000 the US and the UK have, for instance, signed a Memorandum of Understanding for enhanced cooperation on consumer protection, an issue covered by the NTA). In addition to bilateral channels, instances of US-EU consultation involving all Member States have been preserved. The activity of the SLG and the NTA Task Force runs parallel with, for example, that of the Political Directors – since 1997, they even share the same work plan. Such 'institutional thickening' induced by the tendency to preserve back-up options for Member States poses, by definition, a problem of duplication. Éric Remacle has, for instance, recommended a merging of 'the SLG and Political Directors dialogue into one single structure of dialogue called SLG'.[13] Each case needs to be examined on its own merits, taking into account the problems of national endorsement and implementation of measures defined at the US-EU level. Considering that, on the whole, the actual mechanisms provide many possibilities to prevent *faits accomplis*, there should be room for further rationalization of the representation of the EU in the US-EU structures.

Secondly, the trilateral format benefited from the rather consistent backing of the US administration. This was politically more attractive for the US because the European Commission was seen as a more amenable negotiation partner (on trade liberalization for instance). Tactically speaking, as Y. Devuyst notes, this format did in addition provide the

---

[13] Éric Remacle, 'The Foreign Policy and Security Dimension of the New Transatlantic Agenda. Which Added Value of the NTA for Transatlantic Security Cooperation?', in TEPSA, *Implementation of the New Transatlantic Agenda and Future Prospects* (Brussels, Final Report, 1998).

US with an extra opportunity to pull different strings at different levels. Variable geometry, created in this instance by the coexistence of different formats of negotiation, favors *a priori* those who play at all tables.

Finally, the constitutional evolution of the EU also helped the trilateral format to prevail. The acceptability of this format is largely a function of what Member States recognize as the legitimate zone of influence of the Commission. For 'new' trade issues such as intellectual property protection, international services and investment, as well as for foreign and security policy (the EU Second Pillar) or for justice and home affairs (the EU Third Pillar), the close involvement of the Commission was long seen by several European governments as problematic. The latter suspected the Commission of wanting to capture progressively more competencies by taking advantage of its key role in the NTA, and particularly of its frequent interaction with the State Department. By strongly advocating trilateralism, the Commission probably fueled these suspicions. On the other hand, the Commission's insistence on a team approach with the Council presidency and its adoption of a lower profile on Second and Third Pillars issues, contributed to acclimatizing the Member States to this format. More importantly, the EU undertook a number of revisions of its Treaties, which reallocated several competencies in favor of the Community pillar and blurred some of the differences between the pillars. Even if tensions over the role of the Commission have not disappeared with the reforms decided in Amsterdam and in Nice, this constitutional evolution contributed to a better acceptance of a central role for the Commission, and hence of the trilateral format.

The combination of the trilateral format and a light Council comitology is now well-established. There is no expressed desire on either the American or the European side to change it at this stage. The number of policy areas and countries (among others, Canada, Japan and Russia) concerned by this format has even been increased. Although it does not conform to the dominant pattern in EU external relations, it is no longer exceptional. We could thus recommend that this format be adhered to for the coordinating organs, but that the process be further lightened by focusing on key tasks, by making rescheduling commonplace and by progressively working towards the suppression of instances of duplication. Institutional reforms would also be necessary to improve the effectiveness and efficiency of the US-EU negotiation process. The actual organization of the EU presidency is, in particular, not satisfactory. The position of the presidency and/or the Commission needs to be reinforced.

Formal Opening to New Categories of Public Actors

As mentioned earlier, the US-EC/EU interface was long restricted to traditional foreign policy and international trade bureaucracies involved in rather classical intergovernmental negotiations. While the TD merely encouraged contacts between the European Parliament and the US Congress, the NTA and the JAP invited the participation of new sections of the American and European executives and various categories of private actors. Direct contacts between governmental bureaucracies with similar remit leading to transgovernmental coalitions on particular policy questions has already been observed and studied in the 1970s.[14] The innovation here was to co-opt them officially into the US-EU general framework and to promote direct contacts on a much larger scale. This opportunity was indeed given and taken in the 1990s like never before: US-EU sectoral dialogues started between the Directorate General of the US Commercial Service and the European Commission's Directorate General for Enterprise, the Department of Education and the Education and Culture DG, or the Labor Department and the Employment and Social Affairs DG; they further expanded between services in charge of competition, safety standards, humanitarian and development aid and environment. As to the other branches of government, they were simply encouraged to develop their transatlantic contacts. For obvious reasons linked to the separation of powers, the language used was particularly cautious. The American and European executive branches acknowledged and welcomed initiatives to enhance parliamentary or court links (the Transatlantic Legislators Dialogue and the Transatlantic Court Dialogue), but stopped short of any invitation or promise of direct involvement in their policy-making exercise. The aim here is to assess the organizational development of these transgovernmental networks, the characteristics of their output and the place they acquired in terms of US-EU policy-making. On this basis, the extent to which the NTA reached its objective in terms of institution building (creating new links and opening US-EU policy-making to new sources of input) is evaluated.

---

14 Robert O. Keohane and Joseph S. Nye, *Power and Interdependence* (New York, Harper Collins, 1989, 2nd edition), pp.34-5.

Considerable differences between transatlantic executive-based networks have unfolded over the years. Some rapidly became very active and well structured, and also established themselves as rather independent from the NTA's central players. Networking among competition authorities is a good case in point. The anti-trust division of the US Justice Department headed by Joel Klein, Assistant Attorney General, the US Federal Trade Commission, chaired by Robert Pitofsky, and the Competition DG, headed by European Commissioner Mario Monti, were almost simultaneously confronted with a proliferation of big mergers. Their workload also increased because these agencies were inclined to widen their remit, up to the point of prosecuting a foreign company for alleged misconduct outside their national territory (cf. US action taken against the former Nippon Paper Company prosecuted on price-fixing charges outside the US market). Ideological proximity helped these agencies to minimize turf battles on mergers with a transatlantic dimension. They indeed share a lot in terms of core policy beliefs and political objectives. In addition to this common 'untouchable'-like ethos, there was sufficient common ground at the implementation level, in particular on the definition of an adequate timetable for dealing with anti-trust cases or remedies. Thus, pooling resources increasingly made sense. Closer cooperation on an informal and formal basis rapidly developed. A first and limited anti-trust cooperation agreement signed in 1991 was supplemented in June 1998 by a far-reaching US-EC agreement on the application of positive comity principles in the enforcement of their competition laws, pertaining to mergers, monopoly, cartel and joint venture cases. The agreement committed the parties to such things as sharing documents and information about trade conspiracies and exchanging views to avoid inconsistent remedies. The competition authorities also defined 'circumstances under which they will refer cases of anti-competitive activities to each other', the obligations of the competition authority handling these cases and the range of confidential information that could be shared. Representatives of the Federal Trade Commission were furthermore allowed to sit in on the decision-making conference of EU regulators, and vice versa. With respect to their place in US-EU policy-making, the competition authorities seem to have used the high degree of autonomy they enjoy *vis-à-vis* their domestic political system to build transatlantic solutions independently. However, this first evaluation would need to be confirmed by an in-depth study of hard cases, *i.e.* those in which a US-EU transgovernmental network did manage to impose its views, even if they were in contradiction with the general preferences of the NTA's central players. The blocked attempts of the telecom merger between World-Com and Sprint or the internet-entertainment merger between AOL, Time Warner and EMI could be revealing in this respect.

Trade or development aid sectors offer additional examples of well developed networks. Yet these exhibited less coherence. Although the political and administrative culture of their members tended to converge, they were to some extent undermined at two other levels. Functional pressures were strong but not symmetrical (on the EU side there was no equivalent to the US Congress' threat to cut the budget of the Commerce Department; although agencies on both sides had to face the consequences of the multiplication of internal and inter-state conflicts and humanitarian crises since the end of the 1980s, the European Commission's Development DG and the ECHO programme did not suffer budget cuts, contrary to the USAID). In addition, these networks seem to have been more affected by turf battles. Despite the more limited autonomy of their members, these networks managed to work rather independently in the framework of the NTA.

Many more networks remained either embryonic or very divided, and entangled in a rather classical form of intergovernmentalism, with the Senior Level Group continuing to act as the gatekeeper of the relationship. The case of the transatlantic transgovernmental network standards and certification issues is exemplary in many respects. When dealing with safety and sanitary issues, the US and EU standard-setting bodies often had different notions on what to do and how to do it. For instance, in the hormone-treated beef question, they were strongly divided over the meaning of the precautionary principle and over the boundaries of relevant scientific evidence. A second element hampering US-EU development was linked with the policy option favored by the NTA's central players. Because the uniformization or harmonization of standards is a very time-consuming option, they pleaded for a system of mutual recognition. This principle was however perceived by the sanitary agencies as a zero-sum game which would dispossess them partially of the final decision over their territorial remit. The conditions for the quick development of a strong transgovernmental network were clearly not met. After a framework for cooperation was eventually established by the US-EC Veterinary Equivalence Agreement signed in July 1999 (which recognized the equivalence of US and EC sanitary regulatory and legislative requirements), it took another year for its joint management committee to hold its first meeting. The latter only managed to discuss how to improve the exchange of technical information on these topics and which technical working groups should be established. If network build-up was not helped by the relatively large autonomy granted to these agencies – who even used it occasionally to slow down the process – it was further weakened by the inclusion of many other actors.[15] When dealing with highly politicized issues, such networks had to live with many godfathers. Their output was ultimately channeled through the NTA's central structures for arbitration.

On the whole, it appears that – as far as executive-led transgovernmental networks were concerned – strong institutional development and independent input in US-EU policy-making resulted from a combination of intense and symmetrical pressures to co-operate, a high degree of ideological proximity, limited ground for turf battles among members of the network (areas of zero-sum game) and a high degree of autonomy of the members vis-à-vis their domestic political system. If the contacts established generally contributed to the creation of new constituencies around US-EU relations, rare were the networks able to produce, and even less to impose, strong policy positions developed among themselves. Thus, few acquired a status of independent players in US-EU policy-making. Using the terminology of the Multi-Level Governance model, there are many more nested networks than interconnected ones.[16] Evidence that the NTA is heralding a new transgovernmental age is at best elusive. For now, the intergovernmental mode of governance still largely predominates. This would also seem to indicate that the changes introduced in the management of US-EU relations did not lead to a significant increase of the technocratic input in policy-making. At this level, one should speak rather of *status quo* (strong transgovernmental networks are basically restricted to policy areas already largely depoliticized domestically) or lost opportunity for the political controllers (the definition of transatlantic structures could have been an occa-

---

15 On the first meeting of the joint management committee, the US side was represented by the Department of Agriculture, the Food and Drug Administration, the State Department, the Department of Commerce and the US Trade representative office, while the EU delegation comprised officials from the European Commission, the Secretariat of the Council of Ministers and several Member States of the Union.

16 Gary Marks, Liesbet Hooghe & Kermit Blank, 'European Integration from the 1980s: State-Centric v. Multi-level Governance', *Journal of Common Market Studies*, 34:3 (1996), p.346.

sion to redefine the principal-agent relationship). But if the NTA has not created much in terms of avenues for the technocratization of new policy areas, it has probably increased the capacity of US and EU independent agencies to resist political challenges.

Transatlantic transgovernmentalism goes beyond the above-mentioned executive-to-executive developments. The legislative and judicial branches of government have indeed also established institutional links at their level. Greeted by the SLG report of December 1998 as 'the first ever judicial branch activity under the NTA', members of the US Supreme Court paid a visit to the European Court of Justice in July 1998. The objective was to initiate a series of contacts meant to encourage a dialogue on common legal problems. Various low-key activities were also envisaged. This 'Transatlantic Court Dialogue' remained embryonic and was hardly integrated into the NTA framework at all.

The contrast with the legislative branch is striking. Regular interparliamentary meetings were established in 1972, way before the adoption of the TD and the NTA. Biannual meetings – held alternatively in Europe during the first semester and in the US during the second semester – are organized by the 'Delegation for Relations with the United States' of the European Parliament and the 'International Relations Committee' of the House of Representatives of the US Congress. Although not excluded *de jure* from the scheme, the US Senate has been traditionally much less involved, a direct consequence of its relative indifference but also, according to officials, of the US House's willingness to keep this tool of parliamentary diplomacy for itself. As the EP progressively acquired more power thanks to the extension of co-decision to new policy areas, members of other Congressional committees became interested to join in. The effects of this change and of the adoption of the TD and the NTA took a long time to lead to a revision of the pre-existing institutional arrangement. It was indeed not until 1999 that the parties decided to give more structure and continuity to their dialogue. On the occasion of the 50th meeting of delegations from the EP and the US House of Representatives, a 'Transatlantic Legislative Dialogue' (TLD) was eventually launched; it established additional interfaces which allow for 'permanent co-ordination' and 'structured periodic contributions' to US-EU common work via additional meetings and videoconferences. Yet implementation was hampered not only by overstretched resources on both sides, but also by intra-parliamentary rivalries. For instance, the question of the *aegis* under which the TLD task force and permanent secretariat would operate raised problems within the European Parliament. A solution was only found recently between Elmar Brok, the chair of the 'Committee on Foreign Affairs, Human Rights, Common Security and Defense Policy', and Imelda Mary Read, the chair of the 'Delegation for Relations with the United States'. By contrast with the announced web site which is still in limbo, the first official videoconferences which target specific issues such as e-commerce or access to public documents, and which are open to all parliamentarians active in the field, started in June 2000.

On both sides, officials insist that the TLD is valued 'as an opportunity for an informal exchange of views that improves understanding and eventually policy-making.' Indeed most issues listed on the NTA and more besides were discussed during these meetings. In theory, 'parliamentary diplomacy' could conceivably go further, for instance, by adopting joint resolutions and recommendations. This is, however, not the habit of the US-EU interparliamentary meetings. A first problem is that, according to observers, many members of the delegation have specific agendas and often leave for other meetings. As a result, some discussions end up with too few representatives around the table to adopt any resolution. A more fundamental problem is that the delegations have no mandate to negotiate or commit their respective institution. The dialogue has therefore very little to offer in terms of concrete and direct contribution.

The integration of the Legislators' dialogue into the NTA organizational framework remained rather limited too. While, according to a senior EP official, 'there is no correlation between the EU-US summits and the interparliamentary meetings', contacts were nevertheless initiated in May 1999 on the margins of SLG meetings. In line with the logic set by the separation of powers, there was no question of formal consultation or deliberation. On the parliamentarians' side, these meetings were seen as an opportunity to receive an update on the state of US-EU relations prior to the summit. For the SLG, the objective was less to initiate upstream consultation or get policy advice, than to shape the opinion of key ratifiers.

These recent efforts in terms of institutional development and integration should certainly not be played down. During the 1990s, Congressional action has frequently served to muddy the transatlantic waters and contributed to rock the boat, in particular with the adoption of controversial extraterritorial legislation (such as the Helms-Burton Act and the D'Amato Act) or with the non-ratification of international conventions which are central for the construction of transatlantic and global modes of governance (such as the Kyoto protocol on climate change). Much can therefore be said in favor of educating Congress about the EU and establishing closer relations between Congress, the EP and national parliaments in EU Member States, in an attempt to avoid what John Peterson calls in his chapter 'irresponsible posturing on both sides.' Interactions with the US Senate in particular must be upscaled. The consequences of the November 2000 elections on the presidential leadership and the 107th US Congress (with a dramatic narrowing of the Republican majority in the House of Representatives and a split Senate) make such endeavors all the more necessary. It would however be naive to think that more information leads automatically to mutual understanding and smoother cooperation. The past has shown that, in specific circumstances, it even opens the doors wider for wedge politics and blockages. Greater exposure should then be seen as a necessary but insufficient condition to combat the rise of isolationist and unilateralist attitudes.

Formal Opening to Private Actors

Besides the direct involvement of technical ministries and the promotion of transgovernmental networks, the NTA/JAP marked the start of a new approach in terms of civil society participation. Commercial, social, cultural, scientific and educational ties between the USA and Europe are centuries old and among the closest ones. Worried by the possible consequences of the end of the Cold War on these ties, the TD and the NTA had as one of their main declared ambitions to foster 'an active and vibrant transatlantic community'. The solution chosen was to build more bridges across the Atlantic. Most people-to-people links initially envisaged were, however, not supposed to be directly connected to US-EU decision-making. Examples of these include educational and research projects between universities, matchmaking of small and medium-sized enterprises or exchange of information among private foundations. The sponsoring by the European Commission of the 'European Union Centres' in the US, initiated in 1998, is one of the latest initiatives to enlarge the US-EU academic constituency. Its backers hope that the ensuing increase in the number of courses, Ph.D.s and conferences on EU issues will have a positive mid-term effect on American opinion leaders. The 'Transatlantic Small Business Initiative' (TASBI), conceived in 1996, is the main instrument for trade and business alliance activity between SMEs through in-person matchmaking or business partnering events (such as an exhibition about franchising opportunities or a healthcare technologies matchmaker). Formed in 1998, the 'Transatlantic Donors Dialogue' (TADD) serves as a forum for private foundations and governmental agencies that fund US-EU people-to-people projects. Its main aim is to share information and avoid duplication in grant-making. Another bridge-building tool, the 'Transatlantic Information Exchange Service' (TIES) was established in 1998. This internet portal dedicated to the development of a transatlantic civil society provides an US-EU on-line directory of web-links about US-EU relations and information about joint US-EU projects, in particular about the activities of the transatlantic Dialogues.

In addition to this type of people-to-people links, the new scheme envisaged to further knit the Atlantic by involving interest groups in policy-making. The novelty resided less in the principle than in the terms of their involvement: structured dialogues bringing together US and EU stakeholders were officially offered joint political encouragement, financial support, formal status and direct access to the US-EU central organs. In return, they were asked to give policy advice in the form of joint recommendations on key NTA issues. Their inclusion was expected to bring extra legitimacy to the process and foster support for its output.[17]

Mirroring the analysis of the transgovernmental networks, the following paragraphs aim to assess the organizational development of the US-EU transnational networks, their policy orientations and the place they acquired in the NTA decision-making framework. The detailed analysis of the dialogues meant to have a direct input in US-EU policy-making – *i.e.* the official dialogues between business, labor, consumers and environmentalists – is preceded by a brief overview of the 'bridging' record of the NTA in general.

The formal opening of US-EU policy-making to 'structured dialogues' was progressive. 'Business' was the only interest group mentioned in the NTA. As the *de facto* monopoly of the 'Transatlantic Business Dialogue' (TABD) raised many questions about the balance of the

---

[17] Horst Krenzler, 'The Potential of the New Transatlantic Partnership: A European Perspective', in Jörg Monar (ed.) *The New Transatlantic Agenda and the Future of EU-US Relations* (London, Kluwer Law International, 1998), pp.13-18.

organizational framework, labor organizations were soon invited to develop a 'Transatlantic Labor Dialogue' (TALD). The idea of establishing additional dialogues took more time to gather pace. Although SLG reports echoed calls to co-opt other categories of stakeholders, the defining moment did not come before May 1997, with the Washington Conference on 'Bridging the Atlantic: people to people links' organized under the patronage of the European Commission and the State Department. In order to foster a 'Transatlantic Civil Society Dialogue', the conference proposed to back efforts of NGOs, foundations and associations of citizens on consumers rights, the environment, development and humanitarian aid, or social exclusion issues. The TADD or TIES, among other actions, grew out of these recommendations. One year later, the top US and EU executives renewed their support for the idea. The text founding the 'Transatlantic Economic Partnership' indeed invited 'interested non-governmental organizations to participate and extend this dialogue on consumer protection, scientific, safety and environmental issues relevant to international trade as a constructive contribution to policy-making.' The 'Transatlantic Consumers Dialogue' (TACD) and the 'Transatlantic Environment Dialogue' (TAED) were officially launched in the second half of 1998. Successive attempts to launch a 'Transatlantic Development Dialogue' (TADevD) were made in vain – December 1998 was the last time a SLG report referred to this project. Finally, further institutionalization of the dialogues came in December 1999 with the adoption by the US-EU Summit of a set of 'Principles for government relations with the Transatlantic Dialogues established under the *aegis* of the NTA'. Guarantees were given to the Dialogues at several levels: EU and US authorities committed themselves to transparency, through regular specific updates on the relevant implementation of the NTA and responses to the Dialogues' recommendations; they promised to meet with the Dialogues at least once every six months; Dialogues were guaranteed access to leaders and ministers at Summits (on a rotating basis), equal treatment and continued official support. The understanding also encouraged Dialogues to maintain open structures and to develop contacts between themselves.

The Transatlantic Business Dialogue

Of the dialogues detailed here, the Transatlantic Business Dialogue is the most developed and the most influential. A governmental desire to change the format of business cooperation on transatlantic matters presided over its inception. The main US and EU business organizations –

the US 'National Association of Manufacturers', the 'US Chamber of Commerce' and the 'Union of Industrial and Employers' Confederations of Europe' (UNICE) – had institutionalized contacts for many years. But, as M. Green Cowles recounts, their level of co-ordination on external trade and investment was deemed unsatisfactory by the US Commerce Department. The idea was therefore to approach US and EU Chief Executive Officers and ask them to develop directly a joint transatlantic trade agenda. These CEOs mobilized very effectively. Despite opposition of the existing organizations and some reservations of the European Commission (officially at least, the primary interlocutors of the Commission have traditionally been umbrella organizations such as the UNICE or sectoral associations), organizational questions were quickly solved. Although they were denied membership or veto power, the employers' associations were invited to send representatives to the TABD's main events. The Dialogues established subsequently were also kept at bay: the TABD displayed cautiousness or disinterest for the development of institutional contacts with them. As for the small and medium-sized enterprises, the latest restructuring of the TABD working groups gave them a better opportunity to express their specific views directly. Out of the five main working groups, one is consecrated to SMEs and is invited to react on the recommendations of the other groups (the group on standards and regulatory policy, on business facilitation, on global issues and on e-commerce) and their sub-structures (the 'issue groups' dealing with horizontal and/or sectoral issues). With dozens of 'issue groups', the TABD has by far reached the highest degree of institutional specialization among the transatlantic dialogues. As the release of joint recommendations on its first conference indicates, the TABD also managed to be operational almost instantly. Very rapidly, its structures became sufficiently developed to establish a sophisticated follow-up mechanism of scorecards whereby, according to the TABD 1998 Mid-Year Scorecard Report, 'each sector and issue group highlights the recent progress, current status, and expected date of implementation of their recommendations'. So, although the TABD is keen to depict itself as 'an informal process',[18] it has developed into an organization which is clearly the most structured and best endowed among transatlantic 'private' Dialogues.

---

18 TABD homepage, 'About TABD', http://www.tabd.com/index1.html.

Most recommendations of the TABD are far-reaching, precise, proactive and practical. Aiming at the establishment of a transatlantic-wide market, the safeguard of economic freedom and the creation of a level playing field insulated from political interference, they strongly embrace the neo-liberal ethos. These recommendations denote a growing ideological convergence of American and European businesses or, at least, of US and EU large and export-oriented companies that dominate the TABD.[19] While in a not so remote past it was not unusual to see such companies requesting indirectly protectionist measures, Vogel's claim is that the more stringent domestic regulations adopted over the last years have not been designed to create a competitive advantage.[20] This new convergence is perhaps best emblematized by the TABD's endorsement of regulatory cooperation on the basis of the 'one standard, one test, one time' principle. Globally speaking, the recommendations of the TABD fit neatly into the scheme outlined in the third part of the NTA ('Contributing to the expansion of world trade and closer economic cooperation') and the TEP. Its policy orientations in terms of transatlantic deregulation and negative (economic) integration are, however, closer to the positions of the US administration than to the lowest common denominator of the EU Member States.

This level of organizational development and type of recommendations facilitated the co-option of the TABD in the NTA policy-making. The TABD was associated with the drafting of the JAP attached to the NTA and the Action Plan attached to the TEP. Its representatives were invited to the US-EU Summits from the start. US and EU high-level officials met regularly with business leaders to listen and respond to them. Both governmental sides devoted a lot of attention to the TABD's recommendations and submitted to its scorecard test. While the TABD praised on different occasions the significant and concrete action taken by the US and EU administrations on its recommendations, its positive contribution was explicitly recognized in official documents such as the

---

19 The involvement of the SMEs working group did not change much to this dominance. Its requests remained in a non controversial range. At the TABD Berlin Conference of October 1999, the TABD was asked for instance to endorse recommendations for the creation of a permanent SME mechanism for addressing SME issues at the WTO level and for the reduction of the documentation for the movement of personnel.

20 David Vogel, *Barriers or Benefits? Regulation in Transatlantic Trade* (Washington D.C., Brookings Institution Press, 1997), pp.58-59.

TEP.[21] Despite the representativeness deficit induced by its exclusive CEOs-led format, the TABD remained the only NTA official interlocutor for business. Thanks to this early and close integration in the NTA framework and processes, it has probably been the most influential dialogue. Beyond the success story of this new form of 'industrial diplomacy', there were also indications that it has been instrumentalized by governmental actors for domestic purposes. An endorsement by the TABD was, in particular, seen as a way to recapture 'the bipartisan middle' while containing populist neo-isolationism in the US Congress. Consulting the TABD also served as an alibi: while some of its recommendations were taken into account, others were simply ignored by the US administration and the EU. In other words, the TABD has been used to shape domestic level support for NTA trade initiatives by 'depoliticizing' contentious issues.[22]

The Transatlantic Labor Dialogue

In many respects, the Transatlantic Labor Dialogue is at the other end of the Dialogues' spectrum. It is clearly the least developed and integrated Dialogue in US-EU relations. For labor, the launch of the NTA raised several dilemmas. Many trade unions were opposed to its core objective of further trade liberalization and globalization. Some of them saw participation as bringing to the process an uncalled-for legitimacy. Moreover, US and EU umbrella organizations – the 'American Federation of Labor and the Congress of Industrial Organizations' and the 'European Trade Union Confederation' – had limited human and financial resources. Investing at yet another level of governance would aggravate their structural overstretch, while accepting seed funds could somewhat tie their hands. Finally the AFL-CIO and the ETUC were worried that closer transatlantic cooperation could weaken wider fora, mainly the 'International Confederation of Free Trade Unions' (ICFTU) and the 'Trade Union Advisory Council' to the OECD (TUAC).

The eventual answer of organized labor to the NTA was slow and modest. Efforts of the AFL-CIO and ETUC to initiate a Transatlantic Labor Dialogue started in early 1996. At the 1997 'Bridging the Atlan-

---

21 Cf. point 15 of TEP adopted in May 1998: 'The US and EU recall the imaginative and practical approach of US and EU business in the Transatlantic Business Dialogue which has contributed directly to many of the NTA's successes.'

22 Anthony Gardner, *A New Era in US-EU Relations? The Clinton Administration and The New Transatlantic Agenda* (Aldershot, Avebury Press, 1996), p.83.

tic' Washington Conference, both organizations publicly announced the establishment of a transatlantic dialogue restricted to themselves. If representatives of the ICFTU and the TUAC were welcome to participate in the TALD meetings, there was no question of a direct opening to sectoral or industry trade unions. It meant that these meetings generally involved very few people. Despite the backing of the US Labor Department and the European Commission's DG for Employment and Social Affairs, it was not until April 1998 that substantive issues were tackled in the new transatlantic format. The AFL-CIO and the ETUC invested little resources in the Dialogue: they meet on an *ad hoc* basis and have not developed a specialized structure of working groups similar to those set up by the other Dialogues. The frequency of their meetings has been kept at a low level. If both sides announced their intention to monitor the NTA's development jointly, no instrument comparable to the report card system has yet been established and there is very little evidence of systematic NTA review either. As for the TALD summits (not more than one per year so far), they were held on the fringes of other labor gatherings such as the TUAC conferences. Finally, besides occasional press releases, very little publicity has been given to these activities: there is barely any mention of the TALD on the AFL-CIO or the ETUC websites (for instance, the ETUC press reports referred only once to US-EU summits, in December 1998); no information has been posted on TIES.

The TALD's recommendations are rather general and often defensive or reactive. Not surprisingly, they focused more on international than transatlantic issues: their main concern is with the side-effects of globalization, *i.e.* the larger exposure to social dumping, delocalization and the domino effect of financial speculation. The TALD's April 1998 London summit spoke of the definition of international core labor standards, basic trade union rights, solidarity with third country workers, the inclusion of labor issues on the WTO's agenda or the danger of the 'Multilateral Agreement on Investment'. If the AFL-CIO and the ETUC advocated the widening of the US-EU agenda, they did not reject transatlantic trade liberalization *per se.* In their statement on core labor standards of December 1998, they explicitly supported 'the deepening of US-EU relations which the agreement on the Transatlantic Economic Partnership represents.' At this level, they recommended in particular an upwards harmonization of labour rights, worker protection, health and safety standards. No detailed propositions followed, an indication perhaps of the low priority given to this objective. The much less consensual labor market regulation and industrial relations (judging from the slow pace of EU harmonization on these matters) were left aside.

The role played by the TALD in US-EU policy-making remained very limited. It could be argued that this is the result of the small space offered to Labor. Undeniably, the trade unions were formally invited relatively early on to take an active role under the NTA and their April 1998 contribution was described by the TEP as 'helpful'. But, *de facto*, many governmental actors saw their involvement as dispensable, if not counter-productive, for the pursuit of the transatlantic agenda's main objectives. The crux of the matter lay, however, with the TALD itself. A dialogue restricted to few meetings between a small number of participants with a narrow mandate is barely the kind of settings from which to expect strong initiatives and sustained momentum. The weak presence of labor umbrella organizations was the expression of their lack of interest for the transatlantic level of governance (as underlined again by the 1999 TALD's decision to decline the invitation to participate in US-EU bi-annual summits on a rotation basis). What matters most when pursuing mainly defensive objectives is to be able to veto decisions. Insofar as this veto can be more effectively and efficiently secured at domestic level, where they have a better grip on the processes, or at multilateral level, where they have more allies (WTO), it therefore made sense that the trade unions attach little importance to the NTA framework.

Transatlantic Consumers Dialogue

Consumer associations, for their part, began to mobilize for a dialogue quite early on, but the project was slow to get off the ground. Once launched, the Transatlantic Consumers Dialogue combined a high level of participation with a relatively high degree of institutional development. Its integration in the new organizational framework suffered from the fact that it was not equally welcomed by the negotiators. The TACD nevertheless succeeded to carve out a place for itself, this largely because US consumer groups and the European Commission found that it was a useful instrument to put pressure on the US administration.

If a large part of the agenda and expertise of consumer associations is domestically and locally oriented, there is also a long-established tradition of international and regional mobilization. A successor of the 'International Organization of Consumer Unions' founded in 1960, the London-based 'Consumers International' federates organizations in almost 120 countries. At the European level, the 'Bureau européen des Unions de Consommateurs' (that is the European Consumers' Organization or BEUC), set up in Brussels in 1962 and currently linking twenty-nine independent national consumer organizations from twenty European countries, is one of the main federations protecting and promoting consumer interests in the region. As early as 1995, these associations started mustering support for a transatlantic consumer dialogue. Yet their views on the Dialogue's future format diverged substantially. As most European NGOs were accustomed to neo-corporatist systems, the EU side had little problem with widely opening the dialogue to officials and accepting public funding. After all, this was in line with their experience in the 'Consumer Committee', a consultative body initiated by the European Commission to officially advise its Health and Consumer Protection Directorate-General on all problems in the field of consumer protection, either at the request of the Commission or on the Committee's own initiative. Predictably, the Commission was the first to endorse the idea and propose seed funds. Several major US NGOs had strong reservations both in terms of opening and funding. They were keen to stay closer to the American pluralist model which puts more distance between the administration and the representatives of the stakeholders, but which offers a better protection of the latter's independence.

These differences were reflected in the greater European contribution in terms of seed funds (a mere 30% was provided by the US administration) and the larger number of European NGOs participating in the eventual launch of the TACD in September 1998. Interestingly enough, where the TABD has two chairs and the TAED two coordinators, the founding members decided to appoint only one coordinator for the Dialogue, the already mentioned 'Consumers International'. This decision should be interpreted as being driven by efficiency concerns rather than as the expression of a unified transatlantic community at consumer level. Considering that most American and European NGOs were already members of that international organization, locating the dialogue's secretariat within its 'Programs for Developed Economies' was indeed a way of avoiding institutional duplication and of benefiting from economies of scale. Whatever the reason, it allowed for the development of a more coherent meta-network, which involved no less than sixty major consumer organizations in the US and the EU. The TACD followed the example of the TABD by setting up working groups as well as by issuing recommendations and (simplified) report cards. With three working groups covering food-related issues, electronic commerce and general trade and economics issues, its structure remained, however, comparatively less developed and specialized than the TABD and the TAED.

Despite divisions among consumer NGOs about the pros and cons of globalization, trade liberalization and free trade areas, the Transatlantic Consumer Dialogue was unanimous on its second meeting (April 1999) in adopting about twenty recommendations on higher standards for consumer protection in a wide array of sectors. The objectives of the TACD were clear-cut and independent (insofar as they spared no side). Recommendations on food safety were particularly radical with, for instance, demands for the institution of 'a total ban on the non medical use of antibiotics in animal and food production' as well as the prohibition of the use of the bovine growth hormone. The TACD also targeted drug and product standards or biotechnology, together with various trade issues linked to public procurement or fair trade labeling. Proposals on electronic commerce were perhaps more modest, with the possible exception of the protection of data privacy and the possibility for the consumer to have recourse to the laws and courts of his home country.

Having been completely excluded from the drafting of the action plans attached to the NTA and the TEP, consumer associations came to the conclusion that the best option to counterbalance business interests was to gain equal status with the TABD. They began by vigorously denouncing discriminations in the NTA's institutional format. One particularly sensitive point was the access to US-EU summiteers. From December 1998 onwards, the TACD, together with the TAED, asked for equal treatment. Expectations rose with the German presidency of the EU. Not only was the German government a red-green coalition, but the foreign ministry was for the first time headed by a green politician, Joschka Fischer. Paradoxically, this contributed to raising tensions. The TACD and the TAED were indeed all the more incensed by the failure of the German presidency even to respond to their written requests to be invited to the Bonn Summit in June 1999 (even though this silence was apparently less a political statement than the result of an organizational problem). In a bitter press release, both Dialogues accused US and EU governments of 'favouritism towards business interests'.[23] Equal treatment was eventually instituted a few months later. The TACD showed afterward that, from its viewpoint, the right to participate mattered more than being systematically involved in every transatlantic discussion: after sending representatives to the Washington US-EU Summit in December 1999, the TACD indeed decided to opt out of the Queluz Summit.

Governmental responsiveness to the TACD was rather contrasted. The European Commission often found NGOs to be natural allies in overcoming divisions among EU Member States. Co-opting them into the decision-making process has long been part of its administrative culture. Just as it endorsed the participation of consumer NGOs in view of the WTO Millenium Round and in the working procedure of the *Codex Alimentarius*, the European Commission (at the instigation of its Health and Consumers Protection DG) gave its strong backing to the equal access of the TACD to the Administrations on both sides. Insofar as the position of consumer NGOs on various transatlantic disputes were close to the EU's official stance, it was indeed interesting to involve them in order to put extra-pressure on the US administration. More concretely, the European Commission took the time to respond to the TACD recommendations by establishing a written inventory of what it was doing, as well as of the positions and agendas of its different services on each issue. Seemingly, on occasion, NGOs did receive verbal briefings 'frankly' exposing the nature of the problems and blockages. In the two-level game terminology, the European Commission sought to shape the transatlantic negotiation by resorting to 'reverberation' and by directly targeting the other side's domestic constituencies.

The US governmental side was much more divided on the question of civil society involvement beyond business representatives. Accustomed to fostering accountability and public participation via the administrative procedure of notice and comment rulemaking,[24] many were not comfortable with the idea of institutionalized upstream consultation. The TACD was generally frustrated by the quality of the con-

---

23 TACD & TAED, 'EU-US Summit Rejects Environment and Consumer Groups Participation, Invites Business Representatives', Press Release, 18 June 1999.

24 Francesca Bignami, *The Administrative State in a Separation of Powers Constitution: Lessons for European Community Rulemaking from the United States* (Harvard Jean Monnet Working Paper No.5/99, http://www.law.harvard.edu/programs/JeanMonnet/papers/99/990501.html).

sultative process on that side of the Atlantic. Tellingly enough, the TACD's request for an inventory similar to that of the European Commission was turned down as too difficult considering the number of governmental actors involved in consumer matters and the absence of an official position on several issues (it must however be added that, according to practitioners, US official delegations coming to the EU often go to talk directly to European NGOs, whereas Commission's delegations have usually no contact or only indirect contact with US NGOs). The frustration borne out of the little consideration apparently given to the TACD's recommendations was even higher. Quoting Lori Wallach of 'Public Citizen's Global Trade Watch', the press note released with the May 2000 TACD's Annual Report underlined that 'when you look at all the consumer dialogue recommendations, it is hard to point to one that the US government has fully embraced'. In conclusion, consumers' representatives backed by the European Commission formally gained a direct and equal institutional access to the NTA, but the US governmental practice hampered the balancing of stakeholders' influence. US consumer associations came to see the European Commission as a lever in their transatlantic and domestic fight against the pro-business bias of the US administration. If the TACD was to some extent instrumentalized by the European Commission, it instrumentalized the latter in return.

Transatlantic Environment Dialogue

Slow to come to fruition, the Transatlantic Environment Dialogue has at long last attracted many important NGOs. Very vocal and proactive since its inception, it managed to take a substantial place in the NTA organizational framework. In its development, recommendations and integration into the NTA's structures, the TAED presents many similarities with the TACD.

Officials of specialized agencies and NGOs became progressively alarmed by the strong pro-business bias of the NTA and, more particularly, by the possible ensuing disregard for the environmental dimension in the negotiation of Mutual Recognition Agreements. With the completion of the MRA negotiations during the first semester of 1997, discussions over the establishment of a TAED gathered momentum. On the European side, things moved faster. The European Commission was ready to provide funds for the Dialogue and the NGOs were willing to accept them. The 'European Environmental Bureau', a federation of NGOs which has consultative status at the European Commission, played an instrumental role at that stage. The EEB is the current European coordinator of the TAED. On the American side, things were more complicated because of the greater reluctance to rely on public funding for reasons already exposed in the analysis of the TALD and the TACD. The private money collected was eventually supplemented by a public grant of the Clinton administration to the National Wildlife Federation, one of the four organizations represented on the TAED's US steering committee. Organizational and ideological difficulties were substantial. Indeed, it was not before December 1998 that twenty-three major US and EU environmentalist organizations assembled in Brussels to lay the foundations of the Dialogue and the TAED was only officially established in May 1999.

From then on, the NGOs' mobilization was impressive. By 2000, the TAED had more than 100 members (45 US NGOs and 57 European NGOs, including organizations from some candidate Member States). As with the TABD and the TACD, it held two plenary meetings per year and set up specialized working groups (on climate protection, biodiversity, trade and environment, food and agriculture, and industry). Building on the text adopted ahead of the December 1998 US-EU Summit, the TAED managed to produce its first recommendations by consensus in its May 1999 inaugural meeting. In addition, it established in a follow-up mechanism (each member of the TAED is asked to grade the US and EU efforts) and released in 2000 a first comprehensive 'scorecard' evaluating governmental responses to its various recommendations. All in all, considering the limited resources available, the Dialogue has been properly structured and functioned reasonably well – even if, as of 2000, the US side had no general coordinator and no coordinator for the biodiversity working group.

Like the TACD but perhaps one tone higher, the TAED made clear from the start that it did not intend to legitimize the contents of the NTA or the TEP initiative. Its main policy aim was to correct an excessive focus of the NTA on trade liberalization issues. Keen to demonstrate that its agenda was independent from and broader than US and EU official schemes, the TAED called for a moratorium on the TEP action plan and warned against harmonization and mutual recognition on the basis of the lowest common denominator in terms of environmental, health and social standards. Its (radical) recommendations were not all reactive: for instance, steps were also proposed to secure environmentally sustainable development.

In line with the policy orientations exposed above, the TAED strove to be fully integrated into the NTA structures. The demand to have access on an equal basis to the US-EU summits is one of the clearest manifestations of its *entrisme*. Although realistic in their appraisal such 'brief encounters' with summit leaders (one of the participants of the May 2000 Queluz Summit described them as 'symbolical' occasions to present directly the TAED's priorities and viewpoints), the leaders of the TAED fully embraced the opportunity – whereas the TALD opted out permanently and the TACD opted in only occasionally. Besides organizing the timetable of its main activities according to the US-EU Summits, the TAED was also very eager to involve high-ranking officials in its plenary sessions – and not only from the Office of International Activities of the US 'Environmental Protection Agency', the 'European Environment Agency' and the Environment DG. In addition, environmentalists took the initiative of *ad hoc* multi-dialogues meetings. Following the example of multi-stakeholder activities set by 'European Partners for the Environment', a first informal meeting of the NTA Dialogues was held in June 2000 in Lisbon, where representatives of the TABD, TACD, TADD, TAED, TLD and TIES discussed together the problems of sustainable development.

On the governmental side, the arrival of environmentalist NGOs was not unanimously welcomed. Many central players saw this as a perturbing factor, an impression which was reinforced by the non-consensual, not to say disruptive, approach adopted by the TAED. In its 2000 report card, the highest score awarded to governmental efforts was C+ (*i.e.* adequate performance) of which there were very few. Because of a greater policy overlap, the European side was in a better position to try to instrumentalize the TAED in NTA negotiations (out of sixteen issues reviewed in the report card, the EU obtained a better score than the US eight times, the US scored highest five times, the US and the EU scored even three times). The TAED not only resisted such attempts, but even tried to instrumentalize the EU to put the US administration under pressure on environmental issues not related to trade matters or transborder pollution.

The Transatlantic Development Dialogue

In 1997, the creation of a fifth Dialogue was envisaged which would bring together NGOs and make recommendations on official development aid and technical assistance programs in third world countries. 'InterAction' – the American Council for Voluntary International

Action – and the 'Liaison Committee of Development NGOs to the EU' (that is to say the representative structure of European external cooperation and international solidarity NGOs with respect to the Directorate General for Development of the European Commission) were designated to lead the way. During the autumn of 1998, some discussions were held between an InterAction representative, the head of the Liaison Committee, James Mackie, and a representative of the European Commission. While everyone seemed to endorse the idea of extending the US-EU dialogue from the executive level down to the NGOs, the Transatlantic Development Dialogue never took off. In the meantime, InterAction managed to launch another project using a very similar rhetoric and rationale: the 'US-Japan Common Agenda Public-Private Partnership' (P3). Supported by the US Agency for International Development (USAID), the US Department of State, Japanese official agencies and Japanese foundations, it aims at 'building bridges between the United States and Japan to support global development and sustainability', this by increasing collaboration with Japanese NGOs.

As far as the mobilization of US and EU advocacy coalitions is concerned, this episode showed that, for many of them, contributing to building an Atlantic Community is not in itself appealing enough to invest in new structures. It demonstrated that there is no interest either for a dialogue if the cooperation goals are not sufficiently specific and the benefits sufficiently direct – especially in the case of NGOs already enjoying privileged access to domestic decision-makers, the USAID and the European Commission. The Americano-Japanese counter-example indicated that grants from public and private foundations can act as an alternative mobilization stimulus. The effectiveness of this stimulus varies, however, with the average size of the NGOs in the sector. Many development NGOs are no longer pure advocacy coalitions. Since states subcontract a very large part of the implementation of their development policy, many NGOs have indeed turned themselves into professional organizations providing various services. That explains why they are relatively indifferent to a level of seed funds which was appealing enough for the consumer or environmental sectors where the main organizations remain on average still much smaller. The failure of the TADevD also confirmed the difference in US and EU institutional approaches to the NTA, the European side proving more open to NGOs involvement and ready to suscitate or fund it directly. Here again, the reflex of the European Commission was to build on its 'comitology' to develop new dialogues and to try to replicate at transatlantic level the structures it has developed at the EU level – characteristic of the toolbox approach.[25]

General Evaluation of the New Format

This last sub-section evaluates the organizational framework as a whole, its general state of development, its nature, its strengths and weaknesses. On the first issue, it could be said that, compared to the pre-1990s formula of cooperation, US-EU relations underwent a very substantial development in terms of structure and processes. The main institutional features of the framework are now well established. The opening of the NTA framework went much further than initially envisaged. Together with various incremental changes, this contributed to a thickening process of US-EU institutions – new elements being added rather than replacing existing ones. In this respect, the problem of underinstitutionalization mentioned by Joseph Nye is odd.[26] It might even be considered that the relationship reached a level of overinstitutionalization or should at least beware of going further in some directions – as Smith's chapter or Hindley's article on the Transatlantic Market Place and the TAFTA treaty option suggest.[27]

As to the nature of the new mode of US-EU governance, it appears that traditional players have retained a central role. Timetables and agendas are largely 'summit-driven', and the framework is still dominated by inter-governmental structures controlled by foreign policy and international trade officials circles. There is at this level no indication of hegemonic bias: the US and the EU are strictly on an equal footing. Furthermore the partnership formula respects the principle of the autonomy of the EU's development. Having more to do with cooperation than with integration, the scheme does not presuppose any pooling or transfer of sovereignty. In other words, it does not amount to a seat at the EU table for the US.

---

25 On programming routines and the tendency of decision-makers to apply the favorite methods irrespective of the nature of a policy problem, see Carl V. Patton and David S. Sawicki, *Basic Methods of Policy Analysis and Planning* (Englewood Cliffs, Prentice Hall, 1993), p.11.

26 Joseph S. Jr Nye, 'The US and Europe: Continental Drift?', *International Affairs*, 76:1 (2000) 51-59, p.55.

27 Brian Hindley, 'New Institutions for Transatlantic Trade?', *International Affairs*, 75:3 (1999), pp.45-60.

This being said, the US-EU governance no longer fits into the mould of a strict two-level game. It is nowadays organized in a 'hub and spokes' manner. Intergovernmental sub-structures are at the center of a wide range of transgovernmental and transnational networks with whom they interact bilaterally. Transgovernmental networks have been established in large numbers. Compared with the expectations of the post-modern rhetoric, their level of 'nestedness' remained, however, surprisingly low – their members continued to report to their central governments and/or to the intergovernmental substructures. These changes therefore have not led as yet to a significant increase of the technocratic input in US-EU policy-making, nor to the 'unbundling' of states into separate and functionally distinct parts announced by Anne-Marie Slaughter.[28] Action was even taken to re-politicize some policy areas, with the striking exception of foreign and security policies. Governmental players had very different views on the nature and scope of the further involvement of civil societies. Their differences were not insurmountable and private actors were successively invited to establish transnational networks. These so-called 'structured dialogues' were then given direct access to decision-makers. The opening of the NTA organizational framework was however selective, governmental actors displaying a tendency to co-opt actors from whom they expected some help in the negotiation. Several networks not only refused to be confined to such a role, but moreover tried to instrumentalize one governmental side against the other in the pursuit of domestic objectives. The new participatory dynamics did not push the logic of 'networks of networks' or 'meta-networking' to its ultimate expression.[29] Projects of formal and systematic dialogue between the Dialogues indeed met with the skepticism or the reluctance of too many public and private players. Globally, the Dialogues as they stand today seem to have changed the pattern of intergovernmental negotiations.

Does the formula reviewed in this section constitute a progress for US-EU policy-making? Although some institutional innovations have been introduced only recently and are therefore difficult to evaluate, the record is globally positive. The combination of serial summitry, specific coordinating organs, trilateral format, and co-option of new categories

---

28 Anne-Marie Slaughter, 'The Real New World Order', *Foreign Affairs*, 76:5 (1997), pp.183-97.

29 Wolfgang H. Reinicke, 'The Other World Wide Web: Global Public Policy Networks', *Foreign Policy*, 117 (1999), p.44.

of public and private actors significantly increased the level of US-EU socialization, awareness of the other side's views and mutual understanding. It created the conditions for sustained momentum and more continuity in the policy process. EU-US relations, in spite of trade disputes and occasional manifestations of self-centredness or unilateralism, are on a relatively stable course. Early warning systems and conflict resolution mechanisms have also been improved over the years, as well as co-ordination and follow-up mechanisms (taking into consideration the extra-complexity introduced in the system by the increase in the number of items and players). On the down side, agenda-shaping and agenda-setting mechanisms became more diffuse and complex, while the US-EU programming capacity remained unsatisfactory. Beneath the claim of a global framework, parallel tracks endured and elements of institutional specialization were even re-introduced, in particular with the TEP Steering Group. In addition, various efficiency and visibility problems demand additional adjustments.

Evolution of the Tensions between Transatlantic Partners and Their 'Containment' Strategies

Let us now examine the continuities and discontinuities in terms of tensions, and of American and EU tactics to hold the other party in check. With respect to the latest evolution of the tensions or conflicts, one important general remark should be made: none of the US-EU tensions and frictions originated from threats to 'vital or important interests' of one of the partners.[30] While tensions over monetary issues receded, trade remained the most visible source of tensions. Although still charged with high symbolism, the economic importance of disputes over agriculture subsided.[31] From this point of view, the successive waves of mergers and consolidation in mature sectors, on the one hand, and the definition of rules for the so-called new economy (telecommuni-

---

[30] Robert D. Blackwill, *The Future of Transatlantic Relations* (New York, Council on Foreign Relations, 1999).

[31] In 1999, the Dispute Settlement Body of the WTO authorized US retaliatory tariffs amounting to $ 191.4 and 116.8 million a year against the EU, to compensate for the damage caused respectively by the 1993 EC bananas import regime and by the European ban on imports of hormone-treated beef. Compared to the 1998 trade figures, the combined penalties only amount to 0.09% of total US-EU trade ($325.4 billion) and 0.17% of EU exports to the US ($176.4 billion). Even in terms of the US-EU trade in agricultural products, it amounts to slightly more than 1.7%.

cations, information technology, bio-technology etc.), on the other hand, became the biggest issues. In the field of foreign affairs, the criticism of the other partner's foreign policy has remained a clear and distinctive feature of the relationship. There were significant tensions, in particular with regard to the definition and treatment of rogue states.[32] But these are largely dwarfed when compared with the tensions of the Reagan era. Finally, as the Peterson and Ginsberg chapters show, recent European efforts in the defense field somewhat marred the transatlantic relationship. Indeed, American reactions to the incipient steps in creating a Common European Security and Defence Policy (CESDP) in the wake of the December 1998 Franco-British joint statement of St. Malo, go a long way towards unveiling the ambiguity of the position of the US vis-à-vis a European Union that would cease to be chiefly a civilian power by acquiring a military dimension. The European Councils of 1999 and 2000 fleshed out the St. Malo declaration, partially in ways that added to US concerns about the three 'D's (decoupling of EU decision-making from broader alliance decision-making, duplication of defense resources, discrimination against non-EU NATO members). At Cologne in June 1999 in particular, the French had been toying with the idea of using the new force for (really) autonomous actions. At the same time, developments such as those made in 2000 for the improvement of EU military crisis management capability and the creation of a European Rapid Reaction Force opened up prospects for strengthening the Alliance by enhancing the efficiency of its European military component, a long sought US objective.

If we now consider attempts by either side to control one another, there is, besides positive engagement through partnership proposals, strong evidence that the American side still resorts to Atlantic and multilateral frameworks such as NATO, the OECD, the OSCE or the WTO to hold its transatlantic partner in check. Similarly, the EU has not shied from using such frameworks to similar ends, notably by launching a number of complaints to the appellate body of the WTO. In addition, as during the Nixon administration, the US has displayed a distinct temptation to use divide and rule tactics by instrumentalizing bilateral relations with several EU Member States to control or altogether circumvent the EC/EU framework. A case in point is the open skies agreements dossier. As Y. Devuyst argues in this book, the Clinton administration,

32 Richard N. Haass (ed.), *Transatlantic Tensions – The United States, Europe, and Problem Countries* (Washington D.C., Brookings Institution Press, 1999).

taking advantage of the Member States' reluctance to transfer air services negotiations to the Commission, encouraged them to negotiate bilaterally with the US, thereby undermining the Commission's proposal to foster a united European stance in aviation diplomacy.[33]

Combined use of these tactics also persisted, in particular in defense and security matters. NATO was initially seen as the best tool to frame the development of a European identity in these fields. The main US objective was therefore to hold the European side in check by making sure that the Atlantic Organization would remain involved in any major European-led operation. If the acceptance in 1996 of the concept of 'Combined Joint Task Forces' was a major concession of the Clinton administration, lending NATO forces and equipment to WEU operations was also an efficient means to prolong (comfortable) European dependency in a number of areas.

When the potentially more hazardous project of a Common Security and Defense Policy was put on the table, the US administration multiplied bilateral warnings and pressures on several EU Member States. In order to calm American misgivings, the Helsinki European Council of December 1999 responded by stating that the new force would be used 'where NATO as a whole is not engaged', in other words, as Anne Deighton has pointed out, 'after the Americans had been given the chance to participate'.[34] A couple of days later, the North Atlantic Council ministerial meeting said explicitly that the future EU policy 'does not imply the creation of a European army'. Yet this did not succeed in assuaging American apprehensions. Just prior to the Feira European Council, US Ambassador to NATO Alexander Vershbow once more expressed the fear of a European force that would act (too) autonomously. In his efforts to prevent such an evolution, he chose to state the case for and against a European Security and Defense Policy (ESDP) in terms of the *finalités politiques* of the Union and the importance of the transatlantic link, *i.e.* in a (rather Manichaean) way likely to exacerbate intra-EU cleavages:

---

33 In May 2000, Portugal was the tenth EU Member State to sign a bilateral agreement with the US. While supporting the European Commission proposal for a 'Transatlantic Common Aviation Area' in principle, Portugal wanted to ensure that its bilateral rights would be 'grandfathered' in the negotiation of this TCAA.

34 Anne Deighton, 'Militarising the European Union', University of Quebec at Montreal, CEPES, Research Paper No.15, 2000, p.7.

> Europeans need to think about the reasons why ESDP is important to them. Is ESDP primarily a political exercise, the latest stage in the process of European construction, or is ESDP's main goal to solve real-world security problems in Europe? If ESDP is mostly about European construction, then it will focus more on institution-building than on building new capabilities, and there will be a tendency to oppose the 'interference' of NATO and to minimize the participation of non-EU Allies. The danger here is that, if autonomy becomes an end in itself, ESDP will be an ineffective tool for managing crises, and transatlantic tensions will increase.[35]

For him, the alternative to this was to find practical solutions between NATO and the EU to solve European security problems, with ESDP a means to that end. Emphatically, he went on to describe this option as the path to 'a beautiful 21st century marriage'. On the key point of the links with the EU permanent military structures, Ambassador Vershbow suggested that 'NATO and US representatives meet in the same room together on crisis management.' Here again the desire of the United States to get a seat at the EU table, thereby ensuring that the 'Atlantic collateral' of American support of European unification remains alive and kicking, was all too plain.

All in all, from the evolution in terms of mutual perceptions, formula of cooperation, tensions and containment tactics, it appears that the US is now more inclined to acknowledge that the EU has certain global interests. In contrast with previous American attempts to minimize the importance of the EC as a global power and to demote it to the role of a regional power, the US official line of the 1990s is to recognize that the EU can no longer be confined to a regional straightjacket. As we have seen, this recognition is tinged with a strong burden-sharing element. Coupled with this recognition of global power status, is the (partial) acceptance by the American side of a lesser degree of transatlantic integration and a greater degree of European autonomy, including in the defense field, although in this last case with the transatlantic collateral appearing under the guise of a marriage proposal. No decoupling thus.

---

[35] WEU Institute for Security Studies, Transatlantic Forum, Paris, 'European Defense: European and American Perceptions', remarks by Ambassador Alexander Vershbow, US Permanent Representative on the North Atlantic Council, http://www/useu.be/ISSES/Vers0518.html.

CONCLUSION

Deeds not Words? Evaluating and Explaining the US-EU Policy Output[1]

Éric PHILIPPART and Pascaline WINAND

Fonds National de la Recherche Scientifique (Belgium),
Université Libre de Bruxelles,
College of Europe (Bruges)

This concluding chapter deals with the policy outcomes of the relationship, especially in the post-NTA era. It endeavors to assess and explain what has been decided in terms of level of cooperation, while evaluating the decision-making performance of the system. Two tables provide a survey of the partnership's output until 1998. They are supplemented by a qualitative assessment that runs up to the year 2000. By comparing the intensity of the objectives and achievements of the New Transatlantic Agenda, the tables indicate stagnant or vibrant areas of cooperation, and timid or far-reaching developments. We have highlighted some of the most interesting cases and suggested the most plausible links with the explanations offered in chapter two. Building on the assessments provided by chapter 13 and the first two sections of this chapter, we then venture on to examine briefly the future prospects of the US-EU partnership.

A General Assessment of the Post-NTA Policy Output

Since, according to Jacques Santer, the ambition of the NTA/JAP exercise was to move from 'policies of consultation' to 'the policies of joint action' and to 'a more practical action-oriented approach based on

1 Éric Philippart is the principal author of this chapter. Special thanks are due to Jean-Louis Migeot for his precious contribution in the configuration of the database which analyses the SLG reports.

deeds not words'[2], the aim here is to assess and explain the policy outcomes of the relationship. Owing to the scope of the NTA – around 200 issues if one takes into account the priorities added since 1995 – what follows is necessarily very synthetic and often preliminary. The assessment and explanation of the transatlantic output, as well as the evaluation of the decision-making performance of the US-EU system will be further developed in the next step of this research project.

To assess the results of US-EU cooperation is a difficult task. Studying the progress made over several years on each and every item of the agenda constitutes a formidable workload. An efficient way to obtain a first approximation was to compare the objectives set by the Joint Action Plan attached to the New Transatlantic Agenda with the reports of the Senior Level Group assessing US-EU achievements and setting priorities every six months. The comparison, however, had to be reasonably detailed and systematic. For that reason, we needed more than the general assessment offered in the third section of chapter one.

The first step was therefore to distill the diplomatic language contained in the JAP into a classification of eight types of action or levels of commitment ranging from 1 (lowest) to 8 (highest): (1) statements of US and EU individual commitments; (2) information – exchange of information and/or information gathering; (3) dialogue; (4) consultation; (5) common encouragement and support for third parties' initiatives; (6) co-ordination of initiatives, positions – in particular in multilateral fora – and actions; (7) cooperation – including identification of means of cooperation; (8) joint action. Each action envisaged by the JAP was then measured against this scale. Listed in Table 1 according to the structure adopted by the JAP, these measures give a comprehensive picture of the partnership's initial ambitions and expectations, sufficiently detailed and systematic as to provide an adequate point of reference for our assessment. From there, we measured the fluctuations in US-EU ambitions and the pace of implementation by applying the same scale to the new priorities and intermediary achievements listed in the successive SLG biannual reports (because of resources constraints, our calculations were restricted to the 1995-1998 period). Finally, since our main aim is to take stock of the progress of the partnership, the NTA's cumulated objectives and cumulated achievements have been compared

2 Jacques Santer, 'Speech at the Transatlantic Policy Network (TPN)', Brussels, 30 November 1995.

in Table 2. This table, combined with the discursive use of subsequent SLG reports up to May 2000, allows a clear delineation of dormant and active parts of the NTA, as well as areas of under and overachievement.

This approach, however, has several shortcomings and is vulnerable to various biases. These have been discussed in chapter two and are only summarized here. First of all, the analysis has to rely on official documents drafted by actors who have a direct stake in the assessment. One could therefore imagine, for example, the SLG adjusting the NTA objectives because political reasons demand that the US-EU record be embellished.[3] Secondly, the quantitative assessment is based on a partial account of US-EU accomplishments – the SLG reports are indeed only concerned with 'major achievements'. Moreover, insofar as the reports give no criteria regarding what is 'major' or not, the selection could be easily affected by the subjectivity of the SLG.[4] Thirdly, the reports establish no hierarchy reflecting the relative importance or scope of the various NTA targets.[5] For these various reasons, the quantitative measures presented in the following tables and graphs had to be verified and supplemented by a qualitative assessment of the transatlantic key sectors, based *inter alia* on the previous chapters.

---

3 The graphs 1 to 3 show fluctuations which could be interpreted in such a way. The SLG started by revising ambitions upwards, with an all-time high in December 1996. This optimism was however not borne by concrete results, the achievements for Part I (Promoting Peace and Stability) and Part II (Responding to Global Challenges) continuing to lag significantly behind objectives. In May 1997, a decision was taken to revise the objectives downwards. This contributed to secure positive report cards.

4 For instance, whereas no achievement in demining cooperation was recorded by SLG reports, Frellesen's assessment includes three cooperative projects presented by the US and the European Commission at the Washington Conference on Global Humanitarian Demining on 20-22 May 1998. A complete examination of events vindicates the choice of the SLG (American and European opinions strongly diverge indeed over the main development of the 1990s, that is, the Ottawa Convention on anti-personnel landmines). The judgement of the SLG was, however, sometimes more questionable. For example, the December 1999 report considered it a major achievement that the parties 'have frankly disagreed on several issues including the use of the death penalty, the best approach to dealing with countries where slavery is practiced and on some issues related to the treatment of religious minorities'.

5 It is, for example, problematic that, in the calculations, joint distribution of humanitarian aid, say, in Ethiopia and the 'Mutual Recognition Agreement' concerning \$ 6 billion of US-EU bilateral trade are evenly weighted. Insofar as there were very few actions massively outdoing all the others, the number of cases calling for some kind of corrective coefficient is so far fairly limited.

Table 1. Joint Action Plan Attached to the New Transatlantic Agenda (Dec. 1995)

		Actions										
	Issues	**1**	**2**	**3**	**4**	**5**	**6**	**7**	**8**	**Total**	**μ**	**σ**
I. Promoting Peace and Stability, Democracy and Development around the World	***65***	***17***	***0***	***4***	***5***	***14***	***15***	***20***	***8***	*83*	**4,9**	**1,4**
1. Working together for a stable and prosperous Europe	*17*	*4*	*0*	*3*	*2*	*3*	*4*	*10*	*1*	27	**4,5**	**1,4**
a) Peace and reconstruction in the former Yugoslavia	5	2		1				6		9	**5,2**	**2,6**
b) Central and Eastern European Countries	5			1	1	1	1	2	1	7	**5,7**	**1,7**
c) Russia, Ukraine and the other New Independent States	5			1	1		3	2		7	**5,6**	**1,4**
d) Turkey	1	1				1				2	**3,0**	**2,0**
e) Cyprus	1	1				1				2	**3,0**	**2,0**
2. Promoting the Middle East Peace Process	*9*	*4*	*0*	*0*	*0*	*5*	*0*	*0*	*0*	*9*	**3,2**	**2,0**
		4				5				9	**3,2**	**2,0**
3. Sharing responsibility in other regions of the world	*13*	5	*0*	*1*	*1*	*3*	*1*	*1*	*3*	15	**4,2**	**2,9**
a) Rwanda - Burundi	1					1			1	2	**6,5**	**1,5**
b) Great Lakes (Central Africa, Congo, …)	1					1				1	**5,0**	**0,0**
c) Angola - Mozambique	1						1			1	**6,0**	**0,0**
d) Nigeria	1	1								1	**1,0**	**0,0**
e) El Salvador - Nicaragua	1			1	1					2	**3,5**	**0,5**
f) Guatemala	1	1								1	**1,0**	**0,0**
g) Haiti	1	1								1	**1,0**	**0,0**

Actions

	Issues	1	2	3	4	5	6	7	8	Total	μ	σ
h) Cuba	1	1								1	**1,0**	**0,0**
i) Hong Kong - Macao (return to China)	1	1								1	**1,0**	**0,0**
j) Korean peninsula - Taiwan - South China Sea	1							1		1	**7,0**	**0,0**
k) Burma	1								1	1	**8,0**	**0,0**
l) Cambodia	1								1	1	**8,0**	**0,0**
m) East Timor	1					1				1	**5,0**	**0,0**
4. Development cooperation and humanitarian assistance	*7*	*0*	*0*	*0*	*1*	*0*	*4*	*2*	*2*	*9*	**6,4**	**0,2**
a) Development cooperation	4						3	1	1	5	**6,6**	**0,8**
b) Humanitarian assistance	3				1		1	1	1	4	**6,3**	**1,5**
5. Human rights and democracy	*5*	*3*	*0*	*0*	*1*	*1*	*1*	*0*	*1*	*7*	**3,7**	**2,6**
		3			1	1	1		1	7	**3,7**	**2,6**
6. Cooperation in international organizations	*5*	*0*	*0*	*0*	*0*	*0*	*1*	*4*	*0*	*5*	**6,7**	**0,6**
a) UN	3							3		3	**7,0**	**0,0**
b) OSCE	1						1			1	**6,0**	**0,0**
c) Bretton Woods institutions, OECD	1							1		1	**7,0**	**0,0**
7. Non-proliferation, international disarmament and arms transfers	*9*	*1*	*0*	*0*	*0*	*2*	*4*	*3*	*1*	*11*	**5,7**	**2,0**
a) Promotion of the Nuclear Non-Proliferation Treaty	1						1	1		2	**6,5**	**0,5**
b) Conclusion of a Comprehensive Test Ban Treaty	1						1			1	**6,0**	**0,0**
c) Negotiation on a Fissile Material Cut-Off Treaty	1								1	1	**8,0**	**0,0**

Actions

	Issues	1	2	3	4	5	6	7	8	Total	µ	σ
d) Extension of the Missile Technology Control Regime	1						1			1	**6,0**	**0,0**
e) Revision of 1972 Convention on Biological Weapons	1							1		1	**7,0**	**0,0**
f) Prevention of proliferation of Anti-Personal Landmines	1					1		1		2	**6,0**	**1,0**
g) Multilateral arrangement for (arms) export controls	1	1								1	**1,0**	**0,0**
h) Prevention of proliferation of weapons of mass destruction	1						1			1	**6,0**	**0,0**
i) Korean Peninsula Energy Development Organization (KEDO)	1					1				1	**5,0**	**0,0**
II. Responding to Global Challenges	***65***	***0***	***13***	***2***	***0***	***4***	***11***	***23***	***1***	***54***	**5,8**	**0,9**
1. Fight against organized crime, terrorism and drug trafficking	*13*	*0*	*7*	*0*	*0*	*2*	*2*	*12*	*0*	*23*	**5,2**	**0,2**
a) Organized crime	5		2					3		5	**5,0**	**2,4**
b) Terrorism	*1*		2					4		6	**5,3**	**2,4**
c) Drug trafficking	*7*		3			2	2	5		12	**5,3**	**2,0**
2. Immigration and asylum	*9*	*0*	*4*	*0*	*0*	*0*	*3*	*2*	*0*	*9*	**5,0**	**2,6**
a) Fight against traffic in illegal immigrants and women	2							2		2	**7,0**	**0,0**
b) Illegal immigration, asylum and migration flows	4		4							4	**2,0**	**0,0**
c) Refugees	3						3			3	**6,0**	**0,0**
3. Legal and judicial cooperation	*4*	*0*	*0*	*0*	*0*	*0*	*0*	*4*	*0*	*4*	**7,0**	**0,0**
								4		4	**7,0**	**0,0**
4. Preservation of the environment	*8*	*0*	*2*	*2*	*0*	*0*	*2*	*2*	*0*	*8*	**4,5**	**2,1**
			2	2			2	2		8	**4,5**	**2,1**

	Issues	Actions 1	2	3	4	5	6	7	8	Total	μ	σ
5. Population issues	*2*	*0*	*0*	*0*	*0*	*0*	*1*	*1*	*0*	2	**6,5**	**0,5**
							1	1		2	**6,5**	**0,5**
6. Nuclear safety	*3*	*0*	*0*	*0*	*0*	*1*	*2*	*1*	*0*	*4*	**6,0**	**0,7**
						1	2	1		4	**6,0**	**0,7**
7. Health	*4*	*0*	*0*	*0*	*0*	*1*	*1*	*1*	*1*	4	**6,5**	**1,1**
						1	1	1	1	4	**6,5**	**1,1**
III. Contributing to the Expansion of World Trade and Closer Economic Cooperation	***47***	**2**	***4***	***6***	**3**	***0***	***9***	***21***	***3***	***48***	**4,9**	**1,4**
1. Strengthening the multilateral trading system	*16*	2	*0*	*0*	*0*	*0*	*7*	*7*	*0*	*16*	**5,7**	**1,9**
a) Consolidating the WTO	4						3	1		4	**6,3**	**0,4**
b) Uruguay Round unfinished business (telecom, etc.)	1						1			1	**6,0**	**0,0**
c) Financial services	1						1			1	**6,0**	**0,0**
d) Government procurement	1						1			1	**6,0**	**0,0**
e) Intellectual property rights (IPR)	1							1		1	**7,0**	**0,0**
f) New issues (environment, investment, competition, labor standards)	4	1					1	2		4	**5,3**	**2,5**
g) Market access: creating additional trading opportunities (ITA ...)	2							2		2	**7,0**	**0,0**
h) International customs cooperation	1							1		1	**7,0**	**0,0**
i) Illicit payments	1	1								1	**1,0**	**0,0**

	Issues	Actions 1	2	3	4	5	6	7	8	Total	μ	σ
2. The New Transatlantic Marketplace	*28*	*0*	*3*	*5*	*3*	*0*	*1*	*14*	*3*	*29*	**5,7**	**2,0**
a) Joint study on ways of facilitating trade	1								1	1	**8,0**	**0,0**
b) Confidence building	1							1		1	**7,0**	**0,0**
c) Standards, certification and regulatory issues	4							4	1	5	**7,2**	**0,4**
d) Veterinary and plant health issues	2							2		2	**7,0**	**0,0**
e) Government procurement	1						1			1	**6,0**	**0,0**
f) Intellectual property rights (IPR)	1				1					1	**4,0**	**0,0**
g) Financial services	1			1						1	**3,0**	**0,0**
h) Customs cooperation	1							1		1	**7,0**	**0,0**
i) Information Society, technology and telecom	6		1	3				2		6	**4,2**	**2,0**
j) Competition	1							1		1	**7,0**	**0,0**
k) Data protection	1			1						1	**3,0**	**0,0**
l) Transport	3				2			1		3	**5,0**	**1,4**
m) Energy	1							1		1	**7,0**	**0,0**
n) Biotechnology	2							1	1	2	**7,5**	**0,5**
o) Safety and health	2		2							2	**2,0**	**0,0**
3. Jobs and growth	*3*	*0*	*1*	*1*	*0*	*0*	*1*	*0*	*0*	*3*	**3,3**	**1,8**
a) Jobs and growth	2			1			1			2	**4,5**	**1,5**
b) Macroeconomic issues	1		1							1	**2,0**	**0,0**

Actions

	Issues	1	2	3	4	5	6	7	8	Total	μ	σ
IV. Building Bridges across the Atlantic	***19***	***1***	***7***	***0***	***1***	***5***	***0***	***8***	***1***	*23*	**4,9**	**1,3**
1. Transatlantic Business Dialogue	*1*	*0*	*0*	*0*	*0*	*1*	*0*	*1*	*0*	2	**6,0**	**1,0**
a) Transatlantic Business Dialogue (TABD)	1					1		1		2	**6,0**	**1,0**
2. Broadening science and technology cooperation	*4*	*0*	*1*	*0*	*0*	*0*	*0*	*4*	*0*	5	**6,0**	**2,0**
			1					4		5	**6,0**	**2,0**
3. People to people links	*9*	*0*	*4*	*0*	*0*	*3*	*0*	*2*	*1*	*10*	**4,2**	**1,5**
a) Contacts between citizens	1					1				1	**5,0**	**0,0**
b) Education (higher education, vocational training, school…)	6		3			1		2	1	7	**4,7**	**2,5**
c) Cross-study of systems of government and communities	1		1							1	**2,0**	**0,0**
d) Sister cities	1					1				1	**5,0**	**0,0**
4. Information and Culture	*5*	*1*	*2*	*0*	*1*	*1*	*0*	*1*	*0*	*6*	**3,5**	**2,1**
		1	2		1	1		1		6	**3,5**	**2,1**
TOTAL	**196**	**20**	**24**	**12**	**9**	**23**	**35**	**72**	**13**	**208**	**5,1**	**0,5**

Remarks: **μ**: mean (average value). **σ**: standard deviation (the standard deviation is a measure of how widely values are dispersed from the mean).

Action (type of action and level of commitment):

1 = statement of US and EU individual commitments – **2** = information (exchange of information and/or information gathering) – **3** = dialogue – **4** = consultation – **5** = common encouragement & support for third parties initiatives and actions (*e.g.* support for UN Secretary General efforts in Angola) – **6** = coordination of initiatives & positions (in particular in multilateral fora) and of actions – **7** = cooperation (including identification of means of cooperation) – **8** = joint action

Graphs

Part I - Promoting Peace and Stability

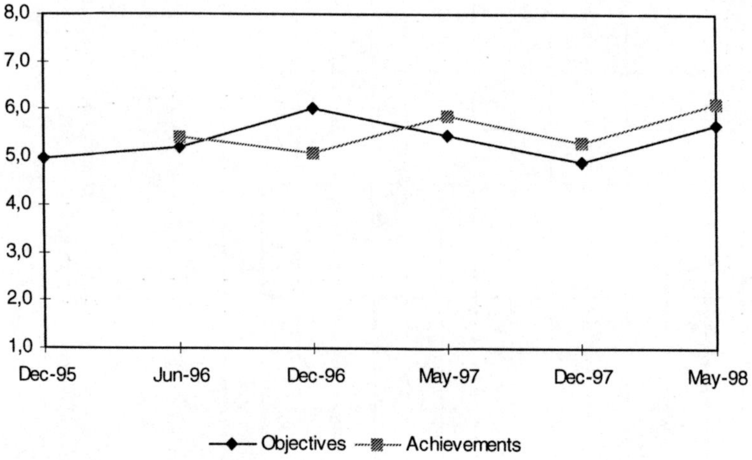

Part II - Responding to Global Challenges

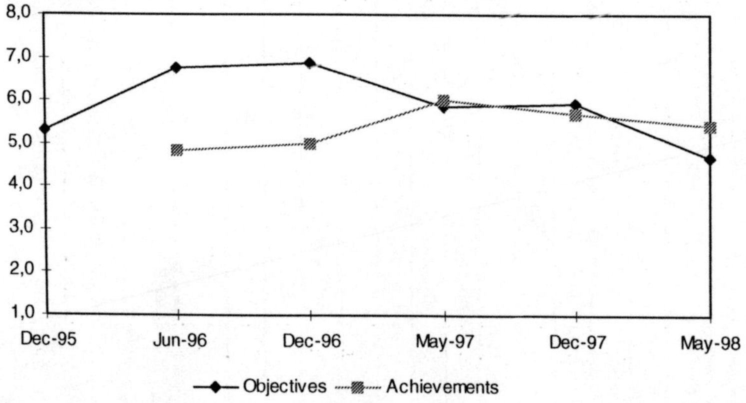

Part III - Expansion of World Trade

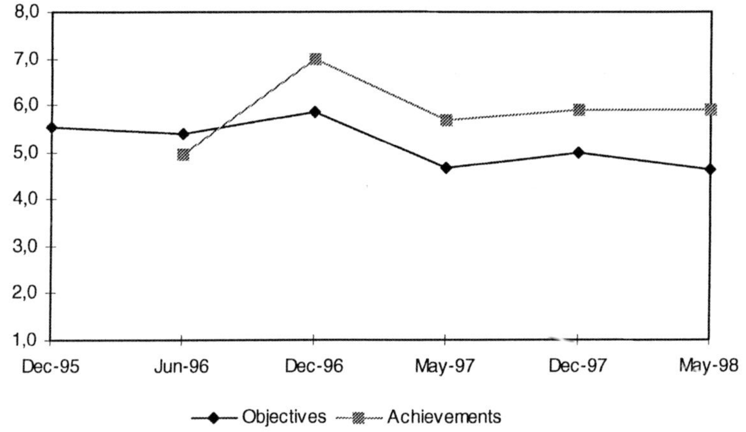

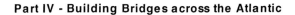

Part IV - Building Bridges across the Atlantic

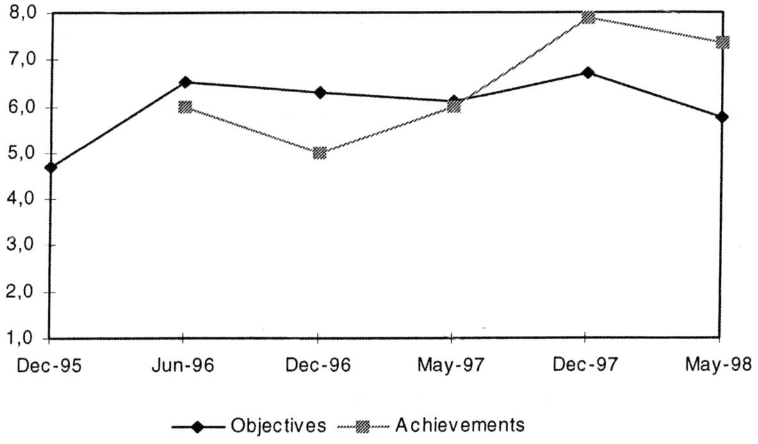

Table 2. US-EU Partnership – Intensity of Actions:
Comparison Cumulated Objectives - Cumulated Achievements
(December 1995 - May 1998)

	Actions						
	In. Obj.	*Cum. Obj.*			*Cum. Achiev.*		
	Total	**Total**	**µ**	**σ**	**Total**	**µ**	**σ**
I. Promoting Peace and Stability, Democracy and Development around the World	*83*	***185***	**5,2**	**2,1**	***109***	**5,2**	**1,7**
1. Working together for a stable and prosperous Europe	*27*	*58*	**4,9**	**2,2**	*30*	**6,4**	**0,8**
a) Peace and reconstruction in the former Yugoslavia	9	16	**5,4**	**2,3**	12	**6,1**	**0,8**
b) Central and Eastern European Countries	7	12	**5,6**	**1,6**	3	**6,7**	**0,9**
c) Russia, Ukraine and the other New Independent States	7	12	**5,8**	**1,3**	6	**6,7**	**0,7**
d) Turkey	2	7	**3,4**	**2,3**	3	**7,0**	**0,0**
e) Cyprus	2	8	**3,5**	**1,7**	3	**6,3**	**0,5**
f) South East Europe *	0	3	**3,0**	**1,4**	3	**6,7**	**0,5**
2. Promoting the Middle East Peace Process	*9*	*15*	**3,7**	**2,4**	*9*	**5,3**	**1,2**
	9	15	**3,7**	**2,4**	9	**5,3**	**1,2**
3. Sharing responsibility in other regions of the world	*15*	*38*	**4,9**	**2,0**	*22*	**3,8**	**1,8**
a) Rwanda - Burundi	2	4	**6,3**	**1,3**	1	**7,0**	**0,0**
b) Great Lakes (Central Africa, Congo, …)	1	8	**5,5**	**1,0**	2	**5,0**	**0,0**
c) Angola - Mozambique	1	2	**5,5**	**0,5**	1	**8,0**	**0,0**
d) Nigeria	1	3	**4,3**	**2,5**	4	**4,0**	**0,0**

	Actions						
	In. Obj.	*Cum. Obj.*			*Cum. Achiev.*		
	Total	**Total**	**μ**	**σ**	**Total**	**μ**	**σ**
e) El Salvador - Nicaragua	2	2	**3,5**	**0,5**	1	**4,0**	**0,0**
f) Guatemala	1	1	**1,0**	**0,0**	1	**6,0**	**0,0**
g) Haiti	1	1	**1,0**	**0,0**	3	**4,0**	**2,2**
h) Cuba	1	1	**1,0**	**0,0**	3	**2,3**	**0,9**
i) Hong Kong - Macao (China *)	1	5	**3,8**	**1,7**	0	**0,0**	**0,0**
j) Korean peninsula - Taiwan - South China Sea	1	1	**7,0**	**0,0**	1	**7,0**	**0,0**
k) Burma	1	3	**6,7**	**1,2**	1	**5,0**	**0,0**
l) Cambodia	1	1	**8,0**	**0,0**	0	**0,0**	**0,0**
m) East Timor	1	2	**5,5**	**0,5**	0	**0,0**	**0,0**
n) Iran *	0	3	**4,7**	**1,7**	3	**3,7**	**0,5**
o) Lybia *	0	1	**3,0**	**0,0**	1	**3,0**	**0,0**
4. Development cooperation and humanitarian assistance	*9*	*32*	**6,4**	**1,4**	*32*	**6,0**	**1,4**
a) Development cooperation	5	15	**6,6**	**1,0**	13	**6,0**	**1,4**
b) Humanitarian assistance	4	17	**6,2**	**1,7**	19	**6,0**	**1,5**
5. Human rights and democracy	*7*	*13*	**4,8**	**2,4**	*3*	**6,7**	**0,5**
	7	13	**4,8**	**2,4**	3	**6,7**	**0,5**
6. Cooperation in international organizations	*5*	*7*	**5,6**	**2,1**	*6*	**4,3**	**1,4**
a) UN	3	5	**5,2**	**2,4**	2	**4,0**	**1,0**
b) OSCE	1	1	**6,0**	**0,0**	1	**5,0**	**0,0**
c) Bretton Woods institutions, OECD	1	1	**7,0**	**0,0**	3	**4,3**	**1,7**

	Actions						
	In. Obj.	*Cum. Obj.*			*Cum. Achiev.*		
	Total	**Total**	**μ**	**σ**	**Total**	**μ**	**σ**
7. Non-proliferation, international disarmament and arms transfers	*11*	22	**5,8**	**1,8**	7	**2,8**	**3,2**
a) Promotion of adherence to the Nuclear Non-Proliferation Treaty	2	2	**6,5**	**0,5**	0	**0,0**	**0,0**
b) Conclusion of a Comprehensive Test Ban Treaty	1	1	**6,0**	**0,0**	0	**0,0**	**0,0**
c) Negotiation on a Fissile Material Cut-Off Treaty	1	1	**8,0**	**0,0**	0	**0,0**	**0,0**
d) Extension of the Missile Technology Control Regime	1	1	**6,0**	**0,0**	0	**0,0**	**0,0**
e) Revision of 1972 Convention on Biological Weapons	1	2	**7,0**	**0,0**	0	**0,0**	**0,0**
f) Prevention of proliferation of Anti-Personal Landmines	2	6	**5,5**	**1,7**	0	**0,0**	**0,0**
g) Multilateral arrangement for (arms) export controls	1	4	**4,8**	**2,5**	1	**6,0**	**0,0**
h) Prevention of proliferation of weapons of mass destruction	1	2	**6,5**	**0,5**	3	**3,0**	**1,4**
i) Korean Peninsula Energy Development Organization (KEDO)	1	3	**5,0**	**1,6**	3	**7,0**	**0,0**
II. Responding to Global Challenges	***54***	***122***	**5,6**	**1,9**	***49***	**5,3**	**1,9**
1. Fight against organized crime, terrorism and drug trafficking	*23*	*56*	**5,6**	**1,9**	*21*	**5,8**	**1,7**
a) Organized crime	5	16	**6,0**	**1,8**	5	**5,8**	**1,2**
b) Terrorism	6	17	**5,4**	**1,9**	6	**5,2**	**1,6**
c) Drug trafficking	12	23	**5,4**	**1,8**	10	**6,2**	**1,8**
2. Immigration and asylum	*9*	*18*	**5,8**	**2,1**	*9*	**5,2**	**2,0**
a) Fight against traffic in illegal immigrants and women (and children*)	2	10	**7,2**	**0,4**	4	**7,0**	**1,2**
b) Illegal immigration, asylum and migration flows	4	5	**3,0**	**2,0**	4	**4,0**	**1,4**
c) Refugees	3	3	**6,0**	**0,0**	1	**3,0**	**0,0**

	Actions In. Obj.	Cum. Obj.			Cum. Achiev.		
	Total	Total	μ	σ	Total	μ	σ
3. Legal and judicial cooperation	*4*	*5*	**6,4**	**1,2**	*3*	**3,3**	**0,5**
	4	5	**6,4**	**1,2**	3	**3,3**	**0,5**
4. Preservation of the environment	*8*	*28*	**5,3**	**1,9**	*9*	**5,0**	**1,8**
	8	28	**5,3**	**1,9**	9	**5,0**	**1,8**
5. Population issues	*2*	*2*	**6,5**	**0,5**	0	**0,0**	**0,0**
	2	2	**6,5**	**0,5**	0	**0,0**	**0,0**
6. Nuclear safety	*4*	*4*	**6,0**	**0,7**	*3*	**5,0**	**2,8**
	4	4	**6,0**	**0,7**	3	**5,0**	**2,8**
7. Health	*4*	*9*	**5,6**	**1,8**	*4*	**6,3**	**1,5**
	4	9	**5,6**	**1,8**	4	**6,3**	**1,5**
III. Contributing to the Expansion of World Trade and Closer Economic Cooperation	***48***	***126***	5,3	1,9	***56***	5,0	2,0
1. Strengthening the multilateral trading system	*16*	*51*	**5,1**	**1,7**	*18*	**4,4**	**1,5**
a) Consolidating the WTO	4	15	**4,5**	**2,0**	4	**5,3**	**1,3**
b) Uruguay Round unfinished business (services a.o. telecommunications, maritime)	1	5	**5,0**	**1,3**	3	**4,0**	**1,4**
c) Financial services	1	4	**6,0**	**0,0**	1	**6,0**	**0,0**
d) Government procurement	1	2	**6,0**	**0,0**	0	**0,0**	**0,0**
e) Intellectual property rights (IPR)	1	1	**7,0**	**0,0**	2	**5,0**	**2,0**
f) New issues (environment, investment, competition, labor standards)	4	10	**5,0**	**1,9**	3	**3,7**	**0,9**

	Actions *In. Obj.*	*Cum. Obj.*			*Cum. Achiev.*		
	Total	**Total**	**μ**	**σ**	**Total**	**μ**	**σ**
g) Market access: creating additional trading opportunities (ITA ...)	2	10	**5,7**	**1,1**	3	**5,3**	**0,9**
h) International customs cooperation	1	1	**7,0**	**0,0**	0	**0,0**	**0,0**
i) Illicit payments	1	3	**4,0**	**2,2**	2	**6,0**	**0,0**
2. *The New Transatlantic Marketplace*	*29*	*63*	**5,5**	**2,0**	*34*	**5,6**	**1,7**
a) Joint study on ways of facilitating trade	1	5	**7,2**	**0,4**	4	**7,5**	**0,5**
b) Confidence building	1	2	**5,0**	**2,0**	3	**7,0**	**0,0**
c) Standards, certification and regulatory issues	5	14	**6,2**	**1,7**	9	**6,2**	**1,5**
d) Veterinary and plant health issues	2	3	**7,0**	**0,0**	3	**7,3**	**0,5**
e) Government procurement	1	2	**4,5**	**1,5**	0	**0,0**	**0,0**
f) Intellectual property rights (IPR)	1	3	**5,3**	**1,2**	2	**5,0**	**2,0**
g) Financial services	1	1	**3,0**	**0,0**	0	**0,0**	**0,0**
h) Customs cooperation	1	2	**7,0**	**0,0**	3	**7,7**	**0,5**
i) Information Society, information technology and telecommunications	6	10	**4,5**	**2,1**	3	**5,0**	**0,8**
j) Competition	1	2	**7,0**	**0,0**	3	**7,0**	**0,8**
k) Data protection	1	3	**3,0**	**0,0**	0	**0,0**	**0,0**
l) Transport	3	7	**5,0**	**1,6**	1	**7,0**	**0,0**
m) Energy	1	2	**5,0**	**2,0**	0	**0,0**	**0,0**
n) Biotechnology	2	4	**7,3**	**0,4**	3	**5,0**	**1,6**
o) Safety and health	2	3	**3,7**	**2,4**	0	**0,0**	**0,0**

	Actions In. Obj.	Cum. Obj.			Cum. Achiev.		
	Total	Total	μ	σ	Total	μ	σ
3. Jobs and growth	*3*	*12*	**4,3**	**1,8**	*4*	**2,3**	**0,4**
a) Jobs and growth	2	7	**5,4**	**1,7**	1	**3,0**	**0,0**
b) Macroeconomic issues (Euro*)	1	5	**2,8**	**0,4**	3	**2,0**	**0,0**
IV. Building Bridges across the Atlantic	***23***	***62***	**5,7**	**1,9**	***29***	**6,5**	**1,5**
1. Transatlantic Business Dialogue	*2*	*12*	**4,9**	**1,0**	*8*	**6,1**	**1,5**
a) Transatlantic Business Dialogue (TABD)	2	8	**5,3**	**0,7**	6	**6,0**	**1,4**
b) Transatlantic Small Business Initiative (TASBI) *	0	4	**4,3**	**1,3**	2	**6,5**	**1,5**
2. Broadening science and technology cooperation	*5*	*10*	**6,7**	**1,6**	*8*	**7,3**	**1,6**
	5	10	**6,7**	**1,6**	8	**7,3**	**1,6**
3. People to people links	*10*	*33*	**6,1**	**1,9**	*12*	**6,2**	**1,5**
a) Contacts between citizens	1	12	**6,8**	**1,1**	3	**7,7**	**0,5**
b) Education (higher education, vocational training, school, stages…)	7	13	**5,9**	**2,3**	7	**7,4**	**1,0**
c) Cross-study of systems of government and communities	1	1	**2,0**	**0,0**	0	**0,0**	**0,0**
d) Sister cities	1	1	**5,0**	**0,0**	0	**0,0**	**0,0**
e) People with disabilities *	0	2	**6,0**	**1,0**	0	**0,0**	**0,0**
f) Non Governmental Organizations Dialogue *	0	2	**5,0**	**0,0**	1	**5,0**	**0,0**
g) Consumers Dialogue *	0	2	**6,0**	**1,0**	1	**7,0**	**0,0**
4. Information and Culture	*6*	*7*	**3,7**	**2,0**	*1*	**8,0**	**0,0**
	6	7	**3,7**	**2,0**	1	**8,0**	**0,0**

	Actions						
	In. Obj.	*Cum. Obj.*			*Cum. Achiev.*		
	Total	**Total**	**μ**	**σ**	**Total**	**μ**	**σ**
*5. Transatlantic Labor Dialogue (TLD) **	*0*	*6*	**5,3**	**0,7**	*1*	**5,0**	**0,0**
	0	6	**5,3**	**0,7**	1	**5,0**	**0,0**
*6. Parliamentary Dialogue **	*0*	*1*	**5,0**	**0,0**	*2*	**6,0**	**1,0**
	0	1	**5,0**	**0,0**	2	**6,0**	**1,0**
*7. Courts Dialogue **	*0*	*3*	**5,0**	**0,0**	*0*	**0,0**	**0,0**
	0	3	**5,0**	**0,0**	0	**0,0**	**0,0**
TOTAL	**208**	**495**	**5,2**	**2,0**	**243**	**4,9**	**2,0**

* = Items added to the Joint Action Plan after December 1995.

At the highly aggregated level of the main parts of the JAP, distinctive features and trends can be observed. Part III ('Contributing to the expansion of world trade and closer economic cooperation') and, in particular, Sub-Part III.1 ('Strengthening the multilateral trading system') were initially the object of the highest expectations. The assignments for Part II ('Responding to global challenges') and Part I ('Promoting peace and stability') were more modest, although not very significantly smaller. The ambitions for Part IV ('Building bridges across the Atlantic') were the lowest.

The initial objectives, cumulated objectives and achievements of the parts of the JAP have in common a rather high standard deviation (average of around 2 – the maximum for a scale from 1 to 8 being 3,5). This indicates that transatlantic endeavors are characterized by a large palette of actions and that there are substantial disparities between the sub-parts of the JAP. For Parts I and IV in particular, the range of the palette has decreased over time (the standard deviations of the objectives set in December 1995 were respectively 2,4 and 2,3: the standard deviations of the cumulated objectives are down to 2,1 and 1,9).

Globally, objectives have been revised upwards with the marked exception of Part III.1, initially the most ambitious part and which has since dropped to the bottom of the list. Part IV, initially the least ambitious part, underwent the sharpest revision upwards to top the list. No less than 287 actions were mentioned in the new priorities from May 1996 to May 1998. Considering that 208 actions were initially envisaged, this bears witness to the dynamism of the NTA revision process, even if some of these actions are recurring priorities (for instance, the Mutual Recognition Agreement was on each list of 'new' priorities until it eventually entered into force on 1 December 1998). Part I emerges as the most expanding or dynamic part with no less that 102 new priorities listed, against 68 for Part II and 78 for Part III. So to that extent, the Transatlantic Agenda remained 'New'.

As for Parts I and II, on average achievements match targets. Part III does not reach its objectives, but the differential is limited thanks the substantial downwards revision of Sub-Part III.1's initial objectives and the good performance of Sub-Part III.2 ('The New Transatlantic Marketplace'). With the largest gap between initial objectives and achievements (-1,4), the average output of Sub-Part III.1 stagnates between consultation and encouragement. Part IV has the highest achievement intensity and is the only part with a score clearly above the one set by the objectives (1,8 above the initial objectives and 0,8 above the cumulated ones). All in all, the parts of the JAP became more homogeneous, but also more ambitious. Although by far not trivial, transatlantic achievements remained on average between consultation and coordination, that is globally below the objectives and far from the generalization of joint actions suggested by the 'Joint Action Plan'. The policy output was however superior to any previous US-EC record and to the record of any similar US or EU partnership (that is to say, with the exception of partnerships with immediate neighboring countries such as Canada and Mexico, or parties such as the Central and Eastern countries candidate to EU accession and the most integrated Mediterranean third countries).

Specific Features of the US-EU Output: A Tentative Explanation

Much starker variations can be observed when looking at sub-parts of the JAP. They call for closer examination and explanation. Insofar as this a policy-oriented book, the aim of this section is to explain specific outcomes rather than to test theories in a systematic way. Therefore what follows simply suggests the most plausible links between a number of remarkable outcomes and the propositions enunciated in chapter 2. The record of Part IV having been assessed and explained in chapter 13 (sub-section 'Formal Opening to Private Actors'), we only focus here on the first three parts of the JAP.

The first part of the JAP, 'Promoting peace and stability, democracy and development around the world', is constituted of a contrasted mosaic of seven sub-parts. Sub-Part I.1 'Working together for a stable and prosperous Europe' has been, in absolute terms, one of the most dynamic areas in US-EU planning (in less than three years, more than thirty priorities were scheduled by the SLG reports). Achievements in Europe reached, on average, what could be considered as the highest intensity of all sub-parts of Parts I, II and III (the three substantive parts of the JAP)[6] and exceeded by far the initial targets. The positive differential of 1,5 – in fact, the biggest of all – is largely due to the very

6 Sub-Part I.1. is surpassed by Sub-Part I.4 'Human rights and democracy', but the different nature of the actions conducted in these sectors of cooperation hedges the comparison. Indeed, it is, politically but also logistically speaking, much easier to design and implement joint monitoring of elections than to cooperate over the reconstruction of Kosovo.

cautious definition of objectives for US-EU actions over Turkey, Cyprus and South East Europe. After initial US-EU tensions, the parties managed relatively quickly to move from dialogue and consultation to coordination and cooperation. The similarly modest objectives listed under Sub-Part I.2. 'Promoting the Middle East Peace Process' were also clearly outperformed, although the achievements remained below the level of intensity reached for Europe. Cooperation picked up in 1998, that is to say, after the EU eventually renounced its ambition to have a seat at the table and accepted to be confined to an auxiliary role.

Sub-Part I.3 'Sharing responsibility in other regions of the world' is characterized by one of the lowest scores in terms of achievement intensity (between dialogue and consultation) and a significant gap between objectives and achievements. Although it potentially concerns all regions outside Europe and the Middle East, the number of new priorities identified by the SLG barely exceeded twenty. Comparatively low-key, US-EU endeavors in Sub-Saharan Africa were basically confined to health programs, crisis management and peace-building. Efforts in the region were therefore very much pro-reactive.[7] There was also clear evidence that the delineation of US-EU cooperation acknowledged implicitly the existence of French, English and American *chasses gardées*. Exceptions were either very limited in their reach or responding to an invitation of the former power in the area.[8] This crisis management orientation was confirmed *a contrario* by the non-listing of stable areas such as South Africa, for which (market) competition between transatlantic players remained the main organizing principle. The region seemingly received more US-EU attention in the run-up and the wake of the 1999 African tour of Bill Clinton in Sub-Saharan Africa.

US-EU priorities followed the same logic in Latin America and Asia, but at a lower level of intensity and with shallower and more patchy results. Exceptions usually correspond to 'symmetrical' issues, *i.e.* having a neutral impact on the parties and their constituents. In accordance to what Lowi and Zimmerman predict, cooperation on issues such as the US-EU support for the Guatemalan peace process benefited

---

7 For instance, mentioned in December 1996 in the context of food security, Ethiopia disappeared from the SLG reports till May 2000 when it was pushed back on the international agenda by its border dispute with Eritrea.

8 The US-EU commitment to 'take strong and appropriate steps to promote the rapid restoration of civilian democratic rule in Nigeria' was the call made by the UK to exert joint pressure at European, Commonwealth and transatlantic levels.

indeed from a low level of adverse mobilization. In these cases, co-operation only materialized when there was a negotiator with a particular motive to take advantage of this permissive consensus, such as the Portuguese presidency of the EU on the reconstruction of East Timor.

There was finally a group of countries of a special nature over which US-EU collaboration was particularly difficult: the 'Rogue States' or 'States of Concern' as they are now called in the official documents of the US State Department. This was to the point that exchange of information or continued dialogue on Iraq, Iran, Cuba or Libya were at times already considered as a major achievement. Despite strong transatlantic divergence on the best strategy to adopt towards these states, the partners did operate some sort of division of labor.[9]

The assessment of these three sub-parts of Part I corresponds to a hegemonic configuration. Although the claim of the parties is to build a global partnership, its core remained largely restricted to European regional issues. The US was the only player at the center of a global system of alliances and took advantage of it. Tensions could be interpreted as moments of wavering, where the hegemonic power had to work harder to impose its leadership. The US managed to do so with the relatively short-lived EU challenge to US leadership in the Middle East Peace Process. It did not in the case of the 'States of Concern' or in sensitive geographical areas such as the Mediterranean (which stayed entirely out of the US-EU agenda, even though the Euro-Mediterranean Partnership is on many issues in direct competition with the US policy for the Middle East and North Africa).

The next sub-part, 'Development cooperation and humanitarian assistance', has been the most dynamic sector of the NTA: between 1995 and 1998, no less than twenty-three actions were added to the nine initially planned. Sub-Part I.4 was also among the most successful ones, with thirty-two major achievements registered for the same period (no other sub-part by far managed to equal the number of actions implemented with the number of actions planned). With a significant proportion of cooperative endeavors and joint actions, these achievements were on average of a high intensity and close to the initial objectives. This success could be linked to several explanations, as the previous

---

9 For instance, in the absence of official channels of communication between the US and Iran, the EU had the responsibility to raise non-proliferation issues with Iran in the framework of its comprehensive dialogue (SLG report of December 1999).

chapters suggest. There is first the interest-based hypothesis, with governmental actors frantically searching for economies of scale after budget cuts in the US and in a number of EU Member States.[10] Clinging onto the facilitating regime hypothesis, there is then the reference to the beneficial effect of transgovernmental networks whose establishment and working are eased by the existence of a widely accepted set of principles (subsumed in the 'Washington consensus'). Finally, there is the hypothesis of the shaping force of EU institutions, according to which the characteristics of EU mode of governance in development aid (more centralized and effective than other domains of external relations) did allow for the success of US-EU cooperation.

As far as 'non-proliferation, international disarmament and arms transfer' is concerned, the US-EU record would appear to be meager, even though the level of commitment and the number of actions envisaged for this sub-part were rather high. For six out of the nine issue areas listed in Sub-Part I.7, there is virtually no entry in the 'achievement' section of the SLG reports from 1996 to 1998 and beyond (hence the very negative differential of -4,3 between cumulated objectives and achievements).[11]

Efforts to promote adherence to international treaties and arrangements already signed by the Americans and the Europeans (the EU and/or its Member States) depend by definition on the willingness of third countries to respond to US-EU encouragement or pressure. The absence of major achievement is therefore not necessarily the result of a lack of cooperation between the US and the EU; it could just as easily indicate the lack of effectiveness of their joint endeavors. In that case, the US-EU record would primarily point to explanations based on the hegemonic supply of regime and the world power structure. The US took the lead as a regime promoter and got the backing of its close allies. This hegemonic coalition was however not strong enough to im-

---

[10] The 1996 joint mission to Rwanda and Burundi carried out by Brian Atwood (Director of USAID) and Emma Bonino (Commissioner in charge of ECHO) is a good example of high visibility actions which, at relatively low cost, allowed the partners to show to their constituencies and to the international community that they were committed to the stabilization of certain regions (in this case by solving the refugee problem in a cooperative spirit).

[11] One exception is the Nuclear Non-Proliferation Treaty (NPT) which eventually surfaced on the SLG list of achievements in the December 1999 and May 2000 reports, following nuclear test in India and Pakistan, on one hand, and the 2000 Review Conference of the Treaty, on the other hand.

pose these key cooperation arrangements to states with sharply diverging interests. The explanation of the US-EU output would thus lie primarily with the insufficient asymmetry in the distribution of power in the international system.

By comparison, the failure to deliver major achievement on the issue of anti-personnel landmines was more clearly the result of the incapacity of the US and the EU to cooperate, in part because of intra-EU divisions. Originally, Sub-Part I.7.f of the JAP only referred to support of international efforts 'to curtail the use and proliferation of anti-personnel landmines'. Following its 1994 call for a ban, the Clinton administration advocated to take the issue to the Geneva-based Conference on Disarmament. This preference was shared by the 'three big' EU Member States, Germany, France and the UK. The international momentum towards a comprehensive ban of anti-personnel mines did however quickly generate tensions among EU Member States. A majority of them decided to participate in the Ottawa Conference of October 1996, and backed the process which led to the signature of the 'Convention on the Prohibition of the Use, Stockpiling, Production, and Transfer of Anti-personnel Landmines and on their Destruction' in December 1997. According to David Long, the EU 'spent much of the landmine campaign divided against itself', failing during most of 1997 'to say anything in common' and struggling to reconcile the different logics of the humanitarian and Community-based aspects of the landmines issue and the security/defense and CFSP-based aspects.[12] Transnational advocacy coalitions obviously managed to take advantage of intra-EU divisions and of the weaknesses of the EU decision-making process to derail US-EU cooperation in favor of a new forum and a more radical solution. In other words, this episode provides a straightforward example of the importance of the EU domestic politics and mode of governance for the explanation of US-EU output.

Sub-Part I.7 only met and even surpassed its objectives on one instance, *i.e.* in terms of support to the Korean Peninsula Energy Development Organization (KEDO). This success brings us back to hegemonic explanations in a most clear-cut form. Of course, on the whole, the US and the EU have a common interest in preventing insta-

---

[12] David Long, *Easier Done than Said; The European Union and Anti-personnel Mines*, paper presented at the International Studies Association-European Consortium for Political Research Joint Convention Panel on the International Politics of the European Union, Vienna, 16-19 September 1998.

bility from spreading or wars from breaking out. The EU was furthermore very keen to underline the global nature of its commitment to strengthen non-proliferation efforts. A contribution of ECU 75 million in a multi-billion dollar project offering energy assistance to North Korea in exchange for an end to its nuclear weapons program was, in that respect, not exorbitant. And yet, Europeans had a number of serious reservations about this instance of US-EU cooperation. Firstly, the KEDO was created as a result of the 1994 US-North Korea Agreed Framework. In other words, the US brokered the arrangement and then prompted Japan, South Korea and Europe to join in to share the costs. The fact that this international consortium would be led by a South Korean manufacturer who would provide two power plants based on a US-designed reactor added to European discomfort. Solutions had to be found to satisfy the EU about its representation on the executive board of the KEDO and about the allocation of the funds. It was not before 1997 that the agreement between Euratom and KEDO entered into force. This eventual US-EU success could therefore be interpreted as the result of a distinctively hegemonic division of labor already mentioned or, to put it more bluntly, as the action of 'a superpower on the cheap'.[13] Here again the hegemonic power had to offer a number of limited concessions to prevent defection and secure burden-sharing.

If we turn to the seven sets of issues constituting the second part of the JAP, 'Responding to global challenges', we find a diversity in ambitions and results no smaller than that of Part I. A large majority of the new priorities were aimed at Sub-Part II.1 'Fight against organized crime, terrorism, drug and immigrants trafficking' and Sub-Part II.2 'Immigration and asylum' (42 out of 68). After Sub-Part II.7 on Health, the achievements for Sub-Part II.1 had the second highest intensity of Part II, with a score of 5,8 – slightly above objectives. Scores for Sub-Part II.2 were roughly similar, with the difference that achievements were below objectives by 0,6. In both cases, actions were at first often limited to an exchange of delegations and discussions over possible agreements.

Beyond the interest-based and regime-based explanations, this positive record supports the set of propositions focusing on the impact of the characteristics of a policy area on the cooperative potential: the nature of

[13] John Peterson and Elisabeth Bomberg, *Decision-Making in the European Union* (London, MacMillan, 1999), p.251.

the policy area determines to a large extent domestic institutional dynamics and some dynamics are more conducive to international cooperation. According to this hypothesis, US-EU cooperation dealing with critical issues should normally benefit from a low level of (adverse) mobilization, organized groups rallying around the flag. With the fight against terrorism, drug trafficking, and to a lesser extent, immigration, asylum and refugee issues being close to the 'pole of power' defined by Lowi, governmental negotiators had therefore more room for manœuvre to conclude US-EU agreements.

As to the slow start of US-EU cooperation, it seems to be best explained by problems linked to European and transatlantic bureaucratic politics. As the experience of the pre-NTA working group on international crime showed, cooperation was hampered for a time by problematic intra-EU coordination, several Member States fearing that the European Commission might use the US-EU format to dilute the (mainly) intergovernmental character of the EU Third Pillar, hence to infringe on their rights. Transatlantic bureaucratic politics also slowed cooperation as the frictions between the French Interior Ministry and the US Drug Enforcement Agency illustrated. In his chapter, Gardner clearly indicates how the French Ministry resolutely opposed a request of the US agency to pass an agreement with the European Commission on sharing information for the control of chemical precursors used in the manufacture of illicit drugs. Interestingly enough, this long-blocked agreement was eventually concluded in 1997, *i.e.* the year in which the EU decided, via the Treaty of Amsterdam, to communitarize a number of these competencies, and the year France changed government. Yet another example of Monnet's postulate that America and Europe will continue to 'come together as fast as Europe unites and no faster'[14], and of the importance of a good relationship between the US and the main EU Member States for transatlantic developments.

Sub-Part II.4 'Preservation of the environment' is, in relative terms, the most dynamic area of this part of the JAP (environmental priorities have been multiplied by three). If the intensity of these sectoral achievements corresponds more or less to the initial objectives (that is, encouragement and support in particular for third party initiatives), there is, however, a strong contrast between the number of actions envisaged (twenty-eight) and implemented (nine). Contrasts are even more dra-

14 Jean Monnet to Gene Rostow, 18 January 1961, MKD.

matic in the case of Sub-Part II.5 'Population issues' whose ambition was US-EU coordination to implement the program of action of the 'International Conference on Population and Development' (the 'Cairo Conference') and support for family planning and expanded access to 'reproductive health programs'. Not a single major achievement could apparently be registered.

In both cases, US domestic idiosyncrasies seem to be the main blocking factor. Powerful interest groups mobilized and, through Congress, managed to restrict substantially collaboration with the Europeans and, beyond, with the main international organizations. The difficulty for the Clinton administration to support family planning programs after a vocal wing of the Republican majority in the Congress portrayed them as promoting abortion is one of the clearest examples of this problem. This illustrates that no significant cooperative development should be expected when, confronted with a hostile Congress, the US President remains indifferent or reckons that the fight would be politically too costly.

If we now examine the respective fortunes of the three sub-parts of Part III, 'Contributing to the expansion of world trade and closer economic cooperation', we see that they also varied substantially. The first sub-part, 'Strengthening the multilateral trading system', was initially the object of high expectations. The fact that the number of actions envisaged was tripled confirmed the central importance of this area and the – sometime uneven – willingness of the parties to redouble their efforts to reach some results. Insofar as the objectives were revised downward, it was also an indication of the depth of the stalemates. For instance, struggling hard on the consolidation of the WTO (Sub-Part III.1.a), the SLG reports referred to this issue no less than eleven times in three years. In the process, however, they decreased dramatically their level of ambition (6,3 for the objectives set by the JAP; 3,8 for the subsequent priorities). If the record for 'Consolidating the WTO' is not as bad as one would have expected on the basis of media coverage, it is largely because it does not reflect the number of deadlocked issues (four results for fifteen priorities). As for the achievements of the sub-part as a whole, their average intensity does not significantly exceed consultation (4,4). Post-1998 records did not improve this score – exceptions such as the successful conclusion in 1997 of negotiations over the Financial Services Agreement or US-EU cooperation over the application of China to the WTO remained too rare. No progress could be registered on the multilateral liberalization of governmental procurement, despite a common US-EU approach on the issue presented at the 1996 Singapore WTO Ministerial, and on international customs cooperation, despite continued efforts underlined in the May 2000 SLG report.

This record in muted colors makes us think of the insights offered by the complex interdependence and the regime approaches. Globalization means more common interests. Undeniably, the transatlantic partners, as the largest world trading blocs, do share an interest in further developing liberal international regimes which open new markets. In order to do so, they should maintain or increase their influence in the WTO. But globalization also means more competing interests. These exacerbated collective action problems between the parties or *vis-à-vis* third countries. For many of these, no solution could be found. Here again, problems have in addition been compounded by the domestic scene. Whereas Congressional actions have frequently created difficulties for the US administration, disagreements among EU Member States and between the Member States and the Commission have weakened the cohesiveness of transatlantic partners and their capacity to become the WTO's 'joint' leaders.[15]

The second sub-part is *grosso modo* dedicated to bilateral economic and trade issues between the US and the EU. Over the first three years of implementation, the SLG reports listed as many new priorities for Sub-Part III.2 as they did for the multilateral issues of Sub-Part III.1, but the average level of intensity was kept constant. Matching its original objectives, Sub-Part III.2 reached an average level of achievements close to coordination (5,8). Even before the JAP of the Transatlantic Economic Partnership came to replace the initial 'New Transatlantic Marketplace', this Sub-Part was among the best performing Sub-Parts of the JAP. Subsequent bilateral accomplishments further increased the contrast with Sub-Part III.1, both in terms of intensity and substance. Among the positive steps taken were the packages on standards and certification (the 1997 MRA package in particular), the 1999 Veterinary Equivalence Agreement, the 1997 Agreement on Customs Cooperation, the agreements on information technology, the Positive Comity Agreement on competition issues, the 2000 Safe Harbor arrangement on data

15 For a more detailed and excellent discussion of these issues, see Bart Kerremans, 'Transatlantic Trade Policy Relations: Bilateral and Multilateral Implications of the Emerging Transatlantic Marketplace in Goods', in *Implementation of the New Transatlantic Agenda and Future Prospects* (Brussels, TEPSA, 1998), pp.18-23.

protection, the 1999 agreement to coordinate labeling programs for energy efficient equipment and 1999 biotechnology pilot project. If these negotiations were longer than scheduled and if the implementation of these agreements has often been slow, at the end of the day there were few topics of Sub-Part III.2 for which no progress was registered. All in all, financial services and the increased coverage of US-EU bilateral government procurement obligations were the only two main exceptions.

Such a policy output is largely consistent with the expected consequences of hyper interdependence and reasonably good management of collective action dilemmas. The existence of international constraining regimes facilitated US-EU cooperation by preventing or limiting defections at bilateral level because the latter could be sanctioned at multilateral level. It was also in this area that the new mode of US-EU governance – in particular, the trilateral format and the direct involvement of non-governmental actors – offered the biggest advantages in terms of effectiveness and efficiency. The parties had indeed a good record in conflict prevention and, to a lesser extent, in conflict resolution (see the honorable performance of Sub-Part III.2.b on 'Confidence building'). In the post-NTA era, the US and the EU did manage to diffuse, among others, trade disputes over leghold traps (resolved in 1997 with an agreement on humane trapping standards for fur-bearing animals) and over the extraterritorial sanctions established by the US Helms-Burton and D'Amato Acts (resolved at the 1998 US-EU Summit hosted by the British presidency of the EU). Except for the notorious conflicts over the EC banana regime and the European ban on imports of hormone-treated beef, bilateral solutions were found within two or three years. Incidentally, this record brings evidence that a mutual understanding of the difficulties inherent in federal systems, as well as a well-endowed and pro-Washington EU presidency, can be a precious asset in US-EU conflict resolution, and henceforth that political purposes at times play an important part in the development of economic cooperation.

The last sub-part of Part III invites little comment. Devoted to 'Job and growth', it is a dormant area in US-EU cooperation. As the assessment of the Transatlantic Labour Dialogue presented in the previous chapter suggests, this is largely due to the existence of competing international regimes and organizations (the 'International Labour Organization', the 'International Confederation of Free Trade Unions' and the 'Trade Union Advisory Council' to the OECD) which specifically undermines US-EU developments. Apparently, the parties did not seize either the opportunity offered by Sub-Part III.3.b to make major progress in terms of monetary collaboration (under this sub-part, both parties pledged to exchange views on macroeconomic issues for the fostering of non-inflationary growth and international financial stability).[16] For certain the Euro was still in its infancy and, just as in other domains, the progress of US-EU cooperation was conditioned by the pace of European integration. But this limited record was most probably also the result of American 'institutional shopping'. The inflexible attitude of the US administration on the issue of the external representation of the Euro in the G7 was rather telling: its objective was to preserve the pre-eminence and more or less the existing format of the G7, this partially because the presence of the Japanese and Canadian governments as well as of several national and supranational European representatives often play to the American advantage. The degree of US-EU cooperation was negatively affected by the existence of regimes offering better alternatives for one of the partners.

On the whole, this section underlines the need to adopt a multicausal approach when explaining the variety of sectoral results. On the basis of the tentative set of explanations used *supra*, one could characterize US-EU relations as a variable geometry partnership, fundamentally based on shared interests and values. American hegemonic reflexes have, however, not disappeared, but are met with increasing European resistance. These reflexes, problems of collective action, as well as specific US and EU domestic idiosyncrasies, have kept the cooperative output at a low level in a number of policy areas. They also led to refocus *de facto* the relationship on a limited number of zones (mainly EU flanking regions) and issues (mainly soft security and economic matters).

Future Prospects for the US-EU Partnership

Although forecasting was not among our main preoccupations, it is difficult to end this book without a few words on the future prospects of the US-EU relationship. Firstly, because the assessment of the format of the

16 Although the third phase of the Economic and Monetary Union was mentioned once in the SLG's priorities (May 1998 report), there was no mention of any major achievement up to May 2000. The late 2000 coordinated intervention of the European and the American Central Banks to boost the exchange rate of the Euro could well be a first in that respect.

relationship and of its policy output leads naturally to address this question. Secondly, because the relationship might be at a crossroads. When new teams are appointed at a relatively short interval, provided that their terms of office largely correspond and that their mandates are sufficiently stable and long, these are indeed traditionally propitious times for taking stock of a relationship. When momentous endogenous and exogenous changes unfold simultaneously, the pressure to revisit the strategy and possibly the institutional framework is even greater. A number of domestic/regional changes with substantial transatlantic and international consequences in economic, monetary and security matters are likely to prompt the Prodi Commission (2000-2005) and the Bush administration (2001-2005) to rework parts of the US-EU partnership relatively quickly.

The economic pillar of the partnership is particularly underdeveloped as far as monetary and fiscal policies are concerned. On the one hand, the coming of age of the European Monetary Union and the probable centralization of European external monetary policy-making will increasingly affect the situation of the Dollar and the international monetary system as a whole. Sooner or later the US should clearly enunciate, as Henning Randall suggests, 'a long-run vision for the institutional arrangements by which it wishes to work with the Monetary Union in bilateral, plurilateral, and multilateral forums in the future'.[17] On the other hand, the American endeavors to ensure an economic soft landing and planned tax cuts will also have major consequences for the EU and for the rest of the world economy. Here too, greater transatlantic consultation and coordination will be much in need. Other cooperation domains such as environment or anti-trust could dwindle down as a result of the Bush administration's policy orientations. As for the security dimension of the US-EU relationship, the ongoing developments could prepare the ground for future contractions and expansions. Contraction with the progressive development of the Common European Security and Defence Policy endowed with decision-making processes formally independent from NATO. Expansion with the development of a EU capacity to address soft security problems linked to international crime, refugees and migrants.

Future geopolitical and geoeconomic systemic frictions could and should be addressed in different ways. For the economic pillar, one

---

[17] Henning, 'US-EU Relations after the Inception of the Monetary Union', p.53.

could consider, following the argument developed in Smith's chapter, that 'notions of strategy should be at least modified and possibly supplanted by those of learning and reflective practice'. In other words, lowering US-EU programmatic ambitions in favor of a more reactive and perhaps pragmatic approach could be a better way to deal with complex interdependence. This would also mean keeping on ice projects of an all-encompassing treaty or even a Free Trade Area. As Henrikson says, in any case 'there is now little interest in formalistic schemes of international organization on the transatlantic level, such as proposals to constitute an Atlantic "Federation" of some kind'. In such a 'pragmatic' approach, informal integration and bottom-up inputs would be the main sources of transatlantic dynamism. This would however not overrule specific forms of US-EU (re-)regulation, nor mean that market competition will be considered as the most adequate organizing principle for transatlantic cooperation as a whole. In security matters, provided that structural problems hampering leadership on both sides lessen, the transatlantic relationship will have to operate 'according to the principles of collective choice to provide a public good'[18] (the protection of its members from an external threat), which supposes the development of a more institutionalized, centralized and formal environment. In these domains, the development of new US-EU regimes should logically still be conditioned by the pace of European integration. Constitutional reforms being necessarily slow in the EU, US-EU redesign is very likely to remain incremental. Adjustment rather than revamping should be the norm.

None of this will however happen if the EU does not accept that, in many cases, its gains will be in relative terms smaller than those of the US. Both the US and the EU have an interest in the preservation of the liberal order and the new hegemonic stability, and could indeed become more closely associated for that purpose. But the US will remain for some time the only state strong enough to be at the center of a global system of alliances. On the other hand, the EU will most probably continue to gradually strengthen its remit beyond the economic field to the monetary, defense and political fields. Its global role is therefore likely to be enhanced, and thus also its potential for entering into a more equal partnership with the United States. Current expressions describing the nature of US-EU relations, such as full partnership and joint leadership,

---

[18] Wolfgang H. Reinicke, *Deepening the Atlantic – Toward a New Transatlantic Marketplace?* (Gütersloh, Bertelsmann Foundation Publishers, 1996), p.19.

might then, in the long run, come to reflect more closely the reality of the relationship. But, for the medium-term, incremental changes in the EU's scope will probably remain insufficient to contribute to the establishment of a genuine joint leadership or of a G2. Provided that the US does not abuse its dominant position and the EU does not engage in a hegemonic race, there is still room for increasing the scope and depth of US-EU relations, be it through informal or formal integration. For the predictable future, structural forces are pushing the relationship towards an ever closer partnership.

About the Contributors

Maria Green Cowles is Assistant Professor at the American University in Washington D.C. She was formerly a Research Associate at the Center for German and European Studies at Georgetown University and taught at the University of North Carolina at Charlotte. Her research focuses on the political activities of multinational firms in EU policy-making and in transatlantic relations. She has published numerous articles and book chapters, including pieces in the *Journal of Common Market Studies*, the *Journal of European Public Policy*, *German Politics and Society*, and *Politique Étrangère*. She is currently writing a book, *The Politics of Big Business in the European Union*, and co-editing another book on *Europeanization and Domestic Change* with James Caporaso and Thomas Risse. Dr. Cowles is an executive committee member of the European Community Studies Association. She received her Ph.D. from the American University in Washington D.C., and served as a Visiting Research Fellow at Harvard University, the University of California-Berkeley, the Centre for European Policy Studies, and the American Institute for Contemporary German Studies. She is a past recipient of the Social Science Research Council-MacArthur Foundation Fellowship on Peace and Security.

Youri Devuyst is Adjunct Professor at the Vrije Universiteit Brussel. He received a Doctorate in Political Science and an LL.M. degree at the Vrije Universiteit Brussel and a M.A. in International Relations at the Johns Hopkins School of Advanced International Studies in Washington D.C. His work has appeared in journals such as the *Journal of World Trade*, *World Competition*, *Global Governance*, the *Journal of Common Market Studies*, the *Journal of European Public Policy*, the *European Foreign Affairs Review* and in several edited volumes.

Thomas Frellesen is an official with the European Commission in Brussels where he is responsible for Common Foreign and Security Policy coordination concerning North America and Asia in the Unit of the European Correspondent. He has previously held the position of Desk Officer for Political Relations with the US. Before joining the Commission, Mr. Frellesen was at the Centre For European Policy Studies (CEPS) in Brussels where he did research on CFSP and transatlantic relations.

Anthony Gardner, an international corporate lawyer with Coudert Brothers in Paris, served as Director of European Affairs in the European Directorate of the National Security Council in 1994-95. As the official in the White House responsible for US-European Union relations, he worked closely with US Ambassador to the EU Stuart Eizenstat in launching the New Transatlantic Agenda in December 1995. He is the author of *A New Era in US-EU Relations? The Clinton Administration and the New Transatlantic Agenda* (Aldershot, Avebury Press 1996).

Roy H. Ginsberg is Professor of Government and Director of International Affairs at Skidmore College. He is the coauthor of *The United States and the European Union in the 1990s: Partners in Transition* (MacMillan 1996) and the author of 'Conceptualizing the European Union as an International Actor: Narrowing the Capability-Expectations Gap' in the *Journal of Common Market Studies* (Fall 1999).

Alan K. Henrikson teaches American diplomatic history, contemporary US-European relations (the Atlantic community), and political geography at The Fletcher School of Law and Diplomacy at Tufts University. Professor Henrikson also serves as Director of the Fletcher Roundtable on a New World Order, a research and discussion group which addresses current questions of regional and international organisation. He has been an Associate of the Weatherhead Center for International Affairs of Harvard University. During 1986-1987, he was in Washington D.C., as the Lloyd I. Miller Visiting Professor of Diplomatic History and Scholar-in-Residence at the Center for the Study of Foreign Affairs in the Foreign Service Institute of the Department of State. Professor Henrikson has written widely on the history and current problems of American foreign policy, the North Atlantic Alliance, US relations with the European Union, US-Canadian-Mexican ('North American') regional cooperation, and political geography. He received A.B., M.A., and Ph.D. degrees in History from Harvard University and also holds a B.A. and M.A. (Oxon.) from the University of Oxford, where he read Philosophy-Politics-and-Economics at Balliol College as a Rhodes Scholar.

John Peterson holds degrees in communications and political science from Ithaca College, the University of California and the London School of Economics. He has taught European politics at the University of California at Santa Barbara, Oxford University, the University of Essex, the University of York and the Institute d'Études Politiques in Grenoble, France. He has twice (1994 and 1995) been a Visiting Research Fellow at the Centre for European Policy Studies in Brussels. He is now with the University of Glasgow. Dr. Peterson is the author of *Europe and America: the Prospects for Partnerships* (2nd edition Routledge 1996). He also has published on US-EU relations in the *Journal of Common Market Studies*, the *European Journal of International Relations* and *Government and Opposition*. In 1995 he prepared a report for DGIA of the European Commission entitled "US Foreign and Security Policies: The Impact of the US 1994 Mid-term Election with Special Reference to US-EU Relations". He co-authored *Decision-Making in the European Union* with Elizabeth Bomberg and *Technology Policy in the European Union* with Margaret Sharp. Both books were published by Macmillan in 1999. As American, he has lived in Canada, Belgium, France and the UK.

Éric Philippart is Research Associate at the Belgian National Fund for Scientific Research (FNRS), Professor at the Political Science Department of the Université Libre de Bruxelles and at the College of Europe (Bruges). Holding degrees in political sciences and international relations as well as public administration and economics from the University of Brussels, he has been a Visiting Fellow at various

American universities including the M.I.T. (Boston), Stanford and Michigan (Ann Arbor) thanks to a 1996 USIA fellowship, as well as at Cambridge University in 1997-8 thanks to the Philippe Wiener & Maurice Anspach Foundation. His main research areas are the external relations of the EU (in particular the economic and political dimensions of the Transatlantic and Mediterranean policies of the EU) and European institutional development (new modes of 'multi-level governance', 'closer cooperation' – 'flexibility' and 'subsidiarity'). He also studies the external relations of federal or regionalized states. He is author or co-author of many chapters in edited volumes and articles published, among others journals, in the *Journal of Common Market Studies*, *European Foreign Affairs Review* and *Études internationales*. He is currently co-editing a book on *Theorising European Integration: Theoretical Approaches and Treaty Reform*, with G. Edwards.

Alberta Sbragia is the Director of the University of Pittsburgh's Center for West European Studies and a Professor of Political Science. A recipient of a Ph.D. in Political Science from the University of Wisconsin-Madison, Professor Sbragia has played a key role in the European Community Studies Association, of which she held the Chair from 1993-95. She has also been active in many national professional bodies, including the Fulbright Fellowship Competition (for Political Science), the Council of European Studies, the Agnelli Foundation's Advisory Committee for Italian Studies, the Conference Group on Italian Politics and Society (of which she is currently President), and the American Political Science Association's section on West European Politics and Society. A Fulbright scholar, she served as a Visiting Associate Professor at the Harvard Business School in 1983-84, teaching "Business, Government, and the International Economy" and directed a Brookings Institution project on the institutional and policy-making evolution of the European Community. Professor Sbragia's scholarly writings are primarily concerned with comparing West European and American politics and policy and have covered a wide spectrum of topics, including comparative federalism. Her current work focuses on the European Union's environmental policy and the EU as an international actor in the global environmental arena. She is the editor of *Euro-Politics: Politics and Policymaking in the "New" European Community* (Brookings, 1992) and the author of *Debt Wish: Entrepreneurial Cities, U.S. Federalism, and Economic Development* (University of Pittsburgh, 1996).

René Schwok, of Swiss nationality, is Associate Professor at the European Graduate Institute and the Political Science Department, University of Geneva. He has been a Visiting Research Fellow at the Center for European Studies in Harvard, as well as at the Institut für Europaïsche Geschichte, in Mayence, Germany. Dr. Schwok has taught European politics in numerous European and American universities. He is the author of *US-EC Relations in the Post-Cold War Era, Conflict or Partnership?* (Boulder, Westview Press, 1991) which has also been published in French and in Japanese. In addition, he has published on US-EU relations in *Études internationales* (Canada) and edited a book with special reference to transatlantic relations: *Security in Europe: towards an interinstitutional flexibility*, Genève, European Graduate & Georg, 1997. Other research interests include the external dimension of the European Union, as well as Switzerland-EU relations. (*Switzerland and the European Common Market*, New York, Praeger, 1991). Forthcoming works include *Enlarging the European Community: Theories, Themes and Policies*, co-authored with Lee Miles and John Redmond (Macmillan).

Michael Smith is Jean Monnet Professor of European Politics in the Department of European Studies at Loughborough University. His principal areas of research are transatlantic relations, relations between the EU, the US and Japan, the making of EU external policies and the role of the EU in post-Cold War Europe. Among his books are *The United States and the European Community in a Transformed World* (1993, with Stephen Woolcock); *Beyond Foreign Economic Policy: The United States, the Single European Market and the Changing World Economy* (1997, with Brian Hocking); *Unsettled Europe: Towards a European Model of Internationalisation* (forthcoming, with Brigid Laffan and Rory O'Donnell). Articles include 'Learning to Cooperate: The Clinton Administration and the European Union', *International Affairs*, July 1994 (with Stephen Woolcock); 'The European Union, Foreign Economic Policy and a Changing World Economy', *Journal of European Public Policy,* Autumn 1994; 'Competitive Co-operation and EU-US Relations', *Journal of European Public Policy*, 1998. He has also published many books and articles in the fields of world politics, foreign policy analysis and British foreign policy.

Pascaline Winand is Research Associate at the Belgian National Fund for Scientific Research (FNRS) and Professor at the Université Libre de Bruxelles (Institut d'Études européennes, Political Science Department and Council of International Educational Exchange). Dr. Winand holds degrees in Germanic studies, political science, international relations and diplomatic history from the Université Libre de Bruxelles, Yale University and Purdue University. She was Visiting Assistant Professor at Carnegie Mellon University, Pittsburgh (1991-1992), Visiting Professor at the Institute of International Relations of Kjiv Taras Shevchenko University (1999) and at the Pontificia Universidad Catolica del Peru (2000), and was a Visiting Distinguished Professor at the University of Pittsburgh in January 2001 where she taught the politics of US-EU relations. She has also been a Jean Monnet Fellow and a Research Fellow at the European University Institute in Florence (1989-1991) and a Research Fellow at the Norwegian Nobel Institute (1997). She was awarded the 1994 Adolph Bentinck Special Mention Prize for her book *Eisenhower, Kennedy and the United States of Europe* published in 1993 by St. Martin's Press and Macmillan. Her research and publications cover a wide range of topics including public and private interest groups in the European Union, the history of European integration, and US/EC-EU relations, present and past.

Index

Series "European Policy"

"European Policy" is an interdisciplinary collection devoted to the study of European integration in a broad sense. Although mostly focusing on the European Union, it also encourages the publication of books addressing the wider, pan-European context, as well as comparative work, including on other forms of regional integration on the world scene. The core disciplines are politics, economics, law, and history. While being committed to high academic standards, "European Policy" seeks to be accessible to a wide readership, including policy-makers and practitioners, and to stimulate a debate on European issues. The collection publishes both in English and in French.

Editor : **Pascaline WINAND**,
Professor at the Université libre de Bruxelles and Research Associate at the Fonds National de la Recherche Scientifique (Belgium)

Published Books

N°23 : *Le pouvoir renforcé du Parlement européen après Amsterdam*, Andreas MAURER, Groupe d'Études Politiques Européennes, 2000, 126 p., ISBN 90-5201-928-2

N°22 : *L'Europe et ses citoyens*, Louis le HARDŸ de BEAULIEU (ed.), Groupe d'Études Politiques Européennes, 2000, 238 p., ISBN 90-5201-929-0

N°21 : *The Euro and European Integration / L'Euro et l'intégration européenne*, EURO INSTITUTE / INSTITUT DE L'EURO, Jean-Victor LOUIS & Hajo BRONKHORST (eds.), 1999, 366 p., ISBN 90-5201-912-6

N°20 : *L'idée fédéraliste dans les États-nations. Regards croisés entre la Wallonie et le monde*, Philippe DESTATTE (dir.), Institut Jules Destrée, 1999, 464 p., ISBN 90-5201-902-9

N°19 : *L'identité européenne de sécurité et de défense. Des coopérations militaires croisées au Livre blanc européen,* André DUMOULIN, 1999, 294 p., ISBN 90-5201-901-0

N°18 : *Union européenne: quels défis pour l'an 2000 ? Emploi, union monétaire, élargissement,* Franklin DEHOUSSE, Jacques VANHAMME & Louis le HARDŸ de BEAULIEU (dir.), Groupe d'Études Politiques Européennes, 1998, 250 p., ISBN 90-5201-810-3

N°17 : *L'Union européenne au-delà d'Amsterdam. Nouveaux concepts d'intégration européenne,* Martin WESTLAKE (dir.), Préface de J. Delors, 1998, 250 p., ISBN 90-5201-809-X

N°16 : *Lobbyisme, pluralisme et intégration européenne – Lobbying, Pluralism and European Integration,* Paul-H. CLAEYS, Corinne GOBIN, Isabelle SMETS & Pascaline WINAND (eds.), Groupe d'étude du Lobbyisme Européen, 1998, 456 p., ISBN 90-5201-803-0